Dedan Kimathi on Trial

Ohio University Research in International Studies

This series of publications on Africa, Latin America, Southeast Asia, and Global and Comparative Studies is designed to present significant research, translation, and opinion to area specialists and to a wide community of persons interested in world affairs. The series is distributed worldwide. For more information, consult the Ohio University Press website, ohioswallow.com.

Books in the Ohio University Research in International Studies series are published by Ohio University Press in association with the Center for International Studies. The views expressed in individual volumes are those of the authors and should not be considered to represent the policies or beliefs of the Center for International Studies, Ohio University Press, or Ohio University.

Executive Editor: Gillian Berchowitz

Dedan Kimathi on Trial

COLONIAL JUSTICE AND POPULAR MEMORY IN KENYA'S MAU MAU REBELLION

Edited by Julie MacArthur

Introductory Note by Willy Mutunga

Foreword by Mĩcere Gĩthae Mũgo and Ngũgĩ wa Thiong'o

Ohio University Research in International Studies
Global and Comparative Studies Series No. 17
Ohio University Press
Athens

Ohio University Press, Athens, Ohio 45701
ohioswallow.com

Printed in the United States of America
The books in the Ohio University Research in International Studies Series are printed on acid-free paper ∞ ™

Cover image: Dedan Kimathi on trial, 1956. Getty Images
Cover design: Beth Pratt

27 26 25 24 23 22 21 20 19 18 17 5 4 3 2 1

Library of Congress Cataloging-in-Publication Data
Names: MacArthur, Julie, 1982- editor. | Mutunga, Willy, writer of introductory note. | Mugo, Mĩcere Gĩthae, writer of foreword. | Ngũgĩ wa Thiong'o, 1938- writer of foreword.
Title: Dedan Kimathi on trial : colonial justice and Kenya's Mau Mau rebellion / edited by Julie MacArthur ; introductory note by Hon. Chief Justice Willy Mutunga ; foreword by Mĩcere Gĩthae Mũgo and Ngũgĩ wa Thiong'o.
Other titles: Research in international studies. Global and comparative studies series ; no. 17.
Description: Athens, Ohio : Ohio University Press, 2017. | Series: Ohio University research in international studies. Global and comparative studies series ; no. 17 | Includes bibliographical references and index.
Identifiers: LCCN 2017036215| ISBN 9780896803169 (hc : alk. paper) | ISBN 9780896803176 (pb : alk. paper) | ISBN 9780896805019 (pdf)
Subjects: LCSH: Kimathi, Dedan, 1920-1957--Trials, litigation, etc. | Kenya--History--Mau Mau Emergency, 1952-1960. | Mau Mau--History.
Classification: LCC DT433.577 .D425 2017 | DDC 967.6203--dc23
LC record available at https://lccn.loc.gov/2017036215

Contents

Illustrations

Maps

Figures

Photographs

Following page 220

Introductory Note

Willy Mutunga

Mau Mau field marshal Dedan Kimathi is a towering historical figure in Kenya, a patriot who stood up against colonial rule and paid the ultimate price. But for too long, Kimathi has remained elusive—his words, his ideas (except for some writing by the Kenyan historian Maina wa Kinyatti), and even his body missing from the public realm. As Kenya looks to its future, it must also look to its past and return dignity and honor to the freedom fighters whose struggle for justice and human rights we carry on in the present.

In the past, many of those who fought for this country have been sidelined and forgotten. On 20 October 1997, I went to Nyeri with a group of committed lawyers and activists to plant a commemorative tree at Karunaini, the spot where Kimathi was shot and finally captured. We hoped planting a mugumo tree would, in some small way, pay tribute to the sacrifices of our fallen compatriots. We were engaged in a series of mass actions to agitate for a comprehensive constitution of Kenya and this visit was part of this struggle. The Kenya police uprooted this tree and all of us were deported from the region.

As part of my activism with various civil-society organizations in Kenya—including the Human Rights Commission, where I served as executive director for six years, and throughout my tenure as chief justice—I have called for the retrieval of Dedan Kimathi's missing body. Our patriotic figures must be given proper burial if we are to honor their service and build upon their revolutionary visions.

Kenya stands at a critical juncture in its history. We are engaged in a deeply transformative process. Transparency and the right of access to information are hallmarks of our new constitution. Access to our historical records must be part of this commitment. The Supreme Court of Kenya is dedicated to honoring this history. In 2015 we opened a museum in the former prison cells located in the basement of the court to allow fellow Kenyans and international visitors to experience the history of transformations within the judicial system in Kenya.

This volume makes a vital contribution toward this goal. This volume will, for the first time, make public and widely available the record of the trial of Dedan Kimathi, a piece of our history long thought lost. The trial, which would end in Kimathi being sentenced to death by hanging, represents an important turning point in the history of struggle in Kenya and thus provides a window into the hopes and unfulfilled visions of Kimathi's time. The scholarly reflections brought together in this volume reveal the deep historical significance of figures like Kimathi, the moral lessons we can learn from the past, and the continuing relevance of the struggle for independence in Kenya today.

We, as Kenyans, must reckon with our past. We must honor our freedom fighters—not just Kimathi but also the many women and men from across this country who have fought for justice and freedom.

I salute the Kenyan contributors to this brilliant volume for their patriotism. I salute and glorify the great global solidarity and commitment to our struggles reflected by our international comrades who are also contributors.

A luta continua, a vitória é certa!

Dr. Willy Mutunga
14th Chief Justice & 1st President of the Supreme Court,
Republic of Kenya

Foreword

By Mĩcere Gĩthae Mũgo and Ngũgĩ wa Thiong'o

I shall not plead to a law in which we had no part in the making.

—Kĩmathi, character in the play *The Trial of Dedan Kĩmathi*

It is in the light of this statement that we offer our observations on Julie MacArthur's publication, a historically significant intervention and addition to existing scholarship on Kĩmathi. MacArthur's work is critical in three main ways. First, makes available to the public, for the very first time, the original transcript of the kangaroo trial of Dedan Kĩmathi and other related documents. Second, it comes on the sixtieth anniversary of that notorious trial and the execution of Field Marshal Dedan Kĩmathi at Kamĩtĩ Prison, Nairobi, in October 1956. Third, the book's appearance during the decade of fiftieth jubilees for independence all over Africa is a reminder that it was the Kĩmathi-led armed struggle, the first of its kind against European colonial powers on the continent, that broke the back of imperialism and so opened the way for the liberation that the various nations are now commemorating.

The publication affords Kenya and the world yet another moment of serious reflection and stock taking in revisiting one of Africa's most compelling moments in the history of resistance against colonialist and imperialist injustice. The colonial script MacArthur makes available reminds us of an ancient African proverb that has many versions, but offers the same caution: "Until the lion tells his story, the tale of the hunt will always glorify the hunter." In Kĩmathi's case the lion never lived to tell his story, and the hunter was relentless in his attempts to define, within his own terms, the lion that died fighting back the colonial hunter. "I would rather die on my feet," Kĩmathi once said, "than live on bended knees." But this is not the spirit of the Kĩmathi that emerges in the colonial mega narrative contained in the court records.

The only complimentary detail that emerges—ironically meant as negative—is the complaint by all Kĩmathi's interrogators, who accuse him of refusing to cooperate or to divulge any security details about the Movement. For instance, John Charles Edward Vidler, ASP, an officer in charge of the Kenyan CID, Nyeri area (with twenty-two years of service), notes, "I have interviewed the accused in custody about other security matters not connected with this offence. He may have had useful information but gave none," adding, "He spoke to me throughout in very good English." Similarly, John Roger Blackman, CID inspector (with five years of service), reports, "Subsequently I interviewed him to see if he could give me security information in respect to other matters. He did not assist me at all. . . . The impression that the accused gave me was that he could assist me in giving information, but he was obstinate and would not do so."

But despite this clear documentation of Kĩmathi's refusal to cooperate with the colonial legal system, a document, purported to be Dedan Kĩmathi's statement to the police under questioning, is filed in court. The statement is so systematically organized and logically presented with dates, locations, and all, that it reads more like a polished report crafted from carefully researched information than a statement put together from verbal information by the prisoner. Since we hear from Kĩmathi's interrogators that he was uncooperative, when and to whom was this statement made, we ask? In our view, it is most likely yet another colonial fabrication.

A glance at some of the documents and the discrepancies, contradictions, and fallacies in them corroborates our conclusion about colonial fabrications against which vigilance is called for:

- Most of the seven witnesses for the prosecution are former members of the notorious British auxiliary army but which the colonial state misleadingly named the Home Guard. To what extent can we trust their testimonies?
- Despite the fact that two of them openly confess during cross-examination that the testimony they originally gave was based on secondhand information, the judge accepts their testimony in total as being

accurate and reliable. Asked if his memory is defective, one Njogi s/o Ngatia responds, "I am liable to forget. Yes, I think I have forgotten about this question. I did not see the accused jump aside, Ndirangu told me what he did." Another one, Mwangi s/o Kahagi, who had testified to corroborate evidence pertaining to the distance from which Kĩmathi was shot, confesses under cross-examination that he is illiterate and is not able to discern distance in terms of measurement. His testimony is also accepted in total.

- The *East African Standard* of 16 November 1956 reports that rewards totaling £500 for the capture of Dedan Kĩmathi had been distributed. Among the recipients are the crown witnesses. Ndirangu s/o Mau, former home guard, stationed at Kahigaini, South Tetu Reserve, for instance, admits on cross-examination that he had already been paid KSh 3,000 as a reward for capturing Kĩmathi. A lot of money in those days. The judge does not even attempt to note any conflict of interest in this and accepts in total Ndirangu's testimony, as well as the testimonies of the other beneficiaries of the reward.
- On 21 October 1956, Kĩmathi is operated on for serious gunshot wounds during his capture and on the very next day Denis William Hamilton Hurley, the provincial surgeon of Nyeri General Hospital, certifies that the prisoner is ready to be interrogated by the police. What medical malpractice!
- At the trial, there are three assessors chosen by the Crown: Tumuti s/o Gakere, Nderitu s/o Muteru, and Kibuthu s/o Kihia! How they were chosen, the records do not reveal, but from the way they behave, it is not unfair to conclude that they were government agents.
- Before delivering their verdict, the judge summarizes the case but tellingly, his summary of the prosecution's submission is fourteen pages, while that of the defense is only four pages. In the summary, the judge virtually directs the assessors to turn in a guilty verdict.
- The assessors readily comply. They retire to deliberate on the submissions at 4:12 p.m. and by 4:20 p.m. (within eight minutes, in other words), they already have a verdict of guilty. According to Kibuthu, "He [Kĩmathi] is guilty. He is a gangster."

A gangster? That was always the colonial label for the soldiers of liberation, who fought the British under the name Kenya Land and Freedom Army (KLFA). Kĩmathi himself had already rejected the label: "I don't lead terrorists. I lead Africans who want their self-government and land. God did not intend that one nation be ruled by another."

It was to refute the entire colonial literature and the demonization of Kĩmathi, along with the Kenya Land and Freedom Army, that in 1977 we wrote the play *The Trial of Dedan Kĩmathi.* Determined to celebrate the true history of Kenya's liberation, we unabashedly embraced Kĩmathi's firm rejection of the colonial terms about the nature and aims of the Kenya Land and Freedom Army. Consequently, our play depicts the trial at the Nyeri High Court as a farce, for Kĩmathi had been sentenced long before the actual trial was staged there. He was being tried by the very system he was sworn to fight. The system became judge, jury, and executioner.

Our play celebrates Kĩmathi as a gallant leader of the Kenya Land and Freedom Army and as the symbol of the masses' struggle to liberate themselves and Kenya from colonialism and imperialist domination. Kĩmathi's letters to the colonial government testify to this, just as they light up the clear vision of the KLFA's struggle as a part of the resistance to international imperialism. As we stated in 1976 in the play's preface:

> We agreed that the most important thing was for us to reconstruct imaginatively our history, envisioning the world of the Mau Mau and Kĩmathi in terms of the peasants' and workers' struggle before and after constitutional independence. The play is not a reproduction of the farcical "trial" at Nyeri. It is, rather, an imaginative recreation and interpretation of the collective will of the Kenyan peasants and workers in their refusal to break under sixty years of colonial torture and ruthless oppression by the British ruling classes and their continued determination to resist exploitation, oppression and new forms of enslavement.

In this regard, the mumbo-jumboish term *Mau Mau* was a British creation to obscure the clarity of the aims in the name Land and Freedom. This very mumbo-jumboism has often fueled a scholarship that tries to diminish the armed wing of the entire anticolonial liberation by describing the struggle that Kĩmathi led as a civil war. Our play, *The Trial of Dedan Kĩmathi,* was based precisely on the rejection of the entire assumptions underlying that British kangaroo court in Nyeri. But it was also a statement against the kind of literature and scholarship that authenticated or condoned that trial.

Forty years since the publication of the play, our position remains basically the same: that the proceedings were a colonial narrative aimed at simultaneously giving legal legitimacy to the British colonial "system of justice" and helping British propaganda obscure the aims of the KLFA struggle. The Kĩmathi of the play characterizes the colonial system of justice as one of protecting the man of property, the exploiter, while silencing the poor, the working masses.

We also stand by what we said in our preface regarding Kenyan literature and scholarship in general. To wit: as scholars, writers, thinkers, researchers, and intellectuals we are on trial. "We cannot stand on the fence. We are either on the side of the people, or on the side of imperialism . . . either fighting with the people, or aiding imperialism and the class enemies of the people."

If the publication of the colonial records, which are pitted against the interpretive narratives of leading scholars on Kenya, including Kenyan intellectuals such as Simon Gikandi and Nicholas Githuku, as well as other international researchers on Kenya, helps reignite the debate about Kĩmathi's legacy to Kenya, Africa, and the world, it will have served a great purpose. We thank and commend Julie MacArthur, her editors, and the publishers for making these important colonial records available for public scrutiny and for the very first time in history. Congratulations!

Mĩcere Gĩthae Mũgo
Emeritus Meredith Professor of Teaching Excellence
Syracuse University

Ngũgĩ wa Thiong'o
Distinguished Professor of English and Comparative Literature
University of California, Irvine

October 2015

Acknowledgments

A long, strange, and winding journey has brought this volume to fruition. It all started with a casual conversation I had over chai in Nairobi with David Anderson and Stacey Hynd in 2008. It was then I first learned of the "mystery" surrounding the trial of Dedan Kimathi. It is nearly impossible to escape the long shadow cast by Kimathi over modern Kenya. But his legacy and the archives of his life remain the subject of much uncertainty and speculation.

Finding the trial indeed proved difficult and perplexing. I have told the full story in the introduction to this volume and elsewhere. Here I would like to acknowledge my indebtedness to the scholars, archivists, public figures, and museum curators who variously opened doors, sent e-mails, located dusty boxes in forgotten corners, and shared with me the intense excitement and sense of possibility when we could finally say we had located the trial of Dedan Kimathi, absent from view, it would seem, for almost sixty years. Finding the trial would not have been possible without the dedicated and enthusiastic support of people across multiple institutions in Kenya: former chief justice Willy Mutunga, former deputy chief justice Kalpana Rawal, Stanley Mutuma, Rose Wachuka, Atieno Odhiambo, Naim Bilal, Richard Otene, Peterson Kithuku, Richard Ambani, Francis Mwangi, James Nyaga, Betty Karanja, Tabitha Kanogo, Maina wa Kinyatti, Aghan Odero, Joseph Karimi, and Billy Kahora. Thanks also to the numerous scholars and students at Dedan Kimathi University of Technology (Nyeri) who provided feedback at a conference in 2014. In London, Richard Temple at Senate House Library provided immense assistance and, as it turned out, the key to finally locating the trial of Dedan Kimathi.

This volume would not have been possible if one of the most influential scholars in African history had not said yes when a young scholar presented him with a crazy idea. John Lonsdale has been unwavering in his support of this project, lending his counsel, his vast networks, his staggering historical recollection, and his name, which undoubtedly encouraged others to sign on as well. Throughout, he has been a steadfast champion and critical intellectual, and personal, resource.

All the contributors to this volume have lent significant time and expertise to realizing this project. Dr. Willy Mutunga, 14th Chief Justice & 1st President of the Supreme Court, Republic of Kenya, was an early supporter of the project and proved a knowledgeable and passionate interlocutor. His introductory note to this volume speaks to the deeply personal and political nature of his relationship to this material. From the start, we were all aware of how important and necessary it was to attempt to engage Ngũgĩ wa Thiong'o and Mĩcere Gĩthae Mũgo in this project. Their groundbreaking 1976 play, *The Trial of Dedan Kimathi,* has provided the entry point for many generations into the continuing relevance of Kimathi and this period in Kenyan history. Ngũgĩ and Mĩcere honored our project by providing a foreword to this volume that is as insightful as it is provocative.

Putting this volume together has been a truly collaborative process. I am grateful to my esteemed fellow contributors—David Anderson, John Lonsdale, Nicholas Githuku, Simon Gikandi, and Lotte Hughes—for their patience, generosity, critical interventions, and scholarly camaraderie. Special thanks also go to Derek Peterson and Joseph Kariuki Muriithi for providing the wonderfully rich and incisive annotations to the Gikuyu-English translation of one of Kimathi's letters (Document 8).

The African Studies Association (ASA) conference in 2016 brought many of the contributors to this project together in one space. A roundtable discussion, featuring myself, Lonsdale, Gikandi, and Githuku, provided an opportunity to present reflections on the trial to fellow Africanists. The comments of Luise White, David Throup, Mickie Koster, and many others helped shape the final product. At the conference, Ngũgĩ and Mĩcere also graced us with a special guest lecture on the fortieth anniversary of their play. The energy and excitement were palpable. Their reflections on the politics of naming and the enduring legacy of Kimathi provided great inspiration in the final stages of this project. My sincere thanks to the executive committee at the ASA and to Simon Gikandi and the Princeton African Humanities Colloquium, who generously provided the funds to make this event possible.

For my own part, I must thank my colleagues in the Africanist Seminar at the University of Toronto. Presenting this work in its early stages to this highly accomplished group of Africanists and having their support throughout the years were critical to the development and completion of this project. The University of Toronto, Mississauga, Office of the Vice Principal, Research and the Department of Historical Studies both provided funds that helped with travel, research, and publication costs. I also thank Brian Balsley for the wonderful maps produced for this volume.

My sincere thanks also go to Gill Berchowitz and the entire team at Ohio University Press for all your patience, professionalism, and commitment to this project and to the field of African history more broadly. Two anonymous readers provided immensely detailed insights, points of critique, and words of encouragement that helped in the revisions to this volume.

This volume is the product of collective labor. It belongs not to any one contributor but to all those who pick it up, read its pages, engage in its sometimes fierce debates, and imagine from its contents their own Kimathis.

Julie MacArthur
University of Toronto

Abbreviations

CID	Criminal Investigation Department
DC	District Commissioner
KAR	King's African Rifles
KAU	Kenya African Union
KCA	Kikuyu Central Association
KHRC	Kenya Human Rights Commission
KG	Kikuyu Guard
KLFA	Kenya Land and Freedom Army
KNA	Kenya National Archives (Nairobi)
MMWVA	Mau Mau War Veterans' Association
NARC	National Rainbow Coalition
NMK	National Museums of Kenya (Nairobi)
TNA:PRO	The National Archives: Public Records Office (London)
TP	Tribal Police
TPR	Tribal Police Reserve

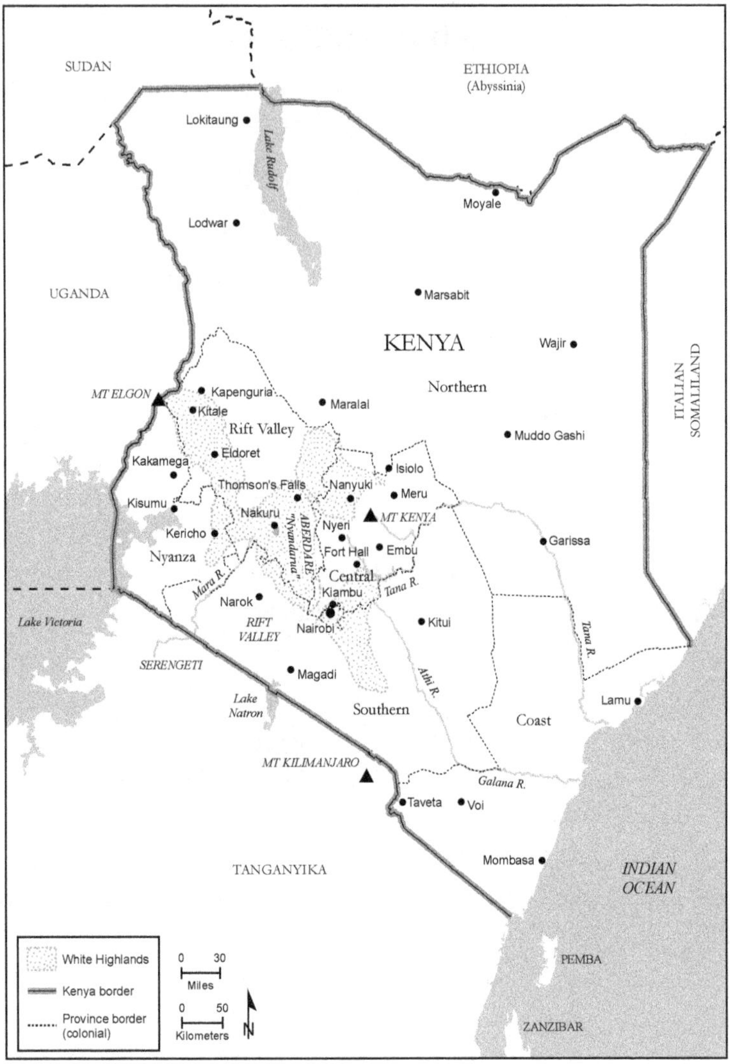

MAP 1 Colonial Kenya, c. 1956. *Map by Brian Edward Balsley, GISP.*

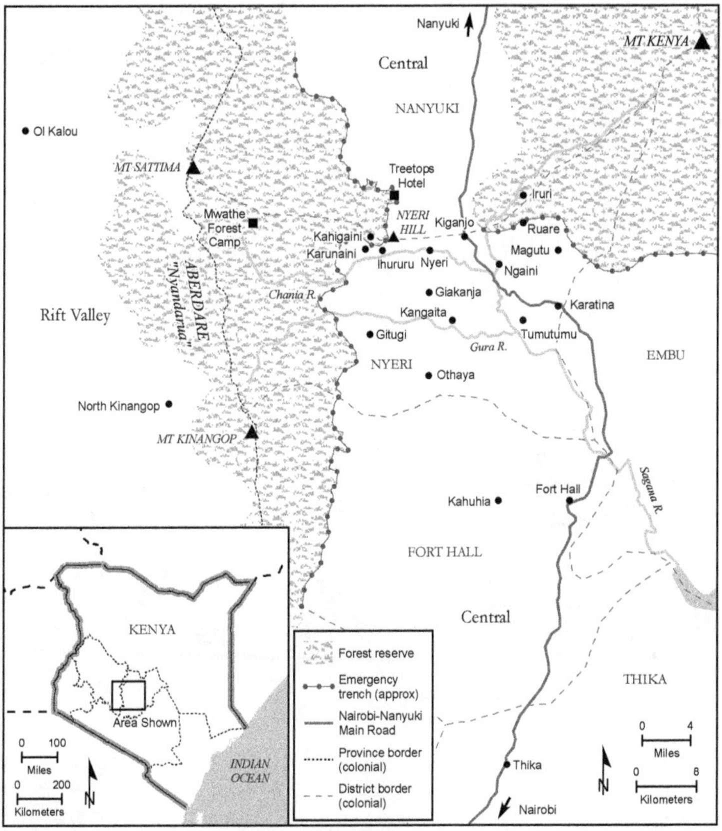

MAP 2 Central Kenya. *Map by Brian Edward Balsley, GISP.*

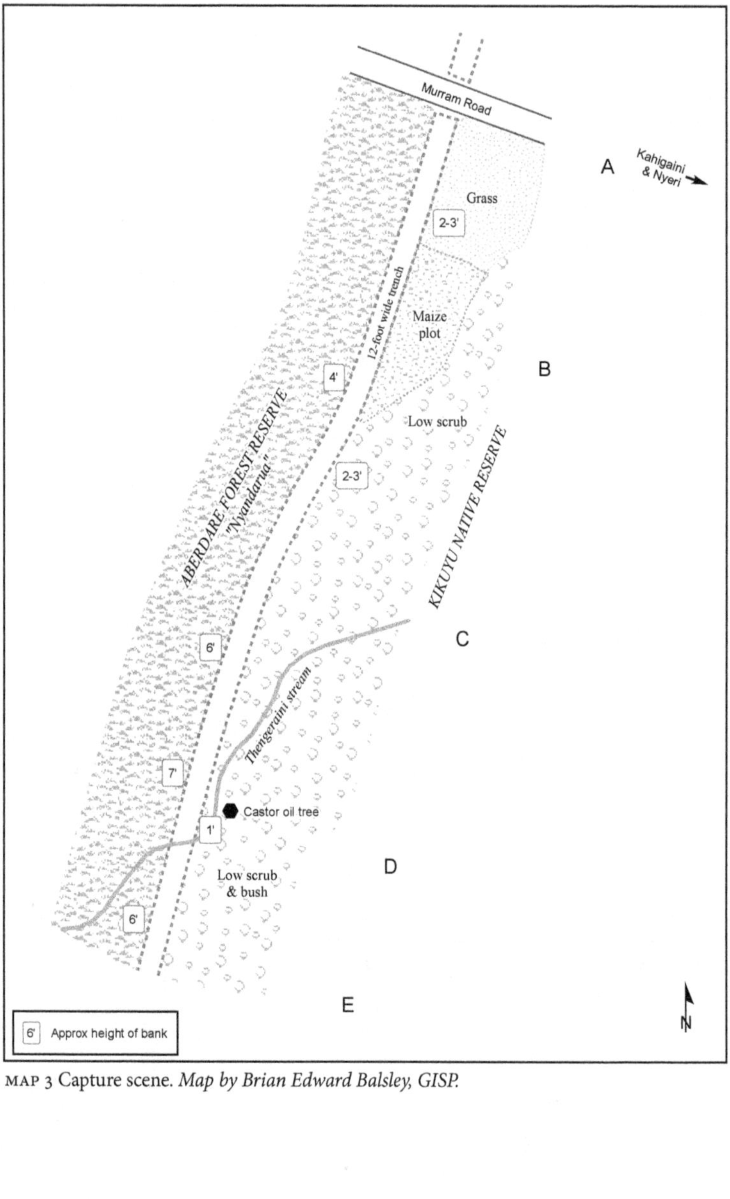

MAP 3 Capture scene. *Map by Brian Edward Balsley, GISP.*

Introduction

The Trial of Dedan Kimathi

Julie MacArthur

ON 19 NOVEMBER 1956, Mau Mau rebel field marshal Dedan Kimathi stood or, more accurately, sat in front of Her Majesty's Supreme Court of Kenya at Nyeri and asserted a "plea of not guilty." After eight days of trial, Chief Justice Kenneth Kennedy O'Connor found Kimathi guilty of unlawful possession of a firearm and ammunition and sentenced him to be "hanged by the neck until he is dead."[1] Early on the morning of 18 February 1957, Dedan Kimathi was hanged to death and buried in an unmarked grave in the grounds of Kamiti prison.

This book centers on the trial of Dedan Kimathi—a piece of the colonial archive long thought lost, hidden, or destroyed. Dedan Kimathi remains a powerful symbol of resistance in Kenyan history. His dreadlocked visage, captured while he sat in the defendant's chair on trial for his life, can be seen on T-shirts, in graffiti art on the sides of Nairobi buildings, and on the sides of *matatu* (minibuses) throughout contemporary Kenya and farther afield. His name has often been considered synonymous with the anticolonial rebellion that engulfed colonial Kenya in the 1950s. He was the self-fashioned Field Marshal of the Mau Mau, a movement that had many names, many faces, and even more interpretations.[2] The Mau Mau rebellion, which emerged predominantly among the Gikuyu, Embu, and Meru populations of Central Kenya, was a radical response both to colonial settler policies of land appropriation and squatter labor restrictions on the one hand, and to the repressive local African governing apparatus in the reserves and the slow-moving constitutional nationalists of the anticolonial movement in Kenya on the other.[3]

Kimathi rose to prominence in the early 1950s out of relative obscurity, first as an administrator of the oaths of loyalty sworn by "Mau Mau" adherents and then as leader of the fighters who moved into the forests after the colonial declaration of a State of Emergency in October 1952. His charisma, flair for oration, and ability to evade British forces became legendary. For the British, Kimathi was a fearsome adversary. Special Branch superintendent Ian Henderson, the man in charge of the "hunt" for Dedan Kimathi, compared him to Hitler.[4] In his memoir, *The Hunt for Dedan Kimathi,* Henderson pictured Kimathi as both a formidable intellect and a cowardly criminal. In 1953 the *East African Standard* compared him to Mussolini.[5] For many in Kenya, however, Kimathi conjured other historical comparisons. William R. Ochieng' argued Kimathi had been "elevated to the ranks of Mao, Lenin and Guevera."[6] Ali A. Mazrui placed Kimathi among the top candidates in Kenyan history to be anointed a national martyr, akin to other global anticolonial heroes the likes of Gandhi.[7] While the Emergency and counterinsurgency operations would officially last until 1960, the capture and execution of Kimathi, in 1956 and 1957 respectively, allowed the British to claim victory over Mau Mau and solidified Kimathi's position among the martyred leaders of a failed rebellion.

But Kimathi's legacy was never a simple exemplar of patriotic martyrdom, and his place in the postcolonial imagination reflected the complicated legacy of the Mau Mau rebellion: at times suppressed or downplayed, at others lauded and filled with mythic importance, but always contested.[8] When Nelson Mandela visited Kenya for the first time, in July 1990, he invoked Kimathi's name in a speech at Kasarani Stadium: "In my 27 years of imprisonment, I always saw the image of fighters such as Kimathi, [General] China, and others as candles in my long and hard war against injustice." He lamented the absence of Kimathi's widow, Eloise Mukami, at the festivities and the lack of a proper burial site for Kimathi: speaking of his desire to pay homage to the fallen heroes of Kenya's independence struggle, Mandela lamented "it is an honor for any freedom fighter to pay respect to such heroes."[9] Mandela's speech provided a pointed, if implied, critique of Kenya's second president, Daniel arap Moi, and his government's treatment of former "freedom fighters." Moi's stolid expression during the speech revealed the more problematic aspects of the choice of Kimathi as hero in postcolonial Kenya.

As Marshall Clough observed in his important study of Mau Mau memoirs, those who exalted Kimathi often failed to "address the incongruence between Gikuyu revolt and Kenyan nation, . . . between guerrilla-martyr Kimathi, champion of the fighting Mau Mau and enemy of loyalism, and living statesman [first president Jomo] Kenyatta, representative of the Gikuyu elders and the constitutional politicians and apostle of peace, reconciliation, and [the policy of] forgive and forget."[10] Clough pointed to the "irony" of elevating Kimathi as a national hero, with many of his contemporaries questioning his revolutionary credentials and pointing to his loss of support due to his notoriously strict disciplinary ethos and his legendary antagonism with the more populist General Stanley Mathenge.[11] Kahinga Wachanga, an early follower but later rival for leadership in the forest, described Kimathi as a great leader who fell from grace, turning jealous and power hungry in his later years.[12] Wachanga was quick to remind his public that Mau Mau was not one man but a movement: "we had no one leader or commander except the oath. The oath was our leader."[13] In memoirs and popular Kenyan literature, Kimathi could be a tragic folk hero, a misunderstood rebel commander, a power-hungry despot, a prophetic patriot, a reminder of the lost dreams of revolution, or a dangerous precedent for future dissidents against the postcolonial order.[14]

As many of the contributions in this volume make clear, Kimathi embodied all these ascriptions. Kimathi came to symbolize many of the contradictions that Mau Mau, and indeed Kenyan anticolonialism and nationalism writ large, represented: rebel statesman, educated peasant, modern traditionalist. Whether Mau Mau was indeed a purely anticolonial struggle or an internal civil war, a nationalist movement or a Gikuyu political project, a hastener or a hindrance to the achievement of independence in Kenya remain hotly contested debates.[15] The position of "loyalists," those who were perceived to work with the colonial state and proved successful in the postcolonial era, has engendered similarly bitter disputes. The line between "rebel" and "loyalist" was blurred and more often reflected colonial impositions rather than discrete social categories.[16] In an important redress, Bethwell Ogot argued further that the narrow focus on Mau Mau as the sole criterion for revolutionary struggle and

Central Kenya as the sole site of nationalist thought have caused the multiple other anticolonial movements and figures from across the country to die "a second death" and "fragment our collective memory and therefore our history."[17] While Ogot and others are undoubtedly right to call for the necessity of rigorous examination of the multiple anticolonial practices and nationalist thought that developed in dialogue with or indeed outside Mau Mau, understanding Kimathi and his contested legacy remains vital to grappling with the histories of dissent and political thought in colonial and postcolonial Kenya.[18]

While much of the renewed memorialization of Mau Mau in Kenya over the past ten years has focused on the figure of Kimathi—with a statue, plaques, and the date of his death being celebrated across the country, though with varying levels of state sanction—he remains a controversial and elusive figure.[19] When the erection of a statute for Kimathi was finally confirmed in 2006, instructions called on the artists and designers involved to create an ideal of "heroic patriotism."[20] Permanent secretary to the cabinet and the head of public service, Francis Muthaura, further called for the need to "correct the negative image" of Kimathi as he appeared in the famous photograph from his trial, "in handcuffs, disabled."[21] Absences and silences, as much as his ubiquitous image and reworked words of resistance, cloud the figure of Kimathi in contemporary Kenya. Archives, like that of the trial and Kimathi's own voluminous writings during the Mau Mau rebellion, have been shrouded in uncertainty: disappeared, destroyed, or mistranslated. Oral accounts and memoirs, as we shall see, also produce contradictions and ambiguities. The fate even of his body remains a mystery, despite multiple attempts to locate and uncover his burial site.[22]

The recovery of the "missing" Kimathi trial file that prompted the creation of this volume provides just such an opportunity. Some of the most heated historiographical debates mentioned above have centered on memory, political partisanship, and the use of sources.[23] Controversies over classified, "missing," or destroyed British archives on Mau Mau in specific and on the British Empire more generally have grabbed headlines in recent years.[24] The activism of Mau Mau veterans seeking reparations from the British government has prompted an opening of files and a court case on the costs of the colonial counterinsurgency in Kenya.[25] Huw Bennett has written the first full study of the "hidden" colonial archive at Hanslope Park, home to Her Majesty's Government Communication

Centre.[26] Historians Bennett, David Anderson, and Caroline Elkins all played prominent roles in the trial itself, offering evidence of the "systematic abuse and abrogations of justice" that Mau Mau veterans suffered due to the colonial counterinsurgency in Kenya.[27] In 2013 the British government announced a negotiated settlement including compensation in the amount of $21.5 million to be paid to fifty-two hundred Mau Mau veterans. In 2014 a further suit, involving over forty thousand Kenyan claimants, was launched against the British Foreign and Commonwealth Office for a range of alleged offences, including false imprisonment, forced labor, abuse, and denial of rights.[28]

Even within this context of secreted or destroyed archives, the absence of Kimathi's trial has been glaring. Mau Mau history has produced a wealth of primary-source texts, including colonial documents, memoirs, and personal archival publications.[29] Archives from the trials of Mau Mau fighters formed the basis for Anderson's acclaimed study *Histories of the Hanged.* In this book, Anderson demonstrated how these meticulously detailed court transcripts allowed the stories of the shadowy, nameless figures of the Mau Mau rebellion to be brought to light and to bring us closer to the violence and lived experiences of the end of empire and the making of a new nation.[30] John Lonsdale has argued that a careful reading of the trial of Jomo Kenyatta on charges of organizing Mau Mau, while secured through perjured testimony, revealed the ways the nationalist leader used "the law's shield to turn the blow, to convert hegemony from mask of empire to argument for nationhood."[31] Myles Osborne has recently added to this literature by publishing the fascinating interrogation and trial of Kimathi rival Waruhiu Itote, or General China as he was known in the forest.[32] Kimathi himself contributed self-consciously to this archival patrimony. He was an avid writer and believed in the bureaucratic work of documentation (see below). In 1987, Maina wa Kinyatti published a collection of letters written by and addressed to Kimathi.[33] But questions of provenance, access, and translation have dogged the veracity of this archival collection.[34] As with Kimathi's contested legacy, irony marks the profusion, and yet also conspicuous absences, of Kimathi's historical records.

If one searches for the "trial of Dedan Kimathi" in a range of search engines, one invariably finds not its archival record but the groundbreaking play *The Trial of Dedan Kimathi* by Kenyan authors Ngũgĩ wa Thiong'o and Mĩcere Gĩthae Mũgo.[35] Written in 1976, the play uses the theater of the trial to reclaim and rehabilitate a lost history for a postcolonial world. Kimathi, in Ngũgĩ and Mũgo's production, stands before the court and declares his undying commitment to the Mau Mau cause. He gives a history of the movement, of the "Kenyan masses," and of the oppression suffered under British rule. While Ngũgĩ and Mũgo make clear in the preface that their work was "*not* a reproduction of the farcical 'trial' at Nyeri" but rather "an imaginative recreation and interpretation of the collective will of the Kenyan peasants and workers," without the actual trial transcript available for academic and public examination, Ngũgĩ and Mũgo became responsible for constructing the popular postcolonial imagination of the trial and the man himself. And yet, as Ngũgĩ and Mũgo submit in their foreword to this volume, theirs was an imagining of the trial, and of Kimathi himself, that rejected "the entire assumptions underlying that British kangaroo court in Nyeri." The absence of the archival record of Kimathi's final stand, at least in part, created a space for popular mythmaking and the continual reimagining of this contested past.

The Hunt for (the Trial of) Dedan Kimathi

The location of the archival record of Kimathi's trial, much like the fate of Kimathi's body, has remained a mystery. Unlike the British intelligence and colonial records described above, the records of colonial trials mostly remained in the colony where they were produced, most often in multiple certified sets kept at various levels of the judicial process that could include, but were not limited to, sites of appeal outside the colony. Many scholars, writers, journalists, politicians, and activists have gone in search of the Kimathi trial. The tireless journalist and author Joseph Karimi lamented the impossibility of locating the file in his 2013 biography of Kimathi.[36] I recently came across a letter from no less than the late J. M. Kariuki, the populist leader assassinated in 1975, requesting the Kimathi file from the High Court of Kenya for a book he planned to write in 1971.[37] The request was denied.

My own search for the trial began inconspicuously enough.[38] After working on the court transcript of another anticolonial rebel, Dini ya Msambwa leader Elijah Masinde, whose trial had been mislabeled in the archives and never before used by historians, I decided, back in 2008, to venture into the High Court of Kenya (now the Supreme Court) in search of Kimathi's trial.[39] I had heard from colleagues David Anderson and Stacey Hynd that the trial was housed there, and that a few had caught glimpses of various versions of the document, but that no one had as yet been able to secure a complete, certified copy. I arrived at the court and was escorted to the head archivist, who instructed me to bring a letter on my university's letterhead—the University of Cambridge at the time—with my request to view the file. Letter in hand, I returned and was told to meet another archivist in the basement where the court archives were held. Navigating the winding basement corridors stacked high with files and trial transcripts from floor to ceiling, I eventually found a young archivist who took my letter, told me to return the following day, and disappeared. The next day I arrived at the courthouse to find a stack of papers containing what appeared to be the trial of Dedan Kimathi lying on a crowded table.

The file was remarkable, containing a fuller picture of the trial than had ever been revealed before. I copied the entirety of the file and excitedly began research into this fascinating historical document. As I began to consult fellow scholars and legal experts, however, doubt was cast on the authenticity of this file. It was filled with strange artifacts. First among them, a header at the top of the file read REPUBLIC OF KENYA—but there was no "Republic of Kenya" in 1956.[40] Indeed in 1956 independence still seemed to many to be a far way off. The paper and typescript also did not match those in use at the time. The file had to have been produced in the postcolonial era. The file was also riddled with typos, omissions, and inconsistencies. At best, it seemed, this copy of the trial was a poor transcription of the original; at worst, it was a fabrication.

In consultation with the staff at the Supreme Court and archivists and scholars across East Africa, North America, and the UK, I attempted to authenticate the file and see if a certified original could be located. During that time, even the copy I had been given access to in 2008 seemed to have gone missing again. Exhaustive searches by archivists, curators, and staff at the Supreme Court and elsewhere seemed to be yielding little.

In 2015, I decided to widen my search. On a trip to the UK, I followed the trail left by the British lawyers who drafted Kimathi's final appeal to the Privy Council. Many interested parties and parliamentarians in Britain followed the case, warning of the danger of executing such a mythic figure in the Mau Mau movement and publicly pushing for the appeal.[41] British lawyer Dingle Foot took up the appeal. Foot had earlier successfully defended the Koinange family from the gallows.[42] It can be assumed that a certified copy of the trial would have been sent to Foot to allow him to craft the appeal, though whether he would have kept a copy in his personal archives was a gamble. Foot's archives, housed at Churchill College at the University of Cambridge, turned out to be under a hundred-year closure, meaning none of his files from the 1950s would be accessible until at least 2050. But from the index of his files and conversations with the archivists at Churchill, it seemed unlikely that the trial would be among its contents.

Next, I went in search of Foot's associate, a lawyer named Ralph Millner. Often described as a "socialist" or "communist" lawyer, Millner defended several African trade unionists and liberation leaders against colonial prosecutions, wrote booklets on Soviet justice, and worked on multiple high-profile cases across the British Empire. Millner's papers were housed at the Institute of Commonwealth Studies at Senate House Library in London. The archivist at the institute informed me on my visit in May 2015 that Millner's papers had only recently been catalogued and that, to his recollection, no scholar had yet made use of them. The files proved incredibly rich, revealing the fascinating career of this "socialist" anticolonial British lawyer.

And there it was, among Millner's eclectic papers, a complete, original, and certified transcript of the trial of Dedan Kimathi. The file's cover contained the proper citing of the trial's case number and was embossed with the seal of Her Majesty's Supreme Court of Kenya. The paper was the thin, semitranslucent sheets that were used at the time to allow for multiple copies to be produced at once. In addition to the trial, Millner's papers also included reproductions of several of the exhibits submitted during the trial, usually destroyed after such proceedings, and marginal notes from both the judge in the case and Millner himself. After consulting again with scholars, archivists, and members of the judiciary, I could now confidently attest that the copy of the trial found among Millner's papers was authentic.

A few weeks later, upon my return to Kenya, ever more material began to emerge. Archivists and curators at the Supreme Court, due in large part to the tireless efforts of Stanley Mutuma, were able to locate two file folders containing an array of material from the trial, including original, handwritten letters by Kimathi submitted as evidence by the prosecution and the X-ray of the contentious bullet wound he received during his capture. From this material, it seemed likely that the copy of the trial I had been given by the High Court was a poor transcription from the original, handwritten notes for the trial, written in an obscure shorthand that made full transcription almost impossible, probably hastily copied down sometime in the 1990s, judging by the paper and typescript. These newly uncovered files still did not contain a certified copy of the actual trial, and so it appeared the record of the trial found among Millner's papers was the only complete copy of the trial left in existence. Copies of the trial have now been "repatriated" to Kenya.[43] The retrieval and availability of this material, due in large part to the support, dedication, and cooperation of a wide range of scholars, archivists, and staff across the chief justice and deputy chief justice's offices, as well as the direct and enthusiastic support of former chief justice Willy Mutunga and former deputy chief justice Kalpana Hasmukhrai Rawal, has made possible the publication of this volume and the opening of a new chapter in the study of the Mau Mau rebellion.

Dedan Kimathi: The Man

Kimathi's biography is filled with questions and contradictions. Indeed, as this volume reveals, multiple Kimathis existed and continue to exist—many still wait for Kimathi to emerge from the forest, as did Ngũgĩ's Matigari, whose visage and material being seemed to morph and change as he moved about the country decades after independence.[44] But the dissonances in these stories provide opportunities; as Justin Willis has argued, "dissonances can tell us very much both about the ways in which people structure and understand the past—that is, about the ways in which they turn disparate fragments of knowledge into history."[45] The account of Kimathi's life given here has been gleaned from multiple sources, both written and oral, but should be read with an awareness that it, by necessity and design, must be partial, filled with dissonances, and open to continued contestation and revision.

Kimathi was born at Kanyinya, Tetu Location, Nyeri District of Central Province around 31 October 1920. He never knew his father but was raised by his mother, Waithuthi, and took her late husband's name, Wachiuri, as his own. From a young age, Kimathi excelled in school. At age fifteen, he entered Karunaini Primary School in Tetu Location, where he became well known for his prowess in debating clubs, his voracious appetite for the written word, and his own eloquent prose.[46] With school fees difficult to secure consistently, Kimathi moved in and out of schooling and odd jobs over the next few years. In 1941, Kimathi enlisted as a sweeper with the King's African Rifles (KAR), work he soon deserted after being exposed to the terrible conditions of African troops.[47] This brief service has led to the popular myth that Kimathi, like other Mau Mau generals, had served with colonial forces in the global theaters of war during World War II. In reality, his service was brief and confined to Kenya, a period even Kimathi omitted when relating his own biography to his interrogators after his capture.[48] In 1942 he enrolled in the Church of Scotland Mission Primary School at Tumutumu but was expelled in February 1944, for reasons that remain a matter of debate. After trying his hand at a variety of jobs, ranging from dairy clerk to farm laborer and contractor, Kimathi returned to his old school of Karunaini as an "untrained" teacher. While his teaching career was short lived, Kimathi is widely remembered for his dedication to education. Eloise Mukami, then a student at Karunaini and later married to Kimathi in 1948, remembered Kimathi as a brilliant and strict teacher: "Mwalimu Dedan Kĩmathi was tough. My schoolmates and I respected him for his intellect but also feared him for his insults when we did not perform well."[49] It is said that during his time at Karunaini Primary School he opened a night school, "teaching simple writing and reading to earn money to pay his school fees."[50] Indeed, the tribal policeman Njeru s/o Karundo, who would confirm Kimathi's identity on the day of his capture, in 1956, was a former Karunaini student and remembered Kimathi from his time there as a teacher.

Some time between 1947 and 1949, Kimathi joined the emerging nationalist movement, becoming a member of the Kenya African Union (KAU), the first national political party in Kenya. Kimathi served as secretary for the Ol Kalou branch, where Kimathi worked as a swineherd, and the Thomson's Falls branch of the KAU, though the exact chronology of his time as secretary remains difficult to pin down. Kimathi's political career and relationships within the KAU, however, seem to have been limited. In his interrogation, Kimathi asserted that he had seen then president Jomo Kenyatta at KAU meetings, particularly at the famous meeting at Thomson's Falls on 26 June 1952, but that he had "never had private conversations with him or with other political leaders."[51] The Ol Kalou and Thomson's Falls branches, where Kimathi served as secretary, were, by his time, controlled by the militant supporters of the Muhimu, an outgrowth of the Anake a Forti (Forty Group) made up of ex-servicemen, urban gangs, and frustrated political activists of the late 1940s. Rumors of a growing movement among the urban youths from the Muhimu, squatters, and a wider range of supporters in the rural areas of Central Kenya were spreading in the early 1950s. The Muhimu committee played a central role in transforming and spreading the practice of oathing from the urban areas to rural villages.[52] Kimathi quickly rose among their ranks, becoming a respected oath administrator and organizer of a growing movement as yet without a name. Violent episodes increased into the early 1950s as attacks on settler farms, arson, and political murders gave shape to an emerging insurgency. Reports of mass oathing ceremonies, growing resistance and acts of arson on settler farms in the White Highlands, and the murder of "loyalist" Senior Chief Waruhiu prompted the colonial government to declare a State of Emergency in October 1952. The following few months would see the murders of white settlers, Senior Chief Nderi Wang'ombe, and prominent Nairobi politician Tom Mbotela. Directly following the declaration of the emergency, the colonial government launched a series of operations aimed at imprisoning political leaders, rounding up Gikuyu residents of Nairobi, and interning in concentration camps both those suspected of Mau Mau involvement and those in the rural areas accused of providing "passive" support to the movement.[53] In November 1952, Kimathi found himself arrested for the first time during one of the frequent "screenings" of farm laborers, on suspicions of his involvement in the murder of Senior Chief Nderi. But Kimathi managed to escape by bribing a local warder (perhaps with the assent of local chief Muhoya, whose relationship with Kimathi is discussed below). Kimathi then headed for the Nyandarua forest, also known as the Aberdare forest.

It was in the Nyandarua forest that Kimathi rose to become one of the most important leaders of the Mau Mau rebellion. His time in the forest is the best-documented, though still greatly contested, period in his life. There he founded the Kenya Defence Council and the Kenya Parliament, both attempts to bring order, hierarchy, and centralization to the scattered Mau Mau forces. Unlike General Mathenge, Kimathi was known less for his prowess as a field general and more for his speeches and ability to draw on global exemplars of revolution and political thought.[54] He was known to tour all *itungati*, troops of young "warriors," giving motivational speeches to the young men and chastising their leaders for any breach of protocol he discovered at their camps.[55] Kimathi was obsessed with the bureaucratic recording of the daily work of his troops and the ever-shifting organization of Mau Mau forces.[56] At a now famous meeting held at Mwathe in August 1953, Kimathi lectured the hundreds gathered on the need for record keeping.[57] Special Branch reports in June 1953 repeatedly reference finding typewriters, printing machines, and other record-keeping materials.[58] According to Derek Peterson, these record books "would make them citizens of a future independent polity. . . . Mau Mau's record keeping was more than a memory bank. In writing, Mau Mau imagined a counter-state."[59] In the forest, Kimathi became a statesman, and imagined himself as a leader of a new polity of citizens of an ordered, lawful, and progressive society.

But Kimathi was also at the center of many of the more contentious conflicts over discipline and moral order in the forest: as Lonsdale put it, "quarrels of gender and education were at the heart of Mau Mau's agonized spirit of manhood."[60] While Kimathi enforced a strict code of legal prohibitions and punishments in the forest, he also drew resentment from fellow fighters when he failed to punish his brother Wambararia for attempted murder. While Kimathi chaired meetings on the question of women in the forest, penned prohibitions on sexual affairs with female fighters, and was the first to allow women to be promoted in the military ranks, he was also well known for his relations with female fighters, often described in memoirs on both sides as keeping a "harem" of lovers in his company.[61] Most famous perhaps was Kimathi's relationship with his long-term mistress in the forest, Wanjiru Wambogo, the only woman in the forest to be awarded the rank of colonel and regarded as the "head of the women and the mother of Mumbi's children."[62]

Kimathi's confrontations with other generals were legendary. Superintendent Henderson noted that "in the rest of Kenya there were a few Africans who could have held their own with Kimathi in council or on the platform. But they were not in the forest and Kimathi was."[63] In the forest, literacy often became a dividing line among the leadership.[64] Kimathi openly criticized the unlettered and they in turn accused Kimathi of having been poisoned by Christianity and Western education. In March 1955, General Stanley Mathenge and his followers broke away from Kimathi's

Kenya Parliament and formed their own association, the Kenya Riigi, which translates as the woven door that secured the opening of a Gikuyu household.[65] As Peterson has argued, "to Riigi critics, the bureaucrats of Kimathi's Kenya Parliament were untrustworthy. . . . General Kahiu-Itina accused Kimathi and other educated Protestant leaders of using their illiterate followers for their own selfish ends."[66]

Of particular interest in relation to his later trial is the question of Kimathi's role in and openness to negotiations with the British. In August 1953, Kimathi sent a letter to prominent politician W. W. W. Awori to be published in his newspaper *Habari za dunia*, which Awori published and then turned over to the colonial police Criminal Investigation Department (CID). The letter was then translated into English and published in the *East African Standard*. In this letter, Kimathi wrote, "I have told all leaders of the war in the forest areas to stop fighting again from August 1, 1953. . . . Now it is only peace we want to maintain."[67] In Special Branch files, Huw Bennett found similar references to negotiations in 1953 indicating the Kenya Intelligence Committee believed these letters to reveal "a sincere wish by many Mau Mau to surrender," though they remained doubtful of the reach of Kimathi's influence.[68] Such discussions led to the first surrender offer by the British government on 24 August 1953. When few surrendered in the first few weeks following the offer, Kimathi again requested negotiations toward a conditional truce, though Bennett was unable to find any evidence that this request was followed up.[69] While this initial surrender scheme yielded little, these records do demonstrate how early in the Emergency lines of communication had been opened and negotiations discussed, with Kimathi at the center.

There also exists a series of letters that discuss negotiations and surrender possibilities between Kimathi and Senior Chief Kagumba wa Muhoya, chief of Ihururu, in the North Tetu division of Nyeri. The relationship between Muhoya and Kimathi revealed the complex and intertwined personal histories of dissent and loyalism within the Mau Mau rebellion.[70] Kimathi was age-mates with Muhoya's sons, and worked with Muhoya during his time at the Ihururu Dairyman Cooperative Society. Members of Muhoya's home guard had gone to school with Kimathi, as had several members of the party who would later capture Kimathi. Indeed, Kimathi pinpointed Muhoya as a possible "go-between" for the rebel leader and the provincial administration. Their relationship was obviously complex. In one letter, Kimathi chastised Muhoya for not controlling his home guard forces and announced that he would "come again in order to see you face to face, Muhoya."[71] He ended the letter by warning Muhoya that if he wanted war, then Muhoya best "enter the aeroplane with your Home Guard and go to Europe." Exhibit No. 25 from Kimathi's trial, a letter dated 2 June 1954 from Muhoya to Kimathi, revealed the regularity of their communications. In this letter, Muhoya informed Kimathi that he may "at any time surrender with your men under the original terms. . . . you and your followers will not be molested if coming in to surrender."[72] Henderson discovered this letter in a discarded skin satchel in 1955. While some in the colonial office remained wary of Muhoya's true loyalties, the chief publicly derided Mau Mau as unruly youths who should return to productive labor and familial obligations. Muhoya managed to not only survive but also profit from the polarizing politics of the era.[73]

The capture of General China, on 15 January 1954, provided the government with a new strategic option in regards to surrender negotiations. General China, born Waruhiu Itote and leader of the Mount Kenya forces, had a complicated relationship with Kimathi, who outranked him but allowed him a "practically unrestricted hand" in the leading of his troops.[74] China's capture came as a result of an accidental gun battle between China's men and government forces, during which China was shot. Though China, like Kimathi, would later claim he had come in to surrender and to negotiate on behalf of Mau Mau, he would be charged with consorting with armed men and the possession of ammunition, both capital charges under the Emergency Regulations.[75] Then assistant superintendent Ian Henderson led the interrogation of China and read in China's detailed depiction of the Mau Mau's structural organization the "sole wish . . . to expound his political testament . . . and then walk to the gallows without trial."[76] Henderson reported that China wanted "no discord between himself and Dedan Kimathi although he does not consider that Kimathi is a good leader." While China claimed Kimathi had lost "a lot of prestige" and that he was "frightened to leave the forest," he affirmed that Kimathi was the undisputed leader and could not "be deposed."[77] Although China was found guilty and sentenced to death, his sentence would be commuted in return for his cooperation with the colonial government in negotiating surrender terms with other Mau Mau generals still at large. After a large-scale surrender scheme negotiated by China and Henderson ended in what seems to have been an unintended slaughter by British forces of Mau Mau forces gathering to surrender, negotiations ceased and China was sent to Lokitaung Prison until 1962, where he was imprisoned alongside future president Jomo Kenyatta.[78]

Subsequent attempts at negotiations caused great internal dissension. Who should represent Mau Mau grievances and what the conditions of surrender should be caused ever-greater rifts to emerge among the leadership. In January 1955 the colonial government made another attempt at negotiations, declaring a two-week cease-fire and dropping leaflets offering amnesty to Mau Mau who surrendered. According to Kahinga Wachanga, Kimathi rejected this offer out of hand, but Wachanga and others felt the offer was genuine and proceeded with the negotiations. What happened next is perhaps best told by Wachanga himself:

> At first light the following morning, we were awakened by Kimathi's *itungati.* We were told to raise our hands and we were searched for weapons. Then we were marched to meet Kimathi and ten Murang'a junior leaders. That morning, Kimathi had his men arrest twenty-seven senior leaders. Kimathi interrogated us upon our arrival in his *mbuci* ["guerrilla camp," derived from the English term "bush"]. He asked us why we had met with the government without him. Kimathi was a very jealous man. He did not want any one to be above him. He did not like it when we negotiated without him. He had wanted to lead the negotiations himself. Kimathi ordered his *itungati* to build a temporary camp to keep us in. We were held and interrogated there by Kimathi and his Lieutenants. We decided to try to escape after the fourth day in that camp. We were able to overpower our guards and get away into the forest. . . . This was truly the lowest point in our struggle. Kimathi had shown himself to the other forest leaders. From that time, he was unable to command the respect or support of any forest fighters.[79]

Kimathi's scribe, Njama, tells a very different story of the circumstances and nature of this encounter, but he comes to a similar conclusion: after this affair, "Mathenge and his supporters had classified the Kenya Parliament and its supporters as enemies."[80] Whatever the motives and intentions, it is clear from these multiple accounts, including those presented in the primary documents in this volume, that Kimathi had been discussing negotiations since at least mid-1953 and believed that if negotiations were to proceed, he was the only man to lead them. Despite the seeming failure of these multiple surrender negotiations, the forest war was all but over by the middle of 1955. Surrenders increased and the divides within the Mau Mau movement were widely publicized in British propaganda. But Kimathi was still at large, a fact that dogged colonial officials and inspired detained Mau Mau fighters and ordinary Kenyans across the colony.

The "hunt" for Dedan Kimathi has been enshrined in multiple accounts and elevated to mythic levels. Early intelligence reports seem to have known the least about Kimathi's movements of any of the leaders in the forest.[81] The elusive figure of Kimathi became a symbol of the entire rebellion. Home Guards training for service used an effigy of Kimathi for target practice.[82] For many British officials, most famously in the case of Superintendent Ian Henderson, capturing Kimathi became "an obsession."[83] Intelligence reports told of Kimathi wearing the overcoat of the "late Mr. Ruck," an image that certainly would have added to his brutal and remorseless image in British minds.[84] A reward of KSh 10,000, or £500, was proffered in 1953 for information "leading to the arrest of a former Secretary of the Thompson's [*sic*] Falls Branch of the KAU, Dedan Kimathi wa Waciuri, who is wanted in connection with the murder of chief Nderi."[85] While British soldiers were not eligible for such rewards, British company commanders, with the knowledge of their commanding officers, made unofficial offers to their soldiers of KSh 100 "to kill the Mau Mau leader Dedan Kimathi"—a matter that prompted great controversy during the McLean Court of Inquiry in 1953 that investigated disciplinary breaches and misconduct among British forces.[86] In October 1954 the colonial government published thirty thousand flyers in Gikuyu asking, "Have you seen Dedan Kimathi lately?" hoping to enlist the public's help and further restrict Kimathi's ability to move throughout the region.[87]

Kimathi's legend grew with every month he eluded the British forces. Detained politician J. M. Kariuki remembered being forced to repeat the phrase "Dedan Kimathi and Stanley Mathenge will be finished in the forest" by the guards at the Langata detention camp.[88] Kariuki and others would subvert this psychological torture through some creative linguistic gymnastics: "fortunately the Swahili word for 'flourish' (ishi) is very similar to that for 'finish' (isha) so by mumbling in deep voices we managed to disguise this one easily." The "Song of Kimathi" elevated Kimathi to godly heights, with Kimathi, like the biblical Moses or perhaps the first Gikuyu man, ascending "into the mountains alone."[89] Kimathi's very name became synonymous with the Mau Mau rebellion, for all sides.

By early 1956, however, Kimathi was increasingly isolated, surrounded by a few loyal followers but constantly harassed not only by colonial forces but also by the *komerera* gangs that roamed the forests. The komerera were often former Mau Mau fighters condemned for their "idleness and cowardice," as the term implied: "as vagrants they perpetrated anti-social violence, refused to cook for their leaders, and failed to fight the British."[90] Kimathi saw in the komerera all the ill discipline and lack of moral order that he abhorred. From the early days, Mau Mau leaders worried that the komerera gangs who operated on the "fringes of guerilla operational areas" would damage their cause and that the unprincipled banditry of these "thugs" could prove "politically disastrous."[91] As Mau Mau forces became increasingly divided, komerera gangs proved ever more successful in stealing their stores, harassing their troops, and causing disorder in the few camps left under Kimathi's command. In addition, Kimathi had to contend with the "pseudogangs," bands of former Mau Mau fighters who had surrendered or been captured and sent back into the forest to infiltrate, capture, or kill the remaining forest fighters.

The hunt for Kimathi was prolonged and aided by the coalescence of these various forces. In June 1956, Henderson's forces captured Kimathi's brother Wambararia, who fed them false information that stalled the search for a time.[92] Henderson, by his own account, ramped up the search after Wambararia's capture, sending "a select group of the very best of our converted terrorists . . . over ninety hard-core Mau Mau" into the forest to search for Kimathi.[93] Although accounts vary, Kimathi's "forest wife," Wanjiru, either deserted him or was told by him to "be caught by yourself!" to allow Kimathi a close escape sometime in mid-October 1956.[94] When Wanjiru was captured, "she swore at her captors, spat at them, bit them and kicked at them as they bound her up."[95] Henderson's account of her initial obstinacy after her capture, sudden turn against Kimathi during interrogation, and surprising release soon after has led some to claim she gave crucial intelligence on Kimathi's movements, though very little evidence exists to support these claims.[96] In Henderson's words, "it seemed that even Ngai [God] was deserting Kimathi."[97] When Kimathi was finally captured, in the early hours of 21 October 1956 in the emergency trenches dug to separate the "native reserve" and the Nyandarua forest, he was alone.[98]

Neither Henderson nor any of his "Mau Mau turncoats" were actually present when a troop of tribal police captured Kimathi on the edge of the forest reserve. While newspaper accounts and subsequent memoirs described the careful planning and the "tightening of the net" leading up to the capture, when read from the multiple accounts given as testimony during the trial the capture appears more accidental. Popular accounts tell of Kimathi entering the reserve that day, as he knew a film would be playing at Karunaini village, an event that would pull the civilian population away from their farms and allow Kimathi to gather some food.[99] Walking along the trench that morning, carrying a few ears of corn and some sugarcane, a troop of tribal police spotted his shadowy figure and began chase.

The actual progression of the subsequent events during the capture proved the most contentious aspect of Kimathi's trial. How Kimathi came to be shot and captured remains disputed. The tribal police reserve constable responsible for shooting Kimathi, Ndirangu s/o Mau, would be alone during the actual shooting, despite earlier claims by his partner on patrol, Njogi s/o Ngatia, that he had witnessed the shooting. Ndirangu claimed he shot Kimathi in the leg as Kimathi attempted to reenter the forest. The evidence, including the X-ray of Kimathi's bullet wound (fig. A.3 in appendix), as noted by Judge O'Connor in his judgment, however, did not support Ndirangu's account. In 1985, at the age of seventy-nine, Ndirangu would recount a version of the capture to a local journalist almost identical to his testimony to the court in 1956, save one addition: after being shot, Ndirangu claimed Kimathi said to him "ni wega (It's okay)."[100]

Kimathi's demeanor after the capture prompts some interesting questions. Kimathi was, by all accounts, an eloquent and effusive speaker. His silence after the capture stood out not only to British officials but moreover to local onlookers.[101] After being read the charges against him, Kimathi stated, "I would like to say that I never knew there was such a law," pausing for a few seconds and then adding, "I have nothing more to say."[102] The trial perhaps offers further insights, but Kimathi's silence following his capture raises questions not only possibly about his own motivations and state of mind at the moment of capture but moreover about the possible colonial omissions or erasures of Kimathi's voice during the period between capture and trial, a point raised by Mũgo and Ngũgĩ in their foreword.

The British press reported Kimathi's capture worldwide. The accompanying photograph pictured Kimathi, stripped of his leopard skin coat and cap, from an extremely high angle, dreadlocks wound tight atop his head, as if a subdued animal or helpless infant (photos 2 and 3).[103] A British Pathé newsreel video proclaimed to the world that the capture of Kimathi "will have a great psychological effect for the Mau Mau leaders still at large are only small fry. Without Kimathi, Mau Mau's days are numbered."[104] The government distributed one hundred thousand leaflets throughout Central Kenya detailing how Kimathi was captured. Special broadcasts announcing his capture were made with the aim of reaching "even the most remote and isolated villages in the Emergency areas."[105] Kimathi's capture also happened to coincide with the royal visit of Princess Margaret to Kenya, making Kimathi's capture share the front page of the *East African Standard* on 22 October 1956 with full images of the princess's arrival. The princess was regaled with stories of his capture, even meeting with the tribal police officers that led the capture outside of Government House.[106] Broadcast around the world, Kimathi's capture brought the special-forces operations in Kenya to a "spectacular conclusion."[107]

The trial would occur almost a month later and last eight days. It would be one of the last in the long parade of Mau Mau trials throughout the 1950s that would lead 1,090 Africans to their deaths by hanging and thousands more to detention camps.[108] The charges against Kimathi were unlawful possession of a firearm and unlawful possession of ammunition.[109] Originally, British officials also charged Kimathi with the murder of Mwai Itufanwa, a forest guard who served outside Aberdare National Park, near Nyeri, and was killed in December 1952.[110] But murder was a much harder charge to prove, and the mere possession of the pistol, a charge never denied by Kimathi, carried the death penalty under the Emergency Regulations. The murder charge was thus "delayed," though according to Prosecutor D. W. Conroy, it was technically never dropped.[111]

Outside the courthouse, hundreds would gather each day hoping to catch a glimpse of the rebel leader, carried in and out of the court on a stretcher, still suffering from the bullet wound to his upper thigh (photo 6). Crowds grew to the point that local police set up roadblocks leading into the town.[112] Among those in the crowd was Kimathi's mother, who would also testify in the trial. *Time* magazine would describe the scene with vivid, and highly prejudicial, imagery:

> Day after day, in the shade of the great jacaranda tree outside the courthouse at Nyeri, an old woman squatted, moodily scratching the vermin beneath her filthy rags. Inside, on trial for his life before a British judge and a jury of three Kikuyu elders from his native village, was her son, Dedan Kimathi, 36, self-styled Field Marshal, Knight Commander of the African Empire, President of the Parliament of Kenya and Commander in Chief of the Land Liberation Army, the man once feared through all Kenya as the leader of some 10,000 Mau Mau terrorists.[113]

The article would go on to describe Kimathi as "riddled with venereal disease . . . a leader with no army, betrayed even by his mistress . . . [having] only the memory of past power to sustain him." As an ambulance drove Kimathi away from the courthouse each day, the article continued, "a crowd of impassive Kikuyu natives watched in stony silence," and Kimathi's mother "stared at her son's Kikuyu judges and spat in the dust." Present in this obviously sensationalized account lurk many of the colonial assumptions regarding not only Kimathi but moreover the wider African public who bore witness to this trial.[114]

Inside the courthouse, Kimathi stood trial with his court-appointed lawyer, Frederick Miller, before Justice O'Connor, Crown prosecutor Conroy, and three Gikuyu "assessors." By all accounts, Kimathi appeared feeble, visibly drugged and in pain from the surgeries performed on his leg and hip after his capture. Indeed, the proceedings had to be suspended on the first day due to concerns over Kimathi's medical condition. This was not to be a soapbox trial, as in the cases of other anticolonial leaders put on trial the likes of Jomo Kenyatta and Nelson Mandela.[115] As litigant, Kimathi proved himself the ever-controlled, measured speaker he had gained a reputation for in debating clubs and in his command of troops in the forest. Kimathi used the complicated internal politics of Mau Mau, the colonial government's often contradictory counterinsurgency strategies, and his own painful, seemingly hidden history of epilepsy to make his case.[116]

It was this last strategy that provided some of the most poignant moments of the trial: in Kimathi's words, "during my life I have suffered from what the Kikuyu call 'devils.' It throws me down to the ground and I become unconscious. . . . It started a very long time ago when I was young . . . when I was a small boy. I have these fits very often. They have continued all my life." While epilepsy remains a highly stigmatized disorder in modern Kenya, its associations with excessive religiosity, mental instability, or prophetic calling have a distinct colonial history.[117] Kimathi spoke of receiving treatment for his condition in the forest: "I have been treated by 'medicine men' (Witness corrects the interpreter's translation to 'Witch doctors') not by African doctors of medicine." Kimathi's correction of the interpreter here raises questions not only about translation but moreover about the role of witchcraft in the movement: in 1955, the district officer and later historian John C. Nottingham voiced the widely held official view that "on witchcraft all movements such as Mau Mau must be built."[118] Indeed, both sides appealed to the power of witchcraft in their propaganda: British propaganda painted Mau Mau fighters and supporters as brainwashed, under the spell of powerful leaders who used witchcraft to control their loyalties, while Mau Mau propagandists similarly invoked their ability to harness witchcraft powers and enlisted Kamba witchcraft practitioners to "employ power and paraphernalia against the state."[119]

Such testimony also raised questions regarding Kimathi's mental state, and indeed the collective mental stability of all those who fought in the forest. While a defense of "insanity" was specifically not sought in this case, and indeed the evidence of epilepsy was presented not as explanation of Kimathi's behavior or leadership but rather as explanation of his failure to articulate his desire to surrender at his capture, the specter of madness and witchcraft raised through this testimony certainly resonated with a much longer history of the pathologization of dissent.[120] The testimony around Kimathi's history with epilepsy also provides a stinging resonance with Maina wa Kinyatti's vitriolic rant in 2007 during the unveiling of the Dedan Kimathi statue (photo 9), in which he argued that the fighters of the Mau Mau Land and Freedom Army were "still being treated like an epileptic orphan."[121] While not examined explicitly in this volume, Kimathi's trial transcript opens up the possibility of new insights and explorations into African and European perceptions of health and disease, witchcraft and power, psychology and rebellion.

For Kimathi, this trial, which would almost certainly end in his death, represented a last opportunity to record his patriotic vision and renegotiate the meaning of the Mau Mau movement. And yet, as a close reading of the trial and as the contributors to this volume suggest, multiple meanings can be drawn from Kimathi's testimony.[122] As General

China wrote in his memoir regarding his own trial, "whether anyone tells the whole truth in a court which is trying him for his life is doubtful; at least, I doubt it."[123]

After the assessors returned their unanimous verdict of guilty, Judge O'Connor sentenced Kimathi to death by hanging. Multiple appeals failed and Kimathi was moved to Kamiti Prison, in Nairobi, where he was held until the day of his execution (see fig. A.5). In his memoir, former Special Branch officer Derek Peter Franklin provided an account of Kimathi's final days, relayed to him by his brother Raymond, who served as one of Kimathi's guards. He described Kimathi's cell as cramped and stench ridden, with Kimathi originally manacled by one hand to the wall above his bed before medical concerns prompted an adjustment of the spatial arrangement in his cell.[124] Another account offered a different image of Kimathi in his final days. On a torn slip of paper telegraphed to London in February 1957, a "Senior Prison Officer" at Kamiti Prison described Kimathi as a model prisoner, and said of his final walk to the gallows, "to the last he was composed and quiet."[125]

Kimathi's death prompted a variety of responses. In the *Daily Worker*, renowned author Doris Lessing called Kimathi's execution "a completely barbarous act of which we should all be deeply ashamed."[126] Solly Sachs, a prominent trade unionist exiled from South Africa, predicted "the execution of Dedan Kimathi will send a wave of horror and indignation throughout the peoples of Africa and Asia, and of Europe and America, who are bitterly opposed to the policy of terror and oppression in Kenya and other parts of Africa."[127] For many Kenyans, mourning for Kimathi would have to remain clandestine with Emergency Regulations still in effect until 1960, thousands still in detention, and no body to bury. The date of his death, however, inspired yearly commemorations and has served as a symbolic reference point for continuing postcolonial struggles.[128]

The Volume

This critical edition provides the first public availability of the complete trial of Dedan Kimathi. The publication of the trial transcript may be shocking, even unsettling to those for whom Ngũgĩ and Mũgo's version provided the reclamation of a collective history of solidarity, heroism, and national fidelity. But a close reading of the trial reveals that much of our historical and contemporary knowledge of Kimathi, the internal structure of Mau Mau, and the political legacies of rebellion and counterinsurgency in Kenya are in need of further public and academic reflection. Annotations have been provided throughout the primary texts to offer points of clarification and context. The audiences for this volume are thus necessarily multiple.

To put the trial in a broader context, this volume also includes material related to the trial and several other important documents. The Judgment and the Appeals for Kimathi's case provide a lens into how the British colonial justice system interpreted and carried out legal procedures in this very high profile case. The thoroughness of these procedures, as Anderson argues in his contribution to this volume, speaks to the recognition of the potential impact of the Kimathi verdict.

If one is looking for a Kimathi closer to that of Ngũgĩ and Mũgo's creation, then one might find him more readily in the pages of his interrogation. By the end of this report, Kimathi's interrogator A. D. Dunn reveals his frustration with Kimathi's unwillingness to give names. Throughout, Kimathi refuses to reveal the true name of his "mistress" and supposed "betrayer." He refuses to name any of those who participated in the "passive wing" of Mau Mau, those who provided food and support from the reserves. Dunn ends by noting that the "subject is a man of tremendous personality, with a well developed sense of humor, and punctuated his obvious lies with a large grin." But, as Anderson and Lonsdale point out in their contributions to this volume, the account offered by Kimathi under interrogation deviates significantly from, and even at times contradicts, his testimony before the colonial court.

Finally, several key exhibits from the trial and letters written by Kimathi have been included in their original form. Considering the voluminous collection of letters Kimathi wrote over the course of the rebellion, the selection of letters chosen as exhibits reveals the selective nature of the prosecution's case as well as the hesitancy of the defense to submit into evidence any further documentation that might prove incriminating. Exhibit No. 22 (Document 7) offers a particularly unique source, as it appears to be the only letter still in existence originally written by Kimathi in Gikuyu. Further, the translation of the document into English (Document 8) for the court proceedings reveals the ambiguous and politically charged nature of such work. I am grateful to Derek Peterson and Joseph Kariuki Muriithi for their insightful and provocative annotations on the work of translation and the relationship between these two versions of this letter. Other documents, including Kimathi's last letter to Father Marino, and further exhibits from the trial, including the contentious X-ray of Kimathi's wound, provide a complex constellation of archival material now available for public and academic analysis.

This volume also includes critical essays by some of the most prominent Mau Mau scholars in the world. David Anderson's chapter provides an incisive look into the mechanics of British colonial justice and the character of the legal proceedings taken against Kimathi. Kimathi's trial, in Anderson's assessment, was "functional and ordinary," and in many ways more rigorous and carefully orchestrated than other Mau Mau trials at the time. But it was also rich with political significance, and filled with revelations on Kimathi's complex motivations and shifting strategies during the course of the rebellion. While encouraging caution regarding the possibility of the "colonial fabrications" that Mũgo and Ngũgĩ point to in their foreword, Anderson demonstrates just how crucial such texts can be in the historical project of "triangulation" and the "balancing of evidence."

There is perhaps no scholar more renowned or respected for investigating the moral economy of Mau Mau than John Lonsdale. In his contribution, Lonsdale draws together threads of arguments he has made throughout his career to examine the ways Kimathi's defense put "Mau Mau's internal debates publicly on trial." Setting Kimathi's defense in a longer genealogy of moral disputes over social obligation, collective action, and generational discipline, Lonsdale investigates the "intimate unease" and necessary subversions such histories engendered.

Placing the Kimathi trial into a broader social and political context, Nicholas Githuku's chapter offers provocative insights and critical reflections on the roles of legality, morality, and identity within the Mau Mau movement and the decolonization of Kenya. Githuku importantly asks readers to think equally about what was "not on trial" in Kimathi's case. Using a broad theoretical and interdisciplinary framework, Githuku unpacks the "uneasy tango" of Britain and Kenya's colonial pasts and reveals Kimathi as a "privileged identity" in contemporary conceptions of nationalism, state building, and social justice.

Simon Gikandi's chapter delves into the spaces between literary representation and historical imagination, memory and forgetting, materiality and absence, the archival and the imaginative. As popular literature has played a prominent role in the making of "Mau Maus of the mind," Gikandi explores the elusive literary figure of Kimathi as a "floating signifier"—a symbolic referent for national imaginaries that resists repression despite the danger his figure continues to pose to the postcolonial state. Popular writing around Kimathi, Gikandi argues, further reveals contemporary "historiographic anxieties" and provides a "space of dislocating the truth claims of colonial and postcolonial history."

Finally, Lotte Hughes's chapter bravely dives into the murky waters of the ongoing battles over the memorialization of Mau Mau in Kenya, battles that have often featured Kimathi at their center. Taking a broader lens, Hughes's contribution offers new ways to think about the so-called "amnesia policy" and "crisis of memory" in postcolonial Kenya, and the state and nonstate heritage projects that reflect the fragmented experiences of rebellion as much as their aims of reconciliation. Examining the activism of Mau Mau veterans themselves in driving for public recognition, Hughes unpacks the national processes of memory making and the search for a "useable" Mau Mau past.

If there is one aspect of this story that is beyond question, it is that Kimathi was a dedicated scribe. By all accounts, he was a careful and charismatic speaker; a bureaucratic leader, who believed in the importance of record keeping and history writing; an intellect to be reckoned with, in person and on the page. In 1953, when the CID complained that they still did not have a picture of the famed Mau Mau leader, Kimathi staged two photographs and had them delivered to the Nyeri police station. In the second, he posed deep in the Nyandarua forest, head high, holding a rifle (see fig. A.4). At a time when the mere possession of a weapon carried the death penalty, Kimathi announced himself to the world holding a rifle. The *East African Standard* would publish a modified version of the photo, cropping out the rifle and centering only Kimathi's face, carrying the caption "This is Dedan Kimathi, the notorious Mau Mau terrorist, on whose head there is a price of £500. . . . It shows him in an arrogant pose—head thrown back and hair brushed out, recalling the pompous manner struck by Mussolini—so that the light exaggerates his features."[129] The prosecution would use this photo as evidence against Kimathi's claims to nonviolence: when asked why he had the photo taken, Kimathi replied, blithely, "It is no harm to have a photo taken. I wished to have it taken. The rifle was not mine."[130]

But in the first, earlier photograph sent to the CID, Kimathi posed holding a different weapon: the pen (see photo 1). Another rebel stands beside him, holding open a notebook as if ready to take down Kimathi's every word.[131] It is in this spirit that this volume presents this material, made public for the first time since Kimathi's death, sixty years ago. The voices captured in this volume, from colonial officials to Kenyan writers to international scholars to Kimathi himself, do not always agree. Archives such as these documents create as much as they record. No one, singular "Kimathi" emerges from this volume. But, as former chief justice Mutunga evokes in his introductory note, through such revitalized public and academic engagements, we hope, "a luta continua!"

Notes

1. Criminal Case no. 46 of 1956, Dedan Kimathi v. Regina, Her Majesty's Supreme Court of Kenya at Nyeri, Papers of Ralph Millner, Archives of the Institute of Commonwealth Studies, Senate House Library, London, ICS165/3/2.

2. As Mĩcere Gĩthae Mũgo and Ngũgĩ wa Thiong'o point out in their foreword, along with several of the contributors in this volume, the term Mau Mau was popularized by British officials and the colonial press, and its origins and meaning remain contested. However, scholars and veterans of the movement alike have largely taken up the ascription in the postcolonial period. For some of the debates over the use of the term and the multiple "faces" of this rebellion, see E. S. Atieno Odhiambo, "The Production of History in Kenya: The Mau Mau Debate," *Canadian Journal of African Studies* 25, no. 2 (1991): 300–307; E. S. Atieno Odhiambo and John Lonsdale, eds., *Mau Mau and Nationhood: Arms, Authority and Narration* (Athens: Ohio University Press, 2003); Donald L. Barnett and Karari Njama, *Mau Mau from Within: Autobiography and Analysis of Kenya's Peasant Revolt* (New York: Monthly Review Press, 1966), 54–55; Bruce Berman, "Nationalism, Ethnicity, and Modernity: The Paradox of Mau Mau," *Canadian Journal of African Studies* 25, no. 2 (1991): 181–206; Frederick Cooper, "Mau Mau and the Discourses of Decolonization," review of *Squatters and the Roots of Mau Mau*, by Tabitha Kanogo, and *Economic and Social Origins of Mau Mau*, by David W. Throup, *Journal of African History* 29, no. 2 (1988): 313–20; John Lonsdale, "Mau Maus of the Mind: Making Mau Mau and Remaking Kenya," *Journal of African History* 31, no. 3 (November

1990): 393–421; Lonsdale, "The Moral Economy of Mau Mau: Wealth, Poverty, and Civic Virtue in Kikuyu Political Thought," in *Unhappy Valley: Conflict in Kenya and Africa,* vol. 2, *Violence and Ethnicity,* ed. Bruce Berman and John Lonsdale (Athens: Ohio University Press, 1992), 315–504; Carl G. Rosberg Jr. and John Nottingham, *The Myth of "Mau Mau": Nationalism in Kenya* (New York: Praeger, 1966). For debates on the term Mau Mau, see also Lonsdale's contribution to this volume.

3. For the sake of consistency, the term Gikuyu is used throughout this volume, though the common form of Kikuyu appears in several of the primary and secondary sources and in references to historical names (e.g., Kikuyu Central Association).

4. Ian Henderson, *The Hunt For Kimathi,* with Philip Goodhart (London: Hamish Hamilton, 1958), 22.

5. *East African Standard,* 7 September 1953.

6. William R. Ochieng', "Dedan Kimathi: The Real Story," *Maseno Journal of Education, Arts and Science* 1, no. 1 (1992): 134.

7. Ali A. Mazrui, "On Heroes and Uhuru-Worship," *Transition* 3, no. 11 (November 1963): 28.

8. Other scholars have argued this point. See, for example, David M. Anderson, *Histories of the Hanged: Britain's Dirty War in Kenya and the End of Empire* (London: Weidenfeld and Nicolson, 2005), 287. For a fascinating account of academic debates over the place of Mau Mau and Kimathi in Kenyan historiography, see David William Cohen, *The Combing of History* (Chicago: University of Chicago Press, 1994), 59–64.

9. As quoted in S. M. Shamsul Alam, *Rethinking the Mau Mau in Colonial Kenya* (New York: Palgrave Macmillan, 2007), 41. For Eloise Mukami's recollections of this event, see Wairimũ Nderitũ, *Mũkami Kĩmathi: Mau Mau Freedom Fighter* (Nairobi: Mdahalo Bridging Divides, 2017), xiii–xix.

10. Marshall S. Clough, *Mau Mau Memoirs: History, Memory, and Politics* (Boulder: Lynne Rienner, 1998), 82.

11. Ibid., 243.

12. H. K. Wachanga, ed. Robert Whittier, *The Swords of Kirinyaga: The Fight for Land and Freedom* (Nairobi: East African Literature Bureau, 1975), 26

13. Ibid., 32.

14. Barnett and Njama, *Mau Mau from Within;* Sam Kahiga, *Dedan Kimathi: The Real Story* (Nairobi: Longman Kenya, 1990); Waruhiu Itote, *"Mau Mau" General* (Nairobi: East African Publishing House, 1967); Itote, *Mau Mau in Action* (Nairobi: Transafrica, 1979); Shiraz Durrani, *Kĩmathi: Mau Mau's First Prime Minister of Kenya* (London: Vita Books, 1986); Tabitha Kanogo, *Dedan Kimathi: A Biography* (Nairobi: East African Educational Publishers, 1992); David Njeng'ere, *Dedan Kimathi: Leader of Mau Mau* (Nairobi: Sasa Sema Publications, 2003); Wachanga, *Swords;* Kenneth Watene,

Dedan Kimathi (Nairobi: Transafrica, 1974). For a comprehensive look at how Kimathi has been portrayed in memoirs and popular literature, see Alam, *Rethinking the Mau Mau,* 53–70.

15. For a recent summary of these historiographical debates, see Myles Osborne, "The Historiography of Mau Mau," in *The Life and Times of General China: Mau Mau and the End of Empire in Kenya,* ed. Osborne (Princeton: Markus Wiener, 2015), 255–61.

16. Bethwell A. Ogot and Mordecai Tamarkin both provided early accounts of the ambiguous position of loyalists within the Central Province. Bethwell A. Ogot, "Revolt of the Elders: An Anatomy of the Loyalist Crowd in the Mau Mau Uprising, 1952–1956," in *Politics and Nationalism in Colonial Kenya,* ed. Ogot, Hadith 4 (Nairobi: East African Publishing House, 1972), 134–49; Mordecai Tamarkin, "The Loyalists in Nakuru during the Mau Mau Revolt and Its Aftermath, 1953–1963," *Asian and African Studies* 12, no. 2 (1978): 247–61. Daniel Branch has written the first full study dedicated to the history of the loyalists: *Defeating Mau Mau, Creating Kenya: Counterinsurgency, Civil War, and Decolonization* (Cambridge: Cambridge University Press, 2009).

17. Bethwell A. Ogot, "Mau Mau and Nationhood: The Untold Story," in Atieno Odhiambo and Lonsdale, *Mau Mau and Nationhood,* 34. See also Ogot, "Britain's Gulag," review of *Histories of the Hanged: Britain's Dirty War in Kenya and the End of Empire,* by David M. Anderson, and *Britain's Gulag: The Brutal End of Empire in Kenya,* by Caroline Elkins, *Journal of African History* 46, no. 3 (2005): 493–505.

18. For one example of such fruitful comparisons, see Julie MacArthur, "Rebel Litigants: The Lost Trials of Elijah Masinde and Dedan Kimathi," Dedan Kimathi University of Technology, Conference Proceedings, July 2014.

19. Godwin Siundu, "Reading the Statue of Dedan Kimathi," *Standard,* 24 February 2007; Mazrui, "On Heroes"; Annie E. Coombes, "Monumental Histories: Commemorating Mau Mau with the Statue of Dedan Kimathi," *African Studies* 70, no. 2 (2011): 202–23; Annie Coombes, Lotte Hughes, and Karega-Munene, *Managing Heritage, Making Peace: History, Identity and Memory in Contemporary Kenya* (London: I. B. Taurus, 2014); Patrick Gathara, "The Spoils of War: Why Do We Celebrate Kenyatta, Not Kimathi, Day?" 19 October 2009, http://gathara.blogspot.ca/2009/10/spoils-of-war-why-do-we-celebrate.html. For Kimathi as an "elusive" figure, see Gikandi's contribution to this volume.

20. Instructions for Dedan Kimathi Statue, no author, n.d. [2006], Kimathi Statue file, Nairobi, National Museums of Kenya (NMK) Archives. For more on the erection of the Kimathi statue, see Hughes's contribution to this volume.

21. See cover image. Francis K. Muthaura, Permanent Secretary to the Cabinet and Head of the Public Service to Alice K. Mayaka, Permanent

Secretary to the Ministry of State for National Heritage, 24 July 2006, Kimathi Statue file, NMK Archives.

22. Daniel Branch, "The Search for the Remains of Dedan Kimathi: The Politics of Death and Memorialization in Post-Colonial Kenya," *Past and Present,* suppl. 5 (2010): 301–20. For a wider discussion of the place of the dead and burial in relation to Mau Mau in contemporary Kenya, see David M. Anderson and Paul J. Lane, "The Unburied Victims of Kenya's Mau Mau Rebellion: Where and When Does the Violence End?," in *Human Remains in Society: Curation and Exhibition in the Aftermath of Genocide and Mass-Violence,* ed. Jean-Marc Dreyfus and Élisabeth Anstett (Manchester: Manchester University Press, 2017), 14–37.

23. See, for example, Caroline Elkins, *Britain's Gulag: The Brutal End of Empire in Kenya* (London: Pimlico, 2005); Derek Peterson, "The Intellectual Lives of Mau Mau Detainees," *Journal of African History* 49, no. 1 (March 2008): 73–91; Ogot, "Britain's Gulag"; John Lonsdale, "Britain's Mau Mau," in *Penultimate Adventures with Britannia: Personalities, Politics and Culture in Britain,* ed. William Roger Louis (London: I. B. Tauris, 2008), 259–73; Joanna Lewis, "Nasty, Brutish and in Shorts? British Colonial Rule, Violence and the Historians of Mau Mau," *Round Table* 96, no. 389 (April 2007): 201–23.

24. Ian Cobain and Richard Norton-Taylor, "Mau Mau Massacre Cover-up Detailed in Newly-Opened Secret Files," *Guardian,* 30 November 2012; Cobain and Norton-Taylor, "Files That May Shed Light on Colonial Crimes Still Kept Secret by UK," *Guardian,* 26 April 2013; Claire Ellicott, "How UK Ordered Mau Mau Files to Be Destroyed: Archives Reveal How Staff 'Cleansed' Dirty Documents Related to Colonial Crimes," *Daily Mail,* 29 November 2013.

25. David M. Anderson, "Guilty Secrets: Deceit, Denial, and the Discovery of Kenya's 'Migrated Archive,'" *History Workshop Journal* 80, no. 1 (Autumn 2015): 142–60; Anderson, "Mau Mau in the High Court and the 'Lost' British Empire Archives: Colonial Conspiracy or Bureaucratic Bungle?," *Journal of Imperial and Commonwealth History* 39, no. 5 (2011): 699–716. For more on these court cases, see Hughes's contribution to this volume.

26. Huw Bennett, *Fighting the Mau Mau: The British Army and Counter-insurgency in the Kenya Emergency* (Cambridge: Cambridge University Press, 2013). See also Aoife Duffy, "Legacies of British Colonial Violence: Viewing Kenyan Detention Camps through the Hanslope Disclosure," *Law and History Review* 33, no. 3 (August 2015): 489–542.

27. Caroline Elkins, "Alchemy of Evidence: Mau Mau, the British Empire, and the High Court of Justice," *Journal of Imperial and Commonwealth History* 39, no. 5 (December 2011), 733.

28. Katie Engelhart, "40,000 Kenyans Accuse UK of Abuse in Second Mau Mau Case," *Guardian,* 29 October 2014.

29. In addition to those already mentioned, see Josiah Mwangi Kariuki, *"Mau Mau" Detainee: The Account of a Kenya African of His Experiences in Detention Camps, 1953–1960* (London: Oxford University Press, 1963); Gakaara wa Wanjaũ, *Mau Mau Author in Detention*, translated by Paul Ngigĩ Njoroge (Nairobi: Heinemann Kenya, 1988); Wambui Waiyaki Otieno, *Mau Mau's Daughter: A Life History* (London: Lynne Rienner, 1998); Wangari Muoria-Sal, Bodil Folke Frederiksen, John Lonsdale, and Derek Peterson, eds., *Writing for Kenya: The Life and Works of Henry Muoria* (Leiden: Brill, 2009).

30. Anderson, *Histories of the Hanged*, 7–8.

31. John Lonsdale, "Kenyatta's Trials: Breaking and Making an African Nationalist," in *The Moral World of the Law*, ed. Peter Coss (Cambridge: Cambridge University Press, 2000), 221.

32. Myles Osborne, ed., *The Life and Times of General China: Mau Mau and the End of Empire in Kenya* (Princeton: Markus Wiener, 2015).

33. Maina wa Kinyatti, *Kenya's Freedom Struggle: The Dedan Kimathi Papers* (London: Zed, 1987).

34. Wunyabari O. Maloba, *Mau Mau and Kenya: An Analysis of a Peasant Revolt* (Bloomington: Indiana University Press, 1993), 128; Christiana Pugliese, "The Organic Vernacular Intellectual in Kenya: Gakaara wa Wanjaũ," *Research in African Literatures* 25, no. 4 (1994): 177–97.

35. Ngũgĩ wa Thiong'o and Mĩcere Gĩthae Mũgo, *The Trial of Dedan Kimathi* (London: Heinemann Educational Books, 1976). For excellent analysis of the play and its role in the "rewriting of history," see Oyeniyi Okunoye, "Dramatizing Postcoloniality: Nationalism and the Rewriting of History in Ngũgĩ and Mũgo's 'The Trial of Dedan Kimathi,'" *History in Africa* 28 (2001): 225–37; James Ogude, "The Nation and Narration: 'The Truths of the Nation' and the Changing Image of Mau Mau in Kenyan Literature," in Atieno Odhiambo and Lonsdale, *Mau Mau and Nationhood*, 268–83. See also Gikandi's contribution to this volume.

36. Joseph Karimi, *Dedan Kimathi: The Whole Story* (Nairobi: Jomo Kenyatta Foundation, 2013).

37. J. M. Kariuki to the Registrar, High Court of Kenya, 26 October 1971, Kimathi file, Archives of the Supreme Court of Kenya.

38. Julie MacArthur, "The Hunt for (the Trial of) Dedan Kimathi," *Africa Is a Country*, 24 March 2016, http://africasacountry.com/2016/03/the-hunt-for-the-trial-of-dedan-kimathi/.

39. See Julie MacArthur, "Prosecuting a Prophet: Rebellion, Psychiatry, and Justice in Colonial Kenya," unpublished manuscript.

40. My thanks to historian Sean Hawkins, who was among the first to note this irregularity.

41. For correspondence and press clippings from the UK on Kimathi's sentence, see UK National Archives (hereafter TNA:PRO), London, CO 822/1219.

42. Anderson, *Histories of the Hanged*, 60, 290.

43. Patel Okumo, "Judiciary Receives Dedan Kimathi File from United Kingdom," *Standard*, 1 March 2016.

44. Ngũgĩ wa Thiong'o, *Matigari*, translated by Wangũi wa Goro (Nairobi: East African Educational Publishers, 1987).

45. Justin Willis, "Two Lives of Mpamizo: Understanding Dissonance in Oral History," *History in Africa* 23 (1996): 321.

46. Anderson, *Histories of the Hanged*, 287.

47. Wachanga, *Swords*, 26; Derek R. Peterson, *Creative Writing: Translation, Bookkeeping, and the Work of Imagination in Colonial Kenya* (Portsmouth, NH: Heinemann, 2004), 165.

48. See Document 5, interrogation report of Dedan Kimathi, in this volume.

49. Nderitũ, *Mũkami Kĩmathi*, 33.

50. Alam, *Rethinking Mau Mau*, 49.

51. See Document 5, interrogation report of Dedan Kimathi.

52. For more on the practice of oathing, see Mickie Mwanzia Koster, *The Power of the Oath: Mau Mau Nationalism in Kenya, 1952–1960* (Rochester: University of Rochester Press, 2016); Anderson, *Histories of the Hanged*, 42–45; Barnett and Njama, *Mau Mau from Within*, 55–67.

53. For more on the role of the "passive wing," see Cora Presley, "The Mau Mau Rebellion, Kikuyu Women, and Social Change," *Canadian Journal of African History* 22, no. 3 (1988): 502–27; Tabitha Kanogo, *Squatters and the Roots of Mau Mau, 1905–1963* (Athens: Ohio University Press, 1987); Caroline Elkins, "Detention, Rehabilitation, and the Destruction of Kikuyu Society," in Atieno Odhiambo and Lonsdale, *Mau Mau and Nationhood*, 191–226.

54. Wachanga, *Swords*, 26. See also Kimathi's letters transcribed as Documents 8 and 9 in this volume. For more on Kimathi's "management of speech acts," see Gikandi's contribution in this volume.

55. Wachanga, *Swords*, 26; Maina wa Kinyatti, *History of Resistance in Kenya, 1884–2002* (Nairobi: Mau Mau Research Centre, 2008).

56. For more on the "paperwork" of rebellion, see Lonsdale's contribution in this volume.

57. For a vivid depiction of the meeting at Mwathe, see Gikandi's contribution in this volume.

58. Weekly Intelligence Report, Nyeri District, 3–9 December 1953, Kenya National Archives (hereafter KNA), Nairobi, VP/8/9; Nyeri ISUM, 28 June 1953, KNA, VP/8/9.

59. Derek Peterson, "Writing in Revolution: Independent Schooling and Mau Mau in Nyeri," in Atieno Odhiambo and Lonsdale, *Mau Mau and Nationhood*, 89–90.

60. John Lonsdale, "Authority, Gender and Violence: The War within Mau Mau's Fight for Freedom," in Atieno Odhiambo and Lonsdale, *Mau Mau and Nationhood,* 61.

61. Lonsdale, "Authority," 63–68; Henderson, *Hunt,* 33; Barnett and Njama, *Mau Mau from Within,* 443

62. "Mumbi" represents the first woman, mother to all, in the Gikuyu origin story; Njama and Barnett, *Mau Mau from Within,* 443.

63. Henderson, *Hunt,* 29.

64. For more on literacy, see Gikandi's contribution to this volume.

65. For more, see contributions by Lonsdale and Githuku in this volume.

66. Peterson, *Creative Writing,* 207–8. For more, see Lonsdale's contribution to this volume.

67. *East African Standard,* 28 August 1953.

68. Bennett, *Fighting the Mau Mau,* 134.

69. Ibid., 135.

70. Branch, *Defeating Mau Mau,* 62–64. For more, see the contributions of Lonsdale and Githuku to this volume.

71. Dedan Kimathi to "Chief Muhoya and your Home Guard," n.d., CID copy, translated as part of a collection of letters found in June 1953, KNA, VP/9/10.

72. See Document 11 in this volume.

73. Branch, *Defeating Mau Mau,* 140.

74. Osborne, *General China,* 19.

75. China was originally charged with four offenses: murder, consorting with "terrorists," possession of ammunition, and possession of firearms. Fearing the difficulty of proving all these charges, the prosecutor opted to drop the murder and firearms charges. Osborne, *General China,* 26.

76. Interrogation report of General China, as reprinted in Osborne, *General China,* 147.

77. Ibid., 194–95.

78. Anderson, *Histories of the Hanged,* 273–76; Bennett, *Fighting the Mau Mau,* 139.

79. Wachanga, *Swords,* 122–23.

80. Barnett and Njama, *Mau Mau from Within,* 477.

81. Weekly intelligence reports, Nyeri District, 1953, KNA, VP/8/9.

82. "100 Kikuyu Guards in Field Exercise: Dedan Kimathi Effigy Shot Up in Mock Attack at Githunguri," *East African Standard,* 9 September 1953.

83. Bennett, *Fighting the Mau Mau,* 27. "Mr. Ruck" most likely referred to British settler Roger Ruck, who was murdered along with his wife and young son in their home on 24 January 1953, an attack widely and graphically publicized.

84. Nyeri ISUM, Special Branch, 28 June 1953, KNA, VP/9/10.

85. Kinyatti, *History of Resistance*, 199.

86. Bennett, *Fighting the Mau Mau*, 118–20.

87. Government flyer, "Muri Murona Dedan Kimathi Thutha Uyu?," 5 October 1954, KNA, AHC/9/95. As Myles Osborne has recently observed, Kimathi's scribe, Njama, recounted that such leaflets merely served to increase Kimathi's popularity and fame. Osborne, "'The Rooting Out of Mau Mau from the Minds of the Kikuyu Is a Formidable Task': Propaganda and the Mau Mau War," *Journal of African History* 56, no. 1 (2015): 88.

88. Kariuki, *"Mau Mau" Detainee*, 49.

89. Ibid., 101. For more on the link to Moses, see Lonsdale's contribution to this volume.

90. John Iliffe, *Honour in African History* (Cambridge: Cambridge University Press, 2005), 324; Lonsdale, "Authority," 61.

91. Clough, *Mau Mau Memoirs*, 164; Lonsdale, "Authority," 61; Lonsdale, "Mau Maus of the Mind," 419–20.

92. Henderson, *Hunt*, 160–62; Bennett, *Fighting the Mau Mau*, 157.

93. Henderson, *Hunt*, 163.

94. Ibid., 257.

95. Ibid., 258.

96. For a discussion of rumors around Wanjiru's involvement in the capture, see Karimi, *Dedan Kimathi*, 249; "Twilight of a Terrorist," *Time*, 10 December 1956; Dennis Onyango, "State Honours Freedom Hero Kimathi Belatedly," *Standard*, 15 December 2005.

97. Henderson, *Hunt*, 193.

98. See photo 7. The trench where Kimathi was captured is now a site of commemoration, ostensibly controlled by the Mau Mau Veterans Association, who provide visitors with tours of the site: "THE DEDAN KIMATHI TRENCH: Measuring approximately 40 by 40 meters, this is the place that the late mau mau [*sic*] field marshall Dedan Kimathi was shot and captured on the 20th of October 1956. The site is located adjacent to the Thengeraini stream and Nyayo tea plantation in Karuna-ini Sublocation, Muhoya Location of Tetu Division, Nyeri County. The late Field Marshall was sentenced to death and later hanged on 18th February 1957. This site was gazetted by the National Museums of Kenya on the 21st of February 2001. To date, it is still unclear where the remains of the field Marshall are. The local community usually commemorates his hanging and his heroic deeds to save the country from colonialism on the 18th of February of every year." Nyeri Museum Facebook page. For more on the constructions of emergency trenches, see footnote 11 in the trial transcript, Document 1 in this volume.

99. Karimi, *Dedan Kimathi*, 250–52; John Mwangi Kingori and James Muchi Ndirangu, interview by the author, Nyeri, 11 June 2015.

100. Machua Koinange, "My Encounter with the Man Who Shot Dedan Kimathi," *Standard,* 20 October 2013; Dr. Waweru, "The Capture of Dedan Waciuri Kimathi: The Untold Story," 24 February 2015, https://creativeconnekt.wordpress.com/2015/02/24/the-capture-of-dedan-kimathi-waciurithe-untold-story/.

101. Charles Mwai Gichuru, interview by author, Nyeri, 11 June 2015.

102. See Exhibit No. 20, signed arrest statement of the accused, 22 October 1956, reproduced as Document 6 in this volume.

103. Ethnographic records point to the precolonial use of leopard skins by Gikuyu warriors and figures in leadership positions. See Ali A. Mazrui, ed., *The Warrior Tradition in Modern Africa* (Leiden: Brill, 1977), 173.

103. British Pathé newsreel, "Mau Mau Chief Captured, 1956," http://www.britishpathe.com/video/mau-mau-chief-captured.

105. "Leaflets Tell of Kimathi's Capture," *East African Standard,* 23 October 1956.

106. See coverage of the trial in the *East African Standard* from 22 October to 25 October 1956.

107. Bennett, *Fighting the Mau Mau*, 158.

108. Anderson, *Histories of the Hanged*; Elkins, *Britain's Gulag*.

109. See Document 6 in this volume.

110. Obituary, Government Notice 106: "The Government Regrets to Announce the Death of Forest Guard 471 Mwai Itubania: He Was Murdered by *Mau Mau* Adherents on 19th December 1954 in the National Park near Nyeri," *Kenya Gazette,* 27 January 1953; "Dedan Kimathi Charged with Murder," *East African Standard,* 23 October 1956.

111. Notes between Mr. Rednall and Mr. Mathieson, 14 January 1957, TNA:PRO, CO 822/1219

112. "Kimathi Trial Opens at Nyeri," *East African Standard,* 20 November 1956.

113. "Twilight of a Terrorist," *Time,* 10 December 1956.

114. For more on the other figures in the trial and the role of the assessors, see Anderson's contribution to this volume.

115. For a similar reference, see Githuku's contribution to this volume.

116. As Anderson indicates in his contribution to this volume, Sloan Mahone was perhaps the first to highlight this last point in her dissertation, in 2004. Sloan Mahone, "The Psychology of the Tropics: Conceptions of Tropical Danger and Lunacy in British East Africa" (PhD thesis, University of Oxford, 2004).

117. Sloan Mahone, "The Psychology of Rebellion: Colonial Medical Responses to Dissent in British East Africa," *Journal of African History* 47, no. 2 (2006): 244. For the stigma and religious interpretations surrounding epilepsy in sub-Saharan Africa, see Roy Baskind and Gretchen L. Birbeck,

"Epilepsy-Associated Stigma in Sub-Saharan Africa: The Social Landscape of a Disease," *Epilepsy and Behavior* 7, no. 1 (2005): 68–73; Louise Jilek-Aall, "*Morbus Sacer* in Africa: Some Religious Aspects of Epilepsy in Traditional Cultures," *Epilepsia* 40, no. 3 (1999): 382–86. For a broader discussion of psychiatry and illness in the colonial world, see Mahone and Megan Vaughan, eds., *Psychiatry and Empire* (New York: Palgrave Macmillan, 2007).

118. John C. Nottingham, "Witchcraft Appendix," 1955, KNA, BB/PC/EST/12/15. For more on the connections between Mau Mau and witchcraft, see Katherine Luongo, *Witchcraft and Colonial Rule in Kenya, 1900–1955* (Cambridge: Cambridge University Press, 2011).

119. Luongo, *Witchcraft*, 186. See also Cooper, "Mau Mau and the Discourses of Decolonization"; Osborne, "Rooting Out of Mau Mau."

120. Colonial psychiatrist J. C. Carothers was perhaps the most famous for articulating the psychological argument explaining Mau Mau. Carothers, *The Psychology of Mau Mau* (Nairobi: Government Printer, 1954). For more on the pathologization of rebellion, see Mahone, "Psychology of Rebellion."

121. Maina wa Kinyatti, "Better Late Than Never," *People on Sunday*, 18 February 2007.

122. Further complicating the reading of Kimathi's testimony is the issue of language and court translation. The trial transcript does not clearly indicate in which language Kimathi spoke during the trial. By most accounts, Kimathi's mastery of English was excellent. At several points in the trial, however, Kimathi's own correction of the court interpreter suggests that he was speaking to the court in either Gikuyu or Kiswahili.

123. Itote, *"Mau Mau" General*, 179.

124. Derek Peter Franklin, *A Pied Cloak: Memoirs of a Colonial Police (Special Branch) Officer* (London: Janus, 1996), 84.

125. Reuter telegraph to London, n.d. [18 February 1956], TNA:PRO, CO 822/1219.

126. Daily Worker Reporter, "Kenya's Leader Hanged," *Daily Worker*, 19 February 1957.

127. Ibid.

128. In the 1990s antigovernment activists in Kenya named their movement the February 18 Movement (FEM) after the date of Kimathi's execution.

129. *East African Standard*, 7 September 1953.

130. See also Exhibit No. 21, reproduced as figure A.4 in the appendix to this volume.

131. According to Kimathi's interrogation, the other person in this photo was Ndungu Gicheru. See the interrogation report, transcribed as Document 5 in this volume.

Primary Documents

Note on Primary Sources

All of the primary sources presented in this volume have been reproduced with minimal editing in an effort to preserve the original presentation, integrity, and sense of the documents. Minor and minimal orthographical corrections have been made for the sake of clarity and consistency.

Annotations are provided throughout to offer further context or clarification. Specific technical or foreign terms are explained in the first instance that they appear. For the sake of clarity, (…) parentheses are used when original to the text, […] square brackets are used to signify corrections/notations original to the source material, and {…} curly brackets indicate any editorial corrections or notations.

Full copies of the original documents presented here have been deposited both at the archives of the Supreme Court of Kenya and at the Kenya National Archives.

Document 1

TRIAL OF DEDAN KIMATHI

IN HER MAJESTY'S SUPREME COURT OF KENYA AT NYERI.
EMERGENCY ASSIZE CRIMINAL CASE NO. 46 OF 1956[1]

REGINA...Prosecutrix.[2]

versus

DEDAN KIMATHI s/o {son of} WACHIURI...............Accused.

19/11/56
10.20 a.m. - Accused Present.
Accused arraigned.

COUNT 1.[3]

> *Plea: I had it in my possession. The reason I had this arm with me was because I was coming out to surrender. I did not leave it behind me. Government instructions were that anyone who intended to surrender should not leave his arms behind.

Plea of Not Guilty recorded.

---

1. Criminal Case No. 46 of 1956, Dedan Kimathi v. Regina, Her Majesty's Supreme Court of Kenya at Nyeri, Papers of Ralph Millner, Archives of the Institute of Commonwealth Studies, Senate House Library, ICS165/3/2. The original transcript was prepared by the court clerk from shorthand notes taken during the trial proceedings. The original shorthand notes can be found in the Dedan Kimathi file, Archives of the Supreme Court of Kenya. Omissions and gaps are common in these kinds of transcripts. Marginal notes throughout the trial document were typed into the final transcript at the instruction of the presiding judge, Chief Justice Kenneth Kennedy O'Connor.

2. Queen Elizabeth II, represented here by colonial government prosecutor D. W. Conroy. Case presided over by Chief Justice Sir Kenneth Kennedy O'Connor. O'Connor had previously served as Attorney General of both Malaya and Kenya, and as Chief Justice in Jamaica before returning to Kenya to take up the post of Chief Justice in 1954.

3. Count 1—Unlawful possession of firearms contrary to Regulation 8A(1) of the Emergency Regulations, 1952.

*COUNT 2.[4]

> Plea: I had the ammunition in my possession. Similarly as I stated in the other count I did not want to leave them behind as I was following Government's instructions to come out with all I had.

Plea of Not Guilty recorded.

> *NOTE. The whole of the pleas have been included in the record and not only "NOT GUILTY" because it may be of assistance to the accused to show that he has been consistent in his defence throughout.

Assessors brought in.[5] Chosen: 1. Tumuti s/o Gakere.
2. Nderitu s/o Muteru.
3. Kibuthu s/o Kihia.

No objection by Defence.

Conroy.[6] with him Havers for the Crown.[7]
Miller for the accused.[8]
Conroy opens: 2 offences. Details them. 1st more serious.

> If guilty of 1st, also guilty of 2nd. Burden on Crown. Crown must prove that on 21/10/56 Dedan Kimathi was in unlawful possession of a firearm. (1) That he possessed it; (2) That it was a firearm. If Crown proves possession it is for him to satisfy you that he had a lawful excuse to possess it. If after you have heard all the evidence

---

4. Count 2—Unlawful possession of ammunition contrary to Regulation 8A(1A) of the Emergency Regulations, 1952.

5. David Anderson provides this summary of the role of the Assessors: "Assessors sat in each trial, drawn from the same ethnic group as the accused. Although they had no powers over the outcome of a case, the judge was required to ask them for their verdicts and to take these views into account." Anderson, *Histories of the Hanged,* 198.

6. Solicitor General D. W. Conroy, Minister of Legal Affairs. Conroy later acted as Attorney General of Kenya during the Hola Camp massacre controversy of 1959, wherein eleven "hard-core" Mau Mau detainees were clubbed to death by their African guards under the direction of the British warders, who subsequently attempted to cover up the incident.

7. Crown Counsel J. K. Havers.

8. Defence Counsel Frederick Henry Miller. Previously appointed as Resident Magistrate Kenya, with effect 12 November 1949. For more on Miller, see Anderson's chapter in this volume.

you are not satisfied that he possessed it with lawful authority or lawful excuse, guilty. Plan marked for identification Ex. 1.[9] (Defence counsel - no objection. Copies given to assessors). Explains plan.

Saturday, 20/10/56.

Ambushes of T.P's {Tribal Police}[10] were put on this ditch. Party of about 24 men under the command of T.P. Corporal Wanjohi - a platoon: there was a smaller party – section – under Sjt. Mwangi, a T.P.R. {Tribal Police Reservist} Sjt.: Cpl. Wanjohi was a Regular Corporal. Corporal posted his men on the reserve side of the ditch, 2 men at one end, 2 in the middle, 2 under Sjt. Mwangi, at the far end. Quiet night. Buffalo. Nothing else. Just as it was beginning to get light on the Sunday morning 21/10, 2 men on the right were moving when they thought that they saw someone ~~coming~~ [in or] at the edge of the ditch – names Ndirangu s/o Mau and Njogi. Ndirangu shouted to what he thought was a man to stop. He appeared to be coming into the forest. He did not stop but started running down the ditch. He appeared to have something on his shoulder which appeared to be sugar cane. Ndirangu fired. Man tried to climb bank into the forest. Bank too high. He could not get up. Ran across ditch into Reserve.[11] Ndirangu fired again. Man got up on top of the bank

---

9. See Exhibit No. 1, plan of capture scene, reproduced as figure A.1 in the appendix to this volume; and map 3 of the capture scene.

10. The Tribal Police were a parallel police force that answered to the provincial administrations rather than to the Kenya police. The Home Guard, a body formed during the Emergency out of militia groups from the civilian population and armed by the colonial state, were specifically tasked with policing the reserves and given legal status as a "Special Tribal Police," which gave them enhanced powers of arrest and the right to shoot in defined, prohibited "no-go" areas. For more, see Branch, *Defeating Mau Mau.*

11. As part of the counterinsurgency, British officials used forced labor from the villages in central Kenya to dig trenches, or ditches, along forest areas in an attempt to prevent movement of people and supplies between the "native reserves" and the forests. These trenches acted as a prohibited area, a "no-go" zone that provided a space for patrols and increased powers to arrest or shoot on sight. Karatina University, in conjunction with the National Museums of Kenya and the British Institute in Eastern Africa, has been working toward excavating, rehabilitating, and restoring some of these "Mau Mau trenches" around Mount Kenya. For the approximate location of the trenches in question, see map 2 of Central Kenya in this volume.

and Ndirangu fired 3rd time and man fell over and disappeared in the bush. Njogi (for fear of hitting Ndirangu) fired into the air twice. Hearing noise, the other 4 men and Sjt. Mwangi came along to see what was happening. Mwangi s/o Kanguru and Maina also came up and joined Ndirangu and Njogi in searching the bush. [After a little they found a man hanging] over an overhanging bush. Thought at first that he was a leopard – dressed in leopard skin, coat and hat. Ndirangu saw it was a man and asked him who he was. He said Kimathi s/o Wachiuri – Dedan Kimathi. Told to come out; he said he could not. Told to creep out, he did and they saw that he was wounded in the thigh. One of the tribal policemen searched him and they saw a pistol in a holster with a strap over his shoulder. On left side a simi {small sword or double-edge knife}. Mwangi took the pistol from him. Shortly after Sjt. Mwangi arrived and was handed the pistol as he was in charge. Stretcher made and they took Dedan Kimathi away. Cpl. Wanjohi had arrived and the pistol was handed to him. He tore up his shirt and tied up wound. He was taken to the police station and the pistol was handed to a European police officer who will produce it. At no time was Dedan Kimathi ill-treated, nor did he at any time say that he was coming in to surrender or that he wished to surrender. That took place on 21.10. Doctor called and wound treated. On 22/10. senior police officer went to see Dedan Kimathi and charged him with two offences. He was asked whether he had anything to say and said (Defence – no objection): "I would like to say that I never knew there was such a law." He then said he wanted to think and after a little interval said: "I have nothing more to say".[12]

Charges.

(1) Unlawful possession of firearm.
(2) Unlawful possession of ammunition.

In reply to this he said "I would like to say that I never knew there was such a law". If he really intended to surrender, he should have said so there and then.

Firearm.

If you think it has the appearance of a firearm, unless someone tells you to the contrary, it is a firearm. But I will also call evidence

12. See Exhibit No. 20, signed arrest statement of the accused, reproduced as Document 6 in this volume.

of two police officers. They first put one of their own police rounds in and fired and it split wood into halves. On S'day there had been 6 bullets in the pistol. When they were testing they put one of those in the pistol, fired and it went through the wood. You may think that that would fire a round which would kill anyone that it hit in a vital part. Evidence will be called. If you think (1) that Dedan Kimathi was in possession of this pistol, (2) that it could hurt or kill a person [then] unless he had a lawful authority or lawful excuse for possessing it, he is guilty on count 1. If you are satisfied of that and that there were 6 rounds in the pistol, you may think him guilty of the 2nd charge.

DERRICK FREDERICK CREW. sworn states

Inspector Kenya Police, Kiganjo. Qualified draftsman. 16 years in drawing office – Served apprenticeship. Reached higher National Standard of drawing.

On 23/10/56, I left Nyeri with A.S.P. {Assistant Superintendent of Police} Vidler and Insp. {Inspector} Blackman and went to the Kahigaini Village, South Tetu. I prepared a plan of an area pointed out to me by A.S.P. Vidler. This is the plan. Line drawn along top is the ditch in relief. Tendered Ex. 1. No objection. Plan admitted. Ex. 1.

Cross-examined.

The relief plan is drawn to scale in order that the Court may have an idea of the distance. The plan at the foot is not to scale. Ditch runs alongside of valley. From lower side of the trench to bottom of valley is a drop of 50 ft. to 80 ft. estimated.
Question explained.

Relief plan is only to scale from end to end – not in height. From where ditch joins road to bottom of valley might be 300 to 400 ft, ~~but~~ difference in altitude.

Q. If you are on that hillside below the ditch looking up you would be looking up rather sharply: it is a steep slope?

A. Yes. The distance from A to D is between 2,300 and 2,500 ft., i.e. about 800 [yds].

No re-examination.
To Court.

Ditch is reasonably flat-bottomed. Heights of bank marked on plan are approximately correct. I was shown where accused

was supposed to have been found – was shown by Vidler and Blackman – I mark it with a cross.
No further questions.

K.K. O'Connor, C.J.
19/11/56.

NDIRANGU s/o MAU. affirmed.

I am a tribal police reserve constable stationed at Kahigaini, South Tetu Reserve. Have been tribal policeman for about 2 years. Before that Homeguard[13] from the beginning – 1952. I remember 20/10/56 – Saturday. I was a member of a party of tribal police and tribal police reserve under Cpl. Wanjohi. He gave us certain instructions that night. I was in a party under Sjt. Mwangi – they were Njogi, Mwangi (not Sjt. Mwangi), Maina, Njeru, Wanjiri. I think that is all. 5 and myself and Sjt. Mwangi. We went to positions on the ditch which separates the reserve from the forest near Kahigaini Village. We reached ditch at 6.45. It was still light. Sjt. Mwangi put us in position along the ditch. He put me with another man – Njogi. To my right was another man from Sjt. Mwangi's group. I was near the road which goes to Nyeri. Others were placed – I could not see them. I was with Njogi. Sjt. Mwangi posted the others along the ditch on the right side (demonstrates). I was on the reserve side.

Ex. 1. I see this and the ditch and the road, the reserve and the forest. I was placed at point F. (Indicated on plan). I was about 18 paces from the road. I don't know where the others were posted. We stayed in our ambush all night – didn't see anything. We didn't move during the night. When it started to get light, we moved left away from the road. Njogi moved with me. We were armed with .303 rifles. We moved very quietly, slowly, upright. I can't say how far. It didn't take long. We intended to go and see whether we could find any tracks. It was getting light. We saw something. We saw a figure of a person carrying something from his shoulder. It was not light enough to distinguish properly. It looked like poles. When we first saw this person carrying something I was at the edge of a shamba {farm plot} and at the edge of the trench. There was nothing growing in the ground at that time. The man I saw was moving towards the forest. The figure had climbed the bank of the trench and was on the forest side, about 3 yards from the trench when I called out to him. When I first saw the figure he was moving slowly. He was about 35 paces along the ditch from

13. See fn. 10 for an explanation of the Home Guard forces.

me when I first saw him. I had not heard him first. When I first saw the man he was climbing the ditch. I said in English, "Who goes there?" I shouted it out. He didn't answer. He began to go back and fell into the trench.

Q. If he had continued on up the hill as he was going what kind of ground is it?

A. Where he intended to enter was open, but there was a kei-apple fence in front of him.

When I shouted, he dropped what he was carrying and ran along the trench away from me. I ran after him. I got into the trench. I shouted "stop" in Kikuyu very often. He did not stop. When we got into the valley I fired a shot at him on the other side of the valley. The man crossed the dry river bed and got out of the trench. The dry river bed crosses the trench from the forest.

When I fired a shot at him he was on top of the trench on the Reserve side. He made an attempt to get out on the Reserve side and I fired and he went back into the trench. I fired 3 times at him. I first fired when he had run about from here to the sign post.[*] He was then in the trench and I had many times told him to stop. He tried to get out of the trench on the forest side and I then fired at him. He then went back into the trench and continued running down the trench and having crossed the dry river bed, he then got out on the Reserve side. When he was about to get into the trench again, I shot at him. He fell and staggered on the Reserve side. He disappeared for some time. After he disappeared Njogi and I searched for him. When I was running after and firing at the man Njogi was running with me – behind. We had no watch. We searched for him about an hour. We were calling out during the search. Two other persons came – Mwangi (not Sjt. Mwangi) and Maina. After searching we eventually found – we saw a thing like a leopard under a small castor oil tree. There were leaves where he lay. Yes, I easily saw him under the tree. I saw it was a man wearing a leopard cap. He was also wearing a leopard coat – like this. (2 for identification). This is the coat. (3 for identification)[14]

[*i.e. 128 yards]

I spoke to him and said, "Who are you". He replied, "It is I Kimathi s/o Wachiuri." I said, "What about the other name?" He said, "I am called Dedan Kimathi". I asked him whether he was

14. For Exhibits Nos. 2 and 3, leopard skin coat and cap, see photo 2, Dedan Kimathi after his capture, in this volume. For the possible importance of leopard skin in Kikuyu culture, see the introduction to this volume.

known by any other name. He mentioned something I could not understand, something like "Billd Macho".[15] I then said, "Come out". He said, "I can't, because you have shot me". I said, "Drag yourself on your side. Put your hands in the air". He obeyed. He came out from under the bush. I saw that he was wounded – (indicated front of right thigh and buttock). It (bullet) came out at the back. I could recognise him. That is he. (Identifies accused). He was searched. I and Mwangi Mwangi {sic} Kanguru searched him. I saw Mwangi Kanguru find a pistol on him – on the right hip (indicates) in a holster. I would not be able to recognise it. The pistol was inside under this leather jerkin (4 for identification) – under 2 jackets.[16] Mwangi Kanguru took the pistol from him. I search him and found a simi. I didn't pull it out of the scabbard. This in its sheath is the one I found (Tendered, Ex. 5). I later gave that simi to Mwangi Kanguru. While this was going on others came. After I had searched accused Sjt. Mwangi came with 2 others of our ambush party. The pistol was handed to Sjt. Mwangi still in the holster. Later Cpl. Wanjohi came. The pistol was handed to Cpl. Wanjohi by Sjt. Mwangi – still in the holster. We dressed the prisoner's wound – tearing up Wanjohi's vest and tied the wound with it. It was not a vest: it was white cloth – like a shirt. We carried the prisoner to Kahigaini Homeguard Post. A European police officer arrived there. The pistol was handed to him by Cpl. Wanjohi. I don't know the European's name. From the time it was taken from the accused to the time it was handed to the European police officer I did not see it taken out of the holster. The European opened the pistol and I saw him remove 6 rounds of ammunition from it. After that I do not know what happened to the pistol. We carried the prisoner to a motor car. The prisoner's hair was then wound on top of his head. He then had a beard and a moustache. On that morning when the prisoner was captured I did not at any time hear him say anything about wanting to surrender.

Adjourned to 2.15
Resumed 2.50.

(Delay because prisoner complained of being unwell and has been medically examined by three doctors).

---

15. Ndirangu clarifies later in his testimony that what he heard was "Field Marshal."

16. See Exhibit No. 6, pistol, reproduced as figure A.2 in the appendix to this volume.

SOLICITOR-GENERAL:

Since the adjournment accused complained of being unwell. I wish to call the Provincial Physician as to his state of health.

PETER PERCIVAL TURNER, sworn, states.

M.D., M.R.C.P. Provincial physician. I have just examined accused. Prisoner is complaining of a very severe headache and abnormal noises in his ears. This started 6 a.m. and has got progressively worse. This headache could be connected with his general state: he has been wounded. I found no symptoms. This depends entirely on his story. There is nothing to show for this and I would not expect there to be. I didn't take his temperature. Whether these symptoms exist or not depends on whether he is telling the truth or not. In my opinion he has a headache such as he describes. He has experienced similar headaches before and he feels that if he were allowed to rest this afternoon, he would be quite well to-morrow.

No cross-examination.

To Court.

If he is granted an adjournment, my colleagues and I are all of opinion that he will be fit to continue his trial to-morrow.

MILLER: I apply for an adjournment until to-morrow.

Adjourned till 10 a.m. 20/11/56.

K.K. O'Connor
19/11/56.

20/11/56. 10 a.m. Resumed.

DENIS WILLIAM HAMILTON HURLEY. sworn, states:

F.R.C.S., M.S. Provincial Surgeon, Nyeri General Hospital. Accused has been my patient since 21/10/56, when I operated on him for a gun-shot wound in the right thigh. In my opinion he is considerably better and progressively improving. I have examined him this morning together with the Prison Doctor Admiral Twigg and the Provincial Physician. He does not complain of headache this morning. This morning he complains of pain in the right hip region. He says it may interfere with his listening to witnesses and actively concentrating on the trial. He is more comfortable in the chair than on a stretcher. He says that he wants to go on with the trial now. I think that he is fit to go on with the trial. I think that he has got the pain, but I do not think that the pain is severe enough to disturb him much. The symptoms of the pain are subjective. I would have thought that the patient would be at the moment almost entirely free from pain, but if he complains of severe pain that is something that I cannot deny. There is nothing but his statement to show whether he is in severe pain or not. At the moment his temperature is normal: and pulse normal, and his general condition excellent at the moment.

Cross-examined Miller:

The sciatic nerve is in some way affected but in my opinion that is not the cause of this pain. I would be able to tell if it was.

To Court.

This pain of which he now complains is something new. I heard of it this morning. In my opinion the accused is fit to continue now subject to a possible adjournment should he complain later: there is no medical reason why that course should not be pursued. It is also the opinion of my other two colleagues that there is no medical reason why the trial should not continue now subject to adjournment if his condition should deteriorate.

No questions.

MILLER: He wishes to proceed subject to this, that symptoms may come on again.

ORDER.

We will proceed; if he feels ill he is to let his counsel know and counsel is to make an application to the Court to adjourn.

NDIRANGU s/o MAU, on former affirmation:

Cross-examined by MILLER:

I am a tribal policeman. On 21/10 I had on the same clothes as I have now (tribal police uniform and T.P. cap); also a blue overcoat. I made a statement to the police, Insp. Blackman, on 21/10 and I put my left thumb-print on it and it was translated to me and was true.

Q. But you say, "About half an hour later as we were reaching the position we intended to stop at I saw something moving along the forest ditch"?

A. Yes, and that is true.

Q. He was not then climbing out of the ditch when you first saw him?

A. Yes, he was.

Q. You said in your statement: "I saw something moving along the forest ditch to my right: it looked to me as if it was a man, because I could see that it was carrying something on its shoulder which looked like sugar cane. I then shouted in English, 'Who goes there'? and as I shouted this I saw the man, who was at this time climbing out of the ditch"?

A. When I said, "Who goes there?" he had already climbed out. I saw this man who was at this time climbing out of the ditch going in the direction of the forest, drop back into the ditch, feet to me; I say I did not see him going along the forest ditch. The first time I saw him he was climbing up the ditch. He completed his climb out of the ditch. At that point the height of the ditch is not high. Having completed his climb, he went 3 yards (indicated) in the direction of the forest. When I saw him I was about as far from the road as from the Court to the sign-post at the cross-roads. (Estimated very roughly at 70 ~~paces~~ [yards]. Estimate afterwards corrected to 128 ~~paces~~ [yards]). The accused was about 35 ~~paces~~ [yards] (indicated) from me. I was about 2 paces from the nearest point to the ditch on the Reserve side.

Q. Does not thick forest come to the edge of the ditch?

A. Yes.

Q. I put it to you that it would be impossible for you to see anyone to a distance of even 2 ft. from the edge of the ditch?

A. At that place there was an open space. There was no bush between me and where I saw the accused.

Q. How far were you from Dedan Kimathi when you fired the first shot?

A. About from here to the road outside – further than the end of that hut. (Counsel agree distance to road is about 40 paces). Before I fired I called out, "Who goes there?" I also said "Stop!" I did not say anything else, except that I kept on saying "Stop" in Kikuyu when I was running after him. I said, "Who goes there?" "Stop" and nothing else before I first fired. When I fired the second shot, I was nearer him then when I fired first shot (indicates 37 – 38 paces). I chased him over a long distance before I fired the second shot. I did not really know how far as I was running after him. I think I ran about half a mile at a rough estimate (indicates from Court to valley). I then saw him climb out of the ditch on the Reserve side. The distance between firing the 2nd and 3rd shots was longer than between the 1st and the 2nd – I ran further. I did not fire a fourth shot.

I am quite sure. I saw him roll over. When I fired the 3rd shot, I was down below and he was above me. I was on the side of a stream and he was on the other side above. He was about 40 or 50 ~~paces~~ [yards] from me (indicated). When I first saw the man it was light. Yes, it was "only nearly daylight". After firing the 3rd shot, I saw the accused roll over and disappear. My companion was running close behind me. I had outrun him as he had an overcoat which prevented him. I could not say how far he was behind. No, I did not commence my search alone. He caught me up. I left him standing where I had seen the man roll over and I went to the stream to find tracks and we both began to search. Others arrived. It was I who first saw him under a castor oil tree. I did not know how high it was. The tree was 9 to 10 ft. high (indicated). He was concealing himself in leaves under a castor oil tree. Yes, I could point out the tree if I went there again.

Q. The tree was not shaded with leaves: it was easy to see anyone?

A. There were growing plants with leaves at the base of the tree.

Q. What was Dedan Kimathi doing when you fired the third shot?

A. After he had gone down into the dry river bed there was undergrowth there: he doubled round (indicated a curved path with finger). He was attempting to go back to the trench.

Q. You told the police, "When I had fired the second shot, I saw the man climb out on the Reserve side"?

A. No. He was on the Reserve side when I fired the 3rd shot. (Witness is confused between the 2nd and 3rd shots).

Question put again.

When I fired the second shot he was climbing the ditch on the forest side where there was a track made by wild pigs. It was the 3rd shot I fired when he had climbed out on the Reserve side. Yes, when I fired the second shot, he was climbing out on the forest side. He fell because I fired at him. No, I don't think I hit him with the second shot. He dashed back into the trench and continued running away from me. After having gone down to the valley, he climbed the ditch on the Reserve side. I fired the 3rd shot and hit him. He staggered and I lost sight of him.

Q. What was the accused doing when you fired the 3rd shot?

A. He intended to come back into the trench. He was going round back into the trench.

Yes, he was on the top of the trench and still running away when I fired the 3rd shot. Yes, he was running away when I fired the 3rd shot. I left my companion where I had seen the man fall and I went down the hill to the stream to look for [tracks.] Yes, I saw Dedan Kimathi lying on his side under the castor oil tree. Yes, I was below him and I saw him about one yard away. I could have leant forward and touched him. That was the first I had seen of him since I saw him roll over.

Q. I put it to you that when you first saw him sitting under the tree you were slightly below him looking up the slope of the hill?

A. No, he was quite close to me: almost at my feet: not above me.

Q. I put it to you that Dedan Kimathi called your attention to himself by saying, "I am Dedan Kimathi; I have come in to surrender. I have a pistol"?

A. That is not so.

Q. Did you not then raise your rifle and say "You have given us enough trouble"?

A. It is not so.

Q. He was squatting on his haunches on the ground and you fired your rifle and hit him in the thigh?

A. No, it is not so. I am quite certain.

Yes, I have been paid a reward for capturing Kimathi – Shs.3,000/-.[17]

Re-examined.

The overcoat I was wearing was a uniform overcoat. Njogi and the others were wearing uniform. When I first saw the accused he was climbing the ditch. At that place the ditch is not high. (Indicates a little more than 1 ft.).

It was a short time between the time I first saw him and when I shouted.

Q. Where you saw him the first time could he easily have run into the forest, or was it too thick?

17. See the introduction to this volume for details on the reward offered and paid for the capture of Kimathi.

A. ~~I~~ [He] did not distinguish where the voice had come from.

In front of him there were kei-apple thorn trees like a fence. When I fired the second shot he was trying to climb out on the forest side. The ditch was about this height. (Indicates 3 ft. 3in.).

Yes, I left Njogi where I had seen him fall and I went down to the stream and later found him under the castor oil tree.

Q. How far was it from where he had fallen to the castor oil tree?

A. (Indicated) About 50 ~~paces~~ [yards].

To Court.

When I first saw him he was climbing the edge of the ditch on the forest side. He was going towards the forest. The kei-apple trees ahead of him were thick enough to prevent a man going through.

Yes, I said there was open ground there between the kei-apple and the ditch. The kei-apple fence was about 7 or 8 ~~paces~~ [yards] from the edge of the ditch and the intervening ground was "plain ground". When I challenged him he did not stop, come forward or put his hands up. He did not say anything. He did not say, "Don't shoot! I want to surrender". I had not fired at him when he first ran away. When I found him under the tree he said nothing about wanting to surrender. From first to last he never said anything of the kind. I am quite sure. The "stream" I spoke of – I meant dry river bed.

Yes, he was on a small knoll and on the point of going back to the trench when I fired the 3rd shot. No, he was not going back towards me.

At Miller's request.

When I fired the 3rd shot, the accused had already got out of the ditch on the Reserve side. He was curving round to go back to the ditch. He was out of breath and sometimes supporting himself on his hands. The country there was quite open.

No further questions by counsel.

NJOGI s/o NGATIA. sworn, states:

Tribal Police Reserve Constable stationed at Kahigaini. On 20/10/56 I went in a party commanded by Cpl. Wanjohi. I was in a party commanded by Sjt. Mwangi. I was in [a "two"][18] with

18. By "two," this witness is referring to the Tribal Police working in pairs.

Ndirangu on the edge of a ditch separating [native] reserve from the forest. During the night a buffalo was shot some distance away. When it was starting to get light the next morning about 6.30, Ndirangu and I left the place where we had been. He was leading. After going some distance Ndirangu said something. I looked in a certain direction – ahead. I saw something which looked like a stump of a tree. He came up to a place where there was some maize plants near the trench on the Reserve side. The thing that looked like a stump was on the forest side of the trench. The stump was near the trench – on the side of it on top of the side of the trench about two paces from the top of the trench. At that time it appeared to be still. It was not easy to see – not light enough. I looked at the stump closely. It moved when Ndirangu shouted "Who goes there?" It went along the trench away from us – in the direction away from the road which crosses the trench and comes to the Aberdare Mountains. He was running. He was carrying something which I did not distinguish – something placed on the shoulder (indicates horizontal position on right shoulder). It looked like trees (poles). When Ndirangu shouted, "Who goes there?" he dropped it. Ndirangu shouted "Stop" in Kikuyu, many times. Then Ndirangu began to run after the running man and I began to run after him. We ran along the trench after the man who was running towards Thengeraini along the trench.

Still in the trench running after this man we saw him try to climb the bank of the trench towards the forest. I fired one shot into the air. We were still running in the trench; we noticed that the man tried to come across and Ndirangu fired another shot. Ndirangu was in front. I fired in the air so as not to shoot Ndirangu. The bank was on the forest side where the man tried to climb out. The bank was about 3 ft. and had been broken down by buffaloes. When I heard the shot the man came back into the trench and began to run in the same direction until Ndirangu fired a third shot. Ndirangu fired 3 shots. I fired 2 shots. Ndirangu fired the 2nd shot when the man was trying to climb out on the forest side. That was when I fired my shot into the air. When Ndirangu fired his 3rd shot, the man was about 38 ~~paces~~ [yards] away from him (indicated). The man was still in the trench. The man who was being shot at was going up the hill and it seems that the shot hit him: he got out of the trench and went into the Reserve side. After the shot was fired I saw him jump to the Reserve side. This was another place where the bank had been broken down by buffaloes. It was about 2 ft. 6 in. high (indicated). He then disappeared completely. There are some bushes there.

I did not go to the place he disappeared. I went along the trench because I thought he might have gone towards the Ngeraini {Thengeraini} stream. I got out and stood on the bank of the trench about 10 paces from where he had disappeared. I stood there to give Ndirangu time to reach the Thengeraini stream. Then 2 other men came. One Maina s/o Chege and the other was Mwangi Kanguru. They were part of the ambush party. We spoke to them. We began to search for a man in the bush. We searched for about 1 hour. Ndirangu found something. He shouted to us saying "the man is here", in Kikuyu. We went there and saw a thing spotted like a leopard. I looked closely at it. It was day-light then. I saw that it was a person. He was wearing a leopard skin (shows shoulders). 2 and 3 for identification. These are the things he was wearing. From where I saw the man disappear to the castor oil tree was about 30 ft. While we were searching we were saying "Surrender" in Kikuyu. We got no answer. The man in the leopard skin coat and hat under the castor oil tree was sitting lying on his side. He was not easy to see on account of the undergrowth under the tree. After Ndirangu shouted "The man is here", Ndirangu said, "Who are you?" He replied "It is I Kimathi s/o Wachiuri". This is the man ~~(indicated)~~ [Identifies accused]. Ndirangu said to him, "What about the other name"? and he replied, "It is I Dedan Kimathi". He also added, "It is I Bild Marshall". (Field Marshall). I do not know what language this is. I do not know what this means. Ndirangu said, "Raise your arms". He raised his arms at once. Ndirangu said, "Come down here". He replied that he could not come down because he had been wounded. Then we began blowing whistles for the others to come.

The man dragged himself out to us. By this time others came – Sjt. Mwangi, Geru {Ngeru} Karundo, Cpl. Wanjohi, another Mwangi – all the people in our ambush group. We were 7 – 8. Mwangi Kanguru searched Dedan Kimathi. I saw him find something like a pistol. It was in a holster. It was on Dedan Kimathi's right side. He had a jacket under the leopard skin. Ex. 4 it is. The pistol was on this. The leopard skin was on top of the jacket and the pistol was between the jacket and the leopard skin.

Mwangi took the pistol from him and held it until the arrival of Sjt. Mwangi to whom it was handed. He kept it until Cpl. Wanjohi arrived to whom it was handed.

Later a European police officer came to whom Cpl. Wanjohi handed the pistol. It was still in the holster – it had been all the time. The police officer opened the pistol and found in it 6 rounds of ammunition. The pistol in the holster was like this. (6 for identification). When the police officer opened the pistol I saw him take out 6 rounds. I did not see what he did with them. We made a stretcher to carry Dedan Kimathi. His wound was dressed by Selah Githahi {Gitahi}[19] near the place where we found him. I only know Selah Githahi by that name. We had carried Dedan Kimathi to Kahigaini Homeguard post before the European police officer arrived. From the time I first saw this man until he was handed over to the police officer, I never heard him offer to surrender. He never said any words like that. When he was under the castor oil tree, he did not say, "Here is my pistol for you".

Adjourned to 2.30

Miller told that I am relying on him to inform me at once if the accused feels unfit to go on.

Miller says that he understands.

Adjourned.

K.K. O'Connor,
20/11/56.

Resumed. 2.30 p.m.
Miller to Court.

Accused is fit to proceed.

NJOGI –
Examined by Miller

When I saw something like a stump, it was not easy to see. It was carrying something on its shoulder like trees or poles. Yes, that was visible when I first saw it.

When Ndirangu shouted "Who goes there?" he dropped it and ran. He was on the edge of the trench when Ndirangu shouted "Who goes there?" He then dropped into the trench. He was a few feet from the trench when we first saw him.

When we first saw him, he was about 20 yards away (indicated), but I could not see him properly. We were about 150 yards (indicated) from the road.

---

19. Sihar Gitahi Ribai was a member of the Tribal Police unit that captured Kimathi. He treated Kimathi's wound, having learned first aid skills during his service with the British army in Asia during World War II. In an interview with historian Daniel Branch, Gitahi recounted his experiences growing up and attending school with Kimathi. Branch, *Defeating Mau Mau*, 118.

When Ndirangu fired the third shot, he was about 23 yards (indicated) away from me.

When Ndirangu fired his third shot, I did not clearly see the accused, because there were some bushes between him and Ndirangu. It was only a short time that I could not see him – about five minutes.

I have been in the witness box 10 minutes since the adjournment. (Actual time is 14 minutes – K.O'C.).

Q. If you could not see the Accused when Ndirangu fired the third shot, why did you say that he was 38 yards (indicated) away and still in the trench?

A. Because I knew the distance Ndirangu was in front of me and how far the Accused was in front of him and after that I saw the accused going towards the Reserve.

Q. Is your memory defective?

A. Yes, I think so. I am not quite certain. I am liable to forget. Yes, I think I have forgotten about this question. I did not see the accused jump aside, Ndirangu told me he did. I saw him before Ndirangu fired the third shot. I next saw him in his hideout – under the castor oil tree.

Q. When Ndirangu fired the third shot you did not see him?

A. No. From some time after the second shot I did not see him, till I saw him under the castor oil tree.

Q. Why did you tell the court that he was 138 yards away in the trench?

A. If I made a mistake in that, I also made a mistake in saying that he was in the trench.

When he was shot a third time, he was on the side of the trench. So Ndirangu told me. He said "The man has crossed into the Reserve. Stay here and I will search."

I was mistaken in saying that the man was in the trench when he was shot. In fact, I did not see him shot. Ndirangu was in front of me when he shot. Ndirangu told me to wait there while he went ahead to cut him off.

After a little time two other men came.

Q. Did you wait there until you were called to the castor oil tree?

A. No. By that time four of us had gone into the bush to search.

I remained on the top of the bank for about 20 minutes to enable Ndirangu to reach the place that he was going. I did not hear a shot fired then or at any time after I left the trench.

From the time I left the trench to when I saw him under the castor oil tree was – I can't say how long. I had no watch. Maybe about half an hour. From the top of the trench where I was to you 20 yards (indicated).

Where Ndirangu called me to the castor oil tree, Ndirangu was 2 or 3 yards from where the man was under the castor oil tree. He was about 10 yards or 12 yards from me when I called him. We did not search for blood.

Q. If Ndirangu told you the man was wounded, would it not have been reasonable to search for bloodstains?

A. We did not think of that. We thought he might run away. Ndirangu went about 40 ~~ft.~~ [paces] ahead (indicated). We searched for him for about half an hour. Yes, I am liable to forget. I think I had only forgotten about him being in the trench. I do not think I have made any other misunderstanding.

The third shot hit him.

Q. How do you know?

A. Because the second shot was fired into the air and I saw him after that.

I know the second shot did not shoot him, because I saw him running in front. It is true that I did not see him shot by the third shot.

Q. It is because Ndirangu told you so that you think the third shot hit him?

A. Yes.

<u>Re-examined</u>

Yes, I saw the accused running easily after the first and second shots. I could not see the man after the third shot. Yes, I saw Ndirangu fire the third shot. I heard no shot fired after the third shot.

<u>MWANGI s/o KANGURU:</u> affirmed, states:

I am a K.P.R. {Kenya Police Reserve} and have been since May 1954, and before that I was a Home Guard.

I am now stationed at KAHIGAKU Home Guard Post.

On the 20/10/56 I was a member of an ambush party under the general command of Corporal WANJOHI. I was in a group under Sergeant MWANGI.

We took positions along the ditch which divides forest from the Reserve. I was with MAINA. We arrived at positions as it was getting dark.

Nothing happened that night.

Next morning something happened – we saw D. KIMATHI.

The first thing was that I heard gunshots – first I heard two. Then I heard a third one. I heard three shots altogether. I began to go in the direction to investigate, with MAINA.

We did not meet anyone. We met NJOGI and NDIRANGU. They were members of our ambush party (identifies NJOGI).

We had conversation with them.

As a result of that conversation we began to search for a person whom they had seen.

I do not know that place, but the search was near the trench on the Reserve side.

We searched for about an hour. We found someone. NDIRANGU s/o MAU first found him. He said "The person we have been seeking for is here". We went and joined NDIRANGU. He was standing where DEDAN KIMATHI was. DEDAN KIMATHI was lying – there was a castor oil tree and under the growth of that tree he was lying.

Exs. 2 and 3.

He was wearing a leopard skin and leopard skin cap. Those are they (Exs. 2 and 3).

NDIRANGU said to him "Come out". The man said that he ~~was~~ had been wounded. NDIRANGU said "Come out". He dragged himself out. This is the man (identifies accused).

He was asked "What have you got with you?"

I didn't know who he was. I knew him afterwards. He himself said that he was DEDAN KIMATHI s/o WACHIURI.

Search C.

No one had asked him "Who are you?"

He was searched by me.

I found a pistol. It was in a holster. The holster was attached to him by a belt slung over a shoulder.

The holster was on the righthand side.

coat {sic} was inside the leopard skin coat. Under the leopard skin he was wearing a leather jacket. This is it (Ex.4). The pistol was above the jacket. The leopard skin coat – I do not remember whether it was buttoned or not. I removed the pistol by inserting my hand below the throat (indicates). This is the pistol (Ex. 6). I kept the pistol until later I handed it to Sjt. Mwangi. I saw another weapon – a simi. The simi was handed to me by Ndirangu. This is it (Ex. 5). I later handed it to Cpl. Wanjohi. The man was wounded. I helped to dress his wound. Selah did it. From the time when I heard 3 shots and went with Maina to investigate I heard no more shots after that. I never heard Dedan Kimathi say he wished to surrender.

Cross-examined.

Altogether I heard 3 shots fired – from dawn until we found the accused under the castor oil tree. I do not know who fired them. I do not know how many statements I have made to the police. I cannot remember. I have not been counting. Are you asking me how many copies? I have only given one statement. I distinctly remember hearing 3 shots. There were 3 minutes between the 1st and 2nd shots. The 3rd shot was fired about one minute after the 2nd. I heard Ndirangu say, "The man whom we have been searching for is here?" I was then about 10 paces away from Ndirangu. Ndirangu was with Njogi when he found the man – when he shouted that he had found him.

Q. Did you see the accused running away from Ndirangu?

A. No, we went afterwards.

No re-examination.

To Court.

I searched the accused. I did not have a pistol before I searched the accused. I had rifle ammunition. I had no pistol ammunition. So far as I know none of our party had a pistol or pistol ammunition before accused was found.

No further questions.

Adjourned to 9.30 21/11/56.

K. O'C.
20/11/56.

21/11/56. Resumed 9.30 a.m.

BESOBEN MAINA s/o CHEGE. sworn, states:

T.P.R., stationed Kahigaini. I have been a T.P.R. since 1953. On Saturday 20/10. I went out on ambush under Sjt. Mwangi. I was put in position with Mwangi s/o Kanguru on the edge of a trench separating the Reserve from the forest. We stayed there all night. On the following morning we heard 3 shots. We went in that direction to investigate. About half a mile on the way we met Ndirangu. He was standing in the trench and he said something to us. We went into the bush on the Reserve side. Ndirangu then called out, "He's here". That was not a very long time after meeting Ndirangu – about 7 minutes (indicated). We – Mwangi, Njogi and self – went to Ndirangu. Ndirangu asked a man who was under a bush, "Who are you?" I could see the man. It was a castor oil tree and under it was some undergrowth. The man was lying down. He was dressed in leopard skins and buck skin.

Up to this time we had all been searching. (It was only Ndirangu who called out). We were searching for a person who had disappeared in the bush. No, we did not call out to him. Ndirangu asked the man who he was. He replied, "It is I, Dedan Kimathi". He was asked to raise his arms and did so. He was then told to come out and he did so, but he said that he had been shot in the leg. He rolled himself out. I saw him searched by Mwangi. He found a pistol. Ndirangu found a simi. Mwangi took the pistol, and he handed it to Sjt. Mwangi. The prisoner's wound was dressed by Selah Gitahi. I used Cpl. Wanjohi's shirt – he tore it and tied up the wound. I see this piece of material. This was the kind of material (7 for identification). We got poles and made a stretcher and carried the prisoner away. I see the prisoner here to-day (identifies accused).

It was as a result of hearing shots that I went and met Ndirangu. We heard 2 shots at first. A third had been fired before we arrived. There was an interval between the 1st and 2nd shots. We went to investigate after hearing the 2nd shot. We did not run at first. We ran part of the way. We ran faster after hearing the 3rd shot. When we heard the third shot we had gone more than half way to where Ndirangu was. After we arrived and started searching we heard no more shots. From the time we arrived until the prisoner was carried away on a stretcher, I did not hear the prisoner say anything about surrendering.

Cross-examined.

We were posted half a mile from Ndirangu. We were in the Reserve, not in the forest. The road was between me and Ndirangu. Facing the forest, I was on the right of the road. I was about 35 paces from the road (indicated). I have a watch.

Q. What period of time separated the 2nd and 3rd shots?

A. About 15 minutes.

I did not see Ndirangu when the 3rd shot was fired. When I first saw him Njogi was near the trench. When Ndirangu saw us, he came to us and said something. When we first saw Ndirangu he was in the trench. When he spoke to us, we went into the bush with Mwangi and Njogi. I know where Ndirangu was. I could see him. He was searching as we were searching. We searched for about 20 minutes.

Q. Did you not tell the Court a few minutes ago that you searched for 7 minutes?

A. No, I never said anything about 7 minutes.

(Note: Witness said about the same time as he had been in the witness box – which was 7 minutes).

Dedan Kimathi did not appear to be suffering much from his wound. There was a little blood. He said, "I am Dedan Kimathi s/o Wachiuri". He was not talkative.

Re-examined:

I did not have my watch with me that morning. I started to go towards the sound after the 2nd shot. From where we started to where we met Njogi was about half a mile. We walked part of the way and ran part. I cannot say how many minutes it took us. Yes, I thought it was 15 minutes between the 2nd and 3rd shot, and after that we started running down hill. It took us considerable time to do the half mile because we were avoiding ditches and climbing up. I fix the time at 15 minutes by the distance we had to go. The man who was with me had a watch. He did not take the time.

JOHN NJERU s/o KARUNDO. sworn, states:

I am a tribal policeman and have been since 1/10/56. Before that I was a T.P.R. since May, 1955. I am now stationed at Kahigaini Homeguard post. On 20/10/56 I went on an ambush party in charge of Sjt. Mwangi. When I got to the forest I was posted with Sjt. Mwangi and Wanyiri Gakuru {Wanjiri Gakuyu}. We were stationed near a ditch dividing the forest from the Reserve. Ndirangu Mau was stationed slightly below the road which runs up to the Aberdare Mountains from Nyeri. Facing the forest the road was on my left.

About 11.30 that night I heard some shots – buffaloes were being shot. In the morning I heard one shot – enquired where it came from. There was a little light then – not enough to see a person who was some distance away. When I heard this shot, we began to move in the direction of the shot. While we were walking along I heard another shot. After that I heard another. I heard no other shots after that. I saw Maina s/o Chege and Mwangi Kanguru, Njogi and Ndirangu, who was with Dedan Kimathi.

I knew Dedan Kimathi. He is from our school and I have known him for a long time. He was a student and afterwards became a teacher in the school when I was there. He did not teach my class.[20] That is he (identifies accused). There was a few minutes between the first and second shots. I cannot say more precisely. We were running towards the place. There was a space between the 2nd and 3rd shots longer than between the 1st and 2nd. From the place of our ambush to where we saw Njogi, Ndirangu and the others was about 500 ~~paces~~ [yds]. Mwangi Kanguru and Maina were posted nearer to the road than we were. I arrived ~~with~~ [when] Dedan Kimathi was being searched by Mwangi Kanguru. I saw Mwangi find a pistol which was slung from Dedan Kimathi's right shoulder. The pistol was in a holster. I could recognise it. This (Ex. 6) is the pistol and holster. Mwangi Kanguru kept the pistol for a short time and when Sjt. Mwangi arrived, he handed it to him. A stretcher was made and Dedan Kimathi was taken to Kahigaini. I went off on a bicycle and reported to a European police officer at Ihururu Police Station. I returned to Kahigaini in a Land Rover with him and others. When I got there I saw Cpl. Wanjohi hand the pistol to the European police officer. It was still in the holster. The police officer took the pistol out of the holster. I saw him open the pistol and take out 6 rounds of ammunition and put them in his pocket. Then he handed the ammunition to his driver to hold.

I did not at any time on this morning hear Dedan Kimathi say anything about wanting to surrender. I never heard anything of that kind.

<u>Cross-examined.</u>

Between the 1st and 2nd shots there was only a few minutes. Yes, I can tell the time.

Q. What amount of time divided the 2nd from the 3rd shot?

A. Not quite 5 minutes.

<u>Re-examined.</u>

Between the 2nd and 3rd shots we were running towards the place we heard the shooting. I work out the 5 minutes by the distance 500 paces – say 5 minutes. We got up after hearing the second shot, realising there was a fight. When we heard the 3rd shot we had crossed the road and were going up. We had not got half way when the 3rd shot went off. We had gone about 100 paces

20. See Kimathi's biography in the introduction to this volume.

from where we had been. We were running in the trench at that time. It was not difficult. There were no bushes in the trench. We were not running fast.

Q. It took you 5 minutes to do 100 paces?

A. No.

Q. How long?

A. At that time one could not tell. There was between one to five minutes between the 2nd and 3rd shots. I tell that by the space of time it took us because we were hurrying to the place.

MWANGI s/o KAHAGI. affirmed, states:

I am a T.P.R. Serjeant {sic}. I have been in the Tribal Police for about 3 years. Before that I was in the Homeguard – since 1952, at the beginning of the Emergency. Before that I was in the K.A.R. {King's African Rifle}[21] for 13 years. I know Dedan Kimathi. This is he (Identifies accused). I first came to know him when he was in the Dairy. He was a clerk in the North Tetu Co-operative Society Dairy and I used to see him when I used to bring milk from the Reserve.[22]

On 20/10. – night – I was in charge of a small section on ambush duty – 7 men including myself. I posted them on the ditch which separates the forest from the Reserve near the road which goes up to the Aberdares. I was under the command of Cpl. Wanjohi. We were armed with .303 rifles only. I put my men on the Reserve side of the ditch. Next morning (21/10.), I heard some shots from the direction I had placed my men. I was with Wanjiri and Njeru Karundo. The shots seemed to come from my right going up the trench where Ndirangu was stationed. I ordered my men to go to the place and went with them – 3 of us. We hurried – trotting. We heard 3 shots. We heard 2 shots while we were at our post and the 3rd while we were on our way. The 1st and 2nd shots were fired one after the other – a little time. Between the 2nd and 3rd there was a space – not little, not long. I can estimate time. I have noticed how long I have been giving evidence.. {sic} Between the 2nd and 3rd shots we had gone about 150 paces (estimated).

---

21. The King's African Rifles were a British colonial army force in East Africa from 1902 to 1960.

22. For the common occurrence of such interpersonal connections, see Kimathi's biography in the introduction to this volume.

We were running along the Reserve side of the trench. We stopped when we arrived at a place where Ndirangu was. He was on the Reserve side. Njogi was with him, and Mwangi Kanguru and Maina Chege. 4 were there and we 3 came up. We were not told something.

We found Kimathi lying down amongst the undergrowth. There was a small, tall, castor oil tree. He was easy to see under it. We asked the others and him who he was. He said, "Dedan Kimathi s/o Wachiuri". Others came. He was wounded. I arrived after he had been searched. After I arrived I was given a pistol. I could recognise it. This is it (Ex.6). Mwangi Kanguru gave me this. I kept this and when Cpl. Wanjohi arrived I handed it to him.

We made a stretcher and carried Kimathi to Kahigaini Home Guard Post. On the way we met a European police officer. I saw Cpl. Wanjohi give him the pistol (Ex. 6).

I did not at any time hear Dedan Kimathi say that he wanted to surrender.

Cross-examined:

Note: Witness appears to have no idea of distances.

I posted myself and my two men on the right hand side of the road facing the forest. Between us and the next post (between us and the road) was about 30 yards. We were about 30 yards from the main road. The next post was the same distance. Yes, my post would be about 60 yards from the main road. Yes, I made and signed a statement to the police 21/10. Yes, I said I heard Ndirangu s/o Mau shout "Stop". I did hear him. He also said "Halt, who goes there?" Yes, I heard that plainly.

Q. How far do you think you were from Ndirangu?

A. About half a mile.

Q. You said: "As I was running towards Ndirangu, I heard 2 shots fired?"

A. Yes.

Q. You had not mentioned hearing a 3rd shot?

A. Yes, I did. I said I heard 3 shots. I did hear 3 shots.

Note: Witness has no idea either times or distances.

I heard the 3rd shot after climbing hill as we were about to go down the slope. After hearing the 2nd shot I cannot say how many minutes it was when I heard the 3rd shot. I did not look at my watch. It was not a very long time and not a short time. I know a little about how to tell the time. I had a watch before, it is out of order. (Watch put to him.) I cannot read this. I could read another watch. Yes, I know what one minute is. Between 1st and 2nd shot was 15 minutes. Between 2nd and 3rd was shorter – about 5 minutes. Ndirangu was found about half a mile from us. I have already said that Ndirangu was posted about 30 yards away from me. Yes, I said the next post was 30 yards away. Ndirangu had moved away. I had posted him about 30 yards from me. Maina Chege and another man were posted between me and the main road. Ndirangu was with Njogi. Yes, Maina Chege and his companion were about 30 yards from me and 30 yards from the main road. Yes, that makes about 60 paces.

Q. How far did you post Ndirangu from the main road?

Note: Seems just a guess.

A. 30 yards.

When I found him by the castor oil tree, he was about half a mile away. No, I do not know the difference between 30 yards and half a mile, but I paced it. I have now forgotten how many paces it was. In half a mile I cannot say how many paces there are. I am illiterate. I would say it was about 170 yards from the main road to the castor oil tree. I have no idea whatever of the time it took us to cover that distance.

Note: A very stupid witness with no idea of times or distances.

No re-examination.

WANYIRI s/o GAKUU {Wanjiri Gakuyu}. affirmed, states:

I am a T.P.R. Constable and have been one for about 1 year, and before that I was in the Home Guard. I am stationed at Kahigaini Post.

In the evening of 20/10 I was in an ambush party under Sjt. Mwangi. We took positions near the ditch dividing the Kikuyu Reserve from the Forest. I was with Sjt. Mwangi and Njeru Karundo. Facing the forest we were on the right side of the road. Maina and Mwangi Kanguru were also on the right side of the road between us and the road.

11.30 a.m. adjourned to 11.50

Resumed 11.50 a.m.

(one Assessor late. Arrives 11.58.)

Resumed – 11.58.

Witness continues:

I heard a shot that morning – altogether I heard 3 shots. Sjt. Mwangi instructed us to go and investigate and we went in the direction of the firing. We set out after hearing the first shot. We were moving when we heard the 2nd and 3rd shots. Before we heard the 2nd shot, we had not gone very far – about 150 yards (indicated). We were not running: we were walking.

After we heard the 2nd shot, we hurried – went faster. Before we heard the 3rd shot we had gone about 250 ~~paces~~ [yds.] to 300 ~~paces~~ [yds.] (indicated). When we heard the 3rd shot we ran and then arrived at the place. When we arrived I found a person lying on the ground – a prisoner. I could recognise him. That is he. (Identifies accused). He was amongst our patrol. Ndirangu was was {sic} there and Njogi, Mwangi and Maina. I did not see anyone search this man. He had already been searched.

Sjt. Mwangi arrived before me. I was behind him. I saw a simi handed to Sjt. Mwangi. Other things had been handed to him when I arrived. To get to where the man was from our ambush position, the ground sloped in places. We ran along the trench. It was easy to run – nothing to prevent us. I saw Sjt. Mwangi hand the simi to Cpl. Wanjohi. The man was wounded. His wound was bandaged and he was taken to Kahigaini Homeguard Post. Njeru left and a Land Rover arrived with a European police officer. Prisoner was placed in the Land Rover and taken away.

I did not at any time hear the prisoner say anything about wanting to surrender.

<u>Cross-examined.</u>

Q. You were posted on the right of the road facing the forest?

A. Yes.

From the main road my post was about 30 paces. Between us and the main road there was another post. They were here and we were at the Post Office. (Post Office estimated to be 250 to 300 ~~paces~~ [yds.] from here).

Yes, they were between us and the main road. They were about 40 ~~paces~~ [yds.] from the main road (indicated). I cannot tell the time properly.

Q. Can you say the time which separated the first and second shots?

A. No, I cannot give any idea.

Q. How long would it take you to walk to the Post Office?

A. I cannot say how many minutes. It was not a long time between the 1st and 2nd shots. After the 1st shot, we began to go and on the way we heard the 2nd shot.

Q. Can you say how far you had travelled?

A. About 100 yards or so.

We were walking. After hearing the 3rd shot, we had walked about to the Post Office (250 yards to 300 yards). I remember the place where we found the prisoner lying on the ground. The trench was not very far from that place – about 9 or 10 yards (indicated). The ground slopes up to the trench.

No re-examination.

WANJOHI s/o WANJAU. affirmed states:

I am a Corporal in the Tribal Police, stationed at Kahigaini.

On Saturday 20/10/56, on instructions, I placed ambush parties on the forest edge along a trench separating forest from the Reserve between Njoguini and Thaina villages in the Tetu Location of South Nyeri. My party was divided into smaller parties. One was under Sgt. Mwangi. We stayed in position all night. About 6.30 next morning there was a little light. It was just beginning to get light. There had not been any rain during the night. I heard 3 shots. They came from my right where Sgt. Mwangi's party was. First a shot was fired. Immediately I heard another. After hearing the 2nd shot we began to run in that direction. We crossed the road going to the right and we went up to the place where we found the enemy. Between the 2nd and 3rd shot there was a little space. The 3rd shot was fired when we were on the way.

We were running after hearing the 2nd shot. We had run as far as from here to the shops – to Osman Allo's {sic} shop.[23] (Counsel says about 280 yards.) I do not know what minutes and seconds are. We ran faster after hearing 3rd shot. We got to the place where we found a man lying down – Dedan Kimathi. He was lying parallel to the trench on the Reserve side. I did not measure how far from the trench. He was under a castor oil tree. When I saw him he was bleeding and I asked the askaris {soldiers} to stand aside. I took off my under shirt and tore it. I handed it to another askari to bandage his leg. These are pieces of the under-shirt (7 for identification). I later showed a European Police Officer the place – a C.I.D. {Criminal Investigations Department} officer whose name I do not know. There Sjt. Mwangi gave me a pistol. This (Ex. 6) is it. I put it into my trouser pocket. Later a

23. The Osman Allu shop is a landmark in Nyeri. Located in the center of town, Osman Allu's was a general shop founded early in the colonial period by a partnership between Indian businessman Adbul Osman Allu and Ismaili trader Mohamedally Rattansi.

stretcher was made and we carried Dedan Kimathi to Kahigaini. A European police officer arrived "Silo". I handed the pistol to him. He opened it and took out 6 rounds of ammunition from it. Before I opened it, the pistol had not been opened or taken out of the holster. When I returned to Kahigaini from the police station I was handed a simi by Mwangi s/o Kanguru. I took it back to the police station (Ihururu) and handed it to the same European police officer. This (Ex. 5) is it.

Until the European arrived I was in charge of all the tribal police there. I did not at any time hear Dedan Kimathi say that he wished to surrender.

Cross-examined.

I heard the noise of buffalo during the night. I heard about 4 shots fired – at about 11 p.m. I presume that the shots were fired by the ambush askaris. They informed me in the morning that they had killed a buffalo.

{8 for identification}

Facing the forest, I was posted on the left hand side of the road. No, I was on the right and Ndirangu on the left. I cannot tell you how far I was from the main road. I would say about as far from here to Osman Allos shop (about 280- ~~paces~~ [yards]). One does not post people too close because of the danger of shooting. There was no one between me and the main road. Facing the forest on my right was an old man named Karundo.

From the main road to where I found the accused lying on the ground is as far as to a tea canteen long the road beyond the Catholic Church (Estimated by counsel at about 350 ~~paces~~ [yards]). I heard the 3rd shot just as I was about to cross the main road. We ran fast to the place where we found Dedan Kimathi. The tree where we found him – he was lying less than a yard from it (Now indicates about 2 ~~paces~~ [yards]). He had moved from the castor oil tree to where he was lying. I was shown where he had been lying. The trench was 6 or 7 yrds. from the tree (indicated). There was a slope down from the trench to the tree.

No re-examination.

21/11/56. Adjourned to 2.30 p.m.

Resumed 2.30 p.m.

RONALD SLOAN. sworn, states:

I am an Inspector of Police, stationed at Ihururu Police Station, of which I am in charge.

On Sunday, 21/10. at 9 a.m. I received a report. As a result I went to Kahigaini Homeguard Post where I saw a wounded prisoner. This is he (Identifies accused). His wound had been bound up. Cpl. Wanjohi gave me a .38 Webley pistol. This is it (Ex. 6 for identification). It was in this holster. It was loaded with 6 rounds of .38 ammunition. I unloaded it and handed the six rounds to Constable Waigwa. I was in possession of .38 ammunition myself and did not was it to get muddled up with my own. He put the rounds in his pocket. I then arranged for the prisoner Dedan Kimathi to be transported to Ihururu Police Station. When I got there and retrieved the ammunition from Const. Waigwa. I later on the same day marked the pistol with a hack-saw blade on the under side of the barrel. I also put 3 marks on the holster.

I look at 5 rounds of .38 ammunition and one .38 cartridge. This is the ammunition I took out of the pistol that morning. I recognise it because I put 3 lines on each round and on the cartridge case. None of the six rounds was fired when I marked them. Later that morning I handed the six rounds and the pistol and the holster to Insp. Blackman of the C.I.D. Nyeri. The prisoner was searched in my presence at the police station. I found on him 3 pieces of snare wire. These are they. I also found a wrist-watch. This is it. I found a chain round his neck. I found one corn-cob (maize). While he was being searched, he did not say anything about wanting to surrender. He answered questions as to his identity. He was wounded, but seemed to be quite comfortable. I was the first European police officer to see him after his capture. He was in my presence that morning for about 1 hour and a half.

{9 for identification}

Later that morning Cpl. Wanjohi came to me and gave me a simi. This is it. (Ex. 5). I handed all the exhibits over to Insp. Blackman.

Cross-examined.

When I said the prisoner was comfortable he did not seem to be suffering from a bad wound. That is what I meant when I said "comfortable".

To Court.

He answered his name and rank in English. He did not volunteer any remark. I speak Swahili. He did not at any time say anything about wishing to surrender. He could have said this if he had wished, but he did not. I have no personal knowledge of how he speaks English.

No further questions.

K.K. O'Connor.

Insp. Sloan released.

WAIGWA s/o GITAHI. affirmed, states:

Constable K.P.R. at Ihururu where Insp. Sloan is in charge.

On 21/10 I left Ihururu and went to Kahigaini Homeguard Post with Insp. Sloan in a Land Rover. When I got in I saw a person on a stretcher. I know Cpl. Wanjohi. I saw him hand Insp. Sloan a pistol holster which Sloan opened. He found a pistol in it. Insp. Sloan opened the pistol and took out 6 rounds of ammunition which he handed to me. I cannot tell what kind of ammunition this was, but it was short in size and had a blunt head. Before the rounds were handed to me by Insp. Sloan I did not have any similar rounds. I have never possessed this kind. I only have .303 ammunition. I put the ammunition in my pocket in which there was nothing else but keys. I kept it there.

We returned to Ihururu Police Station with the wounded prisoner. When I returned I handed the ammunition to Insp. Sloan.

No cross-examination.

BARIKANGE NYANDAYI. affirmed, states:

I am a Police Constable Kenya Police, stationed at Ihururu.

I remember Sunday 21/10. On that day I went with Insp. Sloan into the charge office where I saw the prisoner lying on a stretcher. This is he (Identifies accused). The Insp. asked me to search him, which I did. I found a watch and 2 wires. These are the wires (Ex. 9). I gave everything I took from the prisoner to Insp. Sloan.

No cross-examination.

To Court.

I was there with Insp. Sloan and the prisoner. I do not speak Kikuyu.

JOHN CHARLES EDWARD VIDLER. Sworn states:

I am an A.S.P. and the Officer in charge C.I.D. in the Nyeri area.

On the morning of Sunday 21/10 I went to the Ihururu Police Station and there saw a person lying on a stretcher. He was attended to by a Police Surgeon. At 11 a.m. I took him by car to the General Hospital at Nyeri arriving there just after 11.30. He was hardly conscious. I believe he had had an injection.

Ex.4 Jerkin. I left him at the hospital. I took possession of the clothing he was wearing. I took this leather jerkin and produce it as an Exhibit. (Exhibit 4 admitted).

Exs.13, 14, 15, 16. I took this khaki shirt from him (tendered, no objection, admitted 13, also this vest, 14, this pair of blood stained underpants, 15, and this pair of skin trousers, which he was not wearing at the time, 16)

I went that afternoon to the rear of the Police Station at Ihururu. Inspector Blackman produced Exhibit 6.

I have been a policeman in the Kenya Police and the Metropolitan Police for over 22 years. For 3 years I was in the Royal Navy. I have received training in the use and handling of firearms including pistols.

I have also had practical experience in handling pistols. I myself am armed with a similar weapon to this, a .38 revolver. I have put the pistol open. This is the first thing to do. I have often fired this kind of pistol at targets of varying sizes. I have seen a wound caused by a .38 pistol on a human being. I have seen a fatal would {sic – wound} caused by a .38 pistol similar to this.

I have been armed with this type of pistol for four years. I consider myself thoroughly familiar with this type of pistol.

This pistol (Ex.6) is in perfect order except that the trigger guard is a little loose which does not affect its efficiency.

On that Sunday afternoon Inspector Blackman and I placed this piece of wood which I produce and tender. No objection.
Ex.17. Admitted (Exhibit 17) approximately ½" thick.

This wood was placed on the ground and behind it a sandbag containing earth. I then paced approximately 10 paces from this target.

Inspector Blackman then placed in this pistol, which was at the time empty, one round of normal .38 ammunition – his issue.

From the distance which I had measured I fired this pistol (Exhibit 6) at the piece of wood. The bullet hit this piece of wood fairly high, splitting it in two.

I put a mark against this "1" and initialled the piece of wood. Inspector Blackman extracted the spent cartridge case. I saw him place another round of .38 ammunition in the revolver and fire the shot from it at these two pieces of wood which had been placed together.

The second shot hit the left hand piece and went through it, the bullet going through the piece of wood into the sandbag behind it. I marked the entry of this bullet with the figure "2" and wrote my name in pencil on this half of the wood.

I retrieved the bullet from the sandbag and handed it to Inspector Blackman. This is the bullet (18 for identification).

I then saw Inspector Blackman eject the spent cartridge case from the revolver and I noticed that it had three marks on it. This is it. (8A for identification).

From my experience in firearms and the experiments I carried out I say this is a lethal barrelled weapon capable of discharging a bullet.

On the following day I went to a place where there is a trench separating the reserve from the forest. I went with Inspector Blackman, Ndirangu Mau and Corporal Wanjohi.

A spot was pointed out to me there by Ndirangu Mau and Corporal Wanjohi. It was a castor oil bush about 30' down a bank on the Reserve side of the trench – 30' from the edge of the trench. I look at Exhibit 1 (plan) and point out where this is and mark it "G". There were branches and leaves on the tree which would be about 5' high.

Some of the branches were bending over towards the ground. It was fairly bushy.

By the foot of the tree there was a little undergrowth – fairly long grass and that type of thing. Some of the earth had fallen down the slope and made a small bank about 6" high against the trunk of the tree. You could see through the foliage of the tree.

I searched the vicinity and found two pieces of cloth. These are they (Ex.7 for identification). Blackman took possession of them and marked them with his initials and the date.

These were found about 6 ft. from the tree – N.E. of it. I mark it "H".

I looked for papers – documents. I didn't find any. There was some loose earth and probed to see if anything had been pushed under near that tree.

When I had received the clothing I also searched them and found no papers or documents of any kind.

On Monday 22nd accused was charged before a Magistrate at the hospital with unlawful possession of arm and ammunition. He was remanded and taken into the prison.

On Tuesday 23/10 I took Inspector Crew to the place and showed it to him and he produced a plan, Exhibit 1.

I have been to interview the accused while in custody about other matters, security matters not connected with this offence. He may have had useful information but he gave me none.

When I saw him on the 21st and 22nd October and subsequently, he never at any time said that he wanted to surrender. If he had wanted to do so there was nothing to stop him telling me that.

He spoke to me throughout in very good English.

<u>CROSS-EXAMINATION:</u>

I first met the accused on the 21/10 at Ihururu. Dr. Twigg, the prison doctor, was there already. I saw Dr. Twigg give him an injection. This was about 10.45.

The injection might have been morphine. I heard Dr. Twigg say it was to relieve his pain. That is why I said he was hardly conscious.

The castor oil tree – I would not say it was a good hiding place: I would say it was a fairly good one.

I understand that a reward has been paid to Ndirangu Mau. I only know what I have read in the E.A. Standard[24] - nothing else. I don't know where the money came from. It is usual to give rewards for the capture of people not convicted. I can't quote cases but I think there have been other terrorists who have had rewards paid for their capture.

I understand that the reward paid was £500 some of which was given to Ndirangu Mau.

RE-EXAMINED.

There were no better hiding places in the immediate vicinity – there were on the other side of the ditch.

TO COURT:

It is my opinion that this pistol (Ex. 6) is capable of causing death if a bullet fired from it hit someone in a vital part.

No questions.

JOHN ROGER BLACKMAN.

I am an Inspector, a C.I.D. Officer attached to the S. Nyeri Reserve Division in the Nyeri area.

At 1.20 a.m. on Sunday 21/10 I accompanied Inspector Vidler to Ihururu Police Station where I saw Accused wounded and lying on a stretcher. He was being looked after by Dr. Twigg.

I received from Inspector Sloan the following articles.

Ex. 2 leopard skin cap.
" 3 " " coat.
" 6 pistol, holster and belt.
" 8 6 rounds of ammunition. These are 5 of the 6.

---

24. The *East African Standard* published that "rewards totaling £500 for the capture of Dedan Kimathi were distributed yesterday. . . . The rewards, in the form of Post Office Savings Bank books, were divided between the nine members of the patrol which was responsible for the terrorist leader's capture. Six received £25 each. Ndirangu Mau, who shot and captured Kimathi, received £150, and Njugi {sic} Ngati, who was present and helped Ndirangu, received £75. Cpl. Wanjohi Wanjau, who was in charge, was awarded £50. The remaining £75 was allocated for a big feast for all of the Tribal Police and Tribal Police Reservists in the North Tetu Location of the South Nyeri Reserve." *East African Standard*, 6 November 1956.

" 9 These are they – 3 snares.
" 10 Watch
" 11 Chain
" 12 maize cob.

At 2 p.m. that day I went to the back of Ihururu Police Station with Superintendent Vidler.

I see Ex. 17. I fired a round of ordinary police ammunition. This is the cartridge case of the round I fired. I marked two lines
Ex. 19. on the case with a hacksaw blade. (Tendered. Admitted).

The pistol fired properly. I hit the wood from an approx. 10[x] range.

It hit a knot in the wood and split the wood into two pieces. I then fired another round which had been taken from the Accused. I had obtained it from Inspector Sloan. This is the cartridge of that
Ex.8A. round (Tendered Admitted).

This wood was propped up against a sandbank. The 2nd round fired – the bullet went through the wood which is about ½ an inch thick (soft wood used for making boxes). The bullet went into the sandbag and Vidler recovered it and gave it to me. Vidler in my presence marked the two places by initialling them.

I have done 5 years army service in the parachute Regiment. I received training in small arms including pistols – in .38 pistols similar to this. I have frequently fired one. I have done weapon training courses in which pistols were included. I have been in the Kenya Police 20 months. I have received training in firearms – pistols in the Kenya Police. I am issued with a .45 Webley. The mechanism of that is similar to a .38.

When I saw Ex. 6 on the 21/10 it was in quite good condition except for a bit of dust. It was quite capable of firing. I pulled it through with a "pull-through" but it would have fired without.[25]

In my opinion it is an accurate pistol. I have seen someone fatally shot by a .38 similar to this. This pistol if fired at a human being would kill him if it hit him in a vital spot.

ADJOURNED TO 9.30 TOMORROW 22/11.

(Signed) K. K. O'Connor.
C.J.
21/11/56.

25. A "pull-through" is a cleaning implement consisting of an oily rag attached by a cord to a weight. It is pulled through the barrel of a rifle or handgun for cleaning purposes.

INSPECTOR CREW recalled on former oath (Consults notes made at the time.)

The distance from the murram road to point G is 1950' (650^x). Distance from the road to beginning of maize plot on trench is approx. 500'. Distance from the road to other side of the maize plot is approx. 800' – maize plot measured along trench about 300'.

Murram road is approx. level for 200^x or so.

The forest side of the trench is higher than the Reserve side. Opposite point G the lip of the trench is higher. The ground slopes down at a gradient of about 1 in 7".

The maize plot is flat and the arrows denote that the ground is sloping away from it downwards.

BLACKMAN RESUMED.

On Monday 22/10 I went to the scene. I searched around near a castor oil tree which was pointed out to me by Ndirangu and Wanyiri {Wanjiri}.

I found near the tree two pieces of wh. cloth (7 for identity) which I identified at the time by writing on them. (Tendered. Admitted Ex. 7). Facing the castor oil tree from the trench they were about six feet from the castor oil bush. I should call it a bush. It had a number of branches growing up. It may have a central trunk but that doesn't stand out. There are branches to the ground on the trench side. There was slight undergrowth – I should think growths from the root. You could see through the tree. At the bottom you could see through, but not easily. You could if you peered through.

There were other trees in the vicinity but not similar to that.

There was no tree there which would have offered a better hiding place.

I have spoken to the accused and heard him speaking. He speaks very good English.

He was charged by Mr. Baker. Subsequently I interviewed him to see if he could give ~~more~~ [me] security information in respect of other matters. He did not assist me at all.

The accused has never on any occasion mentioned to me or to anyone in my presence the fact that he wished to surrender. He has made no complaint to me or to anyone so far as I know that when he was coming in to surrender he was shot.

CROSS-EXAMINATION:

The depth of the valley from the castor oil tree to the bottom of the valley was 200' to 300'.

The valley runs more or less parallel with the trench.

The slope at Pt. G from the trench is fairly pronounced. As you stand at the castor oil tree and look at the trench, you would have to raise your eyes.

When I said there was no tree there that would offer a better hiding place, that is a result of my recollection, but not by inspection.

When I asked the accused for security information he did not refuse in so many words; he said that he had no information. His manner was obstinate. He did not indicate that he had information and would not give it.

The impression that the accused gave me was that he could assist me in giving information, but he was obstinate and would not do so. That was my impression.

It is correct that he has made no complaint that he was shot when he came in to surrender. I do not know whether he has ever been asked by anyone as to the circumstances.

RE-EXAMINED:

I am a C.I.D. Officer. I know the Judges Rules.[26] A prisoner in custody must be cautioned before he is asked questions and I would not ask further questions about the circumstances in which he was arrested unless he volunteers information.

---

26. The "Judges' Rules" are a "code of procedure drafted by the judges to aid the police when they question suspects." G. L. Peiris, "The Admissibility of Evidence Obtained Illegally: A Comparative Analysis," *Ottawa Law Review* 13, no. 2 (1981): 309–44. In 1956, these rules, of practice rather than law, included cautioning suspects or persons in custody before proceeding with questions, informing suspects of their right not to speak, and taking down any statements in writing and having them signed by the suspect after having been read and allowed to make corrections to the statement. Hardinge Stanley Giffard, *The Laws of England Vol. 10* (London: Butterworth, 1955), 470–73. The "Judges' Rules" have particular significance in relation to the admissibility of interrogation reports as evidence: the main concern of interrogations "was to secure information about insurgent plans and organizations, not to gather evidence to prosecute individuals. Consequently they did not conduct interrogations under judges' rules and so statements obtained during their interrogations were not admissible as evidence in a court of law." David French, *The British Way in Counter-insurgency, 1945–1967* (Oxford: Oxford University Press, 2011), 89. For more on Kimathi's interrogation and rules of evidence, see Anderson's contribution to this volume.

SOLICITOR-GENERAL:

I do not propose to call Sales;[27] but offer him for cross-examination if required by Defence.

MILLER: No thank you

DENIS WILLIAM HAMILTON HURLEY. Sworn states.

F.R.C.S., M.B. Provincial Surgeon, Nyeri General Hospital.

On the 21/10 about mid-day a man was brought to me by the police. That is he (indicates Accused).

I examined him. He was wounded. His general appearance was good. His standard of nutrition was excellent. He was suffering from shock but not badly. I understood that he had been given an injection earlier.

He had a gunshot wound through the right thigh – an entry and an exit wound. Entry wound was on the medial aspect of the right thigh, i.e. high up on the inner aspect of the right thigh, rather close to the crotch.

Exit wound was situated on the outer side of the hip above the knob of the thigh bone. The bullet had hit the thigh bone. The continuity of the bone had not been affected. It was still one long bone – but the projecting part had be shattered – pieces chipped off. A man with that wound could crawl with difficulty.

I saw no marks of burning on the wound. I did examine the clothing and found no marks of burning but it would be difficult to find any as the clothes were dirty and bloody.

I operated. He stood the operation very well.

I examined him again later that day (21st).

---

27. Eric James Sales appeared on the original list of Prosecution Witnesses, but was not called to testify. According to his statement during the investigation, Sales was the Acting Chief Inspector in charge of the Central Firearms Bureau, Nairobi. In his statement, Sales reported the following: "On the 24th October 1956 at my office on receiving information that a .38 Webley Revolver No. A 37470 had been recovered, I made a search of the records of Lost and Stolen firearms held at this office. The search revealed that a revolver identical with the revolver already mentioned and bearing the same number (A 37470) was reported stolen from a Mr. Francis Aylmer WORTLEY of the Kenya Regiment on 5th January 1953. The duplicate of Kingsway Police Station Case File CAA 39/53 held at C.I.D. Headquarters shows that it was stolen from a motor car between the hours of 12.30 p.m. and 5.00 p.m. on 5th January 1953." Kimathi File, Archives of the Supreme Court of Kenya.

On Monday the 22/10 I again examined him between 8.30 and 9.30 a.m. I thought his mental condition was clear and normal.

One of the purposes of my examination was to form an opinion whether he might be seen by the police. His physical condition was at that time reasonably comfortable.

I formed the opinion that it was quite reasonable for the police to speak to him.

He had not been given any drugs that a.m. He had been given drugs the day before for his operation. The effect of those drugs had worn off by the Monday.

He had been given anti-tetanus, etc., injections. They would not affect his mental condition. When I spoke to him he did not complain. I asked him some direct questions. He mentioned that his leg was sore, difficult to move and uncomfortable when moved. He complained that he could not pass urine. I relieved that condition for him.

After my examination I spoke to Baker of the C.I.D. I understood that he was going to speak to D. Kimathi. After he had seen Baker I inspected the patient again. His condition had not deteriorated in any way.

CROSS-EXAMINATION:

The operation on the accused on the 21/10 was over about 12.50 as far as I can estimate. I went on to perform another operation.

The bullet hit the inner side of the thigh and came out higher up at the back. The exit wound was a little over 3" higher than the entry wound. I should point out that the exit wound would be affected by the bullet having struck the bone and the bullet would revolve (spin). The exit wound would not necessarily indicate the trajectory of the bullet.

I made a careful examination of the wound and took an x-ray photo which I have here. The point of entry was below the point on the thigh bone which was struck by the bullet. It would be a correct deduction that the bullet was travelling upwards.

On an x-ray film I mark the point of entry as point A. The place where it struck the bone I mark B, which is 1½" higher. X-ray film tendered (Exhibit A).[28] That assumes that the man was standing up when shot.

That bullet could not have been fired by a man who was behind a man who was running away from him. I think the bullet could

28. See Exhibit No. A, X-ray photograph of Kimathi's bullet wound to the thigh, reproduced as figure A.3 in the appendix to this volume.

not have been fired from the right side at 90° from the direction the man was facing. It could have been fired by a person on his left side.

Ø Note. Answer read back and confirmed. K.O'C.

I should say the shot was fired from below and very nearly 90° - 75° - to the man's left front.Ø That assumes that he was standing or running, but if he were squatting with the thigh rotated outwards, the shot could have come from more to his front.

Q. If a person were squatting with his knees open and if a person fired at him from a little below and from his left front, would that explain entirely the nature of this wound.

A. It would.

I would say that that wound would cause considerable pain.

On the Monday morning when Mr. Baker saw him he was still suffering pain. That might have affected the ability to give precise replies to questions; but I thought that it would not in the particular case of this patient.

I did not specifically ask him whether he was suffering from any head pains. It might take another two months before the patient makes a full recovery from his wound.

RE-EXAMINED.

On the Monday morning – he had stood the operation very well. I asked him how he was. In answer he did not say he was suffering from any head pains. My examination was conducted for the special purpose of forming an opinion as to his mental condition for an interview with the police.

Q. Is this wound consistent with this ? The person is pursued by a man with a rifle down a ditch where the banks and the bottom of the ditch are sometimes high and sometimes low: two shots miss: the person gets out of the ditch on the bank: the pursuer remains in the ditch: The pursued gets up on top and starts to circle round leftwards to get back into the ditch. Both are running. Distance of pursuit is 500^x odd. Pursued man occasionally supports himself on his hands: the pursued circles round running with legs extended: Would it be possible for the bullet to enter his body in the way you have found?

* Note: Whole question read back by Court to witness again (as it is v. long). He again answers "Yes." K.O'C.

A. Yes. *

The leg and thigh is a very mobile limb. If a person is running hard with the right leg out and left leg behind it, that would

∅ Answer read back and confirmed

open the crotch and allow the bullet to enter in the way this bullet entered. ∅

I was not able to form an opinion from what distance the bullet was fired. It was not spent, and there was no sign of burning.

If a man were squatting on the ground as described, he would have to be squatting in the full "knees bend" position in order to sustain this wound. The right thigh would have to be rotated – the knees would have to be widely separated.

I have been practising for four years in Kenya and Uganda. I have seen Africans sitting on their haunches. Usually the knees are comparatively close together.

Q. If prisoner is squatting on his haunches, a man with a rifle fires and gives him this wound: if man with rifle is close enough to have a conversation and the assailant fires from the shoulder – would this wound be consistent with that?

A. No certainly not. Because the line of the wound was upwards; therefore the gun was fired from below.

The entry wound would have to be horizontally above the muzzle of the rifle. If the rifle were fired by a man standing, he would have to fire upwards.

Q. The slope has been estimated at 1 in 7. Do you think it would be possible to cause the wound in that way if the firer and the man were close enough to talk?

A. It depends on how close is "close enough to talk". I should say it was unlikely.

TO COURT:

I don't think it likely that this would {wound} could have been caused by a rifle fired, from a distance of 10 or 15[x] away, if fired from the shoulder at a man squatting on the ground.

WITNESS TO MILLER (with leave):

My last answer depends entirely on the slope. If the slope is more than 1 in 7, my answer might have been in the contrary sense.

Yes: if I saw this spot I could give much more definite answers to these questions.

MILLER: I apply for the Dr. to go to the place and see it and give his answers then. It is only a few miles from the Court.

SOLICITOR-GENERAL: I have no objection, but would it help?

MILLER: I ask that he go with Vidler or Blackman.

ORDER.

On application of the Defence, witness may go to the place and see the castor oil bush and the slope of the ground with Superintendent Vidler or Blackman.

(Signed) K. K. O'Connor,
C.J.
22/11/56.

Warned not to converse about the case. His further evidence is postponed.

RESUMED 10.55.

JOHN HARRY BAKER. Acting Senior Superintendent Police, C.I.D. Nairobi.

I was in charge of these investigations on the 23/10/56.

On that day I went to the Provincial General Hospital Nyeri about 10 a.m. I had a conversation with Dr. Hurley. I then went in to see the Accused, Dedan Kimathi. I charged him with two offences. The charges were interpreted by an Interpreter Wambugu who read the charges to the accused in Kikuyu. When a reply was made by the accused, that was recorded by me in English and after the usual certificates had been appended to the statement I read the charges again and the replies to the accused both in Swahili and in English and he agreed that these were proper interpretations of the reply he had made.

He affixed his thumb print and signed the statement. I signed them and so did the interpreter. I now produce the statement which was taken and signed.

Tendered as Exhibit 20.[29]

MILLER: No objection.

In my opinion that statement was voluntarily made not as a result of any threat or inducement.

Witness reads charges.

I administered the caution as stated. Statement admitted (Exhibit 20).

Witness reads Accused's statement.

I asked him whether he understood and he said yes: He answered questions sensibly. He made no complaint to me that he

29. See Exhibit No. 20, signed arrest statement of the accused, reproduced as Document 6 in this volume.

had been coming in to surrender. I cannot say whether I was the most senior police officer he had seen.

I have made enquiries through official channels about the payment of a reward.

The offer of a reward originated in a "hue and cry notice" published by the C.I.D. about 3 years ago. This particular Accused was wanted.

This notice would have been issued by the officer in charge of the C.I.D. at that time. Rewards were also offered for other persons. A number of rewards were offered for persons including the accused on the authority of the War Council. The reward has been paid. It was paid by the Special Commissioner and Acting Provincial Commissioner Central Province, i.e. by the Government and not by the C.I.D.

It has been paid to various members of the Tribal Police patrol which was responsible for the capture of the accused.

Statements were taken from those persons and copies of their statements were supplied to the Defence. The reward was paid after those statements were taken and before they gave evidence in this Court.

SURRENDER LEAFLETS.

I have been asked by the Defence about this. I have caused the official records to be searched and have supplied the Defence Counsel with copies of the surrender leaflets. I can produce in most cases photostat copies. I have given my other copies to the Defence.

CROSS-EXAMINATION:

I read the charges to the accused. I did not go into explanations.

He told me that he fully understood the nature of the charges. Yes: I fully understand them. As I understand lawful authority, it would be something like the issue of a firearm certificate.

I should say that lawful excuse would be when the person in the possession of a firearm considers that he has reasonable grounds, permission to possess that firearm. I can't say what the accused thought it meant.

On the 24/8/53 one leaflet was dropped on the forest. This is it (Tendered. Admitted Exhibit B).[30]

---

30. See Exhibit No. B1, Mau Mau surrender leaflet, transcribed as Document 12 in this volume.

This is a further leaflet of the same date (Tendered. Admitted Exhibit C).[31]

This is a third leaflet which was issued about January, 1955.[32]

I found this morning that some other leaflets were issued. This is another. It is undated but it must have been issued after the 18/6/55. (Tendered. Admitted E). That is the day when Government decided to withdraw the last surrender offer – i.e. that issued in January, 1955. Exhibit E would be issued on the authority of the Government itself.

From enquiries I have learned that all these surrender leaflets were distributed in the Reserve and dropped over the forests. The information contained therein was passed through Information loud speakers and "sky-shouting" aircraft.[33]

Q. Have you a letter dated 25/2/55 alleged to be signed by the accused addressed to D.C. Nyeri?[34]

A. I have a letter in Kikuyu and an English translation.

SOLICITOR-GENERAL:

I object to this on the ground that it is wholly irrelevant. It has nothing to do with whether he was in possession of a lethal barrelled weapon on the 20/10/56 or whether he had a lawful excuse for that. It can only be admissible: (1) if relevant to the issues before the Court; or (2) because it assists in assessing credibility.

I ask you to look at the translation and rule.

MILLER:

You have not yet heard all the issues and I propose to bring evidence on a certain point which I feel that this letter will support. I agree that you should read it. (Court reads the document).

---

31. See Exhibit No. C1, surrender leaflet, transcribed as Document 13 in this volume.

32. See Exhibit No. D1, surrender leaflet, transcribed as Document 14 in this volume.

33. "Sky-shouting" was a technique used by the colonial government whereby recorded messages were broadcast on loudspeakers from an airplane flying over the forests.

34. The letter in question has not been traced, but it can be suggested that this letter, like many others written by Dedan Kimathi to the D.C. Nyeri and to Chief Muhoya, contained indications of a willingness to negotiate surrender terms. For more, see the introduction and the chapter by Anderson in this volume.

COURT:

It has no relevance to the facts of this case, except perhaps as to the mental condition of the accused.

MILLER:

I wish to put this document in as illustrating his metal condition.

SOLICITOR-GENERAL: If there is going to be a plea of guilty insane {sic} or a defence of insanity, I do not object to it going in.

MILLER: There is not going to be a defence of insanity but I wish to put this in as illustrating his mental condition which may have influenced his actions at the time. I will submit that his mind is, to a certain degree, affected by epilepsy, on which you will hear certain evidence; and I shall submit that that condition of mind influenced him and prevented him from appreciating as clearly as a normal person would do. I do not submit that his mental condition prevented him from appreciating that he ought not to carry a firearm but it did influence him in his actions subsequent to his arrest. This may affect the issue of why he did not say on a certain occasion that he had come in to surrender.

SOLICITOR-GENERAL: This is a letter written by the accused nearly three years ago and it is therefore difficult to see how he can pray in aid something that he himself said in order to support his own story. This is not the time to try to get this document in as evidence. If the Defence wishes to give evidence on this, they can call for production of it. At that time we can tell whether the issues are relevant or not.

MILLER: I would agree to that if I may now ask the witness if this is from the Special Branch file – from official custody.

RULING.

The relevance of this letter does not at this stage appear. It may become relevant if and when the accused is called on for his defence and if his defence takes a certain line. It will not be admitted now; but Defence Counsel may apply to have it admitted later and may, in the mean time, ask questions of this witness to ascertain whether or not it is produced from official custody.

(Initialled) K. O'C.

22/11.

WITNESS TO MILLER:

This letter is a document produced from official custody.

RE-EXAMINATION:

On the 8/6/55 Government decided to withdraw the general amnesty from a future date. I have inspected the official records and have extracted documents which I see. The date of withdrawal was the 10th July, 1955. Exhibit E relates to that.

TO COURT: The general amnesty offer made in January, 1955 was withdrawn as from the 10/7/55. The 1953 offers still stand.

No questions.

K.O'C.
22/11/56.

ADJOURNED TO 2.30 P.M. 22/11.

RESUMED 2.30.

GITONGA WAMBUGU WAMIATU Sworn states: R.M. Court Clerk and Interpreter stationed Nyeri.

On Monday 22/10 I went with Superintendent Baker to Nyeri Hospital. I went into the ward and saw Accused.

Superintendent Baker spoke to him in English and I spoke to the Accused in Kikuyu. He first informed accused that he was a Superintendent of Police and that he was charging him with two offences: (1) unlawful possession of a firearm and (2) unlawful possession of ammunition. I translated those charges into Kikuyu. I think that Dedan Kimathi understood – I asked him if he did and he said that he did.

I then asked him if he wished to make any reply. He was cautioned that he need not reply if he didn't want to. He made a statement in Kikuyu which I translated to Mr. Baker. Baker took it down on a typewriter. I then read it back to the accused in Kikuyu. He and Mr. Baker signed it and Dedan Kimathi put his thumb print on it as well.

Dedan Kimathi speaks English. Mr. Baker read the charges over to him in Swahili and English and also the statement that had been written down, in both Swahili and English. He agreed that what was read out to him was a correct record of what had been said.

No threats or promises whatever were made to him and he made the statement quite freely and voluntarily.

He was in bed, covered with blankets.

Q. Did he appear to be very ill?

A. No. He appeared to be quite comfortable.

I see Exhibit 20. My signature is on this. This is the statement which was taken down in my presence by Mr. Baker on my interpretation of what Dedan Kimathi had said.

I made some translations this morning. Ex. B is written in Kikuyu. This is a translation of Exhibit B which I have checked and found correct (Tendered Exhibit B1).

I see Exhibit C dated 24/8/53. This is in Kikuyu. This is a translation of Ex. C which I checked and found correct. (Tendered and admitted C2).

I see Exhibit D which is in Kikuyu except on the back which is in English and Kikuyu. There is a sentence in Kikuyu with the same thing in English and in Swahili (Safe Conduct Pass). These papers are translations of the front and back of D which are correct. (Front D1 Back D2.)

I see Exhibit E. This is written in Swahili. This is an English translation of it which is correct (E1).

When I was translating for Mr. Baker on the 22/10 Dedan Kimathi did not say that he wanted to surrender. He did not say that when he had come in to surrender, people had tried to stop him. There was nothing whatsoever to stop him saying that if he wanted to do so.

No Cross-examination.

<u>DR. HURLEY</u> on former oath.

I have seen the place. I found the slope more steep than I had been led to believe. I found that at a distance of between 10 and 12ˣ from the supposed position of the tree taking the castor oil tree at that point it would be possible to hold a conversation with him and to shoot him so as to produce a wound such as he had.

The fact that the man might be squatting and that his knee would be above his buttock with the thigh inclined upward would not affect my opinion. The entry wound was very near the junction of thigh and trunk.

No further questions.

<u>NDIRANGU</u> recalled by Court.

When I fired the third shot I was kneeling on one knee. I was inside the trench. The man was above me. After going along the dry river bed he turned round toward the Reserve. When he came round to the trench he was like this – (turned half left to me and leaning over). I shot him when he was in that position. He jumped and rolled over into the reserve side.

He was on the bank of the trench when I shot him. He was on higher ground than I. The trench sloped down from where he was to me.

At Miller's request:

He was looking towards where I was. (Witness half faces me and again leans over to his left).

INSPECTOR CREW recalled by Court.

The point by the castor oil tree in the trench is the lowest point of a small valley. The trench goes upwards both ways from that point.

35ˣ along the trench towards the road would be between 50 to 20 ft. higher than the bank near the castor oil tree.

ADJOURNED TO 9.30 TOMORROW.

K.O'C.

22/11.

23/11/56 Resumed. 10.35 a.m.

INSP. CREW to Ct. {Court}

I have revisited the scene.

There is no dry river bed. There is no stream.

From the road to the bank of the ditch opposite where the accused was found there is no dry river bed or stream.

I searched along the trench and for a distance of a few yards on either side.

At the bottom of the incline at 'D' on EXHIBIT 1 there was no water yesterday. It is possible that water would collect there but there was none yesterday.

MILLER no questions.

To court at request of S.G. There is slight erosion of the banks of the trench at Pt. D. No great quantity of water has gone over. There is a little erosion caused by water at that spot.

I see Pt. C on EXHIBIT 1. C to D slopes down in general some parts are flattish and slope slightly – two parts are very steep.

From 'D' the slope up to E is very steep.

From D towards C it is almost flat for 100'

After that there is about 45° slope for approximately 100 yds. After that it is very steep to top of first hump. It is flat again sloping slightly down and finally climbing to point 'C'.

TO COURT A person at 100' the 'C' side of 'D' would be considerably lower than a man thirty or forty yds. along towards 'E'

No further questions.

CASE

MILLER asked if accused fit and told he can ask for adjournment if not. Says he is fit and wishes to proceed.

Sec. 302 Criminal Procedure Code complied with.
Accused elects to give evidence on oath.[35]
Defence witnesses:

1. Accused
2. WAITHOTHI his mother
3. JOSEPH WAKABA from Manyani
4. Dr. TURNER Provincial Physician.

All here. No Witness Summonses required.

DEDAN KIMATHI S/O WACHIURI S/S

I normally live in the Tetu Location.
Prior to my arrest on the 21st October, I had been living in the forest. I had been living there with other people – Africans. I had been living in the forest for almost four years.

Q. During that time did you remain friendly with the people you associated with?

A. Please repeat.

Q. When you first went there you were friendly with your associates. Did you remain their friend?

A. No. We began to become unfriendly in July, 1953, and the reason was because I wrote a letter to the Governor.[36]

S.G. I object to secondary evidence of a document which may be in existence. It should be called for.

---

35. Africans appearing before the colonial courts could be sworn in by taking different oaths according to their religious beliefs. Although the transcript is unclear, it can be assumed that Kimathi was sworn on a Christian oath on the Bible, as reported by the *East African Standard* on 24 November 1956.

36. Kimathi is most likely referring to a series of letters sent by Kimathi in July 1953 discussing the possibility of negotiations. In August 1953, Kimathi sent a letter to W.W.W. Awori to be published in the local newspaper *Habari za Dunia* and that was subsequently translated and published in the *East African Standard,* which publicly called for a ceasefire and negotiations for peace. For more on these letters, see the introduction and Anderson's contribution in this volume.

MILLER: does not press.

I have written many letters. I did not discuss all the letters. I discussed one of the letters with three other leaders. These three other leaders were friendly with me. They wished that I should meet the leaders of the Government. Many others – the majority – a large number objected and wished to kill me. I was told by the other three leaders. I moved to another leader's tent and spent the night there. They wanted to kill me because of a letter I had written to the Government.

The following day I shifted and went to my own hideout far away. I went with five others. That was in the second month of 1954. – that was the second dispute. That is when I finally split from the others. My hideout was a long way in the forest.

Q. Since that day, have you carried out any anti-British or anti-Government activity?

A. No – and not even previous to that. Nor have my five companions.

Q. This pistol which was found in your possession. Tell the Court where it came from.

A. This pistol was handed to me on the 2/4/55 by MACHARIA KIMANYA to defend myself against those who wished to kill me, that is forest men. I don't mean Security Forces in the forest. I mean MAU MAU. I had a pistol only for the purpose of defending myself against MAU MAU and no others. MACHARIA KIMANYA told me when he gave me the pistol that the enmity has grown enormous between us and those who objected to the letter which I wrote to the Govt. {sic} the first letter. There was no other reason but that I should defend myself from those people.

I also got six rounds of ammunition from MACHARIA which are the same six rounds as were found in my possession on 21st October. I have never used that pistol or any other.

Since the second month of 1954 I have been alone in the forest living with those five companions. I have seen the surrender notice. It says that people who surrender should not leave behind the arms in his possession.

EXHIBIT C put to me. I have seen this notice calling on persons to surrender.

Q. Does it say this? "If possible, come with your arms."

I brought my pistol because I followed the instructions in

EXHIBIT C.

I left my companions in the forest in February, 1954. I was arrested in October, 1956.

Q. That was a long time and your life was in danger. Why didn't you come down before?

A. Because there was SHS: 10,000 reward. I knew that if I came out either police or home guards would kill me in order to get paid. Also, I have been writing frequently to ~~him~~ [meet] the Government because I knew that if I came out to them I should be shot.

S.G. I object to this evidence of letters. Govt. denies that there are any. The proper course is to call for any letters of this kind and if they are refused, secondary evidence can be given of them.

The object of this is to produce an impression that [witness] wished to surrender. That the Crown contests. Any letters that there are have been produced to Counsel for the Defence. They are available and can be produced, subject to objection as to relevance.

MILLER: I have read them all.

RULING: If Defence Counsel wishes to have any of these letters produced he should call for it, and it can be put in subject to any objection to its relevance. Secondary evidence of its contents is not admissible while the original is available to speak for itself.

MILLER: Discusses with accused whether he wishes to call for those letters. I shall not call for those letters.

WITNESS: My two reasons for not coming in before were

(1) Because I was afraid of being killed and

(2) was awaiting replies to certain letters I had sent to Government.

A. My reason for eventually coming in was because the forest people (commonly known as MAU MAU) and the Security Forces were hunting me and at this time, I was left all alone and I was ill. I said to myself: "It is better to come out either to be killed, or if I am lucky to get to the Government." My intention was to surrender and to give the pistol and the ammunition to the Government according to the instructions which I knew.

I made up my mind to come out on the 20th October, 1956. After making up my mind I started and it got night before I arrived in the reserve. I arrived in the reserve about 7.30 p.m. It was moonlight. I was afraid to go to any of the homeguard posts because I realised that I would be shot and had no light with me. Being hungry I went to find some kind of food. I went along the shambas. I passed through banana plants and through a shamba [of] maize. The maize was ripe – also sugar cane. I got about six sugar canes and four maize cobs.

Whilst I was coming down I noticed a fire in a shamba.

I then went up to the place where I had seen a fire.

I roasted the maize.

It became daylight before I had eaten the maize. I had not eaten anything.

I then began to walk towards the Kahigaini Road which comes from Ihururu towards the forest – the big murram road which leads into the forest. At this time I was down below Thengeraini in the valley. I began to come up towards the trench in order to come along the trench towards the main road. The main road runs past Thengeraini village. I did not come across the country because there was a steep hill and I wanted to come along the trench. The trench was nearer where I was. I was about 200 yds. from the trench. That was where I cooked my maize cob.

There is a rock on my right.

I was in the trench about 150 yards from the main road.

My intention was to come and stop near the main road and have my food and then come along the road to Kahigaini where there was a police post.

NOTE: The accused animated and smiling, gesticulating. Obviously well and not in any pain or discomfort.

K.K. O'C.

I had no intention of returning to the forest. If I had intended to come back into the forest I would have carried more maize or potatoes or bananas or about 20 sticks of sugar cane – more food supplies.

When I was still in the trench I heard a gun shot.

I could not tell from what distance away it was fired – I think about 40 yards away. I did not see who fired it.

There were two shots one after the other. I did not see who fired the second shot.

I dropped the sugar can {cane} and the two maize cobs I had in my hand and ran. I had no idea who was firing at me.

Before I had gone far I heard a third shot.
When I heard the first shot I did not wait for a second.
I dropped what I had and began to run. I turned back along the trench. The shots appeared to come from the direction of the main road to which I had intended to go.
After hearing the second shot I was running very fast along the trench to where I had been. It was beginning to get light – There was light – not full light. You could see across the valley distinctly.
I did not see the person who fired the second or the third shot.
I was still running very fast when I heard the third shot. It did not hit me. I was still in the trench. I got out of the trench on the reserve side. I saw down where there was a castor oil tree about ten yards away on the reserve side. There was a steep hill.
I was sitting under the castor oil tree here. There was a slope down to the Thengeraini River.
(Police Corporal put by accused in position he says he was sitting – squatting on hunkers knees about 2½' apart arms resting on knees and hands hanging forward.
Assessors see this demonstration.)

When I saw a man coming from West to East – I was facing down towards the stream in the valley with my back to the trench. The tree was on my right but I was under it.

The man came from in front of me slightly to the left.

I had been sitting down under the tree for about twenty minutes. I had a watch with me and I looked at it. I had seen no other person that morning.

After seeing him and noticing that he had a gun I raised my arms. I did not know who he was, but I noticed he was wearing a black overcoat and a whitish cap.

I did not know to which group he belonged, but I thought he was one of those who kills others. I did not know whether he was a MAU MAU or Government.

I raised my arms. I had a small stick me with – a staff.
(Accused corrects interpreter and says "Staff.")[37]

I dropped my staff and raised my arms and said: "It is I DEDAN KIMATHI. I have come to surrender. Don't kill me. I have a pistol."

---

37. The trial transcript does not specify the language used by Kimathi in his testimony. At several points, Kimathi's fluency in English is confirmed, but there are moments throughout the trial when Kimathi corrects the interpreter, suggesting that he is speaking in Gikuyu or Kiswahili.

I had then noticed that he was wearing blue puttees and an overcoat and I presumed that he was a policeman.

Witness smiling as he indicates place on interpreter.

The man was not less than ten or more than fifteen yards away. When he heard me saying that I was DEDAN KIMATHI he 'lowered his knee' – got on to one knee. He hit me almost in the groin. It came out above hip bone.

After being shot I lay on my left side – my right side – my head towards the trench. My leg became numb – from that time till now. I felt great pain, perspired, fainted.

When I came to I saw a group of Police who gave me some water to drink. They made me a stretcher but I do not remember being carried.

I remember being given tea on arrival at the Post.

When I opened my eyes at IHURURU I saw a European – I do not know whether he was a Doctor. I believe I was given an injection but I do not know. Then I was taken to NYERI and put into the Provincial Hospital – I was operated on by the Doctor. The next morning I was visited by a Police Officer in plain clothes who charged me.

I have heard him give evidence as to my reply.

(His reply read to witness).

Yes, it was like that, but having read that pamphlet {leaflet} – Counsel: "Never mind the pamphlet." Witness: I was very ill. What I wished to say was that I did not know that there was such a law to a person who wished to surrender.

I meant to say that I did not know there was such a law to a person who was coming to surrender himself.

When I made that statement my leg and my head were paining very much and I had not then passed water or 'going to relief' since I came out of the forest. I could hear noises in my ears and I was feeling giddy.

Q. Why didn't you tell him that you had come in to surrender?

A. I thought that I had completed the sentence: that I did not know there was such a law for one who wished to surrender. I only spoke six words. I was unable to speak more on account of the pain I had.

Q. You were visited by VIDLER – a Police Officer – on certain matters; why have you not told him that you came in to surrender?

A. He asked me several questions and I replied truthfully.

'B' He was in civilian clothes and he did not tell me he was a Police Officer.

Besides you (COUNSEL) I have spoken to the Europeans who were keeping guard over me and have told them that I was shot while coming out to surrender.

Epilepsy During my life I have suffered from what the KIKUYU call 'devils'.[38] It throws me down to the ground and I become unconscious till I feel people carrying me. It started a very long time ago when I was young. I can't say when. My mother will know. It was when I was a small boy. I have these fits very often. They have continued all my life. When I was young I had attacks frequently. Since I have grown up I get attacks every three or six months. Yes, I have had attacks in the forest. I have been questioned by a Doctor in NYERI, while I was in the hospital since my capture. I have been treated by 'medicine men' (Witness corrects the interpreter's translation to 'Witch doctors') not by African doctors of medicine. The fits continued after they (the Witch Doctors) treated me.

XXD.

I see EXHIBIT 6 (pistol) I admit that I was in possession of this the morning I was arrested – the 21st October, 1956.

Yes, I say that I had kept it to defend myself against attacks. I have never fired it so cannot say that it was in good order. I trusted that the man who gave it to me knew that it was good. I have never had any other weapons in the forest. I always have the 'staff' already mentioned. Before I left the others in 1954, I never had any weapon.

Yes, this is a 'photo of me.[39] Yes, I am holding a rifle. I think it was taken in June, 1953.

EX. 21 easily recognisable 'photo of accd. holding rifle, standing proudly.

(Photo, tendered EXHIBIT 21).

Q. Why did you have that 'photo taken?

A. It is no harm to have a 'photo taken. I wished to have it taken. The rifle was not mine. I am called "Field Marshall. Sir Dedan KIMATHI."

Q. Do you call yourself that?

38. For a fuller discussion of epilepsy in colonial Kenya, see the introduction to this volume.

39. Exhibit No. 21, photo of Dedan Kimathi, June 1953, reproduced as figure A.4 in the appendix to this volume.

A. Yes: when they began calling me that, I continued to call myself that. Yes. I used to sign my letters thus and I had a rubber stamp "Field Marshall Sir Dedan KIMATHI," and I used to call myself "President of the Kenya Parliament. The Freedom Armies." The people invented the name "Knight Commander of the African Empire." Yes, I called myself that. Yes, I was called the "Supreme Commander in Chief of the Country of Kenya and the Land Freedom Armies." I called myself that when the people said that it was good.

I was neither head nor bottom of the terrorist leaders.

I did not make myself the top-rank terrorist leader.

After I was given that title I agreed – I can't tell you whether that was top or bottom or middle rank.

Q. Did you not write to the Government as "Supreme Commander in Chief" and speak for the Terrorist Armies?

A. Yes, I did so write, but I did not know whether I was the top or bottom or middle.

22 I see a document. This is my handwriting. I wrote this letter. It is dated 20/10/54. I cannot remember whether that date is correct. It may be; it is my handwriting.

(Marked 22 for identification)[40]

I look at a letter. This is my handwriting.

23 (23, for identity – dated 30/3/54.)[41]

I look at a third letter. This is in my handwriting I think.

24 (24 for identity – dated 10/4/54.)[42]

Q. You said that since February, 1954, when you split, and left your companions, you have not carried out any MAU MAU activity?

A. Yes.

Q. Would you call writing these letters a MAU MAU activity?

A. I never thought them bad letters.

---

40. See Exhibit No. 22, original Gikuyu version of Kimathi letter, 20 October 1954, reproduced as Document 7 in this volume.

41. See Exhibit No. 23, Kimathi letter, 30 March 1954, transcribed as Document 9 in this volume.

42. See Exhibit No. 24, Kimathi letter, 6 March 1954, transcribed as Document 10 in this volume.

EX. 23 (EX. 23 tendered. No objection. Admitted.)

I cannot say if the date on the postmark is 27th March.

I look at the rubber 'receipt stamp'. It says "Nairobi, 30th March, 1954." I cannot find my date on it. I don't dispute that the postmark is the 27th March. That letter is addressed to the A.G. {Attorney General}

Q. Is it headed "My echo will sound peace"?

A. Yes.

S.G. Puts to witness part of letter as far as "once I shout peace, there is never a war in Kenya."

Yes; I said that in March, 1954, and I signed that: "Field Marshall Sir Dedan KIMATHI".

Q. Were you suggesting negotiating peace on behalf of MAU MAU?

A. I wanted to be outside and to negotiate with the Government and the forest men. I wanted peace.

Q. You were offering in that letter to negotiate peace as Field Marshall KIMATHI on behalf of MAU MAU?

A. Yes, my intention was peace.

Yes, according to my evidence that was after I had left my people in the forest.

I was an intermediary – between. At that time I was not with them, but I had not come out of the forest. I did write that letter with the intention of getting peace, but I was not on either side.

Q. Was it untrue when you said "Once I shout peace there is never a war in Kenya."

A. I trusted so because everyone knew me and I thought if I could come out everyone would. I was afraid of MAU MAU and have been ever since.

Q. Were you a Field Marshall able to shout peace and in command of MAU MAU or were you a fugitive, frightened of MAU MAU?

A. I was a fugitive.

Q. So it was untrue to write to the Government and say 'Once I shout peace there is never a war in Kenya."?

A. Although I was not on any side, I wished to write this letter thinking it would be a help to the forest people.

Q. Was it true or untrue?

A. It is ~~not~~ [very] difficult to answer. I would have attempted. What I wrote was not true.

EX. 22 22 tendered. No objection. Admitted. EX. 22 dated 20/10/54

This is my Letter written in KIKUYU Headed "The Kenya Parliament. The Land Freedom Army.... Aberdares." It is addressed to the Kenya Government, Nairobi.

Q. Does it purport to set out what happened at a meeting of the "Kenya Parliament."? Between 15th and 20th October, 1954, and the views of the "Kenya Parliament."?

A. Yes.

Q. Does it end "Those who were present were: "Field Marshall Sir Dedan KIMATHI, President... more than 270 leaders from various corners."?

A. Yes.

It is signed "Field Marshall Sir Dedan KIMATHI. President for and on behalf of the Kenya Parliament."

I still say that I split away from them in February, 1954.

I split from them after I had been elected.

Q. Are you saying that though you had split from them in February, 1954, you were presiding over them in October, 1954, and writing as a Field Marshall from their General Headquarters?

ADJOURNED to 2.30 p.m.

K. O'CONNOR

RESUMED 2.30 p.m.

EX. 24 I see a letter which I wrote to the Deputy Governor on the 6th March, 1954 (Tendered. Admitted. EX. 24)

I there~~fore~~ said that ~~in so~~ [I was] speaking on behalf of my followers.

Q. Did you say: "Notification to the Public I hereby notify the public that though the Kenya public does not regard us as people of brain and wisdom and knowledge etc. ..... I on behalf of all my followers and the Defence Council and the President of the Council and the Knight Commander of the African Empire and the President of the African Empire .... etc. ..... delegates."

By Field Marshall Dedan KIMATHI K.C.A.E. & Supreme Commander of the Country of Kenya and the Land Freedom Armies 6/4/54."

Q. Were you there purporting to write to the Deputy Governor as Supreme Commander and President of the Council?

A. Yes.

Q. You were speaking to the Government as head of MAU MAU?

A. Yes, along with the people I was representing.

Insanity. Yes, I suffer from a mental disease, though I am a big man.

Q, Do you know what you are doing now?

Yes. I know that I am being tried.

When I do a thing I know what I am doing.

Q. Do you know the difference between right and wrong?

A. Yes, I do.

Q. You said that since February, 1954, you left your companions and feared for your own safety from them. Is that right?

A. Yes.

That is 2½ years ago.

Q. You have said that since then you have not engaged in any MAU MAU activity. Why didn't you surrender then?

A. Because of the price on my head. I have seen the surrender pamphlets {leaflets}.

EX. B. I see EX. B.

I saw a copy of that when I was in the forest. It is dated August, 1953. I saw it in 1953.

Q. Why didn't you obey its terms then?

A. Because I was afraid of being killed because of the price on my head.

S.G. Reads: "Gang leaders ….. come out waving green branches ….. this will ensure that you are not shot at ….. unjustly.

Signed by the Governor and Commander-in-Chief.

Q. Do you say that in spite of that, you were afraid to come in because of the price on your head?

A. Yes.

On the 20th October I came in because I did not care if I was killed.

Q. Was that because you were being hunted by the Security Forces and were left all alone and sick in the forest.

A. Yes, the MAU MAU and Security forces were hunting me and I was ill and alone.

If I had not changed in heart I would not have come out and I changed long before.

Q. Are you trying to say now that you had changed heart and wanted to help the Government?

A. Yes, that is what I am saying.

Q. You said this morning "I surrendered because I had been in the forest a very long time and the Security Forces were hunting me and I was left alone; I said better to come and be killed and get the Government."

A. Yes, I said that.

Q. Was it because you were being pursued so closely that you surrendered or because you had a change of heart?

A. The forest is a large area and if I had not had a change of heart I would have moved elsewhere.

I can't say whether all my gang have been captured. They have gone apart from me. When I said: "It's better to be killed, that is when I came out." For a long time I have been thinking of coming out to help the Government but I was afraid. Recently I did not care. In February, 1954, was when I went to live apart. When I decided to abandon MAU MAU was when I came out completely.

Q. When did you abandon MAU MAU?

A. In August, 1953, I wrote a letter.

I don't understand.

Question repeated.

A. When I wrote the first letter I had abandoned MAU MAU.

I was on the Government's side. In February, 1954, on account of writing a letter I ran away from the others.

Though I saw the surrender pamphlets {leaflets} I was afraid to come out because of the price on my head.

I see a letter.

Q. Have you ever seen that?

A. Yes. I received that in the forest and I replied to it.

EX. 25 (Letter shown to MILLER. Letter from D.C. NYERI to Dedan KIMATHI dated 2/6/54 Tendered. No objection. EX. 25)[43]

Letter addressed to him c/o. Senior Chief MUHOYA:[44]

"You are at liberty at any time to surrender with your men of which you are doubtless aware. You should notify me.... so that you and your followers will not be molested if coming in to surrender."

A. I sent a reply to say that I was to be met at Kabalye School. I sent people who were murdered. So I was afraid to come.

Yes, on the 20th October, I decided that life was not worth living. I came down and collected this food, but I did not go back into the forest.

It was not dark when I started to move – just getting day time.

Q. The instructions were "Come out during day time"; you didn't come out during day time.

A. I was walking along the trench intending to sit down by the road and eat, by which time it would have been day time. I would have collected a green branch.

Q. Did you send any message to the D.C. or anyone else that you were coming in?

A. No, I was all alone.

Q. Were you carrying any copy of the surrender pamphlets {leaflets}?

A. No, they were all destroyed by rain.

Yes, I know that one of them contained a safe-conduct Pass.

---

43. See Exhibit No. 25, letter from Chief Muhoya to Dedan Kimathi, 2 June 1954, transcribed as Document 11 in this volume.

44. For Muhoya's relationship with Kimathi, see the introduction and Lonsdale's contribution to this volume.

Q. You told us this morning your version of what happened when you were shot?

A. Yes.

Q. Do you think the policeman intended to kill you?

A. Yes.

Q. What was there to stop him putting another bullet through your head?

A. Nothing.

I believe I was given an injection at IHURURU. I may have said to the Doctor that I wanted one but I have no knowledge.

I was operated on on Sunday and the next day I was visited by a Police Officer who charged me.

I believe I was visited by Dr. HURLEY. I don't recollect it. I may have replied to him.

Q. The Police Officer did not come and charge you until after the Doctor had come and spoken to you.

A. Perhaps

Q. You heard the Doctor give evidence in this court. He said that your condition would not affect your ability to give precise replies on the morning of the 21st October. Was he wrong?

A. I don't say that the Doctor is wrong but he cannot tell whether I was ill when I was coming through the forest, or whether I was feeling giddy.

I don't say the Doctor is wrong but I say he does not know whether I was feeling giddy or ill.

Q. Do you remember how many time the charges and your reply were read over to you that morning?

A. I am sure I did say what was said there. I have had a copy of it. I can't remember how many times it was then read to me.

Q. Wasn't it read in English, Swahili and Kikuyu?

A. I don't dispute, but I don't remember.

Q. Don't you agree that what you said was correct?

A. I replied that I did not know it was wrong for a man to surrender coming out with his arms.

Q. Why didn't you tell the Police Officers that a policeman had tried to shoot you.

A. I didn't have strength to speak or I would have said a lot.

I remember many days later Mr. VIDLER and Mr. BLACKMAN came to see me. They came once together and Mr. BLACKMAN came once again.

I was still ill. I tried to sit up but they told me to lie down. Yes, I was able to think quite clearly that day.

Q. Why didn't you tell them you had tried to surrender?

A. They were not in uniform and I did not know what part of Government they belonged to.

They did not say they were Police Officers and wanted to ask me some questions.

I just thought they were ordinary Europeans.

If I had thought they were Police Officers I would have complained about my being shot when I came in to surrender.

There has been a European in my cell all the time since my arrest.

Q. When VIDLER and BLACKMAN came in didn't he stand up respectfully?

A. I was lying on the bed; when I saw him he was ~~standing~~ [sitting] down.

I remember the Magistrate coming to see me and asking me if I had any witnesses that I wanted.

No, I didn't tell him that I had been shot when I wanted to surrender. I did not know that it was right to tell him. I was informed that he was the Judge.

<u>RE-XD.</u>

This morning I was shown a 'photo of myself carrying a rifle.

Q. Can you tell the Court how you came to be photographed?

A. At the place where this 'photo (EX. 21) was taken there was a man with a rifle and I got it from him for the 'photo to be taken and then I gave it back. I had it only for a few minutes.

Q. You said that you left your companions in the forest and went away with five or six followers in February 1954, and then you wrote those letters signing yourself Commander in Chief etc.

A. When I wrote those letters there were only five people with me.

Q. Why did you give yourself those grand titles?

A. I did not know it was such a big designation.

Q. Were you at that time Commander-in-Chief of the Army, or President of the Parliament?

A. Previously to that I had been elected to those posts, but when I wrote those letters I was not the Commander.

Q. Were you then connected with the Freedom Army?

A. I had split from them when I wrote the letters.

If I had been able to I would have turned them towards me – towards the Government.

Although I was living alone there were some people in the forest who did not hate me and whom I used to visit and who used to visit me.

I wanted them to be on my side to seek for peace with the Government.

Q. This letter of the 20th October (EX. 22) addressed to the Kenya Govt. and sent by you is headed "Kenya Parliament, Land Freedom Army G.H.Q." Since you wrote that letter, or since February, 1954, have you had any contact with either of those bodies?

A. Only those who were on my side and not those I had split from. There were others besides the six who lived with me.

I cannot tell you how many.

No, I have no idea.

Macharia KIMENYA's {Kimanya} men and I were friendly. Those were the ones I used to visit. MACHARIA and I were the leaders of those people and we were threatened with death. The Freedom Army had been formed long before.

I think my reply to the D.C. NYERI's letter (EX. 25) I think I wrote and explained about the dreams I had had.

I am quite sure that when I came in on the 21/10/56, I came in to surrender.

<u>PETER PERCIVAL TURNER</u> S/S

Provincial Physician M.D., M.R.C.P.,

I know the accused. I have examined him. I discovered that he had idiopathic epilepsy. It is a disease which sometimes affects the mind.

Q. Is it always possible in the earlier stages of this disease to detect deterioration of the mind?

A. No. It would not be possible unless one knew the person personally and knew the person over a long period of time. It would be easier for a relative than for me examining him over a short period of time.

It could be detected in ordinary conversation if it were advanced. Otherwise, it could only be detected by some overt abnormal act.

Inasmuch as anaesthesia and operations are a well known precipitating cause of a fit it can be said that an epileptic may have a fit brought on by these occurrences.

If a fit occurred during anaesthesia it would not be noticed. If the epileptic has a fit under anaesthesia, he would be likely to have a severe headache and mental blurring for some hours after he recovers consciousness. This might last for 24 hours afterwards.

I know Price's textbook of the Practice of Medicine.[45] Frederick Price is dead. The authors of this section are alive, but in London. This is a Medical Treatise commonly offered for sale (S.60 Ev. Act.)

No objection by S. G. to this evidence.

Passage put to witness. 7th edn. P. 1707 "Mental deterioration and aberration in Epilepsy… imbecility."

I agree with that passage. There is still a lot to be learned about Epilepsy.

Psychological Medicine by CURRAN & GUTTMAN 2nd edn.[46]

I regard this as an authority. p. 115. This is a medical text book commonly offered for sale. The authors are alive but in London.

No objection by the S.G.

"At least two thirds of all epileptics show progressive deterioration of variable degree … paroxysmal reaction."

I regard Forensic Medicine by SYDNEY SMITH and FIDDLES as an authority (1949) 9th Edn. p. 394.[47] These authors are in Scotland. This is a medical treatise commonly offered for sale.

---

45. Frederick William Price, *A Textbook on the Practice of Medicine* (Oxford University Press, 1926).

46. Desmond Curran and Eric Guttman, *Psychological Medicine: A Short Introduction to Psychiatry* (E. S. Livingstone, 1945)

47. Sir Sydney Smith and Frederick Smith Fiddles, *Forensic Medicine: A Textbook for Students and Practitioners* (London: J. and A. Churchill, 1949).

"Epilepsy may exist without obvious intellectual impairment ..... insanity."

I agree with that.

XXD. S.G.

There are many forms of idiopathic epilepsy. The main symptom is a sudden loss of consciousness. I observed no symptoms in the accused. Usually a diagnosis has to be made on a story from observers.

I based my opinion solely on what I have been told by Dedan KIMATHI himself, his mother and Joseph WAKABA. I do not know whether he has come from a Detention Camp.

I think Dedan KIMATHI is a reasonably intelligent man intelligent above the standard of a man of his education.

I make no suggest that he is insane. He knows what he is doing and he knows the difference between right and wrong.

He has been under constant observation since 21st Octr. and he has had no fit during that month.

If an operation took place about 12.30 on Sunday 21st .....

I first examined him on the 9/11/56. He was then physically fit.

Q. HURLEY said that he stood the operation well and that he examined him again on the following morning. Apart from pain and stricture of urine he did not complain of anything and he appeared to be mentally alert.

If he had had a fit the previous day, would Dr. HURLEY have discovered it?

A. I think it likely he would have discovered that he was mentally cloudy.

If he had had a headache and mental cloudiness, I would have expected him to mention it, particularly if Dr. HURLEY's examination were carried out for the purpose of ascertaining whether he was fit to answer questions.

If he had had an epileptic fit under the operation, the surgeon might still say that he stood the operation very well.

Yes, I would expect the mental clouding to continue for anything up to 48 hours afterwards.

A headache is not necessarily attributable to a fit under anaesthesia.

PRICE's. P. 1707 "Many epileptics ..... while others show no such mental troubles and fulfil a long life."

I have detected no sign of mental troubles.
The usual picture is a gradual mental deterioration.
In this case, I found no sign of mental deterioration.

TO COURT:

I found no evidence in the mental condition of the accused to suggest that either if he were carrying a revolver he would not know that or that through disease of the mind, he would not know that it was wrong to do so.

RE-XD.

I formed my opinion of his mental condition on questions I had asked other people and the accused.

Q. Would it be easy for a person to deceive you on this point?

A. It would not be easy unless he knew the right story to tell. A person trying to deceive is inclined to tell a bizarre story which it is immediately apparent is not epilepsy.
I am quite satisfied that he is an epileptic.

S.G.

22A. Copies have been made of EX. 22 and checked by the Court interpreter and some errors have been corrected.

I tender this. No objection.
(Admitted EX. 22A.)

ADJOURNED to 9.30 MONDAY, the 26th November, 1956.

(SGND) K. K. O'CONNOR, C.J.
23rd November, 1956.

26/11/56RESUMED 9.30 A.M.

WAITHOTHI W/O WACHIURI[48], affirmed states:

I am the mother of Dedan Kimathi. Here he is (~~Indicates~~ [Identifies] accused).

---

48. For the process by which Waithoti w/o Wachiuri was brought from Kamiti prison to Nyeri to testify, see Anderson's contribution to this volume.

He was attacked by epilepsy. He was first attacked after my next child was able to talk. I cannot say how many years ago. He was a boy old enough to work as a herd-boy.

When people suffer from epilepsy, when they grow up they are thrown down. In my presence he was attacked three times. Twice more others saw him. He was thrown down on the ground. I have a daughter. She was the first to be attacked. Her name is Wangechi. She was first attacked the year she was circumcised. She has frequent attacks. She was attacked recently. Sometimes she is not attacked for some time, then she complains of headache and then she is thrown down. Her attacks are quite unexpected. Sometimes she has no attack until the next harvest. Sometimes she has attacks between harvests.
No Cross-examination.

JOSEPH WAKABA S/O MORETHI[49] Sworn states:

I know Dedan Kimathi s/o Wachiuri. This is he (~~Indicates~~ [Identifies] accused).

Once he had a fall, whether it was due to illness or not I could not tell you. This was in 1945. We were both staying in a house. I was cooking. All at once he fell down and I went to pick him up. He was semi-conscious and after five minutes he became conscious.
No cross-examination.

9.40 CASE FOR DEFENCE.

MILLER: I apply for adjournment to enable me to complete my preparations to address.

Adjourned to 10.30 A.M.

K. O'C.
26/11.

Resumed 10.30 A.M.

MILLER ADDRESSES.

Reads Regulation 8A and 8A.1.[50] Submit Accused did have a lawful excuse for possessing a pistol and ammunition. He did not have lawful authority. Accused came in to surrender himself.

---

49. The *East African Standard* reported that Wakaba had been brought to testify from Manyani Camp, 24 November 1956.

50. Emergency Regulation 8A, 1952, read: "Any person who, except with lawful authority or lawful excuse, the burden of proof whereof shall lie upon him, carries, or has in his possession . . . any firearm shall be guilty of an offence and shall on conviction be sentenced to death."

Wong Pooh Yin v. P.P. 3 W.L.R. 474.[51]

Their Lordship doubt if it is possible to define "lawful excuse………"

Defence on lawful excuse may be proved although no lawful authority may exist. It is the excuse that must be shown to be lawful.

Mwangi Wambugu. Cr. Ap. 168/54. (1954) 11 E.A.L.R.

Lawful authority referable to special provision. Lawful excuse justifies that which is prima facie unlawful. Distinction in mind of the accused.

Lawful excuse – intention to hand in. Case of surrendering terrorist exceptional.

FACTS.

Accused is charged with unlawful possession of arms and ammunition, i.e., without lawful authority. Accused had no lawful authority but he did have a lawful excuse.

Submit that acting on Ex. C, calls on Mau Mau to surrender "If possible come with your arms." That concession has not been withdrawn. Acting on that invitation he came in to surrender and brought his arm. He was frustrated.

You have heard statements of Crown witnesses particularly Ndirangu. It is largely on his evidence and on that of Njogi that your decision must largely depend.

Accused has said on oath that he came down and was about to eat sugar cane very near main road. It is agreed that it was then growing light. Seen carrying sticks of sugar cane. One cob of maize in his possession. If he had intended to return to the forest would he not have taken a good supply of food. No food and nearness to road shows his intention to surrender.

He says that at that point he heard a shot fired 40^{X} away. He ran. What was more natural. What would most people do? Shortly after he was fired at again and a third time.

---

51. Following sections refer to precedence set in two previous cases: *Wong Poohyin v Public Prosecutor* [1954]3 AER 31 (PC) from the Court of Appeal of the Federation of Malaya and *Mwangi s/o Wambugu v Reg* [1954] XXI from the Court of Appeal for Eastern Africa 246 (see KNA, AC/3715). Both cases deal with the legal definition of a "lawful excuse" to carry a firearm under colonial Emergency Regulations. See Judicial Committee of the Privy Council, "The Meaning of 'Lawful Excuse,'" *Journal of Criminal Law* 19 (1955): 51–55.

Here is the difference between evidence of accused and Ndirangu Mau.

Ndirangu says that as he ran he hit him with the third shot He rolled over and disappeared.

Accused says that he ran down and stayed under the castor oil tree. Ndirangu says he was there when he was found wounded. Accused says that after 15 minutes he saw Ndirangu come below him on the slope and to his left, and the accused said to him "I am Dedan Kimathi. I wish to surrender and have a pistol." Ndirangu raised his rifle and shot him.

What does Ndirangu say. Posted about 15^x from the road on the Reserve side facing the forest. I saw Accused 35^x from me, i.e. accused 55^x or so from the main road. Accused's statement that he was near the road is supported.

Ndirangu said that after he had shot him he disappeared for about 1 hour. Njogi said also "We search for about 1 hour."

Wanyiri {Wanjiri} said "After hearing the third shot we ran to the place and heard a person on the ground: it was the Accused." Wanjohi also says "After hearing the 3rd shot we ran faster and found the accused under a castor oil tree."

Crew says distance from the road to the castor oil tree – 800^x. Would it take an hour to run 800^x?
Why do they mention an hour? It is to hide what happened or have they made a mistake. It was clearly a matter of minutes.

Nature of wound. Hurley says "if the wounded man were squatting and he was fired at by a man in front on his left on a slope before him, that would explain this wound. This wound could also have been inflicted as described by Ndirangu. But when Ndirangu was explaining, he was repeatedly made gesture curving to the right which if true [it] would not be possible for that wound to be inflicted.

Yours is the task of deciding who is speaking the truth on a vital issue. If you conclude that Accused was squatting under the tree when wounded, Ndirangu's testimony is false and rest of his evidence is unreliable. Burden of that decision heavy. Man's life in balance.

<u>Why didn't Accused say to Baker that he had come in to surrender?</u>

Accused doesn't deny that he said what was recorded. Accused said: I would like to say that I never knew that there was such a law. He said "I meant that I did not know there was such a law to a person who was surrendering himself", i.e. he didn't know that

that law applied to a person who was coming in to surrender in accordance with terms of the pamphlet {leaflet}.

He could have explained this to Vidler. He says he didn't know he was a police officer. He was not in police uniform.

The statement to Baker was less than 24 hours after the Accused had been operated on. Dr. Hurley said that Accused was suffering from shock and that his wound was not a painful one. You have heard evidence of his mother and J. Wakaba which confirms that he is an epileptic.

You have heard Turner say that one of the results of epilepsy in circumstances of shock is to blunt the mental qualities of the subject and that it does in many cases lead to insanity. I am not suggesting that Accused is insane but there is a lot to be discovered and who can say where insanity begins. I suggest that in considering the circumstances in which the accused failed to make plain that he was coming in to surrender which was surely the first thing that any intelligent person would have done, the accused had he been clear of mind and normal would have said "I came in to surrender" to all persons he met subsequent to his shooting.

Before the operation he had been injected and was as Vidler said semi-conscious. Same day he was operated on.

10.30 Baker took a statement. He had been under anaesthetics less than 24 hours before: he was still suffering pain and you must consider the possibility of his epilepsy in those conditions affecting his mind. He himself said that he had a painful headache, was in pain and feeling giddy. How would anyone feel fit to consider all circumstances of such a charge.

Another circumstance: you have heard how Accused sent various letters to Government. He says that that brought about dissension between himself and the other leaders and that he had to flee and hide. Justified in taking reasonable precautions to see that the persons who might murder him do not succeed and he is justified in adopting reasonable means of self defence.

Why didn't he surrender. Afraid of his life because £500 on his head.

You have here an unfortunate man torn between two loyalties – one displaced – but a man who saw the mistake, made futile attempts to come to terms and finally decided to surrender and met with the circumstances you have heard.

If you believe that Dedan Kimathi came down with his pistol – he could easily have thrown it away while running along. If he had that intention he should be acquitted.

SOLICITOR-GENERAL:
11.17.

Law. Address on three aspects:

(1) Lawful excuse.

Wambugu's case and Wong Pooh Yin's case must be read together. Wong Pooh Yin's later and supersedes.

Wambugu's case.

Final sentence. Had everything been accepted....... lawful excuse.

(1954 3 A.E.R. 311 34.

"In so far as excuse [con]notes something more than a change of mind. Proof of particular intent not an effectual defence.[52]

Submit:

I merely had a change of intention is not enough. He has to establish some overt acts of proof of his intention to surrender."

That he seeks to do. He says he went through a course of conduct which was part of the process.

Submit.

It would not be sufficient for him to show that he retained the pistol on the date charged in order to protect himself in a quarrel with his fellow terrorists.

In Wambugu's case it was laid down that whether a set of circumstances can constitute a lawful excuse is a matter of law.

p. 247. "It is a matter of law whether a particular set of circumstances could constitute a lawful excuse.[53]

---

52. Wording comes directly from Privy Council "The Meaning of 'Lawful Excuse,'" 52.

53. The full passage from Mwangi s/o Wambugu's Appeals Judgment reads: "It is a matter of law whether a particular set of circumstances could constitute a lawful excuse: it is a question of fact whether in any particular case those circumstances ought to be accepted as a valid excuse. In every case, questions of honest or dishonest intention are a matter of inference from primary facts: for example, long duration of unlawful possession without any action to surrender the arms would generally weigh heavily against an assertion of honest intention. The case of a surrendering terrorist is exceptional, because in his case there will generally have been long possession anterior to his formation of an intention to surrender with his arms. As the appellant {Mwangi s/o Wambugu} in this matter shrewdly remarked at his trial: 'What is the purpose of inviting terrorists to surrender with their arms and ammunition? If they leave their arms and ammunition behind, what will be the use?'" Judgment, Criminal Appeal No. 168 of 1954 of Regina v. Mwangi s/o Wambugu, in Her Majesty's Court of Appeal for Eastern Africa at Nairobi, 27 March 1954.

It is not a lawful excuse for one terrorist to say he had a pistol to protect himself from his fellow terrorists.

Burden of Proof:

The burden on the prosecution is to establish the facts beyond reasonable doubt except in so far as the statute shifts any part of the burden to the accused.

If prosecution proves possession of weapon beyond reasonable doubt, that is sufficient for them.

Hornell v. Newberger Products Ltd.[54]

Times newspaper for 21/11/56. C.A.

Hodson L. J. "Degree of probability commensurate with the occasion".

No issue of insanity to be left to the assessors.

No issue of insanity (Miller agrees).

Facts.

Accused has pleaded not guilty to two charges

(1) {Count 1} unlawful possession of a firearm. Prosecution must prove to you that accused was in possession of that firearm and that it was a firearm.

He said "The reason I had it was that I intended to surrender. Government instructions were not to leave it behind."

(1) Possession is admitted.

Crown must prove that this is a lethal weapon.

Vidler's and Blackman's evidence (Shows them the piece of wood). Could kill if hit in heart or head.

Law says that it is not an offence if you have a lawful excuse – e.g., a man who in the course of his duties wanted to defend himself against the enemies of Government. Burden of proof of that rests upon Accused. You must say whether you are satisfied that he probably had a lawful excuse.

One convenient test of the evidence. Do you believe Ndirangu or Njogi, or do you believe Dedan Kimathi. If you are satisfied that Ndirangu and Njogi are telling the truth you should convict. If Dedan Kimathi is telling the truth – acquit.

---

54. Reference to the UK Court of Appeal case Hornal v. Newberger Products Ltd., 1956. This decision related to the standard of proof necessary in civil cases in which "a party made an allegation of criminal conduct." The Court of Appeal held that "on an allegation of a crime in civil proceedings the standard of proof is on a balance of probabilities." Adrian Keane and Paul McKeown, eds., *The Modern Law of Evidence* (Oxford: Oxford University Press, 2014), 111.

If after hearing you can't make up your mind which is the more probably true story because it is for Dedan Kimathi to prove the lawful excuse, you must convict.

Count 2:

In that case you should only find him guilty if you are satisfied that he intended to use the ammunition in matters against public safety. If he had a lawful excuse that is a defence. If you think he was a leader of Mau Mau and possessed pistol without excuse you will think that he possessed ammunition for a purpose against public safety.

Issue:

Was Dedan Kimathi intending to come in, and coming in to surrender on that Sunday morning?

Value of assessors.

You saw Dedan Kimathi. Did he strike you as a man who was telling the truth. Or as a very foxy and suspicious individual.

Admits he has been in the forest for four years. Calls himself Supreme C-in-C, President of the Kenya Parliament – i.e. Head of Mau Mau. On the other hand Ndirangu a Tribal Policeman and Home Guard since 1952. Was Ndirangu telling the truth or was Accused?

2nd Test:

Dedan Kimathi said that since February 1954 he had engaged in no Mau Mau activities. He said neither before and certainly not [afterwards]. But letter that he wrote eight months later.

Exhibit 22 written 8 months later on behalf of the Kenya Parliament. Asks Government to enter into peaceful negotiations "We ask "Allow us to meet and speak the words of peace." Signs at the head of the list all others under. Says that there were more than 273 other leaders. Do you believe that. Not truthful.

He said that the only weapon he had was this pistol. Only had that to defend himself against Mau Mau. Had [he] it for that purpose or to kill innocent men. Supreme C-in-C. Said he had never had any other firearm. Photo Ex. 21.

More probable story that he had left his other arms in his Headquarters and this pistol was easy to carry when he slipped down to the Reserve to get food.

3rd test. Had he other arms.

4th " He said he was coming in to surrender in accordance with them but that he was frightened because there was a price on his head.

Date of "C" is August, 1953. Surrendering in October, 1956. Pamphlet {leaflet} says "<u>Now</u>" etc. (Reads it). Did that affect his mind in October, 1956?

Letters produced don't say "I want to surrender". They say "I am prepared to negotiate and have peace."

Examine his story: Ill, alone, etc.

Hurley said very well nourished and fit. Came down to get food and cooked it. Says he was trying to surrender. Don't you think he was coming down to get food or spend the night in the Reserve and was caught on the way back.

Miller said that how he was shot did not seem a very probable story. Ndirangu said Dedan Kimathi was not shot in the trench. "He was circling and going [back] into the trench."

Ndirangu was recalled. He said this "I fired three shots. I thought I hit him with the 3rd – kneeling etc., faced trench and I shot him in that position. Bullet travelled up, that is quite consistent with Ndirangu's story.

Ndirangu is corroborated by Njogi and Maina and Mwangi Kanguru.

Dedan Kimathi says he ran away and ~~said~~[sat] for 20 minutes. But Njogi, Maina and Mwangi say that they were searching for an hour or for 20 minutes. They all say shots fired before they started searching.

<u>Another test.</u>

Dedan Kimathi said Ndirangu deliberately shot him. Would he shoot him in the leg and allow him to give evidence. Would he not have put another bullet through Dedan Kimathi's head.

<u>Next test.</u>

Dedan Kimathi's story is that as he was coming in to surrender Ndirangu tried to murder him. Would not he make a most vigorous complaint. They all say he could speak quite easily. He could say who he was. He is seen by Blackman, Vidler, Inspector Sloan to whom Sergeant Mwangi gave the pistol. No complaint.

<u>Statement.</u>

Hurley's evidence. Early Sunday taken to hospital. Operated on about mid-day, stood operation well. Following a.m. Hurley went to see him to find out if he was well enough to be charged by the police. He went for that purpose.

<u>Hurley said:</u> "Mental condition clear and normal. Purpose was, etc. Dedan Kimathi said "My leg, etc."

Why didn't he tell Hurley that he had a headache, was hearing gun shots and was giddy. But he didn't. He has now made up this story because of the statement that he made.

He was told he need not say anything if he didn't want to. Charges read. He said that he had understood the charges.

I have nothing more to say.

Then was the time for an innocent man to say "I was trying to surrender."

Read over in three languages and he said it was correct. But now he says he didn't understand what went on.

Was he genuinely coming in to surrender, or had he been into the Reserve for a night and was caught on the way back?

If Ndirangu is telling the truth? If so Dedan Kimathi guilty. If Dedan Kimathi, he is innocent. If you cannot make up your minds which is the most probably true story you must say he is guilty of both charges.

12.20.

ADJOURNED TO 1.30.

Assessors warned.

REGINA V DEDAN KIMATHI.

NOTES FOR SUMMING UP.

I propose first to tell you something of your duties as assessors, the nature of the charges, and the way in which you should approach the evidence in a criminal case: secondly to review for you the evidence of the prosecution and for the defence, thirdly to ask for the opinion of each of you separately on each charge. Under the law of Kenya the final verdict rests with the Judge; but in reaching my conclusion I shall pay very great attention to your opinions.

DUTIES OF ASSESSORS.

(1) It is your duty to put out of your mind anything that you may have heard about this case outside and to come to your opinions only upon the evidence which you have heard in this court.

(2) You must put out of your mind any feeling either of sympathy or of prejudice – of sympathy for the accused because he is an accused person on a capital charge, or of prejudice against him because of anything you may have heard of his past activities. Do not hold it against him or in his favour that his name may be well known. In the eye of the law he is exactly the same, and entitled to exactly the same treatment, as anyone else.

BURDEN OF PROOF.

(3) By the law of Kenya every accused person is presumed to be innocent until he is proved to be guilty and the burden of proving him guilty rests upon the prosecution. Generally speaking it is not for the accused to prove his innocence: it is for the Crown to prove him guilty. And if at the end of the case you have a reasonable doubt in your mind as to the guilt of the accused arising from the evidence given either by the prosecution or by the defence then the prosecution has not made out its case and it is your duty to give the accused the benefit of that doubt and to give your opinions in favour of acquittal.

DEGREE OF PROOF.

(4) The degree of proof required of the prosecution in a criminal case is that they must satisfy the court of the guilt of the accused beyond reasonable doubt. That does not mean beyond

any doubt. The standard is "beyond reasonable doubt". Before you give an opinion against this man you must be satisfied in your own minds, satisfied beyond reasonable doubt, that he is guilty of the offences or one of the offences with which he is charged.

CHARGES.

(5)(Court reads Counts 1 and 2).

Two offences. So far as is possible you should consider the evidence on each count separately; but in this case the evidence on both counts is much the same.

Take Count 1 first. Regulation 8A(1) of the Emergency Regulations so far as material reads:

> 8A(1) Any person who without lawful authority or lawful excuse, the burden of proof whereof (i.e. of lawful authority or lawful excuse) shall lie upon him...... has in his possession any firearm shall be guilty of an offence.....

Points which the prosecution has to prove beyond reasonable doubt:

> that on or about 21/10/56 in the Tetu Location the accused had in his possession a firearm – a Webley Scott revolver which they produce.

There are two things there requiring proof by the Prosecution beyond reasonable doubt:

(i) That the accused had this revolver in his possession; and

(ii) that this revolver is a "firearm" within the meaning of the Regulation 8A(i).

If those two things are proved by the Prosecution beyond reasonable doubt then it is open to the accused to prove that he had lawful authority or lawful excuse for possessing that firearm. He does not say he had lawful authority: e.g. a license. He does say he had a lawful excuse. The burden of proof of that is upon him.

DEGREE OF PROOF.

The accused in proving lawful excuse has not to reach such a high degree of proof as is required of the prosecution: he need not satisfy you "beyond reasonable doubt". It is sufficient for him to show that it is more probable than not that he had a lawful excuse. I direct you as a matter of law that if the accused's story is true and he was intending to bring this pistol and ammunition in in order to surrender them to the proper authorities and he had done overt acts in pursuance of that intention, that could in law be a lawful excuse which would entitle him to be acquitted. He has to prove that it was more probable than not that that was so. That is the main issue in the case.

I also direct you as a matter of law that it would not afford a reasonable excuse for one terrorist to carry a pistol and ammunition for the purpose of protecting himself from other terrorists whom he might have offended.

I may here mention that there is no defence of insanity in this case. The epilepsy about which the accused has called evidence is not in itself a defence to either of the charges. In order for it to be a defence he would have to go to the length of saying that through disease affecting his mind he was on the 21/10/56 either incapable of knowing that he possessed a revolver and ammunition or incapable (through disease of the mind) of knowing that he ought not to possess them. He does not say either of those things and his doctor specifically says that his epilepsy would not have had either of those effects. Therefore there is no defence of insanity.

The reason why evidence of epilepsy is called by the defence is for the purpose of showing that the accused's mind was or may have been blurred after his operation when the police officers came to see him and charged him in order that the defence may account for the fact that in answer to these charges he said nothing about having come in to surrender. I will deal with that again later.

I said that on <u>Count 1</u> the prosecution had to prove two things beyond reasonable doubt:

(i) that the accused had this revolver in his possession, and

(ii) that the revolver is a firearm within the meaning of the Regulation.

It will be convenient to deal with the 2nd point first.
<u>Ex. 6.</u> Is this revolver a firearm within the meaning of the Regulation? A firearm is defined in the regulation. So far as material the definition is:
"any lethal barrelled weapon of any description from which any shot bullet or other missile can be discharged....... Provided that it shall be presumed until the contrary is proved that any weapon having the appearance of a firearm is a firearm".

(a) Appearance. You may think that it does look like a firearm and no one has proved that it is not one.

(b) "Barrelled" obvious.

(c) Lethal. What is the evidence?
Inspector BLACKMAN. On Sunday 21/10/56 behind the police station at Ihururu in company with A.S.P. VIDLER, he fired a normal round of .38 ammunition from this revolver which he had received from Inspector SLOAN. The pistol fired properly. The bullet hit a piece of soft wood ½" thick at approximately 10 yards range splitting it in two. Inspector BLACKMAN then fired with this pistol one of the rounds which were alleged to have been found on the accused at one of the two split pieces of wood. It went right through the wood (Ex. 17) into a sand bag filled with earth which had been placed behind the wood. This witness has had weapon training in the army and the police and says that Ex. 6 was in good condition and an accurate pistol and could have killed a human being if it had hit him in a vital spot. Spent bullet retrieved by Vidler and produced.

A.S.P. Vidler corroborates Inspector BLACKMAN as to the test carried out by them of the pistol and the ammunition alleged to have been found on the accused. This witness had been in the Metropolitan Police and the Kenya Police for over 22 years and in the Royal Navy for three years. This witness has had training in the use of pistols, is armed with a .38 revolver himself. Says that this pistol was in good working order except for a loose trigger guard, was capable of causing death and is "a lethal barrelled weapon".

If you believe that evidence you may think that the 2nd point I mentioned is established and that that revolver is a "firearm" within the meaning of the regulation.

NOW AS TO THE FIRST POINT:

(1) Did the accused have this revolver in his possession?

The accused does not dispute that he did. He says he had it; but he was coming in to surrender and bringing his arms in accordance with the instructions in the surrender leaflet.

That is the real issue in the case – Was he surrendering or not? But, in as much as the prosecution have to prove possession and the circumstances in which the accused was found in possession are relevant not only on that but on the question of surrender or not. I will review the prosecution evidence for you.

COUNT 2.

The evidence on count 1 is as I have said largely the same as the evidence on Count 2 because the prosecution allege (and the accused admits) that the ammunition which is the subject of Count 2 was in the pistol which is the subject of Count 1, and that the accused knew that. So if he possessed one, you may think that he also possessed the other. Therefore, to save waste of time in reviewing the evidence twice, I will tell you now what points the Prosecution has to prove beyond reasonable doubt on Count 2 and then I will review the evidence on both counts together.

2nd Count.

In order to justify a conviction on the 2nd Count, the prosecution must prove beyond a reasonable doubt:

(i) that the accused at Tetu in S. Nyeri on the 21/10/56 had in his possession six rounds of .38 calibre ammunition;

(ii) that the circumstances were such as to raise a reasonable presumption that such ammunition was intended to be used in a manner prejudicial to public safety or the maintenance of public order.

If the prosecution prove those two points against him, the accused may then show that it is more probable than not that he had a lawful excuse for having the ammunition and if he does that is an answer to the charge.

As to the second point. The accused says that he possessed this ammunition because he was coming in to surrender it as instructed by the Surrender Leaflets. If that was true, he not only had a lawful excuse, but there would be no circumstance which would cause a reasonable presumption that the ammunition was intended to be used in a manner prejudicial to public safety. If, on the the other hand, that is not true then you have to consider whether or not the circumstances were such as to cause a reasonable presumption that the ammunition was intended to be used in a manner prejudicial to public safety.

The prosecution say that this man was, on the 21/10/56 still a leading Mau Mau terrorist, going about armed and that it is notorious that Mau Mau terrorists do use their arms in a way which is prejudicial to public safety. They ask you to say that it was a reasonable presumption from the circumstances that the ammunition was intended to be so used.

PROSECUTION EVIDENCE.

Ndirangu s/o Mau. Tribal Police Reserve Constable stationed Kahigaini S. Tetu Reserve.

On Saturday 20/10/56 he was a member of a party of Tribal Police and Tribal Police Reservists under Corporal Wanjohi. That night Ndirangu was in a party under Sgt. Mwangi consisting of Njogi, another Mwangi, Maina, Njeru, (?) – 7 in all.

They went to positions on the trench or ditch which separates the reserve from the forest near Kahigaini village, reaching the ditch about 6.45 p.m. while it was still light. Sgt. Mwangi posted them in twos along the ditch. Ndirangu was with Njogi on the Reserve side of the ditch near the murram road.

Ndirangu and Njogi stayed there all night and saw nothing. When it started to get light, they moved left along the trench away from the road. They were looking for tracks. When they had gone a little distance, to the edge of the open space where there had been maize, they saw something. Not correct that they saw something 35 yards from the road as Defending Counsel said. Ndirangu says he saw a figure of a person carrying something over his shoulder. What it was Ndirangu could not distinguish as there was not enough light to see it properly. Ndirangu said it looked like poles. From what accused said you may think that it was sugar canes. When Ndirangu saw the figure it – the man – was climbing the trench about 35 yards away from Ndirangu. Ndirangu was then on the edge of the ditch on the Reserve side. The figure had climbed out of the trench and was moving towards the forest. There was open ground ahead of him and then a line of kei-apple bushes (i.e. thorn bushes) like a fence – thick enough to form an obstacle. When Ndirangu shouted the man dropped what he was carrying and ran away from Ndirangu along the trench.

The main issue in this case is: Did the accused intend to surrender? Was he coming in to surrender? Make up your minds whether you believe Ndirangu. According to Ndirangu:

(i) When first seen accused was climbing forest side of the ditch <u>going in the direction of the forest.</u>

(ii) He had a little open ground and then a kei-apple fence ahead of him. That would have formed an obstruction.

(iii) When challenged instead of turning round saying "Don't shoot" waving a green branch or putting his hands up, he dropped what he was carrying and ran away down ditch away from Ndirangu.

(iv) When called upon to stop he failed to do so.

Ndirangu says that he pursued the man down the ditch with Njogi following behind. The man tried again to get out on the forest side at a place where the bank had been broken down by buffalo. The bank was there about 3 feet in height. Ndirangu said "He failed to get out because I fired at him. He dashed back into the trench and continued running away from me. After he had gone down to the valley he climbed the other side and then climbed out of the trench on the Reserve side". Apparently he was doubling round in a curve to get into the trench again. Ndirangu fired a third shot and apparently hit him. He staggered and Ndirangu lost sight of him. Ndirangu and Njogi went on. Ndirangu left Njogi at or near the place where they had last seen the fugitive and Ndirangu went on to search. Ndirangu went down to the valley to look for tracks. They blew whistles. Others arrived – Mwangi s/o Kanguru and Maina. They searched for some time. Ndirangu said about one hour. Estimates of time by African witnesses usually very vague indeed. Then Ndirangu says he saw someone wearing a leopard skin cap and jacket lying under a tree. These are the clothes (Ex. 2 and 3).

(Read notes pages 7 to 8 "wanting to surrender").

It was put to Ndirangu in cross-examination that Kimathi had drawn attention to himself by saying "I am Dedan Kimathi. I have come in to surrender. I have a pistol". Ndirangu said that that did not happen.

It was put to Ndirangu that he said: "You have given us enough trouble" and he fired his rifle at Kimathi who was squatting on his haunches on the ground and hit him in the thigh. Ndirangu denied that.

Ndirangu has been given a reward for the capture of Kimathi. You must consider whether you think that that has anything to do with the evidence he has given. Defence suggests that it has. Crown do not admit that. He got his reward before he gave evidence in this court and after he had given his statement to the police.

<u>NJOGI s/o NGATIA.</u>

Tribal Police Reserve Constable. Saturday 20/10/56 he went out in a party commanded by Sgt. Mwangi. They reached the forest and were posted in twos. Njogi was with Ndirangu. They stayed there all night. About day break they moved. Ndirangu saw something and pointed it out. Witness then saw something which looked like a stump on the forest side of the trench about two paces from the top. It wasn't easy to see clearly. It moved. Ndirangu then shouted. The man jumped down and ran away along the ditch. He had been carrying something which looked like poles on his shoulder and dropped it when Ndirangu shouted. Ndirangu shouted: "Stop" and fired. They ran after the man. Witness fired. The man tried to climb the bank on the forest side. Ndirangu fired again. Witness fired twice into the air, so he says. If Ndirangu fired three times and Njogi fired twice that would make five shots in all. But no one else seems to have heard more than three. You may think that this young man Njogi is trying to make out that he took a more important part than he did. You may have your doubts whether he fired at all.

The man tried to go across and Ndirangu fired another shot i.e. Ndirangu's third shot. This witness first said that the man was in the trench when Ndirangu fired his third shot. Afterwards he corrected that and said that he had not seen the third shot fired as there were some intervening bushes and he had not seen the man hit.

Maina and Mwangi Kanguru came up and they searched for about one hour. They said: "Surrender". But got no answer. Another witness said that they did not call out. Witness heard Ndirangu shout that the man was there. He saw a man in a leopard skin coat and hat lying on his side in some undergrowth under a castor oil tree. The man said that he was Kimathi. Witness identifies accused as the man.

They blew whistles and the others of the party came including Mwangi Kanguru. Njogi heard no shot fired after Ndirangu fired his third shot. Njogi corroborates Ndirangu as to the finding of the pistol in a holster on the accused by Mwangi Kanguru and says that it was given to Sgt. Mwangi who gave it to Corporal Wanjohi who later handed it to a European police officer. Pistol then still in holster. European officer opened it and took out six rounds of ammunition.

Witness never heard Dedan Kimathi offer to surrender.

MWANGI s/o KANGURU (D4).

Was a member of this party which went out under Sgt. Mwangi on the 20/10. Witness was posted with Maina.

On the 21/10 he heard shots fired from his right. They went there to investigate. He heard something from Ndirangu and Njogi. They began to search. He went to a place where Ndirangu was and saw a man lying down under a castor oil tree wearing leopard skin jacket and cap. Man, being told to come out, first said that he could not as he was wounded. Then came out and, being asked who he was, said: "Dedan Kimathi s/o Wachiuri". Mwangi then searched prisoner found a pistol in a holster on him.

He never heard Dedan Kimathi say that he wished to surrender.

MAINA S/O CHEGE.

Was posted with Mwangi s/o Kanguru. He substantially corroborates Mwangi as to the circumstances. They heard two shots and went to investigate. They went half a mile till they met Ndirangu. Then they searched and Ndirangu found a man whom witness identifies as the accused. They had gone more than half way when they heard a third shot.

With regard to the actual finding of the pistol witness says: "I saw him searched by Mwangi. He found a pistol. Ndirangu found a simi. Mwangi took the pistol. He handed it to the Sgt. Mwangi".

This witness is definite that he heard no shot after he arrived and started searching, and that from the time he arrived until the prisoner was carried away on a stretcher he didn't hear him say anything about surrendering.

Later witness saw Corporal Wanjohi hand the pistol to the European Inspector.

NJERU s/o KARUNDO.

Was also in the party under Sgt. Mwangi. He was posted to the right of the road facing the forest with Sgt. Mwangi and Wanjiri Gakau {Gakuyu}. He was out all night of the 20/10. In the a.m. when there was a little light he heard one shot and went in that direction. While walking along he heard another shot. They ran. After a longer interval they heard a third shot. When they got to where others were Dedan Kimathi was being searched by Mwangi Kanguru. Witness has known Dedan Kimathi since June 1943. Dedan Kimathi was a teacher at Karunaini School which witness attended. Recognised him at once when he saw him. As to the finding of the pistol he says: "I saw Mwangi find a pistol which was slung over Dedan Kimathi's right shoulder. The pistol was in a holster". He identifies exhibit 6 as the pistol. Mwangi Kanguru kept it till Sgt. Mwangi arrived and handed it to him. Dedan Kimathi was taken to Kahigaini.

Having left Dedan Kimathi at Kahigaini Home Guard post i/c {in command} of Corporal Wanjohi and Sgt. Mwangi, witness borrowed a bicycle and reported the occurrence to a European police officer at Ihururu police station. Went back to Kahigaini in the police Land Rover and saw Corporal Wanjohi hand the revolver to the European Inspector and saw him break it and take six rounds of ammunition from it.

At no time did he hear Dedan Kimathi say that he wanted to surrender.

SERGEANT MWANGI.

Tribal Police Sergeant from Tetu location. Knows Dedan Kimathi. Sgt. Mwangi was i/c of this party which went out on the 20/10. They all had .303 rifles only. No revolvers.

He posted his men on the reserve side of the forest ditch. He was with Wanjiri and Njeru Karundo. Nothing happened during the night. In the a.m. he heard shots from the direction of where Ndirangu was stationed. When they had heard two shots witness with two men trotted in the direction where Ndirangu was. There was a short interval between the first and second shots and a longer one between the second and third. They stopped when they got where Ndirangu was. They saw Kimathi lying down amongst the undergrowth wearing leopard skin clothes. They arrived after he had been searched. Mwangi Kanguru gave to witness a pistol (Ex. 6) which the witness later handed to Corporal Wanjohi. They made a stretcher and took Kimathi to Kahigaini. This witness did not at any time hear Dedan Kimathi say anything about wanting to surrender.

WANJIRI S/O GAKUYU. Substantially corroborates Sgt. Mwangi.

CORPORAL WANJOHI.

Corporal Tribal Police. He was in charge of ambush party on the night of the 20/10. Stayed whole night without incident. In a.m. they heard three shots fired. The second followed the first quickly. They began to run in that direction. The third shot was fired while they were on the way. Saw a man lying on the ground under a castor oil tree. Wounded. Dressed wound with his shirt. Sgt. Mwangi produced this black holster and handed it to the witness who kept it in his possession until Inspector Sloan arrived at the Home Guard Post at Kahigaini where witness handed it to him. Prisoner had been carried to Kahigaini Guard Post. Inspector opened it and took out six rounds. The pistol had not been opened previously. Prisoner did not at any time say that he wished to surrender.

INSPECTOR RONALD SLOAN.

Is inspector in charge of Ihururu police station. About 9 a.m. on the 21/10 received a report from Kahigaini village. Went to Kahigaini Guard Post. Saw man lying on the ground whom he identifies as Dedan Kimathi. Corporal Wanjohi handed witness a black leather holster with a .38 Webley pistol in it. It was loaded with six rounds of ammunition. Witness unloaded it and handed six rounds of ammunition from it to constable 7193 Waigwa s/o Gitaki. Witness kept revolver in his possession. Arranged transportation of prisoner to Ihururu police station and on arrival got six rounds back from constable Waigwa. Marked revolver and ammunition. Identifies them now in Court. Later handed pistol and rounds to Inspector Blackman. Prisoner searched in his presence and three pieces of snare wire, watch and chain and corn cob found. He said nothing about wanting to surrender. You may think that important. This is the first European police officer accused has met. If he had tired to surrender and had been shot you might expect him to complain unless he was very ill indeed. Had not then had injection.

WAIGWA S/O GITAKI.

Saw Wanjohi hand Sloan a pistol holster. Saw Sloan take a pistol out of it, open pistol and take out six rounds of ammunition. Sloan gave him the ammunition which he put in his pocket and witness gave back to Sloan at Ihururu police station.

BARIKANGU NYANDAYI.

Was the man who carried out the search of the prisoner in the police station at Ihururu and found the watch, snare wires etc.

A.S.P. VIDLER.

Says that on Monday 22/10 the accused was charged before a Magistrate at the hospital with unlawful possession of arms and ammunition. He never then or at any other interview which VIDLER has had with him said anything about wishing to surrender. If he had wished to do so there was nothing to stop him. Accused speaks very good English.

MR. {DR.} HURLEY

The Provincial Surgeon said that on the 21/10/56 about mid-day the accused was brought to him. He examined him. He was wounded. General appearance good. Standard of nutrition excellent. Suffering from shock but not badly. Had a gun shot wound in his right thigh. The bullet had gone in on the inner side of the thigh near the crutch {sic} and had come out higher up on the outer side of the hip. The bullet had hit the thigh bone and had knocked pieces off it; but had not broken it completely i.e. it was still one long bone. There were no marks of powder near the wound or on the clothes, though it would have been difficult to find such marks on the clothes as they were dirty and bloody. The surgeon operated and the patient stood the operation very well.

Monday 22/10 Mr. {sic} Hurley again examined accused and found his mental condition clear and normal and the surgeon thought him fit to be interviewed by the police. The effect of the injection [and] of the drugs which he had had on the previous day had worn off. Accused mentioned that his leg was sore and difficult to move and he had trouble with passing urine. The doctor relieved that. The doctor gave permission for this man to be interviewed by the police. After that interview the doctor saw him again and his condition had not deteriorated.

As already mentioned the exit wound was higher than the entry wound – about 3" higher. Mr. Hurley explained that that means that the entry wound must have been higher than the muzzle of the rifle from which the bullet was fired. That could either happen if as suggested by the defence, the accused was squatting on the ground under the castor oil tree with his knees open and Ndirangu standing below him and talking to him fired at him as he sat. Or that wound could have been produced if Ndirangu was firing at the accused from the trench and the accused was on top of the trench running and circling round leftwards to get back to the trench and the bullet was fired from his left side and from below him.

Ndirangu says that that was what the accused was doing when he fired the 3rd shot and that the accused was above him because the ground sloped up. Also Ndirangu said he was kneeling and he says that the accused was running and was on top of the bank of the trench (which bank is there only a foot or so high) on the Reserve side.

If Ndirangu's story is true – we do not know exactly where on the bank of the trench the accused was when he was hit – (he says under the castor oil bush) Ndirangu says on top of the trench. If the accused was on top of the trench opposite the castor oil tree he would not be above Ndirangu because the trench slopes down to that point. Opposite the castor oil tree is in fact the lowest point of the trench. Ndirangu could be approximately level with the accused if both were on the 30 yards or so of flat ground at the lowest part of the trench. If, however, the accused had climbed the slope beyond the lowest point and had got some way up it (as Ndirangu says) he could be above Ndirangu when he was hit, and he might have then crawled or rolled back down the hill just inside the Reserve to the castor oil tree. It is said that that tree provided the best hiding place on that side of the trench in that vicinity so he may have made for it.

Except in so far as it affects the credit of the witnesses the question of precisely how the accused was wounded is not an issue in the case. The main issue is: Was the accused coming in to surrender and bringing his weapons for that purpose? How he came to be wounded is not an issue on Count 1 or Count 2 and is important but is only important in so far as it affects the credibility of the witnesses and whether their stories are true or not. You may think, (I am not suggesting that you should), that the accused was shot under the castor oil tree. You would still have to consider whether he was there because he was trying to surrender as he says. Or you may believe all that Ndirangu says, backed up as he is by the other tribal policemen. You may think that the fugitive was shot on the side of the trench as Ndirangu describes. But that though important is not in itself an issue. The real issue in this case is: Is it true or is it not true that the accused had this pistol and ammunition because he was coming into surrender and was bringing his firearm with him in response to the surrender leaflet? The circumstances in which he was wounded are only material to the extent that they may help to decide that issue. You should concentrate on any evidence which helps you to answer the surrender issue.

SENIOR SUPERINTENDENT BAKER C.I.D.

On the 22/10 Baker charged accused with two offences – possession of a firearm and possession of ammunition – each without lawful authority or lawful excuse. Charges were interpreted by Wambugu.

To that the accused replied:

> "I would like to say that I never knew that there was such a law". (Tells the interpreter that he wants to think) After an interval of about 20 seconds says: "I have nothing more to say".

You will consider whether he was then saying that he didn't know that there was a law against carrying a loaded pistol. Accused does not now attempt to say that he didn't know that it was, generally speaking, an offence to possess a firearm and ammunition and he says that he never meant that. He says that what he meant was "I didn't know that there was such a law for a person coming in to surrender himself". He says his mind was blurred with the effect of his wound, his operation, it is suggested that he may have had an epileptic fit while under anaesthetic. (There is no evidence whatever that any such fit did in fact occur. The evidence is merely that anaesthetics do sometimes or often produce fits in epileptics and if he did have one the mind might be blurred for up to 48 hours). One doctor says his mental condition might have been blurred. The surgeon who examined him says that his opinion was that the accused's mental condition was clear and normal. If so, would anyone whose mental condition was clear and who had come in to surrender and had been shot in dastardly fashion while he was attempting to do so and who was then charged with having a firearm, not say: "But I was surrendering. I brought it in because I was surrendering. And that man had no right to shoot me"? Would he forget the surrendering part, do you think – the most important part – the whole point? Is it credible? It is for you to consider. You may think he was unfit and not himself, mentally blurred. He says he was in pain and had noises in his ears and was feeling giddy. The doctor who examined him had passed him fit to be interviewed, but he may have been wrong. It is for you to consider. Or you may think that what he was saying was that he didn't know the law against carrying firearms and that this surrender idea is an afterthought.

Senior Superintendent BAKER produced some surrender leaflets. There are two lots of surrender leaflets:

(i) issued 24/8/53. That says "Come in and surrender without delay". But that still stands. It also says: "If possible come with your arms".

(ii) 2nd lot issued 18/1/55 "Govt. Will not kill you for carrying arms". There was another addressed to gang leaders dated 24/8/53 which says: "You cannot get into any danger when you come to negotiate your surrender with that of your whole gang and your arms. Come out during the day time waving green branches this will ensure that you are not shot at". That says surrender now carrying a green branch and bring in your arms. That has been withdrawn. It was withdrawn in July 1955.

So the only leaflet that could be "lawful excuse" in October 1956 for carrying arms would be the one of August 1953 ones. But the later one might be a "lawful excuse" if he didn't know it had been withdrawn.

Do you believe accused was surrendering? According to the prosecution accused was:

(i) seen going in the direction of the forest,

(ii) he ran away when challenged;

(iii) he said nothing about surrender to anyone in authority – either his captors or Sgt. Mwangi, Cpl. Wanjohi or Inspector Sloan or the doctor or Superintendent Baker or Superintendent VIDLER or the magistrate.

He says that he did not know that Blackman and Vidler were Police officers. You may think that as they came to see him when he was under close arrest to ask him questions about security matters, he must have thought that they were persons in authority. Isn't it odd that he didn't say: "I am wrongly confined. I have been wrongly charged with possessing a firearm, when all I was doing was coming in to surrender it"? If that was true you may think it odd that he didn't say it. Is it something that he has thought of since? It is for you to consider. He says he has told some of his European escorts. He has not called any of them to say so.

<u>WILL NOW REVIEW THE DEFENCE EVIDENCE.</u>

The accused says that prior to his arrest on the 21/10/56 he had been living in the forest for almost 4 years with his associates. In February, 1954, he fell out with most of his associates because of a letter which he had written to the Government. They wanted to kill him and he moved away with five others to a hide-out far away. He says that neither since that – nor previously to it – has he carried out any anti-British or any anti-Government activity. You can consider whether he is there a truthful witness giving truthful testimony.

He says that the pistol which was found in his possession and the six rounds of ammunition were given to him by one Macharya {sic} Kimanya for the purpose of defending himself against the forest men (Mau Mau) who wished to kill him. Since February, 1954, he says that he has been alone in the forest with only five others. Three letters were put to him in cross-examination all dated later than February 1954.

The first was dated 6th March 1954 in one place and 6th April 1954 in another. Accused admits it is in his handwriting. It is addressed to the Deputy Governor, Sir F. Crawford and it contains a passage: "I on behalf of all my followers and the Defence Council and as President of the Council and Knight Commander of the African Empire and Commander in Chief of the Country of Kenya notify that the terms will not be considered etc..." He signs as "F.M. Sir D. Kimathi K.C.A.E. and Supreme C-in-C of the Country of Kenya and Land Federation {sic} Armies". That is what he wrote then. He now says that those had previously been his titles, but that as from February, 1954, he only had five followers. You will consider whether he is a truthful witness.

The second letter is dated 30/3/54. It is addressed to the Ag. Governor and signed "Field Marshal Sir D. KIMATHI" and contains among other things the sentence: "Once I shout peace, there is never a war in Kenya". You must consider whether that was likely to have been written by a man whose associates had already turned from him – all but five – and who needed a revolver for the sole purpose of protecting himself from them.

The third letter is dated 20/10/1954. It purports to come from "The Kenya Parliament The Land Freedom Armies G.H.Q." and is addressed to the Kenya Government. It urges the restoration of peace and is signed by the accused as "Field Marshal Sir D. Kimathi President for and on behalf of the Kenya Parliament". That is dated about 8 months after February 1954 when, according to what accused now says, he split away from the other leaders and Mau Mau and went away with five companions and was given a revolver solely for the purpose of protecting himself from Mau Mau.

He says that he knew about the Surrender Leaflets. He didn't come in before because as there was a reward of Shs. 10,000 offered for him he was afraid of being killed by police or Home Guards in order to get the money. He says that he was awaiting replies to certain letters which he had written to Government, but he does not attempt to produce those letters.

I will read some of what he said as recorded in my Notes:

(Reads p. 59 "My reason for eventually coming in...." to p. 60 "moonlight".) [55]

He said he was afraid to go to a Home Guard Post as he had no light and went through the shambas. He goes on:

(Read page 60 "it became daylight......" to p. 62 "he did not tell me he was a police officer"). [56]

EPILEPSY.

Then he goes on to say that he has suffered from epilepsy. As I have told you, this epilepsy from which doctor Turner says that accused suffers is not a defence to either of these charges. In order for it to be a defence it would have to be shown that the accused either was mentally incapable of knowing that he was in possession of a revolver and ammunition on the 21/10/56 or that if he did know that, from disease of the mind he was mentally incapable of knowing that he ought not to possess them. He specifically does not put forward that defence. He admits

---

55. See pages 92–93 in Document 1 for full transcript.

56. See pages 93–96 in Document 1 for full transcript.

he knew he had the pistol and the ammunition and that he was mentally capable of knowing that that was wrong, but he says it wasn't wrong for a man who was surrendering and that he was surrendering. There is no defence of insanity. The issue in the case is "Was he or was he not surrendering?" The only reason this alleged epilepsy is brought up is as an explanation for the accused not having said anything to Baker about his having come in to surrender in answer to the charges which Baker put to him. That is the only relevance of the alleged epilepsy. Doctor Turner's evidence is to the effect that from what he has been told by the accused, his mother and Joseph Wakaba, he has formed the opinion that the accused has epilepsy. The doctor thinks he is a reasonably intelligent man, intelligent above the standard of a man of his education. The doctor makes no suggestion that he is insane, he knows what he is doing and he knows the difference between right and wrong. He found no sign of mental deterioration in the accused which is a common gradual result of epilepsy. Dr. Turner said: "Inasmuch as anaesthesia and operations are well-known precipitating causes of a fit, it can be said that an epileptic may have a fit brought on by an anaesthetic and an operation. If he did have one under the anaesthetic it would not be noticed and that might cause a headache and subsequent mental blurring up to 48 hours afterwards". This evidence is brought for the purpose of showing that the accused may have been mentally blurred when he was charged by the police the day after he was captured and said nothing then about having come in to surrender. You must take that possibility into consideration and the possibility that the doctor who examined him – Dr. Hurley – that a.m. with the specific idea of ascertaining whether he was fit to answer questions and who gave it as his opinion that the mental condition of the accused was then clear and normal, may have been wrong.

<u>OTHER WITNESSES TO EPILEPSY.</u>

You have heard the evidence of accused's mother and Joseph Wakaba to the effect that the accused has suffered from epilepsy from a child. As to the epilepsy therefore you should consider whether, assuming that he is an epileptic, you think that the fact that in answer to the charge he did not specifically mention the fact of having had the pistol and ammunition because he was coming in to surrender, was due to: (a) forgetfulness, headache, giddiness and mental blurring brought on by a possible epileptic fit while under the anaesthetic the day before, or (b) because it was not true that he was surrendering and he had not then thought of that story. For you to consider.

CONCLUSION.

I want you to ask yourselves these questions:

(1) Are you satisfied beyond reasonable doubt that on the 21st October 1956 at Tetu, the accused had in his possession (a) this Webley revolver; and (b) six rounds of .38 ammunition or either the revolver or the ammunition?

(2) Is the revolver a firearm as defined?

(3) If the accused had the ammunition in his possession, did the circumstances raise a reasonable presumption that such ammunition was intended to be used in a manner or for a purpose prejudicial to public safety and the maintenance of public order?

(4) If you are satisfied beyond reasonable doubt that the accused did have this revolver, this ammunition, or both in his possession then do you think it more probable than not that he had it or them because he was coming in to surrender and bringing them with him?

If you answer question (4) Yes i.e. if you think he had come in to surrender and had brought the pistol and ammunition for that purpose, you should give your opinions in favour of acquittal on both charges.

If you do not think the accused was coming in to surrender and you find he had the revolver in his possession and that it is a firearm you should give your opinions that he is guilty on count 1.

If you do not think he was coming in to surrender and you find also as regards count 2 that he was in possession of this ammunition and the circumstances were such that it can reasonably be presumed that the ammunition was intended to be used for a purpose prejudicial to public safety and order, then you should give your opinions that he is guilty on count 2.

Please consider your opinions. If you wish to do so you may retire. I shall ask each of you his opinion on each count separately.

4.12 Assessors retire 4.12 p.m.
Assessors return 4.20 p.m.

1st ASSESSOR: {Tumuti s/o Gakere}

Accused was not coming to surrender. He had come out to collect food and to go back to the forest with the food.

The weapon which he had in his possession was not intended to be given to the Government: it was for his protection – as well as the ammunition. He is guilty.
To Court: The ammunition was intended to be used for a purpose prejudicial to public safety and the maintenance of public order.
Volunteered: In the Reserve we don't use wire snares. We have no animals to catch with them.

2nd ASSESSOR: Nderitu. {Nderitu s/o Muteru}

I believe the evidence which has been given by the Prosecution witnesses. He was not surrendering. He arrived about 7.30 the previous night he had ample opportunity of surrendering between 7.30 p.m. and 7.30 a.m. He was returning back to the forest. The pistol belongs to him and the ammunition also was his and he had them to defend himself against the Government. He had no authority to have them. He is guilty on both counts.

3rd ASSESSOR: {Kibuthu s/o Kihia}

He did not come out peacefully. He came out fully armed. If his intention was to come out to surrender, he ought to have a big branch of green branches. Therefore I say he is guilty: he is a gangster. I mean he is guilty on both counts.
To Court: The ammunition which he had was to be used for a purpose prejudicial to public safety and order.

COURT:

I will deliver judgment at 11 a.m. tomorrow 27/11/56.

K. O'C.
26/11/56.

Document 2

JUDGMENT

IN HER MAJESTY'S SUPREME COURT OF KENYA AT NYERI
EMERGENCY ASSIZE CRIMINAL CASE No 46 of 1956

REGINA.......................................PROSECUTRIX

VERSUS

DEDAN KIMATHI S/O WACHIURI..................ACCUSED

JUDGMENT

The accused, Dedan Kimathi s/o Wachiuri is charged with two offences against the Emergency Regulations, 1952, as follows:

Statement of Offence: 1st Count.
Unlawful possession of firearms contrary to Regulation 8A(1) of the Emergency Regulations, 1952.
Particulars of Offence: 1st Count.
Dedan Kimathi s/o Wachiuri on or about the 21st day of October, 1956, in the Tetu Location in the Nyeri District in the Central Province had in his possession a firearm, to wit, a .38 Webley Scott revolver, without lawful authority or lawful excuse.
Statement of Offence: 2nd Count.
Unlawful possession of ammunition contrary to regulation 8A(1A) of the Emergency Regulations, 1952.
Particulars of Offence: 2nd Count.
Dedan Kimathi s/o Wachiuri on or about the 21st day of October, 1956, in the Tetu Location in the Nyeri District in the Central Province had in his possession ammunition without lawful authority or lawful excuse in circumstances which raised a reasonable presumption that such ammunition was intended to be used in a manner or for a purpose prejudicial to public safety or the maintenance of public order.

To each of these charges the accused has pleaded not guilty.

The offence charged in the first count is a capital offence. It is not the ordinary practice to join in an information any other offence with a capital offence; but Regulation 10 of the Emergency

> (Emergency Assizes) Regulations, 1953, specifically permits this in the case of scheduled offences tried in a Court of Emergency Assize, where the counts are founded on the same facts. In the present case the counts are founded on the same facts: this is a Court of Emergency Assize and both offences are scheduled offences.

Regulation 8A(1) of the Emergency Regulations, 1952, so far as material reads as follows:

> "8A(1) Any person who, except with lawful authority or lawful excuse, the burden of proof whereof shall lie upon him, carries, or has in his possession… any firearm shall be guilty of an offence and shall on conviction be sentenced to death".

Regulation 8A(1A), so far as material, reads as follows:

> "8A(1A) Any person who, except with lawful authority or lawful excuse, the burden of proof whereof shall lie upon him, carries, or has in his possession… any ammunition in circumstances which raise a reasonable presumption that such ammunition,….. are intended to be used in a manner or for a purpose prejudicial to public safety or the maintenance of public order shall be guilty of an offence and shall on conviction be liable to imprisonment for life".
>
> It will be observed that both the Regulations under which the accused is charged, cast the burden of proof of lawful authority or lawful excuse upon the accused. This (except in special case where the defence is insanity) is a most unusual position in a criminal case; but the wording of the Regulations is clear and unambiguous and I must follow it.
>
> I have, therefore, directed the assessors, and I direct myself, that, upon count 1, the burden of proving: (a) that at the place and time mentioned, the accused had the revolver described in his possession; and (b) that it is a "firearm" as defined; rests upon the prosecution; and that the burden of proving that he had a lawful authority or lawful excuse rests upon the accused. I have also directed the assessors, and I direct myself, that, upon count 2, the burden of proving that the accused had six rounds of .38 calibre ammunition (as defined), in his possession and that the circumstances were such as to raise a reasonable presumption that such ammunition was intended to be used in a manner or for a

purpose prejudicial to the public safety and the maintenance of public order rests or for a purpose prejudicial to the public safety and upon the prosecution; and that the burden of proving lawful authority or lawful excuse rests upon the accused. And I have directed the assessors (and myself) that the degree of proof where the burden rests upon the prosecution is proof beyond reasonable doubt; but that the standard of proof, where the burden rests upon the accused, is a mere balance of probabilities.

The accused does not allege that he had lawful authority to possess either the revolver or the ammunition. He does allege that he had a lawful excuse of possessing both, in that he was (so he says) intending to surrender in response to invitations contained in surrender leaflets issued by the Government (notably Ex C) and he was (as instructed in those leaflets) bringing in his arms and ammunition for the purpose of surrendering them to Government. Having considered the cases of *Mwangi s/o Wambugu v Reg* [1954] XXI EACA {East African Court of Appeal} 246; and *Wong Poohyin v Public Prosecutor* [1954] 3 AER 31 (PC), I directed the assessors, and I direct myself, that if the story of the accused is true and he was intending to bring in the pistol and the ammunition in order to surrender them to the proper authorities in response to an invitation in a Government leaflet and had done overt acts in pursuance of that intention, that could, in law, constitute a lawful excuse which would entitle him to be acquitted. I also directed the assessors (and I direct myself) that it would not afford a lawful excuse for one terrorist to carry a pistol and ammunition for the purpose of protecting himself from other terrorists whom he might have offended.

Briefly, the case for the Prosecution is that on the evening of Saturday October 20th, 1956, a party of about 24 Tribal Police and Tribal Police Reserve under a Tribal Police Corporal Wanjohi went out from Kahigaini Home Guard Post to line part of the continuous trench which divides the Kikuyu Reserve (hereinafter called "The Reserve") from the forest in the South Tetu Location of Nyeri. The trench is a flat-bottomed trench approximately 12 feet wide. The ground slopes upward from a valley in the Reserve to the trench and upwards again from the trench through the forest. The bank of the trench on the forest side, in the section with which we are concerned, varies from approximately 8 feet high to 2'6" high. The bank on the Reserve side is much lower: it varies in height from 2'6" to 1 foot approximately. On the Reserve side there is mainly low scrub and bush with some cultivation. On the Forest side, thick forest cover to the edge of the ditch in most place; but there is at least one place, which will be mentioned hereafter, where it does not.

In the party commanded by Corporal Wanjohi was a section commanded by a Tribal Police Reserve Sergeant – Sergeant Mwangi. He posted his men in twos along the trench on the Reserve side and astride the murram road which runs up from Kahigaini Village and Home Guard Post to the Aberdare mountains. Facing the forest, Sergeant Mwangi and two men, and another post of two men, were on the right of the road: on the left (SW side) of the road were two Tribal Police Reserve Constables Ndirangu s/o Mau and Njogi s/o Ngati.

The night passed without incident except for the shooting of a buffalo.

When it started to get light on the morning of Sunday October 21st, Ndirangu and Njogi moved along the Reserve side of the trench to their left, very quietly and slowly. They were looking for tracks. When they got to the edge of a place where there had been cultivation, Ndirangu saw a figure carrying something over his shoulder which Ndirangu could not distinguish properly in the dim light: it looked like poles. Ndirangu says that when he first saw the man, he was about 35 yards away (the witness later indicated an object further away) along the trench, climbing the bank of the trench on the forest side. Ndirangu saw him moving slowly towards the forest. At this spot there was open ground for seven or eight yards from the edge of the trench and then thick kei-apple (thorn) trees in a kind of a fence which would provide an obstacle to passage. When the man had climbed the bank of the trench and had moved about three yards, in the direction of the forest, moving slowly, Ndirangu shouted "Who goes there?" in English. The man did not answer: he dropped what he was carrying: started back, fell into the trench and made off along it in a direction away from the road. Ndirangu and Njogi ran after him. Ndirangu called him to Kikuyu many times to stop; but he did not do so. Ndirangu fired. The man ran on. He tried to get out of the trench on the forest side and Ndirangu then fired at him a second time. The man continued running down the trench with Ndirangu and Njogi in pursuit. He crossed what is variously described as a stream or a dry river bed, traversing the trench. (This turned out, on examination by the witness who made a map of the scene, to be a steep dip in the trench at which there were traces of erosion as if water had at some time passed over the trench). On the further side of this dip the trench slopes up steeply. According to Ndirangu the man ran some way up this slope and got on top of the bank of the trench on the Reserve side, which is there only about a foot high. Ndirangu says that he (Ndirangu) was then down below on one side of the "stream" (presumably in the dip) and that the fugitive was on higher ground on the other side of the "stream": the man climbed out of the trench on the Reserve side, but was curving round running to come back to it again when Ndirangu knelt and fired a third shot at him. He staggered and disappeared on the Reserve side of the trench. Ndirangu and Njogi went to the spot where they had last seen the fugitive. There was no sign of him. Njogi remained there. Ndirangu started to search.

The two tribal police reservists from the next post, Mwangi s/o Kanguru (not Sergeant Mwangi) and Maina, arrived, attracted by the shooting.

After searching for some time, variously estimated at one hour and 20 minutes, (estimates of times and distances by illiterate African witnesses are usually quite unreliable) Ndirangu says that he saw a thing like a leopard lying in some undergrowth under a small castor oil tree or bush. He saw that it was a man wearing a leopard skin coat and cap. Ndirangu said to the man "Who are you?" He replied "It is I Kimathi s/o Wachiuri". Ndirangu said "What about the other name?". The man replied "I am called Dedan Kimathi": he also mentioned something sounding like "Field Marshal". Ndirangu told him to come out. He said he could not, as Ndirangu had shot him. Ndirangu insisted on his crawling out, which he did. Ndirangu then saw that he was wounded in the front of the right thigh and buttock. The man was the accused.

The accused was searched by Ndirangu and Mwangi Kanguru. They latter {sic} found on him under his leopard skin coat a black holster containing a pistol. Ndirangu found on him a simi (native sword) in a sheath.

Sergeant Mwangi arrived. The pistol in its holster was handed to him. Later Corporal Wanjohi arrived. The pistol, still in its holster, was handed to him. The prisoner's wound was tied up and he was taken on an improvised stretcher to Kahigaini Home Guard Post. A message was sent to Ihururu Police Station and, in response, Inspector Sloan of the Kenya Police arrived at Kahigaini Home Guard Post. Corporal Wanjohi handed to Inspector Sloan the pistol still in its holster. It had not been taken out. Inspector Sloan took the pistol out, opened it and found in it the six rounds of Webley .38 ammunition which are the subject of Count 2. The pistol is the .38 Webley Scott revolver which is the subject of Count 1.

The prisoner was then taken to Ihururu Police Station. He later received medical attention from the Police Surgeon. Assistant Superintendent Vidler who saw him at Ihururu said that he believed the prisoner had received an injection: he was then hardly conscious. Later, the prisoner was taken to the Nyeri General Hospital where Mr Hurley, the Provincial Surgeon examined him about mid-day on the 21st October. Though wounded, his general appearance was then good and his standard of nutrition excellent: he was suffering from shock, but not badly. He had a gun-shot wound through the right thigh. The entry wound was on the inner aspect of the right thigh, high up near the crutch: the exit wound was on the outer side of the hip above the knob of the thigh bone. The projecting part of the bone had been shattered, but the continuity of the thigh bone had not been broken. The path of the bullet was distinctly upwards.

Mr Hurley operated and the accused stood the operation very well.

On Monday 22nd October, Mr Hurley examined the accused for the purpose of ascertaining whether he was fit to be interviewed by the Police. Mr Hurley thought his mental condition was clear and normal and his physical condition reasonably comfortable. Mr Hurley formed the opinion that he was fit to be interviewed by the Police.

The accused was interviewed by acting Senior Superintendent Baker who cautioned, and in the presence of a Magistrate, charged him with the present charges. The accused speaks very good

English. The charges were read to him in English, Swahili and Kikuyu. He replied:

"I would like to say that I never knew that there was such a law". He then told the interpreter that he wanted to think. After about 20 seconds he added:

"I have nothing more to say".

From first to last, neither to Sergeant Mwangi, Corporal Wanjohi, Inspector Sloan, Mr Hurley, nor Superintendent Baker did the accused say one word about having come in to surrender, and he made no complaint that he had been shot while trying to surrender. When charged with possession of a firearm and ammunition, he did not say that he was surrendering and bringing them in for the purpose of giving them up. He now says that that is what he was doing.

On 21st October Inspector Blackman and ASP Vidler carried out tests with a view to establishing that the pistol found on the accused was a "firearm" within the meaning of Regulation 8A(4) of the Emergency Regulations and that the six rounds found therein were "ammunition" within that regulation. In my opinion the practical experience and training of both these officers qualifies them to speak as experts on Webley Scott pistols and ammunition (*Gatheru v Reg* Criminal Appeal 938 of 1954 EACA) and the tests carried out by them established that the pistol in question was a "firearm", and the six rounds found in it were "ammunition" within the definitions in Emergency Regulation 8A(4).

In brief, the story of the accused is:

Prior to his arrest on 21st October, 1956, he had been living in the forest for almost four years with his associates whom he calls "forest men" or Mau Mau.

In February, 1954, he fell out with most of his associates because of a letter which he had written to Government advocating peace. They wanted to kill him and he moved away with five companions to a "hide-out" far away. He says that neither since February, 1954, (nor, indeed, previously) has he carried out any anti-British or anti-Government activity.

The accused admits that he had in his possession on the 21st October, 1956, the revolver and ammunition which are the subjects respectively of Counts 1 and 2. He says that these were given to him in or about February, 1954, by one Macharia Kimanya for the purpose of defending himself against Mau Mau terrorists who wished to kill him. Since February, 1954, the accused has been in the forest with five companions only. Some others used to come and see him.

The accused says that he knew about the Surrender Leaflets issued by the Government.

There were, in fact, two lots of Surrender Leaflets, the first lot issued in August, 1955 {sic - 1953}, the second lot issued in January, 1955. The second lot was withdrawn in July, 1955. The first still stands.

The leaflet upon which the accused relies (Ex C) says *inter alia*:
"All those who have not committed murder are NOW given a chance to save their lives. Decide quickly what to do, to come in and surrender.... If possible, come with your arms. You can surrender to any European officer or to any other Government representative".

The accused was asked why, if he was relying on this leaflet dated August, 1953, he did not come in to surrender before October, 1956. He replied that this was because (1) there was a large reward offered for him and he was afraid that Tribal Police or Home Guards would shoot him to get the money and (2) he was awaiting replies to certain letters which he had sent to Government. The defence were offered production of these letters, subject to objection as to their relevance, but declined to call for them.

The accused said that his reason for eventually coming in was because the Mau Mau and the security forces were hunting him: at that time he was left all alone and he was ill. "I said it is better to go out either to be killed or, if I am lucky, to get to the Government". He said that his intention was to surrender and to give the pistol and the ammunition to the Government according to the instructions which he knew.

The accused said that he made up his mind on the 20th October to surrender. He started: night fell before he got to the Reserve. He arrived in the Reserve about 7.30 pm: he was afraid to go to any of the Home Guard Posts, for fear that he would be shot. Being hungry, he went to find food and got some sugar cane and four maize cobs. He roasted his maize at a fire.

Day broke before he had eaten. He began to walk towards the Kahigaini road. He was down in the valley and went up to the trench as the most convenient route to the road. He was in the trench about 150 yards from the main road. His intention was to stop near the main road, have his food, and then go along the road to Kahigaini where there was a police post. The accused says that he had no intention of returning to the forest. If he had so intended, he would have taken more food with him.

The accused says that he was still in the trench when he heard a gun shot: he thought it was fired from about 40 yards away: he did not see who fired. There were two shots one after the other. The accused dropped his sugar cane and two maize cobs that he had in his hand and ran. He had no idea who was firing at him. Before he had gone far, he heard a second shot. The shots appeared to come from the direction of the road. He ran fast along the trench and was still running when he heard a third shot. He was not hit. He got out of the trench on the Reserve side and sat down under a castor oil tree about ten yards away. There was a steep slope there down to the Thengeraini river. He squatted on his haunches with his knees open. He sat there for about 20 minutes facing down towards the stream in the valley, after which he saw a man come up from below him – in front and slightly to his left. He noticed that the man was wearing uniform and took him to be a policeman. He raised his arms and said: "It is I, Dedan Kimathi. I have come to surrender. Don't kill me. I have a pistol". The policeman dropped on one knee, fired, and hit the accused almost in the groin. The accused felt great pain and fainted. When he came to, he saw a group of police who gave him some water to drink. They made a stretcher. On arrival at the Home Guard Post, the accused was given tea. When he opened his eyes at Ihururu he saw a European, whom he did not know to be a doctor. He was, he believes, given an injection.

The accused was taken to the hospital at Nyeri and an operation was performed. The next morning he was visited by a Police officer in plain clothes who charged him. He admits having made the reply to the charge which is recorded, but says that he was then very ill: his leg was paining very much, he had not yet passed water or otherwise relieved himself since he left the forest: he could hear noises in his ears and was feeling giddy.

The accused says that when he replied that he never knew that there was such a law, what he wished to say was that he did not know that there was such a law for a person who was coming in to surrender himself: he thought he had completed the sentence and had said that: he only spoke a few words and was unable to say more because he was in pain.

The accused says that when ASP Vidler later visited him, he was in civilian clothes and the accused did not know that he was a police officer. He said nothing to the Magistrate about surrender because he thought he was the judge and it might be improper. The accused says that he has mentioned the question of surrender to Europeans of his escort; but the Defence did not call any of them to substantiate this.

The accused says that he has suffered from epileptic fits since he was a child and he called his mother and one-Joseph Wakaba to support this. Dr Turner, the Provincial Physician also says that the accused is an epileptic and he says that anesthesia and operations are a well known precipitating cause of fits, an epileptic may have a fit as a result of an anesthetic and an operation. This would not be noticed if it occurred during anesthesia. If an epileptic had a fit during anesthesia, it would be likely that he would have a severe headache and mental blurring for some hours after he recovered consciousness. These symptoms might last up to 48 hours. There is no evidence that he did in fact have a fit.

There is no defence of insanity in this case. It is not suggested by the defence that on the 21st October, 1956, the mental condition of the accused was such that he did not know that he possessed a pistol and six rounds of ammunition or that, through disease affecting his mind, he did not know that such possession was illegal. The sole reason for this evidence of epilepsy is to try to account for the fact that, when charged with unlawful possession of a firearm and ammunition, the accused did not, in so many words, say that he had the weapons because he was about to surrender and was bringing them in for that purpose.

The points for determination appear to me to be:

I. Have the Prosecution established beyond reasonable doubt:-

   (a) that on the 21st October, 1956, at Tetu, the accused had in his possession a Webley Scott revolver (ex 6); and

   (b) six rounds of .38 ammunition, or either the revolver or the ammunition?

   (2) that the revolver is a firearm as defined and that the ammunition is ammunition as defined.

   (3) If the accused had the ammunition in his possession, did the circumstances raise a reasonable presumption that such ammunition was intended to be used in a manner and for a purpose prejudicial to public safety and the maintenance of public order?

II. If the Prosecution have established these matters or some of them beyond reasonable doubt, has the accused shown that it is more probable than not that he possessed the revolver or the ammunition or both because he was coming in to surrender in response to an invitation in a Government leaflet and was bringing his arms and ammunition with him?

These are the questions which I asked the assessors to consider before they gave their opinions. They gave unanimous opinions that the accused was guilty on both counts and all stated that he was not coming in to surrender.

I considered that Ndirangu and Njogi were clearly telling the truth as to the circumstances when they first saw the accused climbing the trench on the forest side moving towards the forest and his subsequent flight along the trench when challenged and his refusal to stop – all this before he was fired at. They seemed to be witnesses giving a truthful account of what they had seen. And I believed Ndirangu as to the firing of three shots by him. I was dubious about Njogi's statement that he had fired twice into the air. Ndirangu says he fired three shots, and no one else seems to have heard any more than that.

During the hearing I was dubious about Nidrangu's account of the wounding of the accused with the third shot. From the nature of the wound it was the Surgeon's opinion that if the accused were standing or running, the shot must have been fired from below (ie that the muzzle of the rifle must have been lower than the entry wound) and have been fired from about 75 degrees to his left. The wound could have been caused in the manner described by Ndirangu, if he (Ndirangu) was at or near the bottom of the dip kneeling to fire and the accused had gone some way up the steep slope on the other side, had got out of the trench as was running, circling round to his left to get into the trench again, as Ndirangu describes.

On the other hand, the wound could have been caused by a person firing in a kneeling position from 10 or 15 yards down the slope on the Reserve side at the accused sitting squatting under the castor oil tree, from the accused's left front.

If Ndirangu's account was true, the accused must have been circling round to get back into the trench he had just left and in which his assailants were. This seemed intrinsically improbable. I thought it possible that Ndirangu's third shot did not hit the accused, and that he was shot under the castor oil bush where he had taken cover: that Ndirangu having searched and found him and heard who he was, and knowing that he might well be armed, shot him in the leg to make quite sure that he did not run away again; and that Ndirangu and those of the other members of the party who might know of this were afraid to say so. Ndirangu's account of the wounding of the accused was not supported by Njogi who first gave an account of how the man was shot in the trench and afterwards corrected this and said he had not clearly seen the accused when Ndirangu fired the third shot. The exact circumstances in which the accused came to be wounded are not in themselves an issue in the case. They are important, but important only to the extent that they affect the credibility of the witnesses and the answers to the issues which I have set out above. I unhesitatingly accept the evidence of Ndirangu as to the circumstances in which the accused was first encountered and the chase in the trench, except that I am not quite so sure that the accused was hit on the bank by the third shot as described. I also accept without hesitation the evidence of the Prosecution witnesses as to the finding of the pistol and ammunition on the accused, and all the other subsequent circumstances of the case.

I did not consider the accused to be a witness of truth. I thought that, in view of the letters which he had written to Government subsequently to February 1954, his statements that he had ceased his terrorist activities in February 1954, was untrue. I believed little of his evidence. In particular, I did not believe that he was coming in to surrender on the 20th/21st October. I find as facts that he was returning to the forest when challenged and that he made off as fast as he could and did his best to escape. I find it incredible that if he had, as he now says, been shot while trying to surrender, he would not have said so and made some protest on the numerous occasions when he was interviewed by persons in authority.

I find that the Prosecution have established beyond reasonable doubt that on 21st October, 1956, the accused had in his possession the Webley Scott revolver and the six rounds of ammunition which are the subject respectively of charges 1 and 2: that the revolver is a firearm within the meaning of Regulation 8A(4) and that the ammunition is ammunition as defined. I find that the accused was a member of a terrorist organisation – Mau Mau – and had the ammunition in circumstances giving rise to a reasonable presumption that it was intended to be used for a purpose prejudicial to public safety and the maintenance of public order.

The accused has not shown that it is more probable than not that he possessed the revolver or the ammunition or both because he was coming in to surrender in response to Surrender Leaflet and was bringing them for that purpose. I do not believe the surrender story and I think it is an after-thought and a fabrication. The accused has not shown on balance of probabilities that he had a reasonable excuse for possession of the arms and ammunition.

I agree with the unanimous opinions of the assessors and convict the accused on both counts.

Finally, I desire to say that I regret the necessity of holding this trial before the accused was fully recovered from his wound. The accused was, however, medically certified, before the trial commenced, as being fit to stand his trial, and I have repeatedly indicated that if at any time he felt unfit and wished for an adjournment, one would be granted; but I have been told by his Counsel that he felt sufficiently fit and wished to proceed. He has been under constant medical supervision during the trial and I have watched him constantly for any signs of pain or discomfort.

In my opinion, he has not been prejudiced in his defence by the fact that he is not yet able to walk and not fully recovered.

Dated 27th November, 1956.

KK O'CONNOR.
CHIEF JUSTICE.

Resumed 11.05 am 27/11/56.
Court as before.
Section 319 complied with.

Allocutus: I wish to say that the Prosecution witnesses have not told the whole truth. They have given that evidence on account of the reward which they expected to receive. Nothing else.

Sentence: On the second count accused is sentenced to 7 years hard labour.

On the first count accused is sentenced to be hanged by the neck until he is dead.

Right of appeal notified.

No application for a Certificate.

KK O'CONNOR.
CHIEF JUSTICE.
27/11/56.

Pistol and ammunition are confiscated to the Crown.

KK O'CONNOR.
CHIEF JUSTICE.
27/11/56.

30/11/56.
Miller for the accused.
Stratton for the Crown.

Miller: I apply for a Certificate for appeal on fact or mixed law and fact under section 578 Criminal Procedure Code.

Stratton: I don't oppose.
Certificate granted (dubitante) {doubtful}.

KK O'CONNOR.
CHIEF JUSTICE.
30/11/56.

Stratton: I ask for costs.

No order as to costs.

KK O'CONNOR.
CHIEF JUSTICE.
30/11/56.

Document 3

APPEAL TO THE COURT OF APPEALS FOR EASTERN AFRICA

IN HER MAJESTY'S COURT OF APPEAL FOR EASTERN AFRICA.
CRIMINAL APPEAL NO. 290 of 1956.

(Appeal from the judgment of Her Majesty's Supreme Court of Kenya at Nyeri in Emergency Assize Criminal Case No. 46 of 1956 (The Honourable the Chief Justice of Kenya) dated the 27th November 1956.[57]

In the matter of an Intended Appeal

BETWEEN

DEDAN KIMATHI S/O WACHIURI........................APPELANT
(Original Accused).

AND

REGINA..RESPONDENT
(Original Prosecutrix).

MEMORANDUM OF APPEAL

DEDAN KIMATHI s/o WACHIURI the Appellant above named Appeals to her Majesty's Court of Appeal for Eastern Africa against the decision of the Honourable the Chief Justice of Kenya (Sir. K.K. O'Connor) given at Nyeri on the Twenty seventh day of November 1956 whereby the Appellant was convicted on Count No.1 of the charge against him of an offence of being in unlawful possession of firearms contra Regulation 8A(1) of the Emergency Regulations 1952 and sentenced to death, on the following ground, namely:-

1. That having regard to the fundamental principle of self-defence the learned Chief Justice erred in directing himself and the Assessors to the effect that if the Appellant's sole purpose in carrying the pistol (the subject matter of the charge) was to protect his life from terrorists, such purpose could not in law afford a "lawful excuse" within the meaning of Regulation 8A (1) of the Emergency Regulations 1952.

---

57. For more on the process of appeals in Emergency Assize court cases, see Anderson's contribution to this volume.

2. That the learned Chief Justice erred in law in directing the Assessors to the effect that in order to constitute a "lawful excuse" within the meaning of Regulation 8A (1) it was necessary for the Appellant to have done "overt acts" (other than the single act of carrying the pistol for the purpose of surrendering it) in pursuance of his intention to surrender.

3. That having regard to the fact that a reward had been publicly offered for the capture of the Appellant and to the fact that this reward was paid to the various prosecution witnesses alleged to have taken part in that "capture" after statements had been taken from such witnesses and before they gave evidence, there was grave reason to suspect that such statements may have been induced and that such evidence may have been influenced by this reward.

4. That the learned Chief Justice having for good reason rejected or at least doubted the evidence of the Chief Prosecution Witness, Ndirangu Mau, on a matter material to the question depending {sic} before him i.e. the exact circumstances in which the Appellant was shot and wounded, erred in accepting the uncorroborated evidence of that witness that the Appellant had not, before he was shot, raised his arms and said "It is I, Dedan Kimathi. I have come to surrender. Don't kill me. I have a pistol".

5. That the learned Chief Justice misdirected the Assessors by repeatedly emphasising the failure of the Appellant to put forward his defence of lawful excuse until his trial and by impliedly inviting them to infer therefrom that the Appellant had no such lawful excuse.

6. That the learned Chief Justice erred in considering the Appellant's omission to complain as more or less conclusive of the fact that he had not been shot while trying to surrender.

7. That the learned Chief Justice misdirected the Assessors in law by inviting them to infer that the Appellant was not intending to surrender because he had not so stated when charged before a magistrate on the 22nd of October, 1956.

8. That the learned Chief Justice misdirected himself in law by drawing as against the Appellant an adverse inference by reason of the latter's omission to make an exculpatory statement when charged by Superintendent Baker, and further,

misdirected the Assessors by inviting them to draw a like inference.

9. That having regard to the fact that the Appellant had been shot, seriously wounded and was presumably in considerable pain at the time of his meetings with the various prosecution witnesses (apart from Superintendent Baker) to whom it was suggested that he should have claimed that he was attempting to surrender and/or complained that he was shot whilst so attempting, it was unreasonable to draw any adverse inference from the Appellant's silence.

10. That the learned Chief Justice failed to appreciate that, even though a defence of insanity was not open to the Appellant, his reactions to his surroundings after being shot and wounded were unlikely to have been normal when judged by African, much less European, standards.

11. That the learned Chief Justice underestimated the importance of the medical evidence establishing that the Appellant was an epileptic in considering whether the Appellant's failure to complain was due to his mental condition.

12. That allowing for the fact that it was probably impossible to conduct the Appellant's trial without some reference to his alleged connection with the terrorist organisation known as "Mau Mau" such unnecessary prejudice was caused to the Appellant's defence of lawful excuse in the minds of the Assessors by cross examination tending to show that he (the Appellant) was the leader of that organisation and by the finding of the learned Chief Justice (incidental though it may have been) that he was in fact a member of that organisation.

WHEREFORE the Appellant humbly prays that his Appeal be allowed; that his conviction and sentence be set aside and that he be acquitted.

DATED at Nairobi this 21st day of December 1956.

(Sgd) F.H. MILLER
F.H. MILLER
Advocate for the Appellant

The address for service of the Appellant is care of Messrs. Cumming and Miller, Advocates, Rhokatan House, P.O. Box 607, Nairobi.
FILED this 21st day of December 1956, at Nairobi.

....
REGISTRAR.

Copy to:
The Honourable The Attorney General,
Attorney General's Chambers,
Nairobi.

FILED BY: -
Mssrs. Cumming & Miller,
Advocates,
Rhokatan House,
P.O. Box 607,
Nairobi.

COLONY AND PROTECTORATE OF KENYA.
IN HER MAJESTY'S SUPREME COURT OF KENYA
AT NYERI
EMERGENCY ASSIZE CRIMINAL CASE NO. 46 of 1956.

REGINA
Vs.
DEDAN KIMATHI S/O WACHIURI.

Charge.

COUNT 1. Unlawful Possession of a firearm contrary to Regulation 8A(1) of the Emergency Regulations, 1952.

COUNT 2. Unlawful possession of ammunition contrary to Regulation 8A(1A) of the Emergency Regulations, 1952.

Judgment.

Sentenced to death.

K.K. O'Connor. C.J.
Nyeri.
27.11.56.

Appeal summarily Dismissed.

27.12.56.

Document 4

APPEAL TO THE PRIVY COUNCIL OF THE UNITED KINGDOM

IN THE PRIVY COUNCIL
ON APPEAL FROM HER MAJESTY'S COURT OF APPEAL
FOR EASTERN AFRICA[58]

BETWEEN DEDAN KIMATHI s/o WACHIURI

Petitioner

- and -

THE QUEEN

Respondent

TO THE QUEEN'S MOST EXCELLENT MAJESTY IN COUNCIL

THE PETITION

- of -

the Above-Named Petitioner

SHEWETH:-

1. THAT Your Petitioner prays for special leave to appeal to Your Majesty in Council against the order of a single judge (Worley P.) in Her Majesty's Court of Appeal for Eastern Africa summarily dismissing his appeal against his conviction in the Supreme Court of Kenya (Cor. O'Connor C.J.) on the 27th November, 1956, on two charges, namely, unlawful possession of a firearm contrary to Regulation 8A (1) of the Emergency Regulations, 1952, and unlawful possession of ammunition contrary to Regulation 8A (1A) of the Emergency Regulations, 1952. Your Petitioner was sentenced to death on the first count and to seven years' imprisonment with hard labour on the second. A copy of the Order of Worley P. is annexed hereto.
2. THAT the case for the Crown was on the 21st October, 1956 Your Petitioner was observed by certain tribal policemen in or near a trench which divides the Kikuyu reserve from the forest in the South Tetu Location of Nyeri. One of the tribal

58. Petitioner Dedan Kimathi s/o Wachiuri, In the Privy Council on Appeal from Her Majesty's Court of Appeal for Eastern Africa, London, KNA, MAC/KEN/73/11.

policemen fired at and wounded Your Petitioner who was then apprehended and found to be carrying the revolver and ammunition which were the subject of the indictment. At his trial Your Petitioner did not deny the possession of the revolver and ammunition. He testified, however, that these articles had been given to him because his life was in danger from terrorists in the forest who had quarrelled with him because of certain communications which he had made to the Kenya authorities and that thereafter he had retained them for the purpose of self-defence. He further testified that on the occasion when he was apprehended he had left the forest intending to surrender and to hand over the revolver and ammunition in accordance with the instructions given in the surrender leaflets issued by the Government of Kenya.

3. THAT Regulation 8A of the Emergency Regulations, 1952, so far as material, reads as follows:

> "8A (1) Any person who, except with lawful authority or lawful excuse, the burden of proof whereof shall lie upon him, carries, or has in his possession ...... any firearm shall be guilty of an offence and shall on conviction be sentenced to death".
>
> "8A (1A) Any person who, except with lawful authority or lawful excuse, the burden of proof whereof shall lie upon him, carries or has in his possession ...... any ammunition ...... in circumstances which raises a reasonable presumption that such ammunition ..... are intended to be used in a manner or for a purpose prejudicial to public safety or the maintenance of public order shall be guilty of an offence and shall on conviction be liable to imprisonment for life".

4. THAT the principal grounds of appeal are as follows:-

(1) The learned Chief Justice misdirected the assessors and himself that as a matter of law Your Petitioner's plea that he acquired and carried a revolver and ammunition in self-defence could not afford him a defence.

(2) The learned Chief Justice misdirected the assessors and himself that in order to constitute a "lawful excuse" within

the meaning of Regulation 8A on the ground that he was intending to bring in the pistol and the ammunition in order to surrender them to the proper authorities in response to the invitation in surrender leaflets, it was necessary for Your Petitioner to have done "overt acts" in pursuance of that intention.

(3) The learned Chief Justice misdirected the assessors and himself in that while he directed them that a surrender leaflet which had been withdrawn by the Government before the date of the alleged offences could not provide a "lawful excuse" to your Petitioner unless he was unaware it had been withdrawn, he failed to direct them that the defence of "lawful excuse" would be open to a person who intended to surrender even if there had been no surrender leaflet.

(4) The learned Chief Justice misdirected the assessors and himself that Your Petitioner's alleged omission to state, when charged, that he was coming in to surrender could give rise to an inference that Your Petitioner's said defence was untrue. The Chief Justice further erred in inferring from Your Petitioner's alleged omission to state, at any time before the trial, that he was coming in to surrender, that this defence was untrue.

(5) The learned Chief Justice having for good reason rejected or at least doubted the evidence of the chief prosecution witness, Ndirangu on a material question, viz. the exact circumstances in which Your Petitioner was shot and wounded, erred in accepting the uncorroborated evidence of that witness that Your Petitioner had not, before he was shot, stated that he had come in to surrender.

(6) The appeal ought not to have been dismissed summarily by order of a single judge of the Court of Appeal without a hearing.

7. THAT the material facts alleged in evidence at the trial were in outline as follows.

The case for the prosecution was that on the evening of Saturday, October 20th 1956 a party of tribal policemen under Police Corporal Wanjohi were guarding part of the trench dividing the reserve from the forest. In the party was a section commanded by Police Reserve Sergeant Mwangi, whose men included Constable Ndirangu and Constable Njogi.

The capture of Your Petitioner, according to the prosecution evidence, was described in the Judgment of the learned Chief Justice as follows.

"When it started to get light on the morning of Sunday October 21st, Ndirangu and Njogi moved along the Reserve side of the trench to their left, very quietly and slowly. They were looking for tracks. When they got to the edge of a place where there had been cultivation, Ndirangu saw a figure carrying something over his shoulder which Ndirangu could not distinguish properly in the dim light: it looked like poles. Ndirangu says that when he first saw the man, he was about 35 yards away (the witness later indicated an object further away) along the trench, climbing the bank of the trench on the forest side. Ndirangu saw him moving slowly towards the forest. At this spot there was open ground for seven or eight yards from the edge of the trench and then thick kei-apple (thorn) trees in a kind of a fence which would provide an obstacle to passage. When the man had climbed the bank of the trench and had moved about three yards, in the direction of the forest, moving slowly, Ndirangu shouted "Who goes there?" in English. The man did not answer: he dropped what he was carrying: started back, fell into the trench and made off along it in a direction away from the road. Ndirangu and Njogi ran after him. Ndirangu called to him in Kikuyu many times to stop; but he did not do so. Ndirangu fired. The man ran on. He tried to get out of the trench on the forest side and Ndirangu then fired at him a second time. The man continued running down the trench with Ndirangu and Njogi in pursuit. He crossed what is variously described as a stream or a dry river bed, traversing the trench. (This turned out, on examination by the witness who made a map of the scene, to be a steep dip in the trench at which there were traces of erosion as if water had at some time passed over the trench) On the further side of this dip the trench slopes up steeply. According to Ndirangu the man ran some way up this slope and got on top of the bank of the trench on the Reserve side, which is there only about a foot high. Ndirangu says that he (Ndirangu) was then down below on one side of the "stream" (presumably in the dip) and that the fugitive was on higher ground on the other side of the "stream": the man climbed out of the trench on the Reserve side, but was curving round running to come back to it again when Ndirangu knelt and fired a third shot at him. He staggered and disappeared on the Reserve side of the trench. Ndirangu and Njogi went to the spot where they had last seen the fugitive. There was no sign of him. Njogi remained there. Ndirangu started to search.

"The two tribal police reservists from the next post, Mwangi s/o Kanguru (not Sergeant Mwangi) and Maina, arrived, attracted by the shooting.

"After searching for some time, variously estimated at one hour and 20 minutes, (Estimates of times and distances by illiterate African witnesses are usually quite unreliable) Ndirangu says that he saw a thing like a leopard lying in some undergrowth under a small castor oil tree or bush. He saw that it was a man wearing a leopard skin coat and cap. Ndirangu said to the man "Who are you?" He replied "It is I Kimathi s/o Wachiuri". Ndirangu said "What about the other name?". The man replied "I am called Dedan Kimathi": he also mentioned something sounding like "Field Marshal". Ndirangu told him to come out. He said he could not, as Ndirangu had shot him. Ndirangu insisted on his crawling out, which he did. Ndirangu then saw that he was wounded in the front of the right thigh and buttock. The man was the accused."

Your Petitioner was searched and the loaded pistol was found on him. Sergeant Mwangi and Corporal Wanjohi arrived on the scene.

Your Petitioner was taken on a stretcher to a Home Guard Post and then to a Police Station and later taken by A.S.P. Vidler to Nyeri General Hospital where Mr. Hurley the Provincial Surgeon operated upon him for a gun shot wound through the right thigh.

On the 22nd October, 1956 Your Petitioner was interviewed by Superintendent Baker who cautioned him and in the presence of a Magistrate charged him with the charges the subject of these proceedings. After the charges were read to him Your Petitioner replied –

"I would like to say that I never knew there was such a law."

He then told the interpreter that he wanted to think and after about twenty seconds added –

"I have nothing more to say."

Your Petitioner was later interviewed and questioned both by A.S.P. Vidler and an inspector Blackman.

Your Petitioner's evidence was summarized by the learned Chief Justice as follows –

In brief, the story of the accused is:

Prior to his arrest on 21st October, 1956, he had been living in the forest for almost four years with his associates whom he calls "forest men" or Mau Mau.

In February, 1954, he fell out with most of his associates because of a letter which he had written to Government advocating peace. They wanted to kill him and he moved away with five companions to a "hide-out" far away. He says that neither since February, 1954, (nor, indeed, previously) has he carried out any anti-British or anti-Government activity.

The accused admits that he had in his possession on the 21st October, 1956, the revolver and ammunition which are the subjects respectively of Counts 1 and 2. He says that these were given to him in or about February, 1954, by one Macharia Kimanya for the purpose of defending himself against Mau Mau terrorists who wished to kill him. Since February, 1954, the accused has been in the forest with five companions only. Some others used to come and see him.

The accused says that he knew about the Surrender leaflets issued by the Government.

There were, in fact, two lots of Surrender Leaflets, the first lot issued in August, 1953, the second lot issued in January, 1955. The second lot was withdrawn in July, 1955. The first still stands.

The leaflet upon which the accused relies (Ex. C) says inter alia:

> "All those who have not committed murder are NOW given a chance to save their lives. Decide quickly what to do, to come in and surrender.... If possible, come out with your arms. You can surrender to any European officer or to any other Government representative."

The accused was asked why, if he was relying on this leaflet dated August, 1953, he did not come in to surrender before October, 1956. He replied that this was because (1) there was a large reward offered for him and he was afraid that Tribal Police or Home Guards would shoot him to get the money and (2) he was awaiting replies to certain letters which he had sent to Government. The Defence were offered production of these letters, subject to objection as to their relevance, but declined to call for them. The accused said that his reason for eventually coming in was because the Mau Mau and the security forces were hunting him: at that time he was left all alone and he was ill. "I said it is better to go out either to be killed or, if I am lucky, to get to the Government". He said that his intention was to surrender and to give the pistol and the ammunition to the Government according to the instructions which he knew.

The accused said that he made up his mind on the 20th October to surrender. He started: night fell before he got to the

Reserve. He arrived in the Reserve about 7.30 p.m.: he was afraid to go to any of the Home Guard Posts, for fear that he would be shot. Being hungry, he went to find food and got some sugar cane and four maize cobs. He roasted his maize at a fire.

Day broke before he had eaten. He began to walk towards the Kahigaini Road. He was down in the valley and went up to the trench as the most convenient route to the road. He was in the trench about 150 yards from the main road. His intention was to stop near the main road, have his food, and then go along the road to Kahigaini where there was a police post. The accused says that he had no intention of returning to the forest. If he had so intended, he would have taken more food with him.

The accused says that he was still in the trench when he heard a gun shot: he thought it was fired from about 40 yards away: he did not see who fired. There were two shots one after the other. The accused dropped his sugar cane and two maize cobs that he had in his hand and ran. He had no idea who was firing at him. Before he had gone far, he heard a second shot. The shots appeared to come from the direction of the road. He ran fast along the trench and was still running when he heard a third shot. He was not hit. He got out of the trench on the Reserve side and sat down under a castor oil tree about ten yards away. There was a steep slope there down to the Thengeraini river. He squatted on his haunches with his knees open. He sat there for about 20 minutes facing down towards the stream in the valley, after which he saw a man come up from below him – in front and slightly to his left. He noticed the man was wearing uniform and took him to be a policeman. He raised his arms and said: "It is I, Dedan Kimathi. I have come to surrender. Don't kill me. I have a pistol". The policeman dropped on one knee, fired, and hit the accused almost in the groin. The accused felt great pain and fainted. When he came to, he saw a group of police who gave him some water to drink. They made a stretcher. On arrival at the Home Guard Post, the accused was give tea. When he opened his eyes at Ihururu he saw an European, whom he did not know to be a doctor. He was, he believes, given an injection.

The accused was taken to the hospital at Nyeri and an operation was performed. The next morning he was visited by a Police officer in plain clothes who charged him. He admits having made the reply to the charge which is recorded, but says that he was then very ill; his leg was paining very much, he had not yet passed water or otherwise relieved himself since he left the forest: he could hear noises in his ears and was feeling giddy.

The accused says that when he replied that he never knew that there was such a law, what he wished to say was that he did not know that there was such a law for a person who was coming in to surrender himself: he thought he had completed the sentence and had said that: he only spoke a few words and was unable to say more because he was in pain.

The accused says that when A.S.P. Vidler later visited him, he was in civilian clothes and the accused did not know that he was a police officer. He said nothing to the Magistrate about surrender because he thought he was the Judge and it might be improper. The accused says that he has mentioned the question of surrender to Europeans of his escort; but the Defence did not call any of them to substantiate this.

The accused says that he has suffered from epileptic fits since he was a child and he called his mother and one Joseph Wakaba to support this. Dr. Turner, the Provincial Physician also says that the accused is an epileptic and he says that anaesthesia and operations are well know precipitating causes of fits, an epileptic may have a fit as a result of an anaesthetic and an operation. This would not be noticed if it occurred during anaesthesia. If an epileptic had a fit during anaesthesia, it would be likely that he would have a severe headache and mental blurring for some hours after he recovered consciousness. These symptoms might last up to 48 hours. There is no evidence that he did in fact have a fit.

There is no defence of insanity in this case. It is not suggested by the Defence that on the 21st October 1956 the mental condition of the accused was such that he did not know that he possessed a pistol and six rounds of ammunition or that, through disease affecting his mind, he did not know that such possession was illegal. The sole reason for this evidence of epilepsy is to try to account for the fact that, when charged with unlawful possession of a firearm and ammunition, the accused did not, in so many words, say that he had the weapons because he was about to surrender and was bringing them in for that purpose."

6. THAT the learned Chief Justice directed the assessors in relation to Your Petitioner's defence that he was carrying the pistol and ammunition for the purpose of self-defence as follows –

> "I also direct you as a matter of law that it would not afford a reasonable excuse for one terrorist to carry a pistol and ammunition for the purpose of protecting himself from other terrorists whom he might have offended."

It is submitted that this is a misdirection. The issue raised by the defence was not whether there was a "reasonable excuse" for Your Petitioner to carry a pistol and ammunition but whether there was a "lawful excuse" within the meaning of the Regulation. In his judgment, however, the Chief Justice dealt with the point as follows –

> "I also directed the Assessors (and I direct myself) that it would not afford a lawful excuse for one terrorist to carry a pistol and ammunition for the purpose of protecting himself from other terrorists whom he might offended."

It is submitted that the reasons alleged by Your Petitioner for carrying a revolver and ammunition could have constituted a lawful excuse and that, by his said directions, the Chief Justice withdrew from the consideration of the Court a defence which was open to Your Petitioner.

7. THAT the learned Chief Justice directed the assessors as to Your Petitioner's defence that he intended to bring the pistol and ammunition in for the purpose of surrendering them to the proper authorities, and therefore had a "lawful excuse" within the meaning of the Regulation, as follows :-

> "I direct you as a matter of law that if the accused's story is true and he was intending to bring this pistol and ammunition in in order to surrender them to the proper authorities and he had done overt acts in pursuance of that intention, that could in law be a lawful excuse which would entitle him to be acquitted."

Similarly in his judgment the Chief Justice stated as follows :-

> "I directed the Assessors, and I direct myself, that if the story of the accused is true and he was intending to bring in the pistol and the ammunition in order to surrender them to the proper authorities in response to an invitation in a Government leaflet and had done overt acts in pursuance of that intention, that could, in law constitute a lawful excuse which would entitled him to be acquitted."

Your Petitioner submits that the said directions are wrong in that they suggest that in the absence of proof of specific overt acts this defence could not succeed.

It is submitted that proof of the invitation contained in the

Government's surrender leaflets together with Your Petitioner's sworn evidence that the said invitation was the reason for his forming the intention to come in and surrender with his arms was sufficient in all the circumstances, if such evidence was believed, to provide a lawful excuse.

8. THAT the learned Chief Justice directed the assessors with regard to the two lots of surrender leaflets as follows –

"There are two lots of surrender leaflets:

(i) issued 24/8/53. That says "Come in and surrender without delay". But that still stands. It also says: "If possible come with your arms."

(ii) 2nd lot issued 18/1/55 "Govt. Will not kill you for carrying arms". There was another addressed to gang leaders dated 24/8/53 which says: "You cannot get into any danger when you come to negotiate your surrender with that of your whole gang and your arms. Come out during the day time waving green branches this will ensure that you are not shot at". That says surrender now carrying a green branch and bring in your arms. That has been withdrawn. It was withdrawn in July 1955.

"So the only leaflet that could be 'lawful excuse' in October 1956 for carrying arms would be the one of August 1953 ones. But the later one might be a 'lawful excuse' if he didn't know it had been withdrawn."

In his Judgment the Chief Justice mentioned the same point and stated that of the two lots of surrender leaflets "the second was withdrawn in July 1955. The first still stands".

Your Petitioner submits that this is a misdirection and that it is irrelevant that the later leaflet was withdrawn in July 1955 provided that Your Petitioner was coming in to surrender. He therefore submits that the defence of "lawful excuse" would have been open to him even if there had never been any surrender leaflet.

9. THAT in relation to the question as to whether Your Petitioner was coming in to surrender the learned Chief Justice directed the assessors to consider, inter alia, the alleged omission of Your Petitioner to make any statement of this fact to his captors, as follows:-

"Do you believe accused was surrendering? According to the prosecution accused was:

(i) seen going in the direction of the forest;

(ii) he ran away when challenged;

(iii) he said nothing about surrender to anyone in authority – either his captors or Sgt. Mwangi, Cp. Wanjohi or Inspector Sloan or the Doctor or Superintendent Baker or Superintendent Vidler or the magistrate.

"He says that he did not know that Blackman and Vidler were Police Officers. You may think that as they came to see him when he was under close arrest to ask him questions about security matters, he must have thought that they were persons in authority. Isn't it odd that he didn't say: 'I am wrongly confined. I have been wrongly charged with possession a firearm {sic}, when all I was doing was coming in to surrender it'? If that was true you may think it odd that he didn't say it. Is it something that he has thought of since? It is for you to consider. He says he has told some of his European escorts. He has not called any of them to say so."

Similarly in his Judgment the Chief Justice observed:-

> "From first to last, neither to Sergeant Mwangi, Corporal Wanjohi, Inspector Sloan, Mr. Hurley nor Superintendent Baker did the accused say one word about having come in to surrender, and he made no complaint that he had been shot while trying to surrender. When charged with possession of a firearm and ammunition, he did not say that he was surrendering and bringing them in for the purpose of giving them up. He now says that that is what he was doing."

It is submitted that this is a misdirection in so far as it applies to Your Petitioner's alleged omission to state his defence when charged. It is further submitted that the Chief Justice erred in drawing an inference adverse to Your Petition from an omission of Your Petitioner to state to his captors that he was coming in to surrender (assuming that such omission was proved).

10. THAT the learned Chief Justice in his Judgment commented upon the evidence of Ndirangu regarding the circumstances in which he shot Your Petitioner, as follows:-

> "If Ndirangu's account was true, the accused must have been circling round to get back into the trench he had

just left and in which his assailants were. This seemed intrinsically improbable. I thought it possible that Ndirangu's third shot did not hit the accused, and that he was shot under the castor oil bush where he had taken cover: that Ndirangu having searched and found him and heard who he was, and knowing that he might well be armed, shot him in the leg to make quite sure that he did not run away again; and that Ndirangu and those of the other members of the party who might know of this were afraid to say so. Ndirangu's account of the wounding of the accused was not supported by Njogi who first gave an account of how the man was shot in the trench and afterwards corrected this and said he had not clearly seen the accused when Ndirangu fired the third shot. The exact circumstances in which the accused came to be wounded are not in themselves at issue in the case. They are important, but important only to the extent that they affect the credibility of the witnesses and the answers to the issues which I have set out above. I unhesitatingly accept the evidence of Ndirangu as to the circumstances in which the accused was first encountered and the chase in the trench, except that I am not quite so sure that the accused was hit on the bank by the third shot as described. I also accept without hesitation the evidence of the Prosecution witnesses as to the finding of the pistol and ammunition on the accused, and all the other subsequent circumstances of the case."

In view of Your Petitioner's evidence that before he was shot by Ndirangu he raised his arms and said "It is I, "Dedan Kimathi. I have come to surrender. Don't kill me. I have a pistol", and the fact that the rejection of this evidence depended entirely upon the reliability of Ndirangu's evidence, it is submitted that as the latter's evidence was rejected or at least doubted by the Chief Justice as indicated in the above passage, the Court ought not to have found against Your Petitioner on this vital point.

Your Petitioner submits that a further reason why the evidence of Ndirangu on this point should be regarded with grave suspicion is that (as he admitted in evidence) he had been paid a reward for "capturing" Your Petitioner. In order to obtain such reward it might presumably have been thought desirable by this witness to satisfy the authorities that he had effected the "capture" of Your Petitioner as a fugitive and not merely taken him into custody upon a voluntary surrender. In this connection Your Petitioner stated when found guilty –

> "Allocutus: I wish to say that the Prosecution witnesses have not told the whole truth. They have given that evidence on account of the reward which they expected to receive. Nothing else."

11. THAT the three assessors gave their opinions that Your Petitioner was guilty and he was found guilty and sentenced as aforesaid by the learned Chief Justice. Your Petitioner was granted a certificate of the learned Chief Justice that the case was a fit one for appeal on grounds involving fact or mixed law and fact under Section 378 of the Criminal Procedure Code, although it appears from the Record that the said certificate was granted "dubitante" {doubtful}. The said section, so far as material, provides as follows)

    378. (1) Any person convicted on a trial held by the Supreme Court may appeal to His Majesty's Court of Appeal for Eastern Africa –

    (a) against his conviction on any ground of appeal which involves a question of law alone; and

    (b) with the leave of such Court of Appeal or upon the certificate of the judge who tried him that it is a fit case for appeal on any ground of appeal which involves a question of fact alone or a question of mixed law and fact or any other ground which appears to the court to be a sufficient ground of appeal; and

    (c) with the leave of such Court of Appeal against the sentence passed on conviction unless such sentence is one fixed by law.

12. THAT Your Petitioner's grounds of appeal were as follows –

    1. That having regard to the fundamental principle of self-defence the learned Chief Justice erred in directing himself and the Assessors to the effect that if the Appellant's sole purpose in carrying the pistol (the subject matter of the charge) was to protect his life from terrorists, such purpose could not in law afford a "lawful excuse" within the meaning of Regulation 8A (1) of the Emergency Regulations 1952.
    2. That the learned Chief Justice erred in law in directing the

Assessors to the effect that in order to constitute a "lawful excuse" within the meaning of Regulation 8A (1) it was necessary for the Appellant to have done "overt acts" (other than the single act of carrying the pistol for the purpose of surrendering it) in pursuance of his intention to surrender.

3. That having regard to the fact that a reward had been publicly offered for the capture of the Appellant and to the fact that this reward was paid to the various prosecution witnesses alleged to have taken part in that "capture" after statements had been taken from such witnesses and before they gave evidence, there was a grave reason to suspect that such statements may have been induced and that such evidence may have been influenced by this reward.

4. That the learned Chief Justice having for good reason rejected or at least doubted the evidence of the Chief Prosecution Witness, Ndirangu Mau, on a matter material to the question depending before him i.e. the exact circumstances in which the Appellant was shot and wounded, erred in accepting the uncorroborated evidence of that witness that the Appellant had not, before he was shot, raised his arms and said "It is I, Dedan Kimathi. I have come to surrender. Don't kill me. I have a pistol".

5. That the learned Chief Justice misdirected the Assessors by repeatedly emphasising the failure of the Appellant to put forward his defence of lawful excuse until his trial and by impliedly inviting them to infer therefrom that the Appellant had no such lawful excuse.

6. That the learned Chief Justice erred in considering the Appellant's omission to complain as more or less conclusive of the fact that he had not been shot while trying to surrender.

7. That the learned Chief Justice misdirected the Assessors in law by inviting them to infer that the Appellant was not intending to surrender because he had not so stated when charged before a magistrate on the 22nd of October, 1956.

8. That the learned Chief Justice misdirected himself in law by drawing as against the Appellant an adverse inference by reason of the latter's omission to make an exculpatory statement when charged by Superintendent Baker, and further, misdirected the Assessors by inviting them to draw a like inference.

9. That having regard to the fact that the Appellant had been shot, seriously wounded and was presumably in considerable pain at the time of his meetings with the various prosecution witnesses (apart from Superintendent Baker) to whom it was suggested that he should have claimed that he was attempting to surrender and/or complained that he was shot whilst so attempting, it was unreasonable to draw any adverse inference from the Appellant's silence.

10. That the learned Chief Justice failed to appreciate that, even though a defence of insanity was not open to the Appellant, his reactions to his surroundings after being shot and wounded were unlikely to have been normal when judged by African, much less European, standards.

11. That the learned Chief Justice underestimated the importance of the medical evidence establishing that the Appellant was a epileptic in considering whether the Appellant's failure to complain was due to his mental condition.

12. That allowing for the fact that it was probably impossible to conduct the Appellant's trial without some reference to his alleged connection with the terrorist organisation known as "Mau Mau" much unnecessary prejudice was caused to the Appellant's defence of lawful excuse in the minds of the Assessors by cross-examination tending to show that he (the Appellant) was the leader of that organisation and by the finding of the learned Chief Justice (incidental though it may have been) that he was in fact a member of that organisation.

13. THAT the appeal was summarily dismissed after perusal of the Record by Worley P under Rule 4 of the Eastern African Court of Appeal (Kenya Emergency Assizes) Rules, 1953. Rule 4 of the said Rules provides as follows –

> 4. (1) Where the Court has received the record of a case in respect of which such an appeal as aforesaid has been lodged, a Judge of the Court shall peruse the same, and if he considers that the record does not disclose any matter, whether of law or of fact, sufficient to raise a reasonable doubt as to the correctness of the conviction, or to lead him to the opinion that the sentence ought to be reduced, increased or otherwise varied, the appeal shall, without being set down for hearing, be summarily rejected by an order of such Judge of the Court certifying that he has perused

the record and is satisfied that the appeal has been lodged without any sufficient grounds for complaint.

(2) If the appeal is not dismissed summarily under the provisions of this rule, the Court shall cause notice to be given to the appellant or his advocate, and to the Attorney General, of the time and place at which such appeal shall be heard and shall furnish the Attorney General with a copy of the proceedings and of the grounds of appeal.

(2) {sic} An order of a Judge of the Court summarily rejecting an appeal under the provisions of this rule shall be deemed to be the judgment of the Court, and shall operate as a confirmation of any and every conviction and sentence in respect of which the appeal was lodged.

The said Rules are made under the Eastern African Court of Appeal Orders in Council, 1950 and 1953. By the first of the said Orders in Council (the principal Order) the Court of Appeal for Eastern Africa was re-constituted. It is provided by the principal Order inter alia as follows –

16. (1) The Court shall have jurisdiction to hear and determine such appeals for judgments of Courts of the Territories (including reserved questions of law and cases stated) and to exercise such powers and authorities as may be prescribed by or under any law for the time being in force in any of the Territories respectively, subject to the provisions of this Order or of any such law; and, subject as aforesaid, for all purposes of and incidental to the hearing and determination of any appeal within its jurisdiction, the Court shall have the power, authority and jurisdiction vested in the Court from which the appeal is brought.

. . . .

18. (1) Subject to the provisions of this Order the President and any two other Judges of the Court selected by the President, may make Rules of Court for regulating the practice and procedure … in appeals to the Court …

It is provided by the Eastern African Court of Appeal Order in Council, 1953, inter alia, that the principal Order shall be amended by the inclusion therein of the following Section –

14A. Notwithstanding anything contained in this Order, provisions may be made by Rules of Court under section 18 of this

Order for summary dismissal of appeals by order made by one or more Judges of the Court after perusal of the record; and if such provision is made, appeals may be summarily dismissed accordingly, subject to and in accordance with such provision:

Provided that if and in so far as provision is made as aforesaid for dismissal of appeals by two Judges, no order dismissing on appeal shall be made unless both Judges agree to the making thereof.

Your Petitioner makes the following submissions in relation to the said summary dismissal of his appeal:-

(1) That in view of the provisions of Section 378 of the Criminal Procedure Code and Section 16 (1) of the Eastern African Court of Appeal Order in Council, 1950 he was entitled, as a person who had been granted a Certificate of the trial judge under the said Section 379, to have his appeal heard and determined by the Court of Appeal and there was no power in a single judge to dismiss his appeal summarily under Rule 4 of the Eastern African Court of Appeal (Kenya Emergency Assizes) Rules, 1953.

(2) Alternatively, even if there is power in a single judge to dismiss the appeal summarily in such a case, Your Petitioner's appeal ought not to have been summarily dismissed under Rule 4 (1) of the said Rules in view of the fact that a certificate for appeal had been granted by the trial Judge under Section 378 of the Criminal Procedure Code.

(3) That in any event on the evidence in this case and in view of the grounds of appeal put forward by Your Petitioner his appeal could not properly or reasonably be dismissed summarily under Rule 4 (1) of the said Rules.

Your Petitioner therefore submits that his appeal ought not to have been dismissed summarily without a hearing by the Court of Appeal.

14. THAT Your Petitioner submits that by reason of the foregoing he has suffered a substantial and grave injustice.

YOUR PETITIONER THEREFORE HUMBLY PRAYS that Your Majesty in Council may be graciously pleased to grant him special leave to appeal to Your Majesty in Council against an Order of a single judge (Worley P.) in

Her Majesty's Court of Appeal for Eastern Africa summarily dismissing his appeal against his conviction in the Supreme Court of Kenya on the 27th November 1956 on the charges of unlawful possession of a firearm contrary to Regulation 8A(1) of the Emergency Regulations, 1952, and unlawful possession of ammunition contrary to 8A (1A) of the Emergency Regulations, 1952 and for such further or other Order as to Your Majesty in Council may seem fit

AND YOUR PETITIONER WILL EVER PRAY, ETC.

DINGLE FOOT
RALPH MILLNER

IN HER MAJESTY'S COURT OF APPEAL
FOR EASTERN AFRICA
AT NAIROBI

CRIMINAL APPEAL No. 290 of 1956
(From Criminal Case No. 46 of 1956 of H.M. Supreme Court of Kenya (Emergency Assize) at Nyeri).

DEDAN KIMATHI S/O WACHIURI — Appellant (Original Accused)

versus

REGINA — Respondent

ORDER

THIS IS AN APPEAL against convictions by a Court of Emergency Assize constituted under the Kenya Emergency (Emergency Assizes) Regulations 1953 (G.N. 931 of 1953). In pursuance of Rule 4 of the Eastern African Court of Appeal (Kenya Emergency Assizes) Rule 1953 (G.N.1319 of 1953) I have perused the record of this case and having done so I certify that I am satisfied that the appeal has been lodged without any sufficient ground of complaint. The appeal is therefore summarily dismissed.

N. A. WORLEY,
PRESIDENT.

NAIROBI
Dated 27th December, 1956.

I certify that this is a true copy of the original.
N.D. DESHI
ASSOCIATE REGISTRAR
27.12.56.

IN THE PRIVY COUNCIL
ON APPEAL FROM HER MAJESTY'S COURT OF APPEAL FOR EASTERN AFRICA

BETWEEN:

DEDAN KIMATHI s/o WACHIURI
Petitioner.

- and -

THE QUEEN
Respondent.

PETITION

- for -

SPECIAL LEAVE TO APPEAL

T.L. Wilson & CO.,
6, Westminster Palace Gardens
London, S.W.1.

Document 5

INTERROGATION REPORT OF DEDAN KIMATHI

Provincial Special Branch,
NYERI
31st October, 1956.

SECRET
EFI/1/13

INTERROGATION REPORT[59]
DEDAN KIMATHI s/o WACIURI

EARLY HISTORY

Subject was born in 1921 in Tetu Location, GAKANGA Sub-Location. His father was WACIURI s/o KABUGU who died when DEDAN was a child. Subject first went to school in November, 1935, at KARUNAINI and was at school on and off until 1944. When not at school he worked for the forestry department as a wagon cart boy. In 1939, he went to WANDUBI school as he was then living in Thegenge with his older brother, NAMAN GICHUHI. Afterwards he returned to KARUNAINI school.

In 1944, he went to work on SHARPE's farm (now Lamuria) as a schoolmaster for the children of the farm labour. He then went to SQUAIRS as a milk clerk. At the end of 1944, he went to MWERU in S. Tetu as a teacher for Tumutumu Mission, a job that did not last very long as the Mission did not pay him and he returned to SHARPE's in January, 1945. In April, 1945, he worked for W.H.L. Harris at SUBUKIA, staying there until mid-'46. He next worked on THARUA Farm at NARO MORU until the end of '46 when he went to Ol Kalau and Subukia until the end of '48. He returned to Nyeri and went to KARUNAINI as a Mission schoolteacher. He was sacked by the schools supervisor because his relations with the female pupils left something to be desired. He returned to Ol Kalau working on various farms until March, 1950, when he went to THOMSON's FALLS where he ran a commercial (independent) school for a month before returning to Nyeri where he joined the Veterinary Department and was posted

59. Transcription of Interrogation Report, Dedan Kimathi s/o Wachiuri, 31 October 1956, TNA:PRO, WO276/533.

as clerk to Tetu Dairy where he stayed until February, 1951. He then returned to Thomson's Falls where he went into a building and contracting business with capital unwittingly provided by the Tetu Dairy. He had 3 partners in this business and they traded as ESMAS IKIKI and Company. At the same time he worked for the SHELL Company up to the end of July, 1952, when he returned to Nyeri.

At this stage subject became very evasive and would not talk about his life between July-December, '52 when he went into the forest but admitted to a trip to Nairobi which he said was to obtain building materials.

POLITICAL BACKGROUND

Subject states that he first became a member of K.A.U. in December, 1945, when he became Vice-Secretary of the Subukia Branch at its inaugural meeting as he could read and write. He was hazy and evasive about the principals of K.A.U. and stated that he attended 2 public meetings and all they discussed was a code of behaviour for Africans.

He then stated he had nothing more to do with K.A.U. until June, 1952, when he became Secretary of the Thomson's Falls Branch. On 26th June, there was a public meeting at Thomson's Falls and JOMO KENYATTA addressed the crowd. Subject stated that he had only seen JOMO once before and he never had private conversations with him or with other political leaders.

LIFE IN THE FOREST

In October, 1952, subject went to his mother's house and worked on his shamba and he heard that a warrant was out for his arrest for being a K.A.U. official so he hid in Mahiga in the forest. He denied having taken any oaths or having had anything to do with Mau Mau at this stage. He stayed in the forest by himself coming out at night to get food from his wife. In the middle of December, he came to KIANDONGORO and bumped into a group of 12 men, including KAHIUTINA, SORGUM, MATHENGE, WACHIRA and others. DEDAN immediately became the leader of this gang and they built their first hide near KIANDONGORO and he sent them into the

Reserve at night to get food. In January, 1953, he was joined by NDUNGU GICHERU and KIMBO who already had their own gangs but they immediately accepted him as their leader. The gang now swelled to 35 strong and in February, 1953, he was joined by NYAGA and ABDULLA and their gangs. KIMBO in the meantime had left. He then formed his first organisation, splitting up the gang into sections and his first organisation was as follows:-

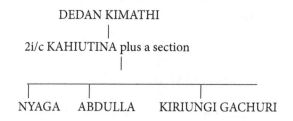

DEDAN KIMATHI

2i/c KAHIUTINA plus a section

NYAGA | ABDULLA | KIRIUNGI GACHURI

KAHIUTINA had a sporting rifle and subject usually stayed with NYAGA's section. By this time his 'fame' was beginning to spread and in early March, '52 {*sic*}, he had a steady stream of visitors, all of whom had gangs of varying sizes. These visitors included NGARE NGUFU from Thomson's Falls, MACHARIA NJAU from Rumuruti, MAKANYANGA from Ol Kalau and THIUNGU GATERU from Subukia. They all came and accepted him as overall leader and his gang rapidly became 500 strong. After about a month the leaders returned to their Districts leaving KIMATHI a pistol and a shotgun.

Subject then gave the first name to his organization. He named it the ITUGATI {sic}[60] Association which means the Association of Military People and he appointed himself the first President.

In May, 1953, subject held another meeting with NDUNGU GICHERU and KIMBO and they agreed to join ITUGATI. They then repaired to MAHIGA with KIMATHI and in the Mahiga Forest met about 400 people who agreed to join ITUGATI. At this meeting NDUNGU was elected Secretary and KAHIUTINA, Treasurer. 'General' KALEBA came across from Mt. Kenya for this meeting and OCHIENG, a Mt. Kenya gang leader was elected Vice-President of ITUGATI under KIMATHI so that the Mt.

60. *Itungati* translated as "warrior" or "freedom fighter."

Kenya Organisation was represented on the Aberdare Council.

After this meeting he went to the Othaya Forest with NDUNGU and met about 800 people led by KIBIRA GATU, WAWERU, KOINANGE and GATEGWA NDIRANGU. They all agreed to join ITUGATI and accepted subject as overall leader. He appointed GATEGWA NDIRANGU as Vice-Secretary of the Committee and WACHIRA GATHUKU as Vice-Treasurer. At this meeting the first ITUMA was used to represent the Nyeri gangs and the word was arrived at in the following way:-

I – ITUGATI
TU – N & S Tetu
MA – MATHIRA

Also at this meeting subject was elected President of the ITUMA and STANLEY MATHENGE was elected Vice-President although MATHENGE was away in Nairobi and did not attend this meeting. Up to this time subject states that he had never met MATHENGE.

In May, 1953, subject went to Chinga and met GIKONYU who had 200 men. GIKONYU told subject that many Fort Hall people had gone into the forest and so on 28th May, he went to Fort Hall with GIKONYU and NDUNGU and there he met MBARIA KANIU who was the senior leader of some 1600 Fort Hall terrorists and also met STANLEY MATHENGE who had just returned from Nairobi. MBARIA's men were mostly Rift Valley repatriates but also included the Loc. 14 gangs. JOHN MUTOATA MACHARIA was MBARIA's Quarter-master General. Subject was at this time in the Loc. 14 forest and states that MBARIA agreed to join the ITUGATI Association and respect subject as overall leader. Subject went to Loc. 12 on 5th June, 1953, and met GAKURI KARURI and IHURA who commanded 600 men between them. They too joined ITUGATI. Taking MBARIA and STANLEY MATHENGE with him subject next went to the Loc. 9 forest and met MACHARIA KIMENIA, MATENJAGWA and STANLEY KIAMA, all for the first time. They all agreed to join ITUGATI and regard subject as leader. Here STANLEY MATHENGE left the party to return to Mahiga Location forest.

Subject, in company with MACHARIA KIMEMIA, STANLEY KIAMA, NGUNGU GICHERU left for Loc. 2 where MACHARIA's gang of 600 were waiting under the command of KAGO and KABANGA. Subject was very impressed with KAGO, whom he described as a brave and fearless leader. The party stayed in the Loc. 2 forest for some time at IRATI and here subject and NDUNGU were photographed together.

In July, '53, the party came back to Nyeri in company of MACHARIA, MBARIA and MURAYA MBUTHIA and at Kiandongoro the party met up with KAHIUTINA once more in company with MAKANYANGA and GATERU. At the end of July, '53, the party went to Chinga forest and rejoined with ABDULLA and subject's younger brother, WAGURA s/o WACIURI alias WAMBARARIA.

At this time subject was contacted by Security Force patrols and the group split up. MBARIA met up with NYAGA and NYAGA sent men to look for subject, and subject duly went to NYAGA's camp. Subject then arranged a leaders meeting for August, '53, and several leaders came, including MACHARI, MBARIA, MATENJAGWA, KIBIRA GATU, NYAGA, ABDULLA, KAHINGA WACHANGA and others.

The meeting was disturbed by patrols and another meeting was arranged for September 12th in the Loc. 13 forest. The leaders then dispersed and subject and his party went to KAGO's camp in Loc. 12. Subject went to Loc. 13 and waited for the leaders to arrive but the meeting did not take place because of poor attendance. On 23rd October, '53, subject and MBARIA KANIU returned to Nyeri and MBARIA departed to join his gang on the KINANGOP.

Previous to this in August, '53, subject wrote his first letter to the Governor and General Erskine and according to him the gist of the letter was an appeal for a cease fire. Also at this time as a result of a dream he formed and wrote down the whole organisation under his command. The organisation was called the ITUMA DEMI and KAHIUTINA was C in C until they quarrelled in December, '53. The ITUMA DEMI was split up into the following Divisions and sections with the following leaders:-

LOCUST DIVISION

Commander	-	NDERITO THUITA (MAGU)
2 i/c	-	VINDO
Section 1	under	MATHENGE WACHIRA
" 2	"	MAKANYANGA
" 3	"	NDUNGU KIMORE
" 4	"	WACHIRA THIRIKWA

Total strength about 400, mostly from TETU.

SNAKE DIVISION

Commander	-	GICHUKI MUGO
2 i/c	-	GIHARA GATANDI
3 i/c	-	GATATA KINGORI
No sections		

Total strength about 80, mostly from THEGENGE.

BEE DIVISION

Commander	-	WACHIRA GATHUKI

This Division was divided by KARARI NJAMA and subject did not know the section leaders.

KAMS DIVISION

Commander	-	KAHINGA WACHANGA
2 i/c	-	WANJOHI GACHUHI
3 i/c	-	WANJOHI JUJI

Nearly all S. TETU people, about 200 strong.

MARATI DIVISION

Commander	-	NYAGA
2 i/c	-	GITAU s/o WAJANI
Section 1	under	WAMBUGU MWAMBIA
" 2	"	NDUNGU MACHARIA
" 3	"	MBOTHO GITHENGE
" 4	"	IHURI GITONGA

Mixed people, about 300 strong.

SALVATION DIVISION

Commander	-	ABDULLA
2 i/c	-	WAMBARARIA
Section 1	under	WAMATHANDI
" 2	"	JUMA ABDULLA
" 3	"	KINGORA (still at large)
" 4	"	NDERITU MUKUNDI

Mostly Tetu people, about 100 strong.

KANYONI KANJA DIVISION

Commander	-	GIKONYU
2 i/c	-	MUNANDI
Section 1	under	MWANEKI GACHONA
" 2	"	WANDERI KIRINYE
" 3	"	MAINA KIRENYE
" 4		cannot remember name of leader

All Chinga people, no idea of strength.

THERIMI DIVISION

Commander	-	JERIKO

No sections, mixed people, about 60 strong.

At this time subject also formed the MBURO army which was a mixed group of people mostly from the settled areas. He has no idea of its strength but it was split up into 3 Divisions. NDUNGU was in command of 1, KIMBO another and MBARIA the third. On his trip to Fort Hall he, together with the Fort Hall leaders formed the GIKUYU IREGI ARMY which was a purely Fort Hall organisation. The organisation was as follows:-

Overall Commander	-	MACHARIA KIMEMIA
Q.M.	-	STANLEY KIAMA

DIVISION 2 (Loc. 13)

Commander	-	NJUGUNA KIRUNYU
2 i/c	-	KIHUMBA GITUKU
Q.M.	-	JOHN MUTOATA MACHARIA

DIVISION 1 (Loc. 12)

Commander	-	IHURA afterwards KAHUNGA KAMAU
2 i/c	-	KIGOMA GAKU

DIVISION 3 (Loc. 2)

Commander	-	KARIUKI NDUATI
2 i/c	-	KAMAU KARICHU
Q.M.	-	KABANGA GATHATWA

DIVISION 4 (Loc. 2)

Commander	-	MUIRURI NJUGUNA
2 i/c	-	KARIITHI KAGI
Q.M.	-	MBOGWA MUKOBO

DIVISION 5 (Loc. 9)

Commander	-	KIHARA
2 i/c	-	could not remember
Q.M.	-	GITHENJI MWANGI

DIVISION 6 (Loc. 14)

Commander	-	KIBIRA {*sic*} WACHIRI
2 i/c	-	NYORO KIRAGU afterwards GATU WATIKI
Q.M.	-	JOMO GAKUNDI

DIVISION 7 (Kiharu people)

Commander	-	WANYEKI WANGOMBE
2 i/c	-	could not remember

Subject also stated that he formed the MUTHASI Army on Mt. Kenya under the command of CHINA, afterwards TANGANYIKA, but later withdrew this and admitted he had nothing to do with the Mt. Kenya organisation.

In December, 1953, subject called a meeting because he was angry because many gangs were going into the Reserves collecting money and seeking all the comforts of home. This meeting was duly held in the Tetu Forest and many leaders attended. At this meeting there was the first serious rift amongst the leaders and subject was accused of not liking fighting. Many leaders left this meeting and arranged a private meeting, without subject, for February, 1954, at KIMBO's camp.

Subject, MAGU (NDERITO THUITA) and VINDO made their way to KIMBO's camp on 8th February, 1954, arriving in the evening at the camp which was in the Aberdares off SQUAIRS. Other leaders there included KIMBO, ABDULLA, KAHIUTINA, MAGU, KARARI NJAMA, OHUMALI and about 50 minor leaders. Before the meeting got under way a quarrel broke out between subject and KIMBO as to whom was to attend. The meeting took place on 11th February, and the first serious attempt to dispose of subject was made by KIBUKU s/o THEURI who was a well known Tetu citizen before the Emergency, being in the movement to stop cattle vaccination by the Veterinary Department in 1946, and a bitter enemy of Chief MUHOYA. At this meeting KIBUKU took the chair and made an attack on subject for writing to the Governor and justified collecting money, saying it was needed to help the children of fallen warriors. Subject got up and replied that the letter to the Governor 'shauri' {issue/problem} was all over and it was too late to alter it and told the meeting to elect a new Chairman in subject's place. The whole day was spent quarrelling without any decision being made.

In the evening, after the meeting had broken up, subject states that he heard of a plot by KIMBO, KAHIUTINA and KIBUKU to kill him. He called MAGU and VINDO to his aid and spent the night in MAGU's tent. Going to the meeting place the next day he met with KIMBO and KAHIUTINA and they waited for the leaders to arrive. They received a message that ABDULLA, VINDO and MAGU had called a separate meeting and about 11 a.m. all the other leaders came to the place where subject was waiting. GATETHU was the spokesman and said that the leaders had rejected the leadership of KIBUKU but that the organisation was to be run by a committee to be elected then. Subject was elected Chairman, KARARI – Secretary and MAGU – Treasurer. It was also agreed to elect Fort Hall and Kiambu members at a later date and that the committee would be known as the Kenya Parliament.

Subject was still in KIMBO's camp on the 14th February, after the meeting was over and they had another bitter quarrel and

KIMBO told subject to get out before he was killed. On 15th, subject left he camp and went to WAMBARARIA's camp in Tetu. On the 17th February, 1954, subject's mistress, GARAI, warned him of an attempt to poison him and for safety's sake he had GARAI taken back to her people in the Reserve. Subject flatly refused to tell me his mistress's real name or village.

On 18th February, 1954, subject states that he received a letter from 'General' CHINA who had been captured on Mt. Kenya. The letter asked subject to appoint representatives for talks with the Government.[61] Subject called a meeting of the Kenya Parliament for March, 1954, but 2 negotiators were appointed by other leaders without subject's knowledge or approval. The Kenya Parliament meeting lasted from 3-18 March, 1954, and the chief bone of contention was whether subject or KARARI NJAMA were to be the representative. The meeting broke up because according to subject, KIMBO and others deliberately wrecked the meeting by objecting to every suggestion and there was no final decision as to whom were to go.

Subject remained with his party until Mid-May, 1954, when he had a visit from Kiambu gang leaders who were led by KIMANI KAHARA. These people stayed until August, 1954, GIKONYU and KANINGA {*sic*} WACHANGA took subject to Chinga Location forest and subject again wrote to the Government to re-open negotiations. (Note:- this letter in fact consisted chiefly of an attack on the Government for dealing with what KIMATHI described as underlings) Also at this time the Kenya Rekalo Memorial Hall and the Kenya Bright Young Stars Memorial Hall, were built and opened.[62]

In September, 1954, subject was bombed and moved back to Nyeri and was again visited by Kiambu gang leaders, including KIMANI KIHARA and MUTARI KALEWA with 18 others. MUTURI had come from MASAI and had been ent {sic} by a

---

61. For the letter from General China to Kimathi, see Maina wa Kinyatta, *Kenya's Freedom Struggle,* 66–67.

62. In the forest, Kimathi called for the construction of memorial halls to house important Mau Mau archives and commemorate the names of fallen fighters. See Barnett and Njama, *Mau Mau from Within,* 326; Peterson, "Writing in Revolution," 89–90.

man called OLE KASIO and MUTURI presented subject with a ceremonial sword. Subject gave MUTURI a letter for OLE KASIO but heard nothing more from him.

In October, 1954, KARIE and NJANGA KARETHI came from Kiambu on a visit and stated that they wanted to join subject's organisation. Subject formed the KENYA INORO Army of Kiambu and put KARIE in charge and NJANGA as Q.M. Both were killed on the way back to Kiambu and MBORO MUKONDO became commander of the KENYA INORO.

At this time STANLEY MATHENGE was with MBARIA KANIU and they were in touch with subject by letter as they were operating in the Rift.

In November, 1954, subject joined up with NYAGA and in December with STANLEY KIAMA, MBARIA KANIU, STANLEY MATHENGE and leaders from Kiambu and a meeting took place on 23rd December, 1954, and the delegates to the Kenya Parliament were increased to include Kiambu people. Another letter to the Government had been written in October, 1954.

In January, 1955, subject in company with STANLEY KIAMA and STANLEY MATHENGE went to Fort Hall and stayed at IHURA's camp waiting for MBARIA KANIU but had to return to Nyeri because of Security Force patrols. On returning to Nyeri, subject built the THERIMI DIVISION Memorial Hall and other Memorial Halls. In February, 1955, subject returned to Fort Hall to meet MACHARIA KIMENIA. Subject did not meet MACHARIA as he was in KIAMBU and he found out that IHURA had been killed. Returning to Nyeri in March 55, subject opened the Kenya Parliament Building in company with STANLEY MATHENGE who went to MAHIGA when the ceremony was over.

In March 1955 subject had a letter from KAHINGA WACHANGA to the effect that he (KAHINGA-) had met the Government representatives on surrender talks and wanted to see subject about it. Subject states that he searched for KAHINGA without success. The same month subject heard sky shout aircraft calling for him, STANLEY MATHENGE and MBARIA KANIU to attend a meeting at CHINGA to discuss surrender. Subject met STANLEY MATHENGE in the GURA Valley and in the

Othaya Forest met KARARI NJAMA, GITONGA, GIKONYU and others. Subject then sent a message to KAHINGA's camp and KAMWAMBA and WARATHITA came from KAHINGA's camp with the news that KAHINGA had gone to Nairobi with Supol Henderson. The fact that he was not the leading figure in the surrender talks made subject angry and he returned to Nyeri. On the 26th March, subject called for a Kenya Parliament meeting, but he got a letter from STANLEY MATHENGE, saying that his (S.M.s) group was going to deal with the Govt. direct without consulting the Kenya Parliament.

Subject states that he was very angry at this and ordered the arrest of MATHENGE. MATHENGE and about thirty others were arrested by people under the command of MACHARIA KIMENIA and they were brought to the Othaya Forest. KAHUIITINA was also arrested. On the night of the first of April 55, they escaped, and subject states that he has not seen Stanley Mathenge since then, although he has had a letter from him asking for co-operation.

Subject then went to GIKONYU's camp and returned to Tetu with MACHARIA KIMENIA. He then went on a journey of no particular point to Fort Hall, Kiambu and the Kinangop leaving MACHARIA KIMENIA there returning to Nyeri early June 55. In his absence quite a lot had happened as KAHINGA WACHANGA, KARARI NYAMA, KINARU GATHUNDI and GATANGA GACHIGWA had surrendered, MAKANYANGA had been killed and NDUNGU KIMORE, MATHENGE WACHIRIA and Gichuki Mugo had been captured.

Subject then went to NYAGA's camp and on the 22nd June 1955 went to ABDULLA's camp. On the 27th June, NYAGA was captured. VINDO went to Thomson's Falls in July and was killed there. Also in July NDERITO THUITA, subject's most senior General next to MACHARIA and MBARIA, was killed in the Nyeri settled area. In November 1955, MACHARIA KIMENIA, NJUGUNA KIRUNYU and KABANGA GATHATWA were killed in Rift and subject's organisation fell apart.

Subject stayed with Abdulla during this time, and little happened until March 1956, when the party was contacted by a pseudo gang, and Abdulla was killed. Subject says that he was only two yards from Abdulla when Abdulla fell down, and this was his narrowest escape to date. Subject escaped with 8 men and his concubine, and they were contacted again by a pseudo gang on the 8th April 1956 without loss.

Subject's organisation at this time consisted of about 40 people split up into groups, the biggest group being under JERIKO, who was feeding him.

In June 1956 subject went to the Moorlands to look for one of his splinter groups headed by WAITWA THEURI and found WAITWA with 5 men. WAMUTHANDI was also with subject. In early July 1956 subject was again contacted by a pseudo team, and WAITWA THEURI was captured, subject escaping with 10. Later in the month subject met up with some 5 stragglers from MBARIA's gang and they took him to the camp of KIMANI KIMARUA and CHEGE KAROBIA. Subject did not get a very enthusiastic reception, but stayed with this gang of 21 until 24th July. CHEGE KABORIA gave him a man (7 K.A.R.) and subject departed for Tetu with 4 men and a woman.

Subject looked for the people he had left behind including KARAU and JERIKO, but they had already been picked up and they did nothing until contacted again on 16th October when WANJIRU, the woman was captured, and the group scattered leaving subject on his own. On the 17th of October subject came into the Reserve and stole maize. He stayed in the forest alone on 18th and 19th Oct. and on the 20th went back into the Reserve at night, to steal food and was on his way back into the Forest when he was shot in the leg by a T.P. ambush and captured.

PASSIVE WING[63]

Subject was very evasive about passive contacts, and it was only under pressure that he admitted that MOFFAT MWAI a local Tetu bad hat was his personal courier. He left other passive contacts to his juniors and flatly denied any direct link with any passive committee.

POLICY AND INTENTIONS

Subject stated that he knew right away from the very start that the Mau Mau could not win, and he was always trying to negotiate

---

63. For further information on the "passive wing," see the Introduction to this volume.

surrender terms. His efforts at negotiation consisted of writing letters to the Governor which contained no practical suggestion for a meeting at all.

Subject would have liked to have been the big shot of surrender negotiations, but made no effort to join the talks once men, whom he considered his junior, had made contact with Special Branch Officers. He has told the story of the surrender talks very much from his own point of view, and never had any intention of surrendering. His juniors realized this and calmly ignored him to his fury.

REASONS FOR FAILURE OF KENYA PARLIAMENT

KIMATHI chiefly blames the failure of the Kenya Parliament to become a fully effective controlling body on the clash of personalities, and his writing of letters to the Government. He says that KIMBO and KAHUIITINA deliberately sabotaged any meetings that they attended, and prevented working decisions from being reached, whilst other influential leaders such as NDUNGU GICHERU ignored requests to attend. Subject also stated many times that the Policy line that he laid down over the Reserves, brought him into sharp conflict with other leaders. KIMATHI forbade the residence in Reserves of gangs, and also forbade the collection of money and the prostitution of young girls, on the grounds that if patrols caught gangsters in huts in villages, many people who were not of the forest would be killed. As subject had all the comforts of home in the forest, at least in the early days, and many of his minions were not so well placed, this argument rather fell on deaf ears.

At times, subject's vicious temper became apparent under interrogation, and this, and this coupled with his domineering personality was obviously another factor, which led to his many quarrels with other gang leaders.

SPHERE OF INFLUENCE

Subject stated that he considered he was at the height of his power around December 1953, when he had some 5000 people under his command. He stated that whichever area in the Aberdares he was in at that time, he was accepted as a leader. He admitted that he had no control whatsoever over Mt Kenya, as he had fallen out with KALEBA on the only occasion that they met, over gangs living in the Reserves, and he had little influence in KIAMBU, although the KIAMBU gangs regarded him as senior leader and "prime minister". His authority in Rift was delegated to MACHARIA and MBARIA two of his most loyal Generals, although they seem to have ignored his frantic appeals for meetings later on in the Emergency.

GRADING OF INTERROGATION

Subject's record of his life in the forest ties up very well with his diaries,[64] and apart from his memory slips is comparatively accurate. He denies that he planned any actual raids, and makes no mention of some of his less endearing methods of keeping discipline in his own gang. Subject flatly refused to incriminate anybody in the Reserve who helped him in the very early days, and according to him behaved like an angel the whole time he was in the forest, never killing anybody.

Subject is a man of tremendous personality, with a well developed sense of humour, and punctuated his obvious lies with a large grin. The main body of the interrogation, his life in the forest, is graded B.2., but the rest is how Kimathi would like things to have happened, rather than how they did happen.

A.D. Dunn (Interrogator)
for SUPOL, SPECIAL BRANCH, NYERI

64. If these diaries survived, their current location remains unknown.

SELECT LETTERS AND EXHIBITS FROM THE TRIAL

Document 6

Exhibit No. 20—Signed Arrest Statement of the Accused

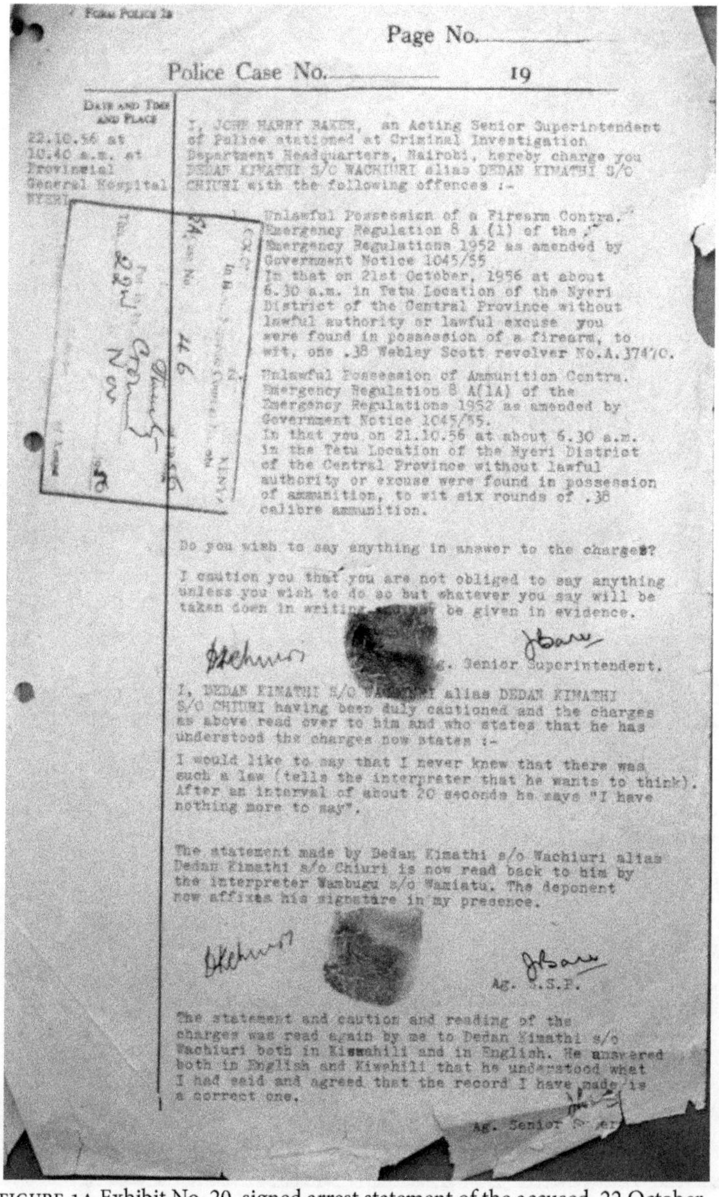

Form Police 13

Page No.

Police Case No. 19

Date and Time and Place	
22.10.56 at 10.40 a.m. at Provincial General Hospital NYERI.	I, JOHN HARRY BAKER, an Acting Senior Superintendent of Police stationed at Criminal Investigation Department Headquarters, Nairobi, hereby charge you DEDAN KIMATHI S/O WACHIURI alias DEDAN KIMATHI S/O CHIURI with the following offences :-

1\. Unlawful Possession of a Firearm Contra. Emergency Regulation 8 A (1) of the Emergency Regulations 1952 as amended by Government Notice 1045/55
In that on 21st October, 1956 at about 6.30 a.m. in Tetu Location of the Nyeri District of the Central Province without lawful authority or lawful excuse you were found in possession of a firearm, to wit, one .38 Webley Scott revolver No.A.3747C.

2\. Unlawful Possession of Ammunition Contra. Emergency Regulation 8 A(1A) of the Emergency Regulations 1952 as amended by Government Notice 1045/55.
In that you on 21.10.56 at about 6.30 a.m. in the Tetu Location of the Nyeri District of the Central Province without lawful authority or excuse were found in possession of ammunition, to wit six rounds of .38 calibre ammunition.

Do you wish to say anything in answer to the charges?

I caution you that you are not obliged to say anything unless you wish to do so but whatever you say will be taken down in writi[illegible] be given in evidence.

[illegible] Senior Superintendent.

I, DEDAN KIMATHI S/O WA[illegible] alias DEDAN KIMATHI S/O CHIURI having been duly cautioned and the charges as above read over to him and who states that he has understood the charges now states :-

I would like to say that I never knew that there was such a law (tells the interpreter that he wants to think). After an interval of about 20 seconds he says "I have nothing more to say".

The statement made by Dedan Kimathi s/o Wachiuri alias Dedan Kimathi s/o Chiuri is now read back to him by the interpreter Wambugu s/o Wamiatu. The deponent now affixes his signature in my presence.

Ag. S.S.P.

The statement and caution and reading of the charges was read again by me to Dedan Kimathi s/o Wachiuri both in Kiswahili and in English. He answered both in English and Kiswahili that he understood what I had said and agreed that the record I have made is a correct one.

Ag. Senior S[illegible]

FIGURE 1A Exhibit No. 20, signed arrest statement of the accused, 22 October 1956, p. 1. Supreme Court of Kenya, Kimathi File.

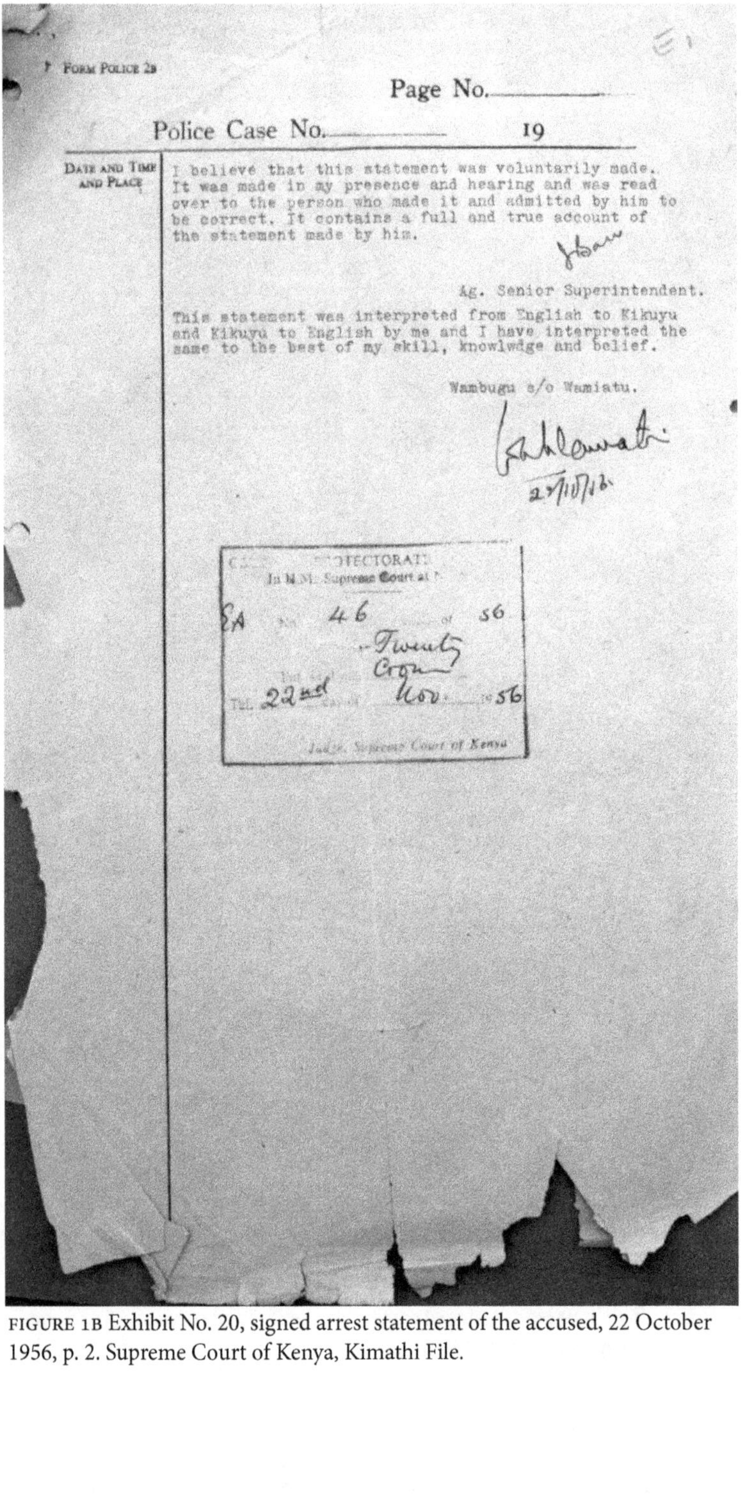
FORM POLICE 28

Page No.

Police Case No. 19

DATE AND TIME AND PLACE

I believe that this statement was voluntarily made. It was made in my presence and hearing and was read over to the person who made it and admitted by him to be correct. It contains a full and true account of the statement made by him.

Ag. Senior Superintendent.

This statement was interpreted from English to Kikuyu and Kikuyu to English by me and I have interpreted the same to the best of my skill, knowlwdge and belief.

Wambugu s/o Wamiatu.

In H.M. Supreme Court at

EA 46 of 56

Twenty Crown

22nd Nov. 56

Judge, Supreme Court of Kenya

FIGURE 1B Exhibit No. 20, signed arrest statement of the accused, 22 October 1956, p. 2. Supreme Court of Kenya, Kimathi File.

Document 7

Exhibit No. 22—Original Gikuyu Version of Kimathi Letter, 20 October 1954[65]

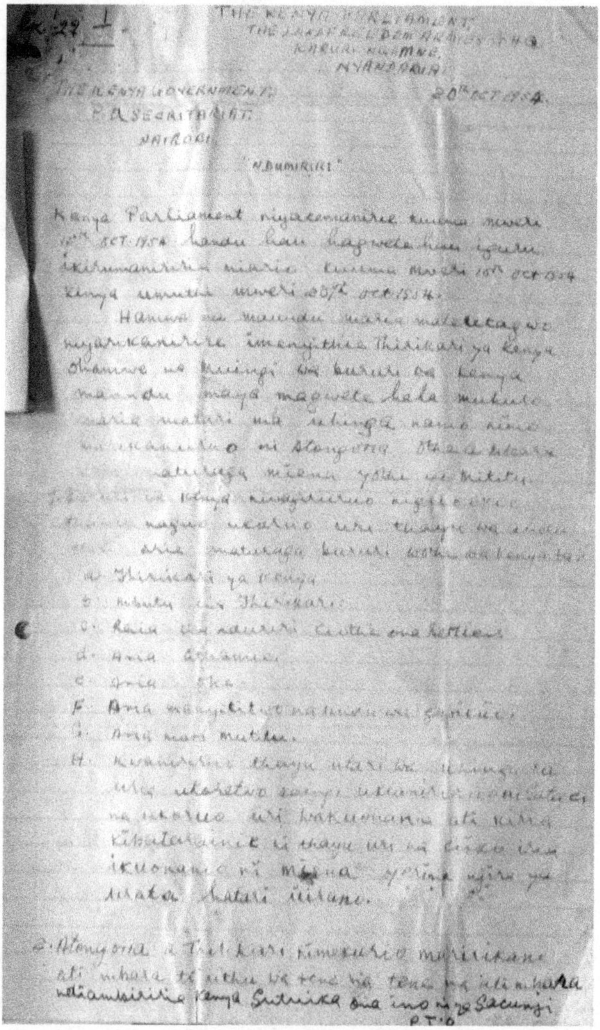
THE KENYA PARLIAMENT,

NYANDARUA.

THE KENYA GOVERNMENT,

20th OCT 1954.

NAIROBI

"NDUMIRIRI"

FIGURE 2A Exhibit No. 22, original Gikuyu version of Kimathi letter, 20 October 1954, p. 1. Supreme Court of Kenya, Kimathi File.

---

65. Exhibit No. 22, original Gikuyu version of Kimathi letter, 20 October 1954, Criminal Case No. 46 of 1956, Dedan Kimathi v. Regina, Her Majesty's Supreme Court of Kenya at Nyeri, Kimathi File, Archives of the Supreme Court of Kenya.

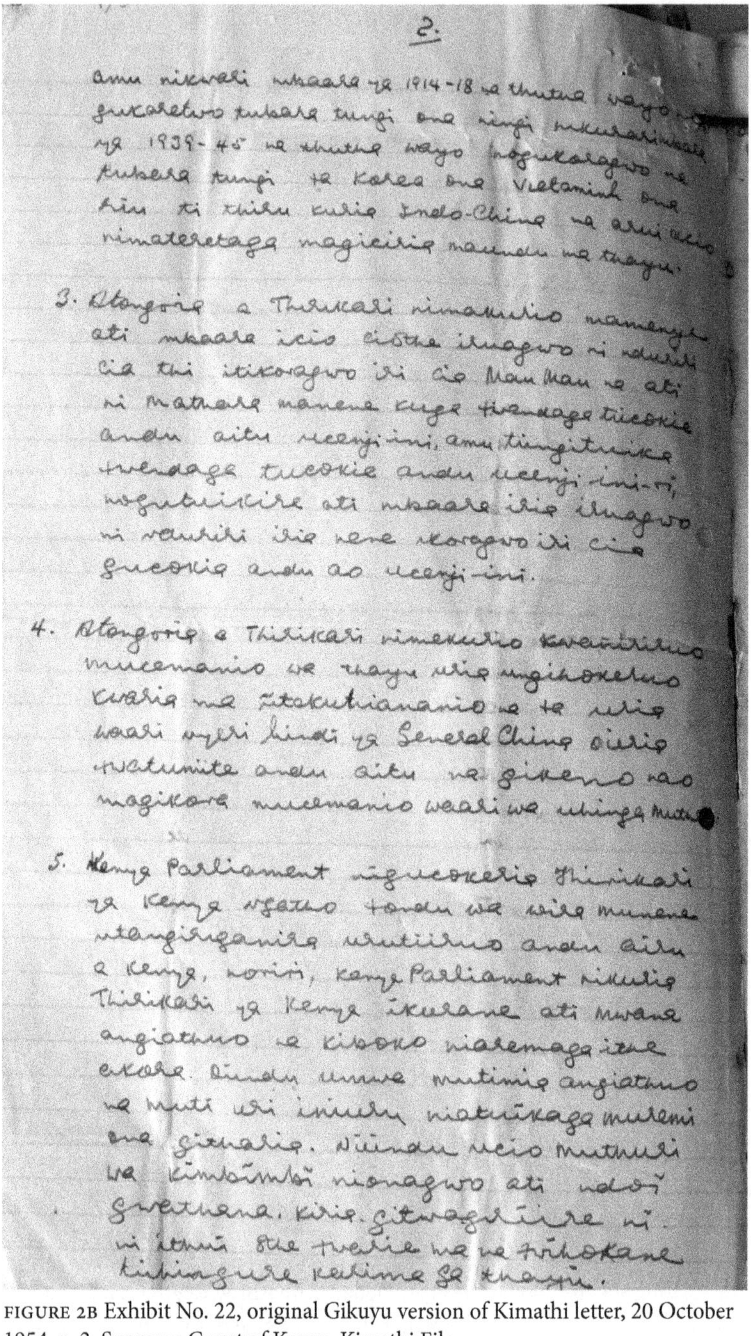

2.

amu nikwari mbaara ya 1914-18 na thutha wayo nĩ gũkaretwo tũbara tũingĩ ona ĩngĩ nĩkũrarĩirwo ya 1939-45 na thutha wayo nĩ gũkaragwo na tũbara tũingĩ ta Korea ona Vietaminh ona rĩu ti thiru kuria Indo-China na arũi acio nimaterететaga magiciria maundu ma thayu.

3. Atongoria a Thirikari nimaũkĩrio mamenye ati mbaara icio ciothe ĩrũagwo nĩ ndũriri cia thĩ itikoragwo iri cia Mau Mau na ati nĩ mathare manene kuga twendaga tũcokie andu aitũ ũceenji-inĩ, amu tũingĩtũrĩka twendaga tũcokie andu ũceenji-inĩ-rĩ, nĩ gũtũĩkĩire ati mbaara ĩria ĩrũagwo nĩ ndũriri ĩria nene ikoragwo iri cia gũcokia andu ao ũceenji-inĩ.

4. Atongoria a Thirikari nimekũrio kwaĩtĩrĩrio mũcemanio wa thayu ũria ũngĩhoteka kwaria na ũtakũthianio na ta ũria waarĩ ngerĩ hindi ya General China ũiria twatũmite andu aitũ na gĩkeno rao magĩkora mũcemanio waarĩ wa ũhinga mũtũ.

5. Kenya Parliament nĩgũcokeria Thirikari ya Kenya ngatho tondu wa wira mũnene ũtangĩrĩganĩra ũrũtĩĩrio andu aitũ a Kenya, norĩrĩ, Kenya Parliament nĩkũria Thirikari ya Kenya ĩkũrane ati mwana angĩathwo na kĩboko niaremagaa itũe akora. Ũndũ ũmwe mũtimia angĩathwo na mũti ũri ĩnũnu niatũũkaga mũlemi ona gĩtharia. Nĩ ũndũ ũcio mũthuri wa Kĩmũũmũ nionagwo ati ndoĩ gwathana. Kĩria gĩtwagĩrĩire nĩ nĩ ithuĩ othe twĩrie wa na tũhokane kĩhingũre kahima ka thayũ.

FIGURE 2B Exhibit No. 22, original Gikuyu version of Kimathi letter, 20 October 1954, p. 2. Supreme Court of Kenya, Kimathi File.

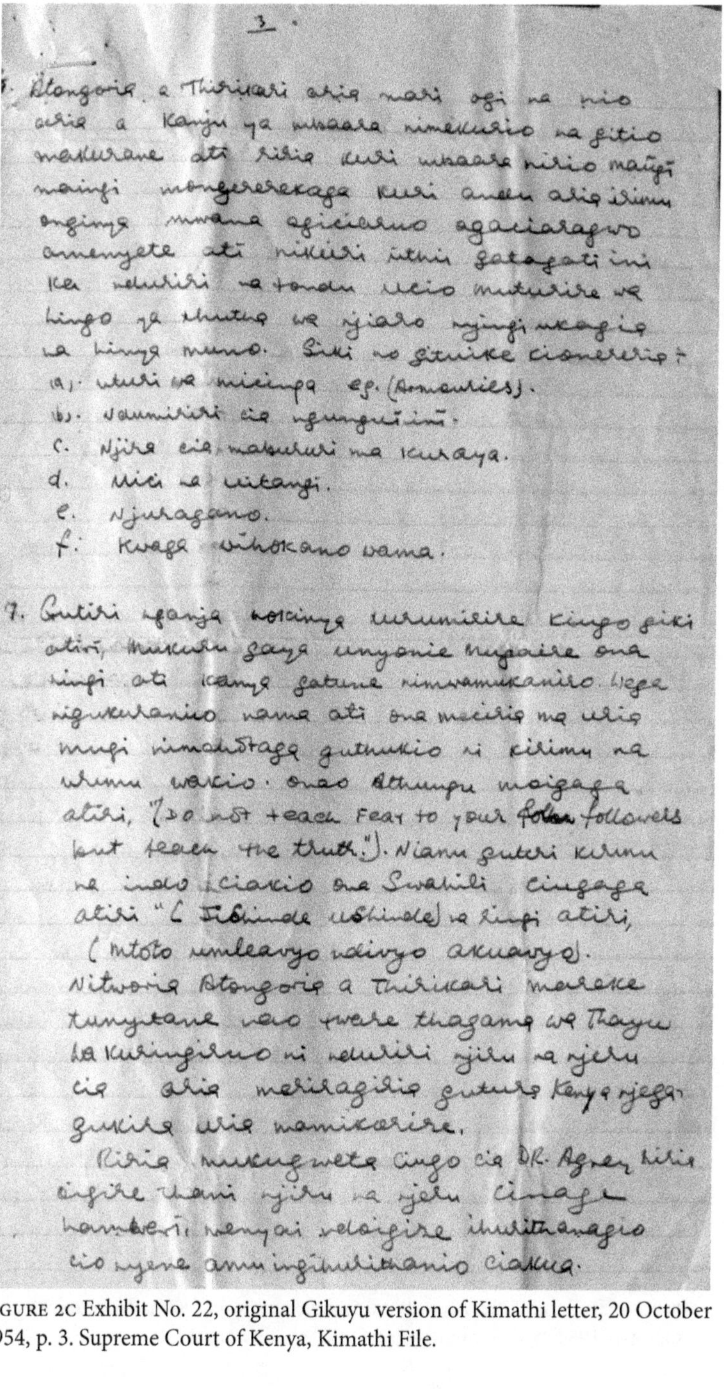

3.

6. Atongoria a Thirikari aria mari ogi na nio aria a Kanju ya mbaara nimekuririo na gitio makurane ati riria kuri mbaara ririo maũgĩ maingi mongererekaga kuri andu aria irimu ongima mwana agiciarwo agaciaragwo amenyete ati nikuri ũthiu gatagati ini ka ndurĩri na tondu ucio muturire wa kingo ya thutha wa njiaro nyingi ukagia na kinya muno. Ciiki no gitũike cionererio:-
(a). uturi wa micinga eg. (Armouries).
(b). Ndumiriri cia ngunguĩ inĩ.
c. Njira cia mabururi na kuraya.
d. Mici na mitangi.
e. Njuragano.
f. Kwaga wĩhokano wama.

7. Gutiri ngania nokinya nurumiriire kingo giki atiri, Mukuru gaya unyonie mugaire ona ringi ati kanya gatune nimwamukaniiro. Wega nigukuranio wama ati ona meciria ma uria mingi nimahutaga guthukio ni kirimu na urimu wakio. Onao Athungu moigaga atiri, ("Do not teach fear to your ~~follow~~ followers but teach the truth."). Niamu gutiri kirimu na indo iciakio ona Swahili cingaga atiri "(Ushinde ushinde) na ringi atiri, (mtoto umleavyo ndivyo akuavyo).
Nitworia Atongoria a Thirikari mareke tunyitane nao tware thagama wa Thayu wa kuringirwo ni ndurĩri njiru na njeru cia aria merikagiria gutura Kenya njega gukira uria mamikoririre.
Riria mukungweta cingo cia DR. Agrey kiria ingiire thami njiru na njeru cimagia hamberi nenyai ndaigire ihuthithanagio cio nyene amu ingĩhuthithanio ciakua.

FIGURE 2C Exhibit No. 22, original Gikuyu version of Kimathi letter, 20 October 1954, p. 3. Supreme Court of Kenya, Kimathi File.

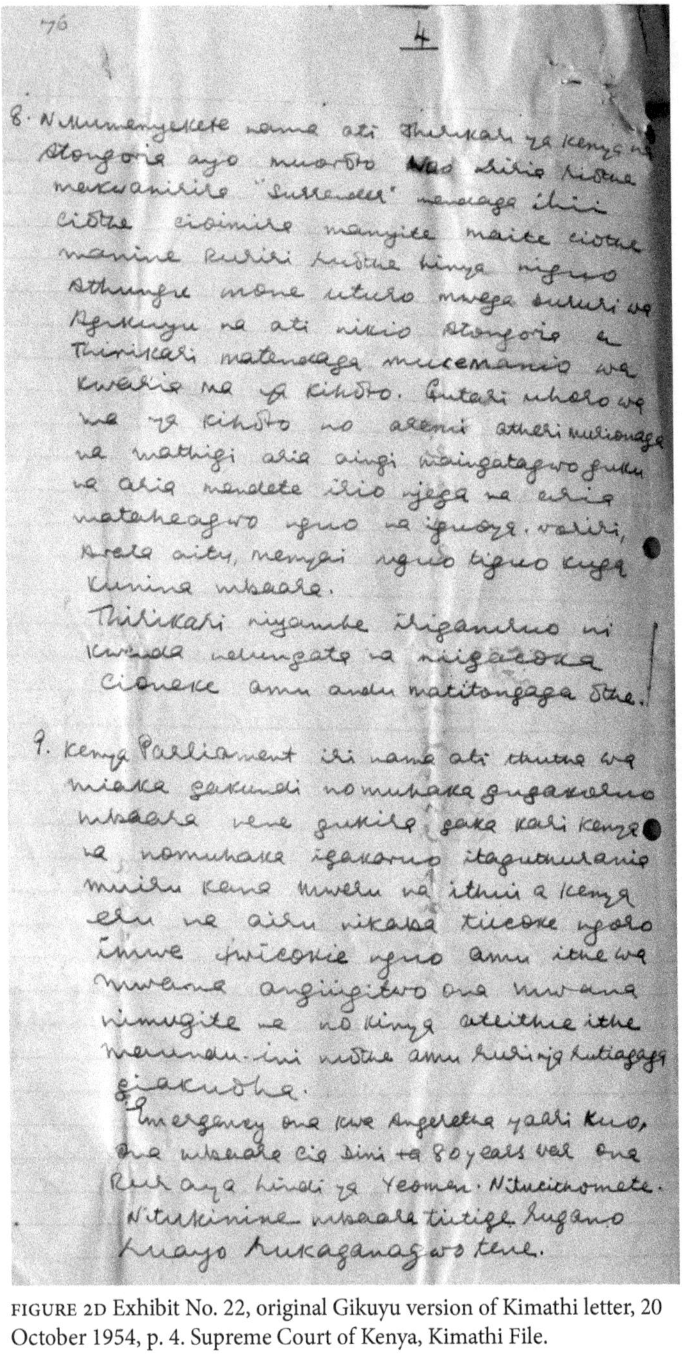

76

4

8. Nimumenyekete nama ati Thirikari ya Kenya na
Atongoria ayo muoroto wao airia aria
makwaniriire "Surrender" menaga ihii
ciothe cioimire mangika maitu ciothe
manine Rurira kuothe kinya nigwo
Athungu mone uturo mwega guthiri wa
Agikuyu na ati nikio Atongoria a
Thirikari matendaga muceman'io wa
kwaria na ya kihoto. Gutari uhoro wa
ma ya kihoto no aremi atheri mukionaga
na mathigi aria aingi maingatagwo guku
na aria mendete irio njega na aria
mataheagwo nguo na igwoya. Variri,
Arata aitu, menyai nguo tigwo kuga
kunina mbaara.
Thirikari niyambe iriganirwo ni
kwenda nduungata na niigacoka
Cioneke amu andu matitongaga otho.

9. Kenya Parliament iri nama ati thutha wa
miaka gakundi no muhaka gugakorwo
mbaara rene gukira gaka kari Kenya
na no muhaka igakorwo itaguthurania
muiru kana mweru na ithii a Kenya
eru na airu nikaba tucoke ngoro
Imwe twicokie nguo amu ithe wa
mwana angiiigitwo ona mwana
nimugite na no kinya ateithie ithe
memunda-ini uothe amu kuri nja kutiagaga
giakuoha.
Emergency ona kwa Angeretha yaari kuo,
ona mbaara cia Dini ta 80 years war ona
Ruraya hindi ya Yeoman. Nitucithomete.
Nitukinine mbaara tutige rugano
kuuo rukaganagwo tene.

FIGURE 2D Exhibit No. 22, original Gikuyu version of Kimathi letter, 20 October 1954, p. 4. Supreme Court of Kenya, Kimathi File.

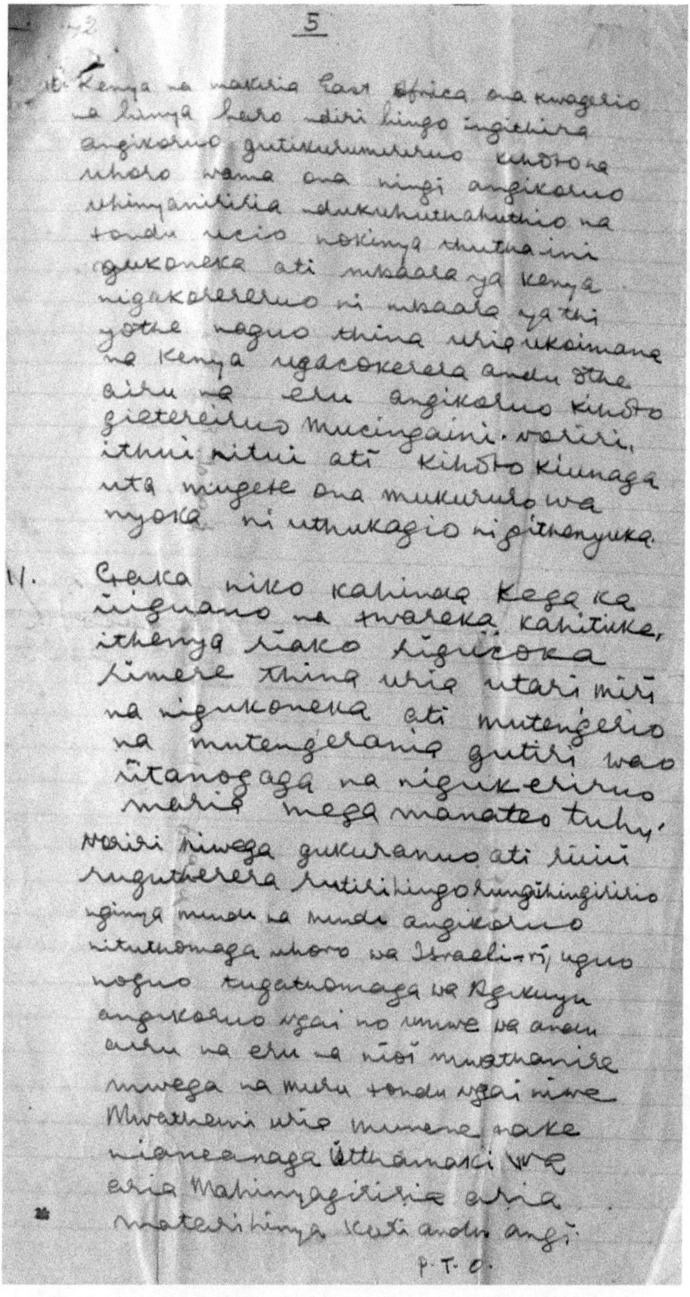

5

ati Kenya na makiria East Africa ona kwagerio
na hinya haro diri hingo ingithira
angikorwo gutikuhumbururwo kihoto na
uhoro wama ona ringi angikorwo
uhinyanirirria dukuhuthahuthio na
tondu ucio nokinya thutha ini
gukoneka ati mbaara ya Kenya
nigakorerereruo ni mbaara ya thi
yothe naguo thina uria ukoimana
na Kenya ugacokerera andu othe
airu na eru angikorwo kihoto
gieterirwo mucingaini. Nariri,
ithui nitui ati kihoto kiunaga
uta mugete ona mukururo wa
nyoka ni uthukagio nigithenyuka.

11. Gaaka niko kahinda kega ka
iiguano na twareka kahituke,
ithenya riako riguicoka
rimere thina uria utari miri
na nigukoneka ati mutengerio
na mutengerania gutiri wao
utanogaga na nigukeririruo
maria mega manateo tuhu,
Nariri niwega gukuranuo ati ruiui
ruguthererera rutiri hingo hungihingiririo
ugima mundu na mundu angikorwo
nitutuomaga uhoro wa Israeli-ri, uguo
noguo tugatuomaga wa Agikuyu
angikorwo ngai no umwe wa andu
airu na eru na nioi mwathanire
mwega na muru tondu ngai niwe
Mwathani uria munene nake
nianeanaga ithamaki wa
aria mahinyagirirria aria
materi hinya kati andu angi.

P.T.O.

FIGURE 2E Exhibit No. 22, original Gikuyu version of Kimathi letter, 20 October 1954, p. 5. Supreme Court of Kenya, Kimathi File.

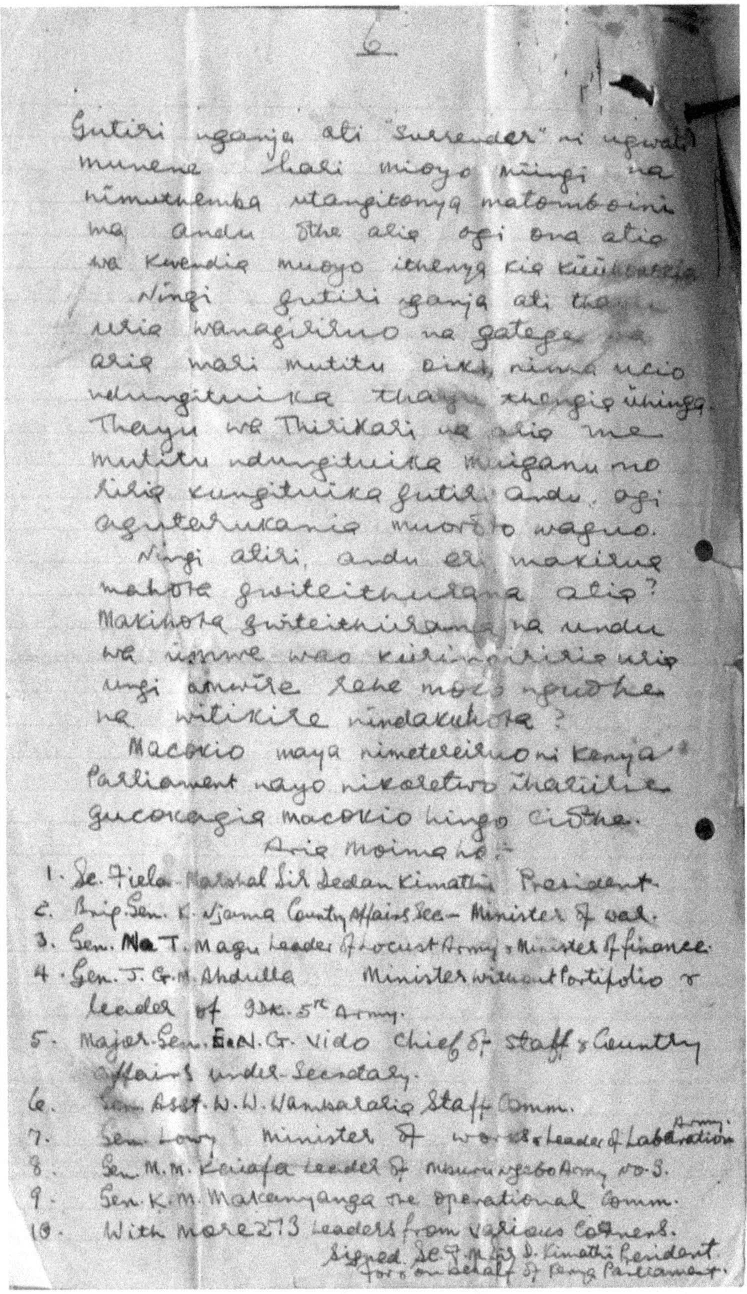

6

Gutiri ugania ati "surrender" ni ugwati
munene. Kahi mioyo ningi na
nimuthemba utangitonya matomboini
ma andu othe aria ogi ona aria
wa Kwendia muoyo ithenya kia kuuragwo.
Ningi gutiri ugania ati thayu
uria wanagiriruo na gatega kia
aria mari mutitu oiki, nimua ucio
ndungitunika thayu thengia uhinga.
Thayu wa Thirikari na aria me
mutitu ndungituika muiganu no
kiria kungituika gutiri andu ogi
agiutarukania muoroto waguo.
Ningi ariri, andu ari makirue
mahota gwiteithuranga atia?
Makihota gwiteithiranga na undu
wa iguma wao kuringiriria uria
ungi amwite kene moto nguthe
na witikire nindakuhota?
Macokio maya nimeteteiruo ni Kenya
Parliament nayo nikoletwo ihaitile
gucokagia macokio hingo ciothe.
Aria moimaho:-
1. Ge. Field-Marshal Sir Dedan Kimathi President.
2. Brig. Gen. K. Njama Country Affairs Sec— Minister of war.
3. Gen. ~~Ma~~ T. Magu Leader of Locust Army & Minister of finance.
4. Gen. J. G. M. Abdulla Minister without Portifolio & leader of GDK. 5th Army.
5. Major-Gen. ~~E~~. N. G. Vido Chief of staff & Country affairs under-Secretary.
6. Gen. Asst. W. W. Wambarario Staff Comm.
7. Gen. Lowy Minister of works & Leader of Labaration Army.
8. Gen. M. M. Kariafa Leader of Mburu Ngebo Army No. 8.
9. Gen. K. M. Makanyanga the Operational Comm.
10. With more 273 Leaders from various Corners.

Signed. Ge. F. M. Sir D. Kimathi President.
for & on behalf of Kenya Parliament.

FIGURE 2F Exhibit No. 22, original Gikuyu version of Kimathi letter, 20 October 1954, p. 6. Supreme Court of Kenya, Kimathi File.

Document 8

Exhibit No. 22A—Official English Translation of Kimathi Letter, 20 October 1954[66]

Annotations on translation provided by Derek Peterson and Joseph Kariuki Muriithi

EMERGENCY ASSIZE CRIMINAL CASE NO. 46 of 1956 Exhibit No. 22A

TOP SECRET

COPY OF LETTER ADDRESSED TO THE GOVERNMENT BY DEDAN KIMATHI[67]

The Kenya Parliament,
The Land Freedom Armies, G.H.Q.,
Karuri, Ngamne,
Nyandarua (Aberdares)

20th. October, 1954.

THE KENYA GOVERNMENT
P.O. SECRETARIAT,
NAIROBI.

MESSAGE

The Kenya parliament assembled on the 15th. OCTOBER, 1954 at the above named place and continued on with its discussions up to the 20th. OCTOBER, 1954.[68]

---

66. Exhibit No. 22A, English translation of Kimathi letter, Criminal Case No. 46 of 1956, Dedan Kimathi v. Regina, Her Majesty's Supreme Court of Kenya at Nyeri, Kimathi File, Archives of the Supreme Court of Kenya.

67. This document is a word-for-word copy of the English translation of the original Gikuyu-language letter, prepared by government translators and admitted as evidence during the trial of Dedan Kimathi. The identity of the translator is unknown, but clearly he works with the political categories of the colonial state. The translator is quick to render Gikuyu words in politically and legally actionable nomenclature: thus Kimathi's term "ĩhĩĩ," a word meaning "uncircumcised young men" (or "boys"), is rendered as "terrorists" in this translator's usage. The translation was made in haste by someone who was not looking for nuance. As a result there are numerous mistranslations and misreadings of the text. In these footnotes we elucidate alternate meanings and highlight vocabularic references that might have occurred to Dedan Kimathi, the author of the Gikuyu original.

68. The Gikuyu says "up to today, the 20th of October 1954."

Amongst other matters discussed it was agreed that the Kenya Government should be informed, as should all other people in Kenya,[69] of those matters which would have to be resolved. These matters were unanimously agreed upon by all the war leaders from all of the areas of the forest.

(1) Peace should be restored to the whole of Kenya which should become a country where all its inhabitants[70] are at peace, particularly the following -

A) The Kenya Government

B) The Government security forces

C) The civilian population,[71] including the settlers,

D) Those detained,

E) Those in prison,

F) Those otherwise in custody,

G) Those in the forests

H) A call for a sincere surrender instead of sly calls for surrender by sky-shouter. It must be a call for negotiations where both sides are sincere with the ultimate aim of friendship.[72]

(2) We would remind the leaders of government that war does not imply that there should always be enmity and hatred. War as such did not have its origin in Kenya. Kenya is but a small place. There was the 1914 – 18 war and then the 1939 – 45 war. Then we have other wars such as the Korean struggle with the classes such as Vietminh, even at this moment there is war in Indochina. Is it not fact that in all these recent wars those engaged have paused to negotiate for peace?

---

69. The Gikuyu is more definite about the identity of the people who are to be informed: it is the "muingi wa bururi wa Kenya," the "general public of the country of Kenya" who are to be engaged.

70. For the term translated as "inhabitants," the Gikuyu says "andu othe aria maturaga bururi wothe wa Kenya," "all people who stay in the whole of the country of Kenya."

71. The original gives the word "raia," a Swahili term meaning "the people." It goes on to define "the people" as being of "nduriri ciothe," of "all tribes."

72. The Gikuyu original has the word given as "friendship" as "urata hatari ũirano," "friendship without backbiting [or belittlement]."

(3) We would ask the government to recognize the fact that all those wars amongst the peoples of different places were not Mau Mau and it is wrong to say that we fight to revert ourselves to barbarism.[73] If this is what we fight for it is evident that other nations have fought for the same purpose.

(4) The leaders of government are asked to announce that they are ready to enter into peaceful negotiations aimed at complete peace. This should not culminate in the same end as that which applied to the surrender negotiations involving General China. In the latter case we sent our representatives and were enthusiastic in spirit but we found that everything was a pure trap.

(5) The Kenya Parliament appreciates the work done for the Africans by the Kenya Government and thanks them for it. That work will never be forgotten. But the Government is asked to remember that a child brought up by the cane[74] alone he goes astray and causes the father to leave him.[75] If a woman is controlled by a rope tied to her nose she becomes fearless and evil.[76] It is said that he who smoulders like a fire of wrath cannot ever rule. What we should do is to tell one another the frankest truth. Trust each other, and thereby open up the way to a life of peace.

(6) The wisest on the government side are surely those on the War Council. It is to those gentlemen that we respectfully ask whether they realize what damage can be done by the continuance of war. Even those who are dumb cannot fail to see that war breeds hatred and a baby born and reared in a time of battle cannot fail to see the hatred that exists between the races involved. It is likely that the attitude of future generations will

---

73. The original is "ucenji," a Gikuyu word borrowed from the Swahili "shenzi," an "uncultured person."

74. In the original the child is not "brought up by the cane," it is "ruled by the cane."

75. The translator renders this phrase wrongly. The original says that the child who is "ruled by the cane" deserts his father.

76. The sense of the original here is "In the same way, if a wife is ruled with a whip by the nose, she becomes defiant and even adulterous." The relevant Gikuyu word is "gĩtharia," an "adulterer" or a "seducer." In a different form, the same word stem also means to "pull down a house," or to "pull a fence to pieces."

be different and dangerous and as those generations who come after us will inevitably be more powerful,[77] We must watch for indications and their effects.[78] i.e.

a) The manufacture of arms,

b) Channels of underground activities

c) The course of events in other countries

d) Thieving and the lack of thriftiness.

e) Assassinations[79]

f) Lack of trust between races.[80]

(7) We must all be aware of the saying – "elder divide so that you may show me the way of dividing".[81] A gourd is made red by the way it is handled.[82] The thoughts of the wise may be foiled by the actions of the foolish. Englishmen say "Do not teach fear to your followers – teach them the truth".[83] But there is no fool with his own property. Swahilis say "Jishinde ushinde" (Conquer yourself to win) also they say "Mtoto

---

77. The government translator has misinterpreted this sentence. The original reads "Because of this, life for the future generations will be very difficult."

78. This last phrase—"we must watch for indicators and their effects"—is not in the Gikuyu original. The Gikuyu simply says "The following can be examples."

79. This term is better translated as "murders."

80. The original simply says "lack of genuine trust"; there is no reference to trust between races.

81. This proverb had appeared in a 1939 book of Gikuyu proverbs collected by Catholic researchers in the vicinity of Nyeri. See G. Barra, *1000 Kikuyu Proverbs* (Nyeri: Consolata Catholic Mission Printing School, 1939), number 496. As we point out in the footnotes below, many of the proverbs that Kimathi cites are identical to the Barra book in their phraseology and orthography. It is possible that he had a copy of the book at his elbow as he composed this missive. It is also possible that Kimathi was relying on oral memory, and that the overlap between Barra's proverbs and Kimathi's proverbs is the result of their shared relationship to Nyeri's oral culture.

82. This proverb—"Kanya gatune ni mwamukaniro"—is better translated as "a red snuff gourd is a symbol of mutual giving and acceptance." It had been published as number 243 in the 1939 collection mentioned above.

83. In the original the English proverb is given in English, and enclosed in parentheses.

umleavyo ndivyo akuavyo" (as you bring up a child, so he grows).[84]

We humbly ask the government to allow us to meet and speak the words of peace with them and prepare the way to a future of peace, understanding and prosperity for all those races who wish to live their lives in Kenya. When Dr. Aggrey said that a black record can sing as well as a white one he did not mean that if you knocked one against the other both would not break.

(8) It is now generally realized that whenever the government calls upon those in the forest to surrender[85] the motive behind such call is to enable the terrorists[86] to be picked up easily and then hanged, the aim being to diminish the tribe so that the European may have a nice place to live in in Kenya.[87] This may be the reason why the leaders of government do not want surrender negotiations which could lead to a satisfactory solution for all.[88] Only those who desert through weakness or those who want nice food will surrender by the green branch terms, and these persons include those who are cowardly or have no clothing.[89] But the majority know that such surrenders will never mean the end of the war.[90] Government should forget having servants though they will be got later as it is realized that all person cannot be rich.

---

84. In the Gikuyu original these last two proverbs are given in Swahili, with no translation. The parenthetical translations are an addition from the government's translator.

85. The word "surrender" is given in English in the Gikuyu original.

86. The Gikuyu original does not refer to "terrorists" but to "ihii," the "young (uncircumcised) men" of the forest.

87. In the Gikuyu original the Europeans plot to have a nice place to live in the "bururi wa Agikuyu," the "country of the Gikuyu people."

88. This sentence was added to the text by the government's translator. The original says "That is the reason leaders of government never want a meeting to discuss truth and justice."

89. The original is somewhat more elaborate in describing the desires of those who surrender: they are said to be "those who desire good food and to be given clothing and furs."

90. Here the writer of the Gikuyu original is addressing himself to "Our friends," saying "Our friends, know that this does not mean the ending of the war."

(9)The Kenya Parliament is of the opinion[91] that after a few years a great war may occur which will effect Kenya and in this war there will be no choice between black and white therefore we of Kenya – Blacks and Whites – should be of one heart and have a common desire to end this war and return our clothes.[92] If the father of the son is pressed, the son helps the father naturally. There have been emergencies before in British countries,[93] even wars over religion such as the 80 Years War and those of Europe during the era of the yeomans. We have learned.[94] We should finish this war so that it goes to posterity.[95]

(10) In Kenya and most of East Africa war is inevitable unless justice is done and use is made of the truth. If some races do not relax the pressure they have put on other races, there is every chance of great future troubles.[96] If there is no way of peacefully ending the present struggle in Kenya, is it not most likely that this struggle will continue up to the time of a world war. All races in Kenya are affected by the situation. Truth and fairness is not a product of the gun.[97] Justice breaks a tied bow[98] as a

91. In the original the Kenya Parliament is "certain," not "of the opinion."

92. The phraseology is unclear here, and it is possible that the writer is in fact calling for the return of clothing. Read in this way, the phrase would say "And us in Kenya, white or black, it is better to be in a common accord, we put back the clothes, for if the father is captured the son will free him, and he will help the father in all matters." But it seems unlikely that clothing would have been so much on Dedan Kimathi's mind. It is likely that instead of "twĩcokie nguo" (we put back the clothes) Kimathi meant to write "twĩcokie ngoro" (we mutually assist ourselves).

93. The original says "There has been an Emergency even in Britain." The word "Emergency" is given in English.

94. The Gikuyu verb means "We have read about these things."

95. In the original this sentence says "Let us therefore end this war and leave a story that will be told for a long time to come."

96. This sentence is better translated as "If exploitation will not be stopped, it can be foreseen that another world war will have to find the Kenyan war still going on."

97. The government translator has modified this sentence and the one immediately preceding it. A better translation is ". . . and the problems that will come from Kenya will affect both black and white people if justice is expected to come from the gun."

98. This proverb is given in a slightly different form in Barra's 1939 collection (mentioned above). In Barra the proverb is "kihooto kigeturaga uta mugete," "The convincing argument relaxes the bent bow."

snake's line is severed by anything which intersects it.[99]

(11) This is the time for agreement.[100] If we let this time pass, in the place of peace and understanding there shall develop greater trouble which shall have endless roots.[101] Let us remember that he who chases tires equally as much as he who is chased.[102] We may well regret the opportunity of this time. It is good to know that a running river cannot be permanently checked. In learning the history of the Israelites we also learned the history of the Kikuyu.[103] As there is but one God for all, there is but one just form of government and that form is known to God. He (God) always gives away the kingdom of the one who seeks to suppress.

(12) Surrender is a great danger to life but the present offer cannot be accepted by those who are wise.[104] In it there is the threat

---

99. This proverb is given, in a slightly altered form, in Stanley Kiama Gathigira's *Ng'ano na thimo cia uGikuyu,* which was published in Nairobi by Eagle Press in 1950. The manuscript had been completed as early as 1938, and it is possible that Kimathi would have read it during the time he spent in Tumutumu's school system.

100. This sentence is better rendered as "This is the time for reconciliation." The verb is "ũiguano," meaning "mutual hearing." It is the same term that translators of the New Testament had used when referring to Christ, the "reconciler" between the old covenant and the new.

101. Kimathi is referring to the proverb "thĩna ndũri mĩri." The thĩna is a leafless plant that grows on trees and saps their energy. The proverb says that the thĩna plant has no roots. Like all troubles, plagues and maladies, it will pass quickly. The proverb was printed as number 838 in the 1939 collection mentioned above.

102. Here Kimathi refers to another proverb: "mũteng'erania na mũteng'erio gũtiri ũtanogaga," "both he that chases and he that is chased become tired." The proverb was printed as number 557 in the 1939 collection.

103. The verb used in the original is "–thoma," "to read." The phrase is better translated as "In reading the history of the Israelites we also read the history of the Kikuyu."

104. There is no number 12 in the Gikuyu original. This paragraph is a continuation of paragraph 11. The translator has garbled the first sentence in this paragraph: it is better rendered as "There is no doubt that surrender is a great danger to the existence of many, and is something that cannot get into the mind of all those intelligent people at all. It is better to sell a soul instead of having it surrender."

of losing rather than saving ones life. Know definitely that the peace offered by the sky-shouter is not the offer of fairness but instead a cunning device. Peace between government and those in the forests is insufficient unless there is a judgement {sic} on the points. How can two fighting bodies stop and judge the points by themselves? Can anything be solved by the one saying to the other – bring forth your hand, admit defeat and go to prison, and at the same time expect agreement. The reply to this letter is awaited by the Kenya Parliament. It is always ready to answer any questions raised by the Kenya Government. Those who were present were:-

FIELD MARSHALL {sic} SIR DEDAN KIMATHI	- PRESIDENT
BRIGADIER GENERAL K.NJAMA	- Country Affairs Secretary, Minister of War.
GENERAL N.T. MAGU	Leader of Locust Army and Minister of Finance.
GENERAL J.G.M. ABDULLA	Minister without portfolio Leader of I.D.K. 5th Army.
MAJOR GENERAL ENG. VIDO	Chief of Staff Country Affairs Under Secretary
GENERAL ASSISTANT W.W. WAMBARARIA	Staff Commander
GENERAL LOWI	Minister of Works and Leader of Liberation Army.
GENERAL M.M. KAIAFA	Leader of Mburu Ngebo Army No.3.
GENERAL K.M. MAKANYANGA	Operational Cmdr.

More than 273 leaders from various corners.
Signed

FIELD MARSHAL SIR D. KIMATHI Pres.
for and on behalf of the Kenya Parliament.

Document 9

Exhibit No. 23—Kimathi Letter, 30 March 1954[105]

<u>EMERGENCY ASSIZE CASE NO. 46 of 1956</u> <u>Exhibit No. 23</u>

[Stamped Land Freedom Army, Marshal D. Kimathi]

[Stamped: Attorney General Chambers 30 MAR 1954]

<u>MY ECHO WILL SOUND PEACE.</u>

Sir,

Kindly please forward this document to your Kenya Government and to the Government Counsels. My first word is, let the Kenya Government not behave as childishly through Mr. Lytellon {sic} and Mr. Blundell[106] who definitely are rueing the British reign.

Any Governmental official or a Member of whatever sort may not suggest an ever enmity or hopelessly think that there is an end of Mau Mau in East Africa and chiefly Africa as a whole. The war ministers you suggest to set up for Kenya will shortly be regarded as tower of Babel and will cause another new Emergency to break out. Let us dress the paining part of the body and the patient will soon recover. Who is not Mau Mau and who is Mau Mau among black and white in Kenya today? How far wide has Mau Mau spread daily while the Government watches behind instead of ahead? You better trust in me a hundred times more than your present home-guards who have no trust in your struggling Government. Once I shout peace, there is never a war in Kenya.

But, my dear, how can a rat come out of the pit while the cat watches to catch it?

---

105. Exhibit No. 23, Criminal Case No. 46 of 1956, Dedan Kimathi v. Regina, Her Majesty's Supreme Court of Kenya at Nyeri, Kimathi File, Archives of the Supreme Court of Kenya.

106. Oliver Lyttelton, Secretary of State for the Colonies, 1951–54. Michael Blundell, Kenyan farmer and politician—Legislative Council Member (1948–63) and Minister on the Emergency War Committee (1954–55).

Regard us as humanly and the whole will get settled within a week. Refuse us and the world will turn against you soon. I am a better citizen, seeking peace for Kenya but if it be that the Kenya Government is just a dry weather that nothing of so called peace will peacefully germinate I will leave such a desert to be manured by one of the big four or three with its auxiliaries whenever desired.

Surely I pity the British Empire, so strong, so rich, so clever, so wise and well unified whilst being led astray by beast like leaders who are surely an anthrax to both cow and the calf. British law became temporary, no Christianity but greediness. See now, this is Kenya, Uganda, Tanganyika, Rhodesial {sic}, Bechuanaland, Sudan, Nagiria {sic}, Egypt, British Guiana, Jamaica, Korea, Spain, Tunisia, Moroco {sic}, Indo-China and Indonesia and the rest weak nations who you laugh at. What are they sounding? Do not you pity the British Isle in time of atomic? I prophesy that so the African continent is known as dark continent the first, British Isle will be the last dark island however strong you are. Because you never pity even a widow nor even a child who God himself has created.

Your Great City is fallen down. Your trade communications are cut up. Your Empire is sold to another nation, your wealth is deprived. Woe, the Great Britain where world rulers rejoice. Woe, the British Empire who felt mercy for my Africa. Will the British rulers here my word and receive my saying or will they say, bloody Mau Mau will be crushed to death?

Can everyone not wonder of so called Mau Mau? Where did they get weapons? How did they telephone to one another and how did they come to agree the same? Where do they get clothes? Where do they get food? Where do they get ammunitions? Where do they get grenades? Where do they get books, papers and where do they really get all their supplies?

Troops, home-guards & Police enter the bushes for searching the Mau Mau, will they ever meet 20 together or have they ever met 20 together? Bombers in large numbers started early in Feb.1953 and have only killed 9 while God is my witness over it and when I swear in the name of Gikuyu & Mumbi. How many do you think are here? How many do you think are watching in towns & Reserves?

Please turn to God not to Mau Mau. Repent to God not to Mau Mau. In the name of God, do not tear it out but read it publicly. It is sorrowful that God the Almighty Father fights against you while you are fighting against Dedan Kimathi & his Mau Mau gangs.

(a) Let Bishops pray in Kenya Churches from Wednesday to Friday. Do not discriminate the colour.

(b) Every mission will do the same and at the same hour.

(c) African Gospel preachers will do the same.

(d) After the Three days' prayer let the Tribes of Kenya sacrifice with a brown pure ram as a sign of exchanging the human being's blood with that of a ram. After doing all that we both end the war peacefully or otherwise we shall continue untill another world war breaks out and disperse this naughty fights in Kenya.

Signed and Stamped

Field Marshal Sir Dedan Kimathi

Document 10

Exhibit No. 24—Kimathi Letter, 6 March 1954[107]

EMERGENCY ASSIZE CRIMINAL CASE NO. 46 of 1956 Exhibit No. 24

{Addressed on envelope to: The Artony {sic} General
P.O. Secretariat, Nairobi, Kenya}

[Government House, Nairobi
Official Stamp,
10 APR 1954]

[Stamped LAND FREEDOM ARMY,
Date: 6th March 1954]

NOTIFICATION TO PUBLIC

I hereby notify the public that though that the Kenya Government does not regard us as people with brain and wisdom or knowledge that negotiation talks could not be attended by our own elected delegates while we were ready to do so, and as now the Kenya Government has nominated its own delegates to attend the negotiation talks, I on behalf of all my followers and the Defence Council and as President of the Council and the Knight Commander of African Empire and the Commander-in-Chief of the Country of Kenya notify that the terms proceeding and the discussions will not be considered and are in all the circumstances extremely rejected, as this encourages a further progress of rebellion.

The Government should consider of either to continue with fighting or to co-operate with our own elected delegates.

By F.M. Sir D. Kimathi K.C.A.E. and Supreme C-in-C of the
Country of Kenya and the Land Freedom Armies.

Nyandarua
6/4/54

Copy to: -
Acting Governor of Kenya
P.O. Secretariate Nairobi.

---

107. Exhibit No. 24, Criminal Case No. 46 of 1956, Dedan Kimathi v. Regina, Her Majesty's Supreme Court of Kenya at Nyeri, Kimathi File, Archives of the Supreme Court of Kenya.

Document 11

Exhibit No. 25—Letter from Chief Muhoya to Dedan Kimathi, 2 June 1954[108]

EMERGENCY ASSIZE CRIMINAL CASE NO. 46 of 1956 Exhibit No. 25

Office of the District Commissioner,
P.O. Box 32, Nyeri.

2nd June 1954.

Sir,

I have received your letter of 21st May and note its contents. You are at liberty at any time to surrender with your men under the original terms, of which you are doubtless aware.

You should notify me through the channels proposed by you as to place and date, so that you and your followers will not be molested if coming in to surrender.

DISTRICT COMMISSIONER, NYERI

Dedan Kimathi,
c/o Senior Chief Muhoya,
Ihururu.

[Recovered by Supt. Henderson
from a skin satchel discarded
in the Tree Tops Sahen.
Found on 19th Aug, 1955.]

108. Exhibit No. 25, Criminal Case No. 46 of 1956, Dedan Kimathi v. Regina, Her Majesty's Supreme Court of Kenya at Nyeri, Kimathi File, Archives of the Supreme Court of Kenya.

Document 12

Exhibit No. B1—Surrender Leaflet, 24 August 1953[109]

GANG LEADERS.

You will not be in any danger if you come to negotiate a surrender along with the whole of your gang and your weapons.

Come out during day-time waiving green branches as a sign to show that you are surrendering. This will ensure that you are not shot at.

Come to any Police or Military Camp.

If you surrender with your gang and your arms you will be placed under military order and you will be given sufficient food. We shall endeavour to see that you are not treated unjustly.

E. BARING.
Governor of Kenya.
August, 24th, 1953.

GEORGE ERSKINE,
General
Commander-in-Chief, East Africa.

---

109. Exhibit No. B1, Criminal Case No. 46 of 1956, Dedan Kimathi v. Regina, Her Majesty's Supreme Court of Kenya at Nyeri, Kimathi File, Archives of the Supreme Court of Kenya.

Document 13

Exhibit No. C1—Surrender Leaflet, 24 August 1953[110]

NOW IS THE TIME YOU CAN FINISH THE WAR.

Up to the present moment, very many Mau Mau terrorists have been killed. And now the Government have increased the police and the military to track down and kill the Mau Mau gangs. The loyal Kikuyu, Embu and Meru who defend the country are getting stronger every day.

If you do not stop fighting, only hunger and death wait for you. Many of your men have surrendered to the Government, and now some of your leaders have asked the Government to end the fight.

SAVE YOUR LIFE NOW.

We know that many of you were forced by Mau Mau men to join their gangs to help them in their violent and murderous actions. Now the Government gives you a chance to save your life.

Come and give yourselves up to the Government. If you do that the Government will not forget the trouble you have lived in and they will not kill you for carrying arms or for consorting with Mau Mau against your wishes.

This more concerns you if you have not committed murder. All those who have not committed murder are Now given a chance to save their lives. Decide quickly what to do, to come and surrender.

ONLY A LITTLE TIME REMAINS FOR YOU.

But now there is a chance. Therefore decide quickly what to do for our fight against Mau Mau will go on relentlessly, fighting all those who do not surrender.

SAVE YOUR LIFE NOW.

Take courage. Plan Now and escape from Mau Mau, come and surrender without any delay.

---

110. Exhibit No. C1, Criminal Case No. 46 of 1956, Dedan Kimathi v. Regina, Her Majesty's Supreme Court of Kenya at Nyeri, Kimathi File, Archives of the Supreme Court of Kenya.

IF POSSIBLE COME WITH YOUR ARMS.

You can surrender to any European officer or to any other Government representative. Come voluntarily just now.

E. BARING.
Governor of Kenya.
August 24th, 1953.

GEORGE ERSKINE.
General
Commander-in-Chief, East Africa.

Document 14

Exhibits Nos. D1 and D2—Surrender Leaflet and Safe Conduct Pass, 18 January 1955[111]

FRONT. (Leaflet for the forest).

To all MAU MAU leaders and their followers.

NEW SURRENDER TERMS.

This is a chance to save your life.

As you know the Government is intensifying its operations against Mau Mau and will continue these until every terrorist has been captured or killed, or has given himself up.

Now is your chance to save your life.

The Government makes the following new offer to all Mau Mau leaders and their followers.

If you surrender now with your arms you will save your life.

You will not be prosecuted for any Mau Mau offence which you have committed prior to the date of these terms. That is January 18th., 1955. This means you will not be hanged, whatever you have done, if you commit no further acts of violence after that date.

On surrender you will be fairly treated and properly fed. And afterwards you will be detained. How long you will be detained will depend on the Government's examination of each one's case.

You can surrender to any of the Security Forces wherever they may be including any member of the Military, Police, Kikuyu, Meru and Embu Guards, or any Administrative Officer or at any of their Posts.

This offer will not remain open indefinitely.

Surrender NOW wherever you are – in the forest – in the Reserve – in the settled area or in the towns.

When you surrender you must bring in your arms or weapons.

Your chance to save your life is to surrender NOW.

SURRENDER BY GIVING YOURSELF UP CARRYING A GREEN BRANCH.

---

111. Exhibit No. D1, Criminal Case No. 46 of 1956, Dedan Kimathi v. Regina, Her Majesty's Supreme Court of Kenya at Nyeri, Kimathi File, Archives of the Supreme Court of Kenya.

Sir. Evelyn Baring.
Governor.

General Sir. George Erskine.
Commander-in-Chief.

18th. January, 1955.

EMERGENCY ASSIZE CRIMINAL CASE No. 46 of 1956

Exhibit No. D2—Safe Conduct Pass[112]

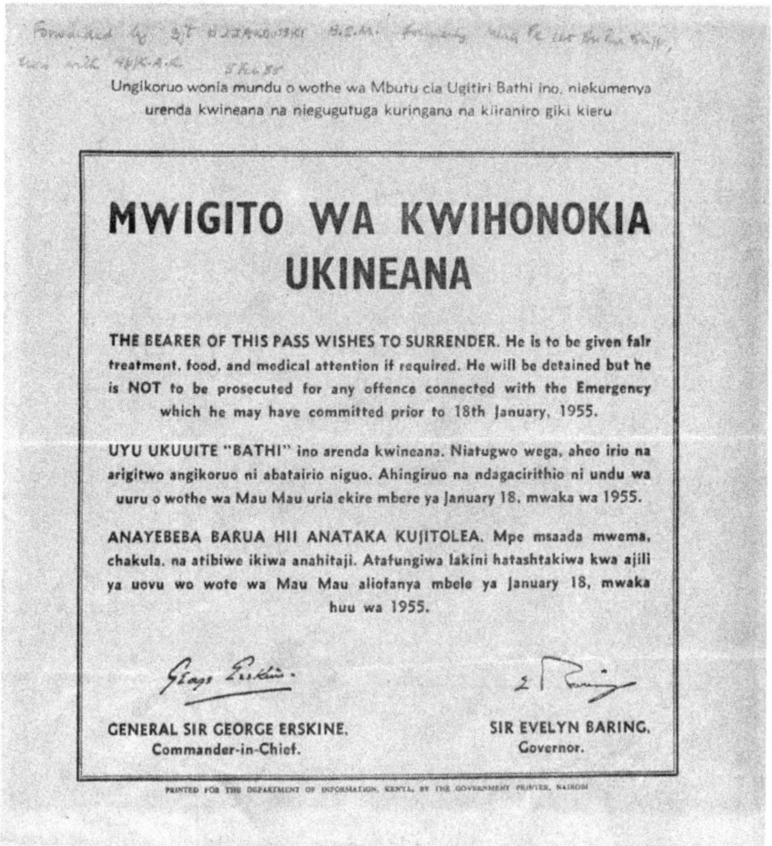

Ungikoruo wonia mundu o wothe wa Mbutu cia Ugitiri Bathi ino, niekumenya urenda kwineana na niegugutuga kuringana na kiiraniro giki kieru

MWIGITO WA KWIHONOKIA UKINEANA

THE BEARER OF THIS PASS WISHES TO SURRENDER. He is to be given fair treatment, food, and medical attention if required. He will be detained but he is NOT to be prosecuted for any offence connected with the Emergency which he may have committed prior to 18th January, 1955.

UYU UKUUITE "BATHI" ino arenda kwineana. Niatugwo wega, aheo irio na arigitwo angikoruo ni abatairio niguo. Ahingiruo na ndagacirithio ni undu wa uuru o wothe wa Mau Mau uria ekire mbere ya January 18, mwaka wa 1955.

ANAYEBEBA BARUA HII ANATAKA KUJITOLEA. Mpe msaada mwema, chakula, na atibiwe ikiwa anahitaji. Atafungiwa lakini hatashtakiwa kwa ajili ya uovu wo wote wa Mau Mau aliofanya mbele ya January 18, mwaka huu wa 1955.

GENERAL SIR GEORGE ERSKINE,
Commander-in-Chief.

SIR EVELYN BARING,
Governor.

PRINTED FOR THE DEPARTMENT OF INFORMATION, KENYA, BY THE GOVERNMENT PRINTER, NAIROBI

FIGURE 3 Exhibit No. D2, Mau Mau safe conduct pass, 18 January 1955. Supreme Court of Kenya, Kimathi File.

112. Exhibit No. D2, Criminal Case No. 46 of 1956, Dedan Kimathi v. Regina, Her Majesty's Supreme Court of Kenya at Nyeri, Kimathi File, Archives of the Supreme Court of Kenya.

Document 15

FINAL LETTER FROM KIMATHI TO FATHER MARINO[113]

DEDAN KIMATHI
C/O H.M. PRISON
17TH FEBRUARY, 1957

Father Marino
Catholic Mission
P.O. Box 25
NYERI

Dear Father,

It's about one O'clock night that I have picked up my pencil and paper so that I may remember you and your beloved friends and friends before the time is over.
I am so busy and so happy preparing for heaven tomorrow the 18th February 1957. Only to let you know that Father Whellam came in to see me here in my prison room as he received the information regarding my arrival. He is still a dear kind person as I did not firstly expect. He visits me very often and gives me sufficient encouragement possible. He provided me with important books with more that all have set a burning light throughout my way to paradise, such as-:

1. Student Catholic Doctrine
2. In the Likeness of Christ
3. The New Testament
4. How to Understand the Mass
5. The Appearance of the Virgin at Grotto of Lourdes
6. Prayer book in Kikuyu
7. The Virgin Mary of Fatima
8. The Cross of the Rosary etc

I want to make it ever memorial to you and all that only Father Whellam that came to see on Christmas day While I had many

113. A copy of this letter hangs in the gallery at the Kenya National Archives. The original letter is housed in the Consolata Archives, Rome.

coming on other weeks and days. Sorry that they did not remember me during the birth of Our Lord and Savior. Pity also that they forgot me during such a merry day.

I have already discussed the matter with him and I am sure that he will inform you all.

Only a question of getting my son to school. He is far from many of your schools, but I trust that something must be done to see that he starts earlier under your care etc.

Do not fail from seeing my mother who is very old and to comfort her even though that she is so much sorrowful.

My wife is here.[114] She's detained at Kamiti Prison and I suggest that she will be released after sometime. I would like her to be comforted by Sisters, e.g Sister Modester, etc. for she too feels lonely. And if by any possibility she can be near the mission as near Mathari so that she maybe so close to the sisters and to the church.

I conclude by telling you only to do me favor by getting education to my son.

Farewell to the world and its belongings, I say and best wishes I say to my friends with whom we shall not meet in this busy world. Please pass my complements and best wishes to all who read Wathiomo Mukinyu.[115] Remember me too the Fathers, Brothers and Sisters.

With good hope and Best wishes,
I remain dear Father
Yours loving, and departing convert
D. Kimathi

---

114. For more on Kimathi's wife, Eloise Mukami, see Nderitũ, *Mũkami Kĩmathi.*

115. *Wathiomo Mukinyu,* or "The True Friend," was the first vernacular Gikuyu newspaper. It first appeared in 1916 and was owned and edited by the Consolata Catholic Mission. Muoria-Sal et al., *Writing for Kenya,* 41n68.

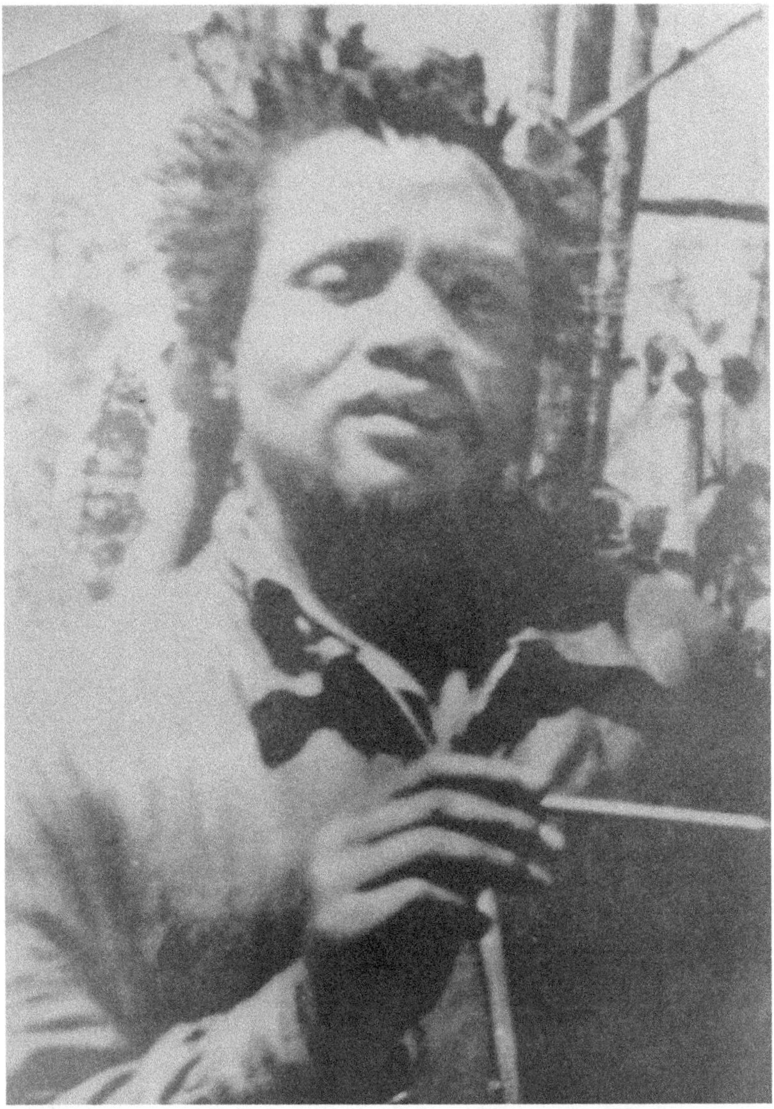

PHOTO 1 Dedan Kimathi with pen, June 1953. Kenya National Archives.

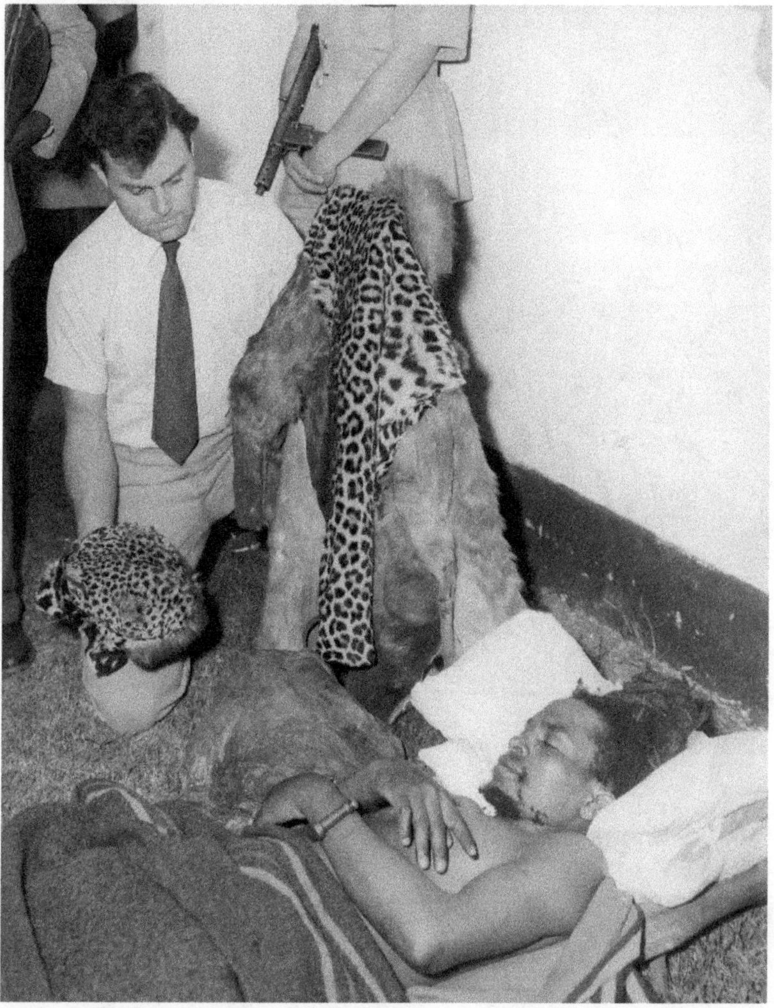

PHOTO 2 Dedan Kimathi after his capture, 21 October 1956. Getty Images.

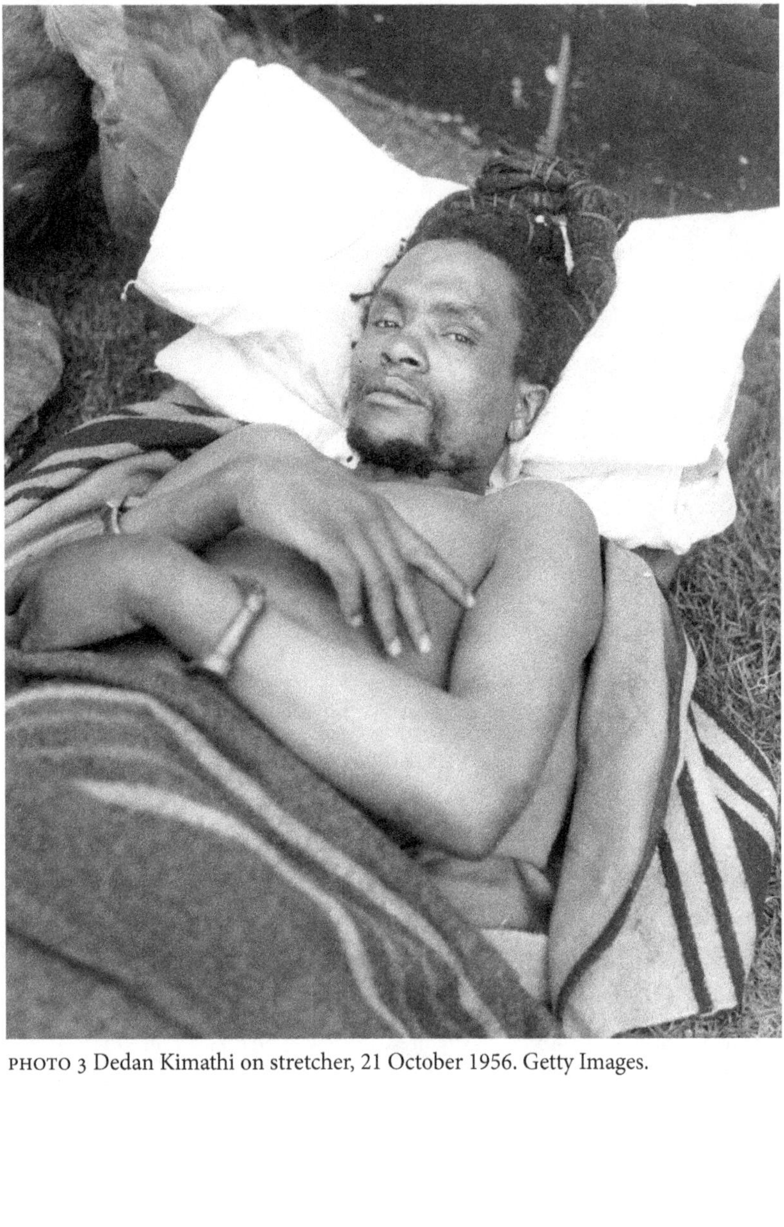

PHOTO 3 Dedan Kimathi on stretcher, 21 October 1956. Getty Images.

PHOTO 4 Superintendent Ian Henderson, c. 1956. *The Hunt for Kimathi*. 1958.

PHOTO 5 Corporal Wanjohi s/o Wanjau and Tribal Police Officer Ndirangu s/o Mau, 21 October 1956. British Pathé.

Daily 20 cents

Nairobi, Thursday, November 22, 1956

HY ALLIES REFUSE

Kimathi trial draws crowds

PHOTO 6 Outside courthouse, Nyeri, 22 November 1956. *East African Standard.*

PHOTO 7 Kimathi's trench, Aberdare forest. Photo by author.

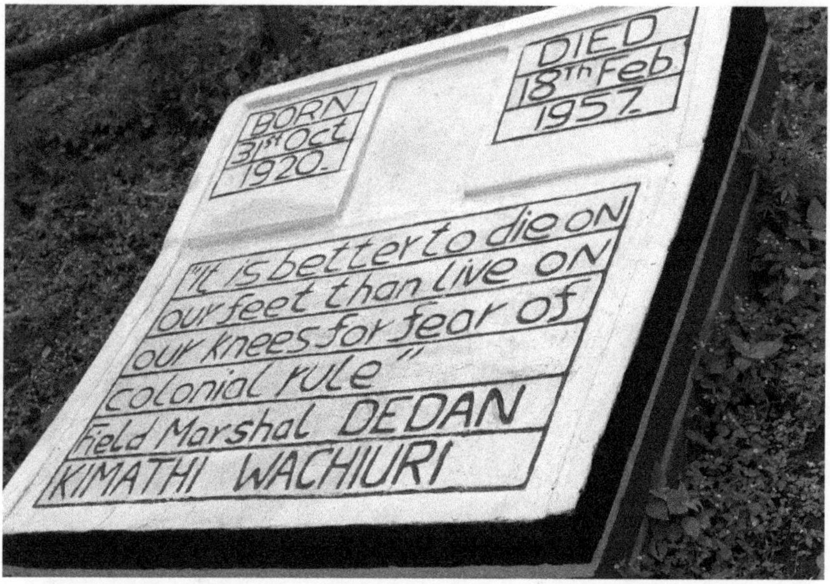

PHOTO 8 Memorial plaque at Kimathi's trench. Photo by author.

PHOTO 9 Kimathi statue, Nairobi. Photo by author.

Kenya Land and Freedom Army
(Mau Mau)
Men and women fighting in the armed struggle
rated mainly from the Mount Kenya and Aberdare forests.
Other women, who also formed part of the struggle,
ght them food. They both looked away when the food

PHOTO 10 Mau Mau memorial, Nairobi. Photo by Simon Gikandi.

PHOTO 11 Dedan Kimathi mural, Nairobi. Photo by author.

Critical Essays

1

Mau Mau on Trial

Dedan Kimathi's Prosecution and Kenya's Colonial Justice

David M. Anderson

The trial of Mau Mau leader Dedan Kimathi has been vividly portrayed by Kenyan authors as political theater[1] and as revolutionary rhetoric,[2] yet it has featured only fleetingly in the historical retelling of Kenya's struggle to be free from colonialism.[3] Dedan Kimathi is the leading heroic figure in Kenya's national narrative. As Ali Mazrui reminded us long ago, all national histories must have their heroes, but heroes are more easily made the less we know about them.[4] So it is that Kimathi's heroism has been made in an imagined nationalism, and not in the real world of historical events, human relationships, and personal struggles. The ambiguities surrounding Kimathi's leadership of the Mau Mau movement, first highlighted in Karari Njama's account of the forest armies, published in 1966,[5] have been largely ignored in subsequent nationalist histories, leaving plenty of scope for fictionalized speculation and mythmaking.[6] Kimathi's iconic status in Kenya's nationalist history surely remains undeniable, yet his behavior in the forest among his comrades, his relations and negotiations with the British, and his reputation as a rebel leader, all bear much closer scrutiny than they have had from historians thus far.[7]

The circumstances of Kimathi's capture, trial, and execution, as recounted through the documents assembled by the British for his prosecution in the Special Emergency Assize Court at Nyeri, in November 1956, therefore presents an opportunity to review what is known of his life during his four years in the forests of Nyandarua (the Aberdare), and what this tells us about the Mau Mau movement and its ultimate defeat in the face of a fierce British counterinsurgency campaign.[8] This chapter contributes to this revisionist task by providing a detailed, factual examination of the character of the legal proceedings under which Kimathi was prosecuted, contextualizing the trial in the colonial justice system imposed under Kenya's Emergency Powers. The trial was functional and ordinary, but also laden with political significance and potency—factors of which the British were acutely aware. Kimathi's trial was but one among more than twelve hundred Special Emergency Assize hearings conducted to prosecute alleged Mau Mau adherents between July 1953 and December 1956.[9] The processes and procedures of the court followed a well-established pattern, nothing of which was compromised to accommodate Kimathi's celebrity, but some of which was elaborated in ways that were not generally available to other accused in such trials. Keen not to offer a political platform for Kimathi, and aware of the dangers of making a martyr of the wounded rebel leader, the British adhered rigorously to the rules of the court while also ensuring that no obstruction was placed on Kimathi's defense. Few other Mau Mau defendants had been treated with such courtesy and regard.

To appreciate how the trial was conducted it is first important to understand that although the Special Emergency Assizes were a division of the Supreme Court and heard capital cases, they functioned in a radically different way from that normally expected in a courtroom under British jurisdiction. These assize courts offered a stripped-down and truncated version of "British justice," with the legal practicalities specifically shaped to the circumstances of a colonial war of insurrection. It is a striking paradox of the Special Assize Courts that because they had been set up to deal specifically with Mau Mau crimes under Emergency Powers there was seldom any attempt to establish the motive for a crime, even an act of murder, in the cases brought to trial. This avoided any discussion in court of the aims and objectives of Mau Mau as a movement, and so denied the accused any opportunity to present a political case. These cases are therefore all about Mau Mau, but Mau Mau is hardly ever mentioned in the proceedings.

The background to the creation of the Special Emergency Assizes and the character of their proceedings will be explained in the opening section of this chapter. The second section will then address the specifics of the

Kimathi trial, highlighting the distinctive aspects of the case. The conclusion reflects on the place of Kimathi's trial in the wider history of the Mau Mau insurrection, and, returning to Mazrui, in the making of a hero.

The Special Emergency Assize Courts

With the declaration of a State of Emergency in October 1952, Kenya's colonial government was granted significant new powers in the making of legislation and in the administration of the colony. These powers were permitted under the authority of the 1939 Emergency Powers Order-in-Council, a piece of catchall British colonial legislation that could be applied in any colony, giving the governor discretion to pass and apply new laws without the restriction of being under martial law and having to subordinate ordinary governance to military command. As David French pithily explains, this allowed colonial governments "to maintain the outward appearance of legality and simultaneously employ as much or as little coercion and violence as they chose."[10] In each colonial context the interaction with existing local legislation forged its own characteristic outcomes under such conditions, and in Kenya two distinctive features were dominant: first, Emergency Powers had the effect of militarizing Kenya's colonial administration; second, in design and imposition the new regulations fell prey to the stern influence of Kenya's white-settler population, whose vociferous political campaigning drove Governor Baring toward increasingly draconian Emergency measures.[11]

The powers granted to the governor included the right to alter the types of cases that could be heard by different levels of court and to extend the range of offenses for which a capital sentence could be handed down by the courts. At the outset of the Emergency magistrates' courts had been granted powers to hear cases relating to Mau Mau oathing ceremonies, for which the penalty could be life imprisonment. This development had been opposed by the attorney general, John Whyatt, on the grounds that it gave administrative officers (most magistrates were district commissioners or district officers, and hence part of the political service of the government) unwarranted judicial powers.[12] But the argument in favor of the extension of powers was driven by the simple fact that the Supreme Court was being rapidly overwhelmed by the sheer number of cases, and in November 1952 several resident magistrates were temporarily elevated to the role of acting judges in order to deal with the enormous backlog of cases then awaiting trial in the Supreme Court.[13]

In the wake of several murders of Europeans on farms in the White Highlands in the early months of 1953—most notoriously the killing of the Ruck family, following which the white settlers had angrily protested on the governor's lawn[14]—the Nairobi government was already preparing to take further steps to speed up the processing of cases by the Supreme Court when the Lari massacre of 26 March 1953 took place. This slaughter of more than seventy Kikuyu loyalists, most of them women and children, heightened the anxieties of African and European alike and proved to be the catalyst in bringing about a new set of judicial changes. Over the next two months steps were taken to extend the death penalty to a wide range of offenses related to Mau Mau insurgent activity—acts of sabotage; the illegal carrying of arms, ammunition, or explosives; consorting with persons in possession of arms; the administration of Mau Mau oaths; and the supplying of material aid to insurgents were all now made capital offences.[15] This went some way to placate the settler clamor for firmer government action against the insurgents, but it also threatened to increase further the immense pressures on the Supreme Court. The settler leader, Michael Blundell, pushed for a more rapid system of justice to be imposed, one that would clear the backlog of pending cases and ensure that those found guilty of crimes would be more speedily brought to the gallows. Though Attorney General Whyatt was again reluctant to sanction changes that seemed to him to undermine the principles of English law, Governor Baring worked hard to persuade the secretary of state, Lyttelton, that such measures were urgently needed. By 12 June 1953, Lyttelton had overcome opposition to the scheme in the Colonial Office and the regulations for the new Special Emergency Assize Courts were formally approved.[16]

These courts would sit in Nairobi, Nakuru, Githunguri, Thika, Nyeri, Nakuru, and (latterly) Thomson's Falls, Meru, and Embu, and would hear only cases relating to the Emergency Powers regulations. A number of magistrates were declared as special acting judges to preside at the new courts, and given the full powers of a High Court judge. Special sittings of the appeals court were also provided for, so as to speed up the processing of cases after conviction, with the intention of moving convicts more rapidly to execution and preventing a buildup of persons awaiting appeal under sentence of death. Baring also managed now to get approval for the summary dismissal of appeals where no obvious legal ground could be established—a measure that London had previously refused to sanction.[17]

Locating all trials close to the areas where offences were committed and trimming down the appeals procedure had an immediate impact in accelerating cases, but the most significant legal change was the removal of the requirement for a committal proceedings before a Supreme Court prosecution of a capital offense. The committal proceedings, ordinarily undertaken in Kenya before a magistrate, provided the opportunity to establish the basic facts of the case, to review the essential evidence that would be brought before the court, and so to determine the relevant charge. Despite the fundamental nature of this change, the chief legal adviser to the Colonial Office, Roberts-Wray, failed to fully understand the implications of the removal of the committal proceedings until four days *after* his office had approved the new regulations: "Any accused person will be grossly hindered in his defence," Roberts-Wray now wrote, "if he comes to his trial knowing nothing of the evidence to be given against him."[18] When London pointed out this dangerous aspect of the new legislation, Nairobi's response was to permit the defense counsel to see witness statements for the prosecution in court, but in practice this came much too late to be of any real use. Court procedures also removed the requirement for the prosecution even to provide the defense counsel with the list of witnesses that were to be called in Special Emergency Assize cases. This limitation was intended to protect witnesses from intimidation and was a direct response to the fact that Mau Mau supporters had been extraordinarily successful in the early months of the Emergency in interfering with witnesses. Defendants therefore had no idea who would appear against them in the dock until they arrived in court. While the prosecution assembled as many witnesses as they required, the court procedures and the lateness of notifications meant that the defense counsel usually found it practically impossible to call witnesses. Defense witnesses were therefore only very rarely called in Special Assize Court hearings, and when they did come to court it was usually only to provide a testimony as to the good character of the accused and not to speak to the facts of the case.[19]

These limitations might have been acceptable in a situation where the defense team had opportunities to discuss the case with the accused and at least give time to preparing a defense against the specific charges made. However, under the Special Assize Court regulations, notifications of hearings were given only a few days before trial, which allowed very little time for defendants to engage an advocate of their choice. No formal provision for the instruction of advocates was made in the police stations or Kikuyu Home Guard posts where suspects were often held, and many accused did not even meet their appointed advocates until hours before the trial. While some suspects were able to engage advocates through their relatives, this could only be done where the relatives were aware of the arrest and its circumstances. For the majority of those coming to trial, especially those captured as members of Mau Mau forest gangs, it was not a possibility. Though a handful of wealthier accused did manage to engage defense lawyers, notably in the Lari trials, very few Kikuyu defendants came to court with an advocate of their own choosing.[20]

The often hasty scheduling of cases at the Emergency Assizes could also present difficulties for the prosecution in assembling a sufficiently robust body of witnesses to give evidence. Officers of the Crown were obliged to attend cases when summoned, even at short notice, and so for the most part pathologists, police officers, and even Home Guard and Tribal Police could be relied on to be present, although there were frequent difficulties with army officers, who might be on operations in a more distant location. The burden of the evidence sought from these prosecution witnesses was descriptive and factual—establishing the identities of the protagonists and circumstances of the arrest, describing the nature and cause of any wounds, and dealing with simple matters of the date and time of events. Evidence provided by prosecution witnesses would be challenged by the defense in an effort to expose any discrepancies or contradictions between witnesses, or to reveal any uncertainties or ambiguities. Over time, there was a clear move on the part of the Crown to call fewer prosecution witnesses, thus lessening the opportunities for the defense to unpick the case. By the time of Kimathi's trial, at the end of 1956, in cases with a single accused it was rare for the prosecution to call more than half a dozen witnesses.[21]

The majority of the defense lawyers appearing in the Special Emergency Assize Courts did so under what were termed Paupers' Briefs. Allocated by the office of the attorney general, this system allowed the state to impose a defense counsel to ensure that an accused person was properly represented in court, and it lessened the possibility that Mau Mau accused, if allowed to defend themselves, might seek to politicize trials.

However, Whyatt quickly found that Kenya's European lawyers were generally reluctant to take on Emergency Assize cases, declining the Paupers' Briefs when they were offered. Though this was considered improper behavior—members of the bar were expected to take such briefs as an act of professional citizenship—Whyatt was reluctant to air the issue in public and so instead steered the briefs toward Kenya's many Asian lawyers. They were prepared to take these briefs despite the low fee rate, while some, such as Fitz de Souza, Ajeet Singh, and A. R. Kapila, also did so out of a political conviction that such cases should be defended on principle. The one Kenyan African lawyer practicing in Nairobi at this time, Chiedo Argwings-Kodhek, worked on little else but Mau Mau cases throughout the Emergency and was harried and harassed by European administrators and police officers because they suspected him of harboring Mau Mau sympathies.[22] As a consequence of these arrangements, the proceedings of the Special Emergency Assizes therefore invariably had a racial complexion: European judges presided, with European lawyers for the state mounting the prosecution, while Asian lawyers predominated for the defense, and Africans stood accused in the dock.

The regulations governing the Special Emergency Assizes also allowed for mass trials. Approximately 70 percent of the cases heard between 1953 and 1956 involved multiple accused—usually between two and five codefendants standing together in the dock—but in the largest trials, deriving from the Lari massacre, more than fifty accused were arraigned in a single case. Mass trials of this kind tended to come in relation to the more infamous cases, such as the murders of Europeans, large-scale massacres of African loyalists, or the capture of large gangs of Mau Mau. Multiple defendants appearing together raised greater dangers of a miscarriage of justice, with the individual pleadings and evidence of each defendant sometimes being lost in the generalities of the case, especially when the trial was in the hands of inexperienced acting judges—a fact remarked upon at length by the appeals court whenever the opportunity arose.[23]

All Special Emergency Assize trials were heard before a single judge, without the assistance of a jury. Trial by jury in Kenya for any criminal case had always been an entitlement for Europeans but was not extended to Africans accused even in Supreme Court hearings. The decision to deploy a single judge in the Emergency Assizes, rather than a panel of three, was done entirely for reasons of expediency. This placed a considerable burden on the judge, working alone and often dealing with complex prosecutions of multiple accused and sometimes handling opaque or incomplete evidence. Kenya's most senior and experienced judges preferred to continue with their work in the Supreme Court, and so rarely appeared in Special Assize cases, leaving the vast majority of the trials to be presided over by the acting judges, many of whom were temporarily elevated from their role as resident magistrates. In consequence, the most difficult and politically charged cases to come through Kenya's judicial system in the 1950s were in the hands of the most junior and least experienced members of the judiciary.

Presiding judges, however, were assisted in every case by a team of three African assessors. The assessors were selected from the same ethnic group as the accused, so that matters of custom or local belief and practice could be properly attested where they might arise during the trial, and so that a link would be established between the proceedings of the court and local communities. Assessors were not there to pass judgment, nor could they "direct" the judge: their function was merely to offer commentary and advice. But the judge was not obliged to follow the advice offered by assessors, nor need he act upon anything raised in their comments. The role of assessor thus brought an African presence to the judicial process in the courtroom but gave Africans no authority or power in that process.[24] Assessors were, in theory, permitted to question witnesses and the accused during the trial, and might therefore have served the useful purpose of bringing out or clarifying aspects of the case that might otherwise have remained obscure, but this was never encouraged and did not happen in any Special Emergency Assize case for which papers survive. There was a requirement that assessors give a view on the case at the conclusion of the proceedings, however, following the summing up from the judge, but before the pronouncement of the judgment. Judges were formally instructed to give weight to the views expressed by the assessors, but there is no substantive evidence from any surviving trial papers from the assizes that they ever did so. On the contrary, judges often expressed themselves as exasperated and mystified when assessors choose not to concur with the verdict handed down by the court, or to raise matters that seemed tangential to the key questions before the court. Given the risks of attack by Mau Mau, relatively few Africans were willing to volunteer as assessors, and those appointed were invariably staunch loyalists, who were often prominent members of Christian churches, active in the colonial administration, or involved in the Kikuyu Home Guard.[25]

The court proceedings were conducted in English and recorded in that language by a clerk, who produced a full transcript of each trial. Translation from and into Kikuyu or Swahili was provided for any accused person who could neither speak nor understand English, but it is not clear from the surviving records how thorough or effective this procedure was. The transcripts of proceedings contain many sections where it is apparent that only an abbreviated version of a statement has been recorded, or where questions are omitted, so they do not properly constitute a verbatim account. Many defendants were thought by the judges to be "disinterested" in the proceedings, and many comments from the bench indicate that the defendants may not have understood the nature of the charges against them, the character of the evidence, or the likely consequences of the court's decisions. This may have been due to language difficulties, but it may also indicate that many accused were resigned to their fate, believing that the court would find them guilty come what may.

That impression may have been largely substantiated for the accused by the way in which the court treated certain kinds of evidence. This related to amendments made to the Evidence Act under Emergency Regulations. Special Emergency Assizes cases were frequently characterized by allegations of the mistreatment and especially beatings of prisoners. Accused persons commonly claimed to have been beaten when arrested, and again (often repeatedly) during interrogations. Those coming before the court frequently bore the physical scars of these attacks. Extrajudicial statements gathered during the questioning of prisoners in Mau Mau cases often assembled evidence that amounted to a full confession; but if such statements had been gained under duress, then they would not be admissible in court. The court could accept such statements in evidence only if they had been made before either a magistrate or a senior (European) police officer. The extension of this power to senior police officers was the critical factor, this amendment being introduced as yet another way to relieve the burden on magistrates as the press of legal work caused by the insurrection built up. This had been firmly opposed by the attorney general, who rightly pointed to the dangers of an arresting officer being responsible for attesting what might amount to a confession that would condemn the prisoner. Whyatt's objections were swept aside on the grounds of practicalities, but he gained the proviso that the court would have the right to exclude any such statement from the record of evidence if the judge had any doubt that the statement was freely made and a correct record.[26]

This placed the burden squarely on the judge: if the accusations of abuse and duress made by the defense counsel related to the extrajudicial statement, then it was incumbent on the judge to establish the facts so that the statement could be held as evidence. Failure to treat such accusations properly might result in the appeals court overturning a guilty verdict. This led to a series of "trials within a trial," with the judge asking the court to be cleared and the assessors withdrawn, while the attesting officer (normally a police officer, more rarely a magistrate) was called to deny the accusation of duress, or doctors were called to examine the prisoners. While it was evident by their injuries that prisoners had been abused, judges were reluctant to wholly dismiss the extrajudicial statements and so steered a careful course between allowing the statement to stand—on the basis that the timing and circumstances of the beatings could not be established—and ensuring that any conviction did not rest solely on the confessional evidence contained in the statement. While judges did, from time to time, express their unease at this situation,[27] and it is clear that the appeals court seized upon evidence of the abuse of prisoners by officers of the state whenever it was presented to them,[28] the routinized beatings of prisoners in interrogations was vividly reflected in the proceedings of the Special Emergency Assizes.

The success of the Emergency Assizes in accelerating the pace of capital-case prosecutions in Kenya is evident, and was often praised by the more conservative senior members of the judiciary.[29] The figures are indeed striking: between July 1953 and December 1956, the Special Emergency Assize Courts heard 1,211 cases in which 2,609 African suspects stood trial. The courts acquitted 1,033 persons and convicted 1,574 persons—all of whom received sentences of death.[30] This does not entirely account for all persons prosecuted for Mau Mau offences, as between October 1952 and April 1953 such cases were heard in the magistrates' courts and in the Supreme Court, and there were a handful of other cases prosecuted between January 1957 and October 1959. When these figures are added, the total number of convicts who were executed stands at 1,090, with 240 death sentences having been commuted and 160 appeals against conviction allowed. All female convicts were reprieved, but they numbered fewer than thirty.[31] All adult convicts who were reprieved, whether male or female, were sentenced to life imprisonment with hard labor, while juveniles were detained at the governor's pleasure.[32] Well aware of the extent of judicial execution and the fate of other Mau Mau accused, on finding himself in the dock in Nyeri's courtroom, Dedan Kimathi could only have expected one outcome.

Dedan Kimathi in the Dock

In terms of procedure, the trial of Dedan Kimathi was very typical of the Special Emergency Assize Court hearings we have already described, but certain aspects of the prosecution were distinctive and reflected Kimathi's notoriety and status as Mau Mau leader. From the moment of his capture, on the fringe of the Nyandarua forest on the morning of 20 October 1956, Kimathi was treated as no ordinary prisoner.[33] Like that other wounded Mau Mau leader to be captured earlier in the Emergency, Waruhiu Itote (a.k.a. General China),[34] Kimathi had immense intelligence value, so the state was keen to treat his wounds and ensure that he could be properly and thoroughly interrogated. Kimathi was therefore spared the "roughing up" at the hands of Home Guard and police that was so often the fate of other captured Mau Mau forest fighters. There was no accusation to be made here of beatings or abuse of the prisoner—in contrast to the musings of Kinyatti in his unreferenced and misleading account of Kimathi's treatment[35]—although the conditions to be endured in the basic concrete-block structure that was the Nyeri jail were far from comfortable.

The record of Kimathi's interrogation suggests that he was far more guarded than had been the talkative and sometimes boastful Itote, but he nonetheless provided his interrogator with a detailed account of the structure and organization of the forest gangs, much of this proffered in demonstration of Kimathi's claim to overall command of the Mau Mau movement.[36] This interrogation report directly contradicts many of the statements that Kimathi would make from the dock during his trial—claims that he had been disaffected from the Mau Mau movement since February 1954, that he had been attacked by other members of the movement, and that he moved about the forest in fear of his life from further assaults—and hence needed to carry a weapon. However, although the prosecuting counsel challenged these points, the court was not presented with the evidence of the interrogation report. Though it might be argued that withholding Kimathi's interrogation report served a specific political purpose for the British, it was in fact normal practice *not* to present such reports in the courtroom. Police officers took separate statements from the accused that were specifically intended for use in the courtroom—Kimathi was interviewed by a police officer on 22 October 1956, when in the hospital and still recovering from the surgery on his wound,[37] more than a week before he met with Dunn, on 31 October 1956, to conduct the formal Special Branch interrogation. Police "evidence" intended for the trial was therefore collected in an entirely separate process from interrogations of key prisoners that were intended for intelligence purposes, and would be added to the database gathered and analyzed by staff at the Mau Mau Interrogation Centre.[38] Interrogation reports were never attested in the same legal way required for a statement to be used in court. Moreover, interrogation reports were likely to contain information that might be used operationally, and so to allow such matters to be presented in court might risk the integrity of any future actions by the security forces.

The choice of judicial staff for the case was both surprising and revealing of British attitudes and apprehensions. Sir Kenneth O'Connor was selected as the judge to hear the case. O'Connor was Kenya's chief justice and one of several prominent Irish-trained colonial-service lawyers.[39] He was the most senior judge then in Kenya, yet he had very limited experience of the Special Emergency Assizes or of Mau Mau cases. Justices serving in these courts would normally hear several cases in a single day and take sittings at circuits lasting more than a week, yet since returning to Kenya in 1954 the archive records show that O'Connor had presided in only three Special Emergency Assize hearings, all in Nairobi. In these cases O'Connor acquitted one accused and convicted four others. One of these convictions, that of a female accomplice of an oath administrator, was overturned on appeal, while two other death sentences were commuted.[40] Dedan Kimathi would therefore be only the second Mau Mau convict who would go to the gallows after being sentenced by O'Connor.[41] If O'Connor's appointment was therefore surprising, given his lack of previous involvement in Mau Mau cases, it clearly revealed the importance attached to the case by the British in Kenya. Cases were normally simply added to the circuit list for the Nyeri courtroom, and Kimathi would have been tried by whatever judge was assigned to the court at that time. But O'Connor would come to

Nyeri *only* to hear the Kimathi case: as the senior government legal officer, this case was seen to be his responsibility.

A similarly careful and high-profile approach was taken in the selection of the Crown's prosecuting counsel. Diarmaid Conroy was the most experienced state prosecutor available, having over previous years acted in many important cases. But like O'Connor, he rarely appeared in court by 1956, being by then fully absorbed in his administrative roles as solicitor general and minister of legal affairs in the colonial government of Kenya. Dusting off his robes and wig for the Nyeri appearance, Conroy would be assisted by the most highly regarded and competent junior prosecutor then working in the Legal Department, J. K. Havers—who would later in his colonial career rise to the post of attorney general in Gibraltar. Sir Diarmaid Conroy, CMG, OBE, as he became, went on to serve as chief justice in Northern Rhodesia as Kenneth Kaunda led the country to independence, before returning to the Lord Chancellor's Office in the UK as President of Industrial Tribunals, during the difficult years of the 1960s and 1970s. This was a formidable prosecution team.

In court, the prosecution went to unusual lengths to clearly establish the circumstances of Kimathi's capture and arrest, as his possession of arms and his malicious intent were at the center of their case. No fewer than seventeen witnesses for the Crown were brought into the dock, including eight Tribal Police and Tribal Police Reservists who had been involved in Kimathi's capture, and two African constables of the Kenya Police and five European police officers, including CID staff, who had been responsible for his detention in Nyeri and his questioning. The Nyeri surgeon Dr. Denis Hurley also gave evidence as to Kimathi's injuries. The final prosecution witness was Gitonga Wambugu Wamiatu, court clerk and interpreter stationed at Nyeri, who was summoned to clarify the recording of Kimathi's statement to the police from his hospital bed on 22 October 1956, confirming that he did not then mention that he was coming in to surrender.[42] These witnesses were determinedly consistent in their evidence, leaving little for the defense to work with. The thoroughness of their answers, when compared with the transcripts of other trials of this kind, suggests either that they had been made aware of the significance of the case and the need to be focused and informative, or that the court clerk was more careful in recording their words than was usually deemed necessary in such cases.

If it can be seen that great care was taken in the construction of the prosecution case, it was also decided that there should be no room for criticism of Kimathi's defense, and so highly unusual steps were taken here also. Any ordinary Special Emergency Assize trial would most likely have seen the appointment of a lawyer working on a Paupers' Brief, perhaps one of the able and energetic Kenyan Asian lawyers who so often filled this role: but the government decided they could not leave Kimathi's defense to chance, and keen to be seen to be doing everything possible to facilitate the smooth process of the case, the state paid to secure the services of a leading and highly respected Nairobi European advocate, Frederick Henry Miller. It is not clear that Kimathi had any say in this appointment, or even whether he was fully aware that he had a choice in accepting or rejecting the advocate proposed by the court, but it is certainly apparent that Miller was properly remunerated for the task and given every opportunity to consult with his client in an effort to build a credible defense.[43] Miller arrived in Nyeri several days before the hearing, giving him plenty of time to speak with Kimathi, and from the character of the trial it seems that Kimathi did indeed cooperate with the advocate, putting forward a defense that differed markedly from the initial statement he had made to police officers on 22 October 1956. All this, again, was far from normal in Special Emergency Assize hearings.

Kimathi's initial statement became a bone of contention during the trial, as the accused sought to modify, correct, and sometimes refute the information contained in the transcript of the interview. In their preface to this volume, Mĩcere Gĩthae Mũgo and Ngũgĩ wa Thiong'o suggest that Kimathi's statement may have been a "colonial fabrication." Pointing to its formulaic structure, laying out a well-ordered sequence of "facts," and its many incriminating admissions, they describe the statement as resembling a "polished report crafted from carefully researched information."[44] In one sense, this is surely correct. Statements of this kind were taken from all suspects soon after their capture, in preparation for the court hearing. The typed document presented to the court and headed "Statement of the Accused" was not a verbatim account of the interview but rather a reconstruction from the notes taken by the police officer during the interrogation. The process of "reconstruction" inevitably gave scope for the interrogator to impose specific interpretations and nuances on the words of the accused, ironing out inconsistencies, and perhaps even omitting details that were considered either irrelevant or unhelpful to the prosecution. Kimathi's pretrial statement, like all others by accused persons brought before the Emergency Assize courts, must therefore be treated with the greatest of caution.

The defense that Miller developed in court on Kimathi's behalf challenged the pretrial statement in many details but hinged on two key issues: first, that because of his long-standing condition of epilepsy,[45] the statement Kimathi made to police officers when he was recovering from the effects of anesthetic following his operation should not be accepted by the court. The condition, it was claimed, had caused the accused to be confused and unclear in his responses. On this point, it appears that Miller's purpose was to have the statement made to the police on 22 October discounted principally because it contained within it comments that amounted to a confession: Kimathi admitted that he not only held the revolver with which he was arrested but also a shotgun. Proof of possession of arms was sufficient for the death sentence to be passed, and Kimathi's statement therefore amounted to a clear admission of guilt.

However, the issue of epilepsy also touched on the question of Kimathi's acknowledged volatile behavior and might therefore also be construed, in part at least, as a plea in mitigation. The epilepsy mitigation defense had precedent in the Kenyan Supreme Court, of which an advocate of Miller's local experience must certainly have been aware. In the case of a murdered colonial officer, Grant, from 1946, the advocate defending the accused, Karamba ole Sentue, claimed that an epileptic fit had temporarily affected his mind, causing him to thrust his spear through Grant's chest. Two brothers of the accused were brought as witnesses to testify to ole Sentue's history of epileptic fits. While the court accepted that ole Sentue suffered from epilepsy, it did not lessen his sentence when convicted of murder.[46] In another case, more than thirty years earlier (1913), an epilepsy-suffering European settler, Cornelius Grobler, murdered his wife and then tried to take his own life. In court, it was claimed that an epileptic fit had temporarily deranged Grobler and that this was the cause of his violent, aberrant behavior. Though the court treated Grobler with some sympathy, the plea of epilepsy as mitigation it did not prevent his conviction, on this occasion by a European jury.[47]

Other than pleas relating to the mental health of accused, no similar defense on the grounds of the personal circumstances of any Mau Mau defendant is to be found in the cases brought before the Special Emergency Assize Courts after July 1953. Moreover, Miller called three witnesses to give testimony on the question of Kimathi's epilepsy. The first was a government physician, Dr. Turner, who was asked about the general effects of the condition. Kimathi's mother, and a friend from his school days, then gave testimony as to the depth and extent of Kimathi's past epilepsy. The mother, Wachiuri, had been brought to the court from a prison camp, where she was held under a government detention order. Though we have no documentation on this, her presence in court would have required careful negotiation with the government. Similarly, it was reported in the *East African Standard* that Joseph Wakaba, the friend who gave testimony as Kimathi's defense witness, had been brought to the court from the Manyani detention camp.[48] There is no record in any other Emergency Assize hearing of a defense witness being allowed to leave detention to come to court, or of any defense counsel even making such a request.

Having used the epilepsy plea to thwart the apparent confession to possessing arms contained in Kimathi's statement to the police, the second line developed in Miller's defense then sought to explain why Kimathi was, in fact, legitimately in possession of the weapon. Miller now lead with the claim that, when apprehended and shot, Kimathi had in fact been coming out of the Nyandarua forest to surrender, bringing his weapon with him only for his own protection. This claim resembled the defense offered by other accused in cases heard before the Special Emergency Assize courts, and, once again, Miller was well aware of the precedent. The specific case he had in mind was that of Mwangi Wambugu, prosecuted before Justice Law in Nyeri late in February 1954.[49] Wambugu claimed that he came out of the forest to surrender, bringing his *simi* (short sword) with him because he needed it for his own protection and to prove that he really was a Mau Mau fighter. The Tribal Policemen who apprehended Wambugu took him to the Ngobit police post, where he voluntarily handed them a single round of ammunition he had in his possession. On coming before the court, Justice Law doubted the claim that he had intended to surrender and so convicted Wambugu for possession of ammunition, sentencing him to be hanged. On appeal this verdict was overturned, and Wambugu acquitted, the Criminal Appeal judgment pointing out that the judge had failed to give any reason to disbelieve Wambugu's story.

Evidence regarding the intention of Mau Mau captives to surrender was a common feature of Special Emergency Assize cases, especially following the first surrender offer, of August 1953, and then again between January and August 1955, after the second offer. In 1953 the so-called green-branch offer had asked the rebels to give themselves up to the security forces clutching a green branch, to indicate they were not hostile. The leaflets issued to advertise this offer also asked that Mau Mau rebels should bring their weapons with them when surrendering. This offer, though superseded by later developments, was never formally withdrawn, whereas the second surrender offer, coming as part of an amnesty that also "cleared the slate" for Home Guard and others who might have committed offences in their counterinsurgency activities, was annulled by government order on 10 July 1955.[50] Documents were produced in court to establish the precise nature of each surrender offer, and it was accepted by O'Connor that a Mau Mau fighter might still, in October 1956, legally surrender under the terms of the 1953 offer and not be prosecuted. The question then became whether or not this had in fact been Kimathi's intention. The court would eventually rule against Kimathi on this point, giving greater weight to the evidence of the Tribal Police who had arrested him, and to others who also confirmed that he had made no mention of surrender until getting to court—that is, until after he had been in consultation with his defense counsel.

The grim irony of this discussion, and a matter that was not indicated in the court proceedings, and has only become apparent with the release in 2012 of additional British documents on the Kenyan Emergency,[51] is that it was precisely letters that Kimathi had written to the government during 1953 that had promoted the first surrender offer to be framed.[52] The surrender leaflet issued on 24 August 1953 was authorized by a meeting at Government House four days earlier that "was called to consider the implementation of a general surrender policy in view of the attached two communications which had been received from Dedan Kimathi."[53] The letters prompting the 1953 surrender offer were thus sent more than six months before the earliest of Kimathi's letters referred to in the courtroom, the first of which dates to March 1954, and are therefore almost certainly the letters Kimathi himself mentions in this 1954 correspondence as not having been replied to.

Justice O'Connor's summing up in this case is among the longest and most thorough in any Special Emergency Assize hearing where just a single accused stood in the dock. Dismissing the epilepsy claim as largely irrelevant, the bulk of his comments deal with the issue of whether Kimathi's claim to have been surrendering was credible. With one eye firmly on the appeals court and the other on the assessors sitting in front of him, O'Connor's summing up skillfully blocked off any possible angle from which a further plea might be made, carefully weighing each of the points favoring and against Kimathi's defense. Though the opinions of the assessors need have no impact on O'Connor's judgment, the government would have been greatly embarrassed, and open to criticism, had the Kikuyu assessors dissented from the view of the court and suggested that Kimathi should go free or that clemency be shown. In the event, their comments gave the British no cause for concern. The first assessor, Tumuti Gakere, asserted that Kimathi had come out of the forest to collect food, and not to surrender, and that he had every intention of going back into the forest when he was captured. The second assessor, Nderitu Muteru, declared his faith in the evidence given by the prosecution witnesses, dismissed Kimathi's surrender claim, and stated that he believed that the pistol and ammunition belonged to Kimathi. Finally, Kibuthu Kihia, making reference to the terms of the 1953 surrender offer, declared, "If his intention was to come out to surrender, he ought to have had a big bunch of green branches. Therefore I say he is guilty: he is a gangster."[54] O'Connor's final judgment in the case left no room for doubt that Kimathi was guilty as charged, and the death sentence was passed.

The verdict against Kimathi was challenged in the East African Court of Appeal but was summarily dismissed on 27 December 1956.[55] The case then went to the Privy Council.[56] There, Kimathi was represented by Dingle Foot, the British barrister who had saved the Koinange's from the gallows when they stood accused of involvement in the murder of Senior Chief Waruhiu.[57] But even the optimistic Foot must have realized that the path to the Privy Council was opened only to ensure there could be no accusations leveled at the British of having restricted Kimathi's opportunity to seek justice. With the dismissal of the case by the Privy Council, all possible legal pathways had been exhausted. Dedan Kimathi was executed by hanging on the morning of 18 February 1957.

Criminal trials under English law are adversarial. The prosecuting and defense counsel construct arguments, assembling evidence in support of their case and seeking to convince the court—whether a single judge or a full jury—of the guilt or innocence of the accused. Truth may emerge from this process, but truth it is not the primarily goal of either the prosecuting or the defense counsel. Advocates, along with judges and juries, consider only the evidence laid before the court, being explicitly instructed to ignore other factors.

Historians, by contrast, have the advantage of being able to triangulate other kinds of evidence, from beyond the courtroom, in order to come to judgments. This may not necessarily bring historians any closer to truth than courtroom advocates can manage, but it does allow for a rather different "balancing of evidence." Dedan Kimathi's interrogation presents evidence that was not offered to the court but that historians must weigh against the arguments made before Justice O'Connor by Conroy and Miller, respectively. If we assume that the interrogation is accurate, reflecting what Kimathi actually said to the Special Branch officer Dunn on 31 October 1956, then it is difficult to avoid the conclusion that Miller's defense of Kimathi was constructed entirely post hoc, designed purposefully as a legal strategy that might succeed in sowing sufficient doubt in the mind of the judge so as to avoid a capital sentence. There is, accordingly, reason to doubt that Kimathi intended to surrender when shot by Tribal Policeman Ndirangu, and, moreover, reason to doubt that his epilepsy—though genuine enough as a condition from which he suffered and one that might well have had a strong influence on his behavior at times in the forest—had any bearing on the circumstances of his capture, questioning, interrogation, or trial.

The circumstance of Kimathi's capture was also only partially revealed in the courtroom. By October 1956, Kimathi was being hunted in the Nyandarua forest by a security team under the direction of Special Branch officer Ian Henderson. According to Henderson's own account, the Mau Mau leader's hideout had been found by 16 October, and the security forces had laid a careful ambush there to catch Kimathi on his return. There was nothing at the camp to indicate that Kimathi had left without intending to return—clothing and equipment were left in the hideout, neatly arranged and ready for use, and there was buck meat and vegetables in the food store.[58] The next day, 17 October, Kimathi was seen by one of Henderson's Kikuyu officers, Ruku, darting across a clearing after he had fired on the security patrol. On the following day Kimathi was encountered again, this time he and his remaining companions being chased through the forest as they conducted a firefight with their pursuers. Kimathi escaped yet again but was now separated from his final comrade, Maragua, while his female companion, Wanjiru, was captured. These dramatic events left Kimathi alone, without food, and with only his revolver and simi for protection, and now knowing that his camp had been located and was probably ambushed. Henderson calculated that Kimathi's only course would be to leave the forest to get food from the Kikuyu Reserve area, and so stop lines were set along the forest boundary of Tetu Location at the two points where the Mau Mau leader was most likely to emerge. Men of the Tribal Police, the Kenya Police, and the King's African Rifles took up positions on the night of 18 October, and on 19 October the security forces tracking Kimathi confirmed that he had, indeed, moved to the forest fringe along the boundary with Tetu. It was at the southernmost of the Tetu stop lines that Ndirangu shot Kimathi, at 6:30 a.m. on the Sunday morning of 21 October.

Nothing in Kimathi's behavior over these days suggests a man who was contemplating surrender, though his situation was increasingly desperate. Evidence on all of this might have been revealed had Henderson been summoned as a witness, but given the character of the charges against Kimathi—the possession of arms and ammunition—there was no need to air details of security operations in the courtroom in order to secure a conviction. Far from interpreting the trial papers as indicating Kimathi had "given up" on the insurrection, and was ready to submit himself to the British through surrender, a wider reading of the historical context therefore suggests that his nationalist fervor was as strong as ever on the day of his capture.

Kimathi's wider motives, behavior, and intentions as a rebel leader, and the broader context of his situation in the Nyandarua forest, all matter greatly because it affects how Kimathi is to be judged not by a colonial court but by history. For Kenya's nationalists, the trial itself brings revelations about Kimathi's willingness to surrender at an earlier stage of the insurrection, and about the deep and painful divisions between Mau Mau fighters in the forests. How should these disputes be judged? Can they be reconciled within a nationalist history that holds Kimathi as a national hero? There is certainly much more history yet to be written on these matters, not least on the place of surrenders and amnesty in the history of the Mau Mau rebellion, and on the cohesion and leadership of the Mau Mau forces in the forests of Mount Kenya and the Nyandarua. Ali Mazrui's perceptive essay on heroism and Kenya's history, written in 1963, suggested that Kenyans would need to adopt a "selective memory" if they were to find national heroes for their newly independent nation. "Kenya's candidates are the returning rebels from the Aberdares," wrote Mazrui. "Perhaps we can now take it fairly for granted that Kimathi is a strong candidate for inclusion tomorrow in the Book of Kenya Martyrs."[59] The documents on the trial of Dedan Kimathi add to our knowledge and understanding of the complex history that surrounds him, but more than half a century on he still stands as the iconic hero of Kenya's rebellion against colonial rule, his statue adorning one of the main thoroughfares in Kenya's capital, Nairobi. His heroism, as Mazrui understood it must be, is symbolic as well as historic.

Notes

1. Ngũgĩ and Mũgo, *Trial.*
2. Kinyatti, *Kenya's Freedom Struggle*; Kinyatti, *History of Resistance*, 331–36.
3. Karimi's *Dedan Kimathi* is the most thorough account of Kimathi's life yet published, but Karimi acknowledges (p. 261) that he was unable to locate the trial papers. Kanogo discusses Kimathi's capture but says nothing about the trial. Kanogo, *Dedan Kimathi,* 26–27. Njeng'ere, *Dedan Kimathi,* a Kenyan secondary school textbook, recounts his hanging and burial in an unmarked grave at Kamiti Prison but, again, says nothing about the trial. Kahiga's *Dedan Kimathi,* styled as a "documentary novel," ends with Kimathi's capture. Maina wa Kinyatti offers an essay on Kimathi's supposed "revolutionary philosophy." Kinyatti, *Mau Mau: A Revolution Betrayed* (New York: Mau Mau Research Center, 1991), 79–93. Maloba presents an account of Kimathi's role in Mau Mau strategy, but makes no mention of the trial or execution. Maloba, *Mau Mau and Kenya,* 127–33.
4. Mazrui, "On Heroes."
5. Barnett and Njama, *Mau Mau from Within.*

6. Branch, "Search," 301–20; Marshall S. Clough, "Mau Mau and the Contest for Memory," in Atieno Odhiambo and Lonsdale, *Mau Mau and Nationhood,* 252–67; Coombes, Hughes, and Karega-Munene, *Managing Heritage.*

7. For examination of some of these themes, see Lonsdale's contribution in this volume.

8. David M. Anderson, "Exit from Empire: Counter-insurgency and Decolonization in Kenya, 1952–63," in *At the End of Military Intervention: Historical, Theoretical, and Applied Approaches to Transition, Handover, and Withdrawal,* ed. Robert Johnson and Timothy Clack (Oxford: Oxford University Press, 2015), 107–36; Bennett, *Fighting the Mau Mau;* Branch, *Defeating Mau Mau;* Elkins, *Britain's Gulag.*

9. This and following comments on the Special Emergency Assize Courts draws largely upon evidence presented in Anderson, *Histories of the Hanged,* esp. 7–8, 114–16, 152–56, 164, 174–77, 290–91, 354–55.

10. David French, *The British Way in Counter-insurgency, 1945–1967* (Oxford: Oxford University Press, 2011), 74.

11. For discussion, see Bennett, *Fighting the Mau Mau,* 34–40. On the significance of the administration, see Bruce Berman, *Control and Crisis in Colonial Kenya: The Dialectic of Domination* (Athens: Ohio University Press, 1990).

12. Discussion of the use of Emergency Powers began in Nairobi in August 1952; see "Minutes of a meeting held at the Secretariat, 17 August 1952," TNA:PRO, FCO 141/6595.

13. Anderson, *Histories of the Hanged,* 70. For the relevant decisions, see "Extracts from record of meeting held at Government House, 26 November 1952, to discuss certain matters connected with the present Emergency," TNA:PRO, FCO 141/6595.

14. Anderson, *Histories of the Hanged,* 93–98, 152–53.

15. Anthony Clayton, *Counter-insurgency in Kenya: A Study of Military Operations Against Mau Mau* (Nairobi: Transafrica, 1976), 14–15.

16. "The Emergency (Emergency Assizes) Regulations, 1953," Govt. Notice 931, 12 June 1953, *Kenya Official Gazette, Supplement 45.* For the correspondence between Nairobi and London over this, see TNA:PRO, CO 822/734.

17. See the lengthy correspondence on this in TNA:PRO, CO 822/735.

18. Minute by Roberts-Wray, 16 July 1953, TNA:PRO, CO 822/734.

19. Anderson, *Histories of the Hanged,* 156–57.

20. Ibid., 156.

21. This assessment, along with other general comparative comments made below, is based on a study of more than a thousand cases, held between 1953 and 1956, the papers for which are found at KNA, MLA 1/463 to KNA, MLA 1/1365, and in the KNA, RR series.

22. Anderson, *Histories of the Hanged,* 156–58.

23. In one Lari trial, forty-eight convictions were overturned on appeal: Criminal Case 165/1953, "Chege Mwauri and 51 others," trial transcript, KNA, RR 11/31–36; for the judge's summing up, and judgment, KNA, RR 11/37; and for the appeal papers, "Court of Appeal for Eastern Africa at Nairobi, Criminal Appeals Nos. 339–386 of 1953," 1 December 1953, TNA:PRO, CO 822/702.

24. John Gray, "Opinions of Assessors in Criminal Trials in East Africa as to Native Custom," *Journal of African Law* 2, no. 1 (1958): 5–18. For a discussion of juries and assessors in Kenya, see J. H. Jearey, "Trial by Jury and Trial with the Aid of Assessors in the Superior Courts of British African Territories: Part II," *Journal of African Law* 5 (1961): 40–43, and for general comments on the purpose of assessors, Jearey, "Trial by Jury: Part III," 95–98.

25. On loyalist motivations, see Branch, *Defeating Mau Mau,* 117–47.

26. Early cases of this kind are discussed in Anderson, *Histories of the Hanged,* 101–11. See especially, Criminal Case 55/1953, "Ndirito Gikaria and 11 others," KNA, MLA 1/467.

27. For example, see the comments of Justice Law in Criminal Case 118/1953, "Muchiri Gathothwa and Ndambini Kiambuni," KNA, MLA 1/586.

28. For examples, see Criminal Case 584/1954, "Criminal Appeals 988 and 989 of 1954," KNA, MLA 1/1098; Criminal Case 178/1953, "Criminal Appeal 541 of 1953," KNA, MLA 1/613.

29. For example, see Paget Bourke to Attorney General (Cyprus), 3 June 1957, TNA:PRO, FCO 141/4403, recommending that Cyprus might follow Kenya's example if they needed to clear a backlog of cases from the Supreme Court.

30. Figures compiled from returns in "Emergency Assize Returns," KNA, DC/KSM/1/15/122; "Emergency Assize Returns 1954," KNA, DC/KSM/1/15/286; "Capital Cases—speeding up, 1954–55," KNA CS/1/16/17.

31. For prosecutions of females, see Marina E. Santoru, "The Colonial Idea of Women and Direct Intervention: The Mau Mau Case," *African Affairs* 95, no. 379 (1996): 253–67.

32. TNA:PRO, CO 822/1256. Some convicts had sentences overturned because they were juveniles, others died in custody, and others still were declared insane; but even when these are accounted for there remain small discrepancies in the overall figures.

33. For an account of Kimathi's capture and treatment, see Anderson, *Histories of the Hanged,* 288–90.

34. For Waruhiu Itote's trial papers, see Criminal Case 35/1954, "Waruhiu Itote," KNA, MLA 1/677. For the full context, see Osborne, *General China.*

35. Kinyatti, *History of Resistance,* 332.

36. A. D. Dunn (Interrogator, Special Branch, Nyeri), "Interrogation Report—Dedan Kimathi s/o Waciuri," 31 October 1956, TNA:PRO, WO 276/533, reproduced as Document 5 in this volume.

37. Exhibit No. 20, signed arrest statement of the accused, 22 October 1956, reproduced as Document 6 in this volume.

38. On the use made of interrogation reports, see "Mau Mau Unrest: Mau Mau Interrogation Centre, Embakasi, 1953–1957," TNA:PRO, FCO 141/6179.

39. For an indication, see Helen O'Shea, *Ireland and the End of the British Empire: The Republic and Its Role in the Cyprus Emergency* (London: I. B. Tauris, 2014).

40. These cases are Criminal Case 655/1954, "Ndungu Ngang'a and Wakenya w/o Kiata," KNA, MLA 1/1166; Criminal Case 64/1955, "Mukwate Leti and Njuguna alias Mthakyo Mutinda," KNA, MLA 1/1276; Criminal Case 69/1956, "Mutahi Guama," KNA, MLA 1/1365, which was a retrial ordered by the Court of Appeal.

41. Mukwate Leti was the other person to be hanged, on 2 September 1955, having been convicted as an oath administrator in Criminal Case 64/1955, ibid.

42. Evidence of Gitonga Wambugu Wamiatu.

43. Judicial Department (Nairobi) to Cumming and Miller (PO box 607, Nairobi), 19 December 1956, Payment Order from the "Emergency Expenditure Fund," for the sum of KSh 4,405, in the papers of Ralph Millner, Archives of the Institute of Commonwealth Studies, Senate House Library, ICS 165/3/2.

44. See the foreword by Mũgo and Ngũgĩ to this volume.

45. For what I believe to be the first scholarly discussion of Kimathi's epilepsy, see Mahone, "Psychology of the Tropics."

46. "Accused's Mental Health to Be Examined," *East African Standard,* 13 September 1946; "Narok Crime: Death Sentence," *East African Standard,* 27 September 1946.

47. "Unanimous Verdict and Sentence of Death," *East African Standard,* 21 April 1913.

48. Report on the trial in the *East African Standard,* 24 November 1956.

49. Justice Law to Governor Baring, 3 March 1954, and Criminal Appeal no. 168 of 1954, Judgment, both in Criminal Case 80/1954, "Mwangi Wambugu," KNA, MLA 1/725.

50. The relevant documents can be found in "Offer of Amnesty and treatment of surrendered terrorists, 1952–54," TNA:PRO, FCO 141/5685; and "Surrender terms for Mau Mau terrorists, 1955," TNA:PRO, FCO 141/6450.

51. On the discovery and release of these documents, as the consequence of a legal action brought by Kenyan victims of British tortures during the counterinsurgency in the 1950s, see Anderson, "Mau Mau in the High Court," 699–716; Anderson, "Guilty Secrets," 142–60.

52. "Top Secret—Meeting with the C-in-C, 11.00 am, 20 August 1953," Government House, 20 August 1953, TNA:PRO, FCO 141/6557. Unfortunately, the two letters referred to are not with the file.

53. Exhibit No. B1, transcribed as Document 12 in this volume.

54. See the Statement of Assessors, in Document 1 in this volume.

55. Appeals could only be lodged on grounds of procedural or technical irregularities in the trial and not on the basis of the interpretation of the evidence. Appeals involved the review of the documentation on the case by senior judges, and did not involve any hearing. Appeals were lodged in approximately 15 percent of the cases that came before the Special Emergency Assize Courts. Anderson, *Histories of the Hanged,* 290.

56. Appeals to the Privy Council in London were rare, owing to the expense and the difficulties in securing a barrister to present the case, but also because there was little chance of success unless the appeal could be linked to a contentious point of law that had determined the judgment. "Privy Council Petition, Dedan Kimathi Wachiuri," and related papers, KNA, MAC/KEN/73/11.

57. Anderson, *Histories of the Hanged,* 60. See also the trial papers in KNA, MLA 1/468. Ex–paramount chief Koinange and his son were accused of having planned the murder of Senior Chief Waruhiu, whose death was the event that triggered the declaration of a State of Emergency in October 1952.

58. This and what follows is drawn from Henderson, *Hunt,* 253–66.

59. Mazrui, "On Heroes," 22, 34.

2

Mau Mau's Debates on Trial

John M. Lonsdale

Kimathi's Defense

On the morning of 23 November 1956, a month after he had been shot, severely wounded, and taken into custody, Dedan Kimathi took the defendant's chair in the Nyeri courtroom dock. He faced two charges: the possession of an unlicensed revolver and of six of its .38-caliber rounds. Under Kenya's Emergency laws each was a capital crime—unless, that is, he could show "lawful excuse" for carrying them. If found guilty on either charge he would be hanged, as one thousand of his fellow insurgents had been before him.[1] His evidence suggests that he had no wish to follow them; to the contrary, he argued that he had had to arm himself against them for fear of their murderous discontents. By choosing self-defense as his lawful excuse—his only possible means to secure an acquittal and escape the gallows—Kimathi had also chosen to put Mau Mau's internal debates publicly on trial.

For four days he had heard the prosecution evidence given by members of the Gikuyu Tribal Police (TPs). They claimed to have shot and captured him as a fugitive terrorist. As dawn was breaking on 20 October, so they said, they had caught him returning to the forest that had been the

Mau Mau realm for the past four years. He was carrying maize and sugarcane stolen from Gikuyu households at the forest's edge. The TPs had challenged him, he had fled and, after a few misses, one of them, Ndirangu, had shot him in the groin, so preventing his escape. On the TPs' evidence, then, Kimathi had come out of the forest because he was hungry; he had said nothing about wanting to surrender, or about his gun.[2]

Kimathi told a different story when he came to be examined by Kenya's solicitor general, Diarmaid Conroy, an Irish Catholic. He rested his defense on two grounds. First, he had lawful excuse for being armed in his fear of being killed, not by the colonial security forces but by the "forest men" from whom he had "finally split" more than two years earlier. This admission may not have surprised the court. Whites wanted to believe him to be a deranged psychopath, the supreme embodiment of the horror in which they held Mau Mau as a whole. Equally, many of his own men were known to hate him as a dictator, however much they stood in his awe; his bodyguards strangled critics.[3] Kimathi himself held that his would-be killers resented not his discipline but his strategy, his proposed peace talks with the British. In bringing his arms with him, moreover, he was simply complying with the terms of the government's surrender offers.[4] He had told the TPs of his intention to surrender and of his gun but had been too shocked and sick to repeat this statement when questioned in hospital by a white police officer; he suffered from what Gikuyu called "devils," what whites called epilepsy.[5]

Conroy pressed Kimathi further. Had he really broken with Mau Mau all that time ago? Had he not written to the government, months after the alleged split, under such grand titles as Field Marshal, Knight of the East African Empire, and President of the Kenya Parliament and Land Freedom Army?[6] Did this not prove he was still in command? Kimathi disagreed. His followers had promoted him, not he himself, so he did not know how important his ranks were, whether "top or bottom or middle." Moreover, in his letter of 27 March 1954 (Exhibit No. 23) he had written not as a commander but as "an intermediary—between. . . . I did write that letter with the intention of getting peace but I was not on either side. . . . I was afraid of Mau Mau and have been ever since."[7]

In that case, why, asked Conroy, did he take so long to "come in" and surrender?[8] Kimathi explained: it was dangerous, some fighters had been shot in the attempt. It was riskier still for him; there was a price on his head—KSh 10,000, or £500.[9] Members of the security forces might think it easier to secure that reward by killing rather than capturing him (as perhaps Ndirangu had tried?). It was not until he was sick, deserted, and hunted on all sides that he had decided to take his chance. Without this "change of heart" he could well have continued to hide in the vastness of the Nyandarua or Aberdare forests.

Kimathi had to convince three assessors, fellow Gikuyu and the chief justice Sir Kenneth O'Connor, a Protestant Irishman and Indian army veteran of the First World War. We cannot know how he came to agree with his defense counsel, Frederick Miller, a Nairobi lawyer, how to present his case. However, the police interrogation he had faced three weeks before the trial must have helped him think out his best line of defense. On 31 October, a week after capture, he had been questioned by a Police Special Branch officer, Anthony Dunn, seconded from the army's Kenya Regiment, a surprisingly young and inexperienced choice to handle so important a prize.[10] Dunn's report was not presented in court, for reasons that would have been at once political, operational, and legal.[11] It recorded a story that in four respects was strikingly different from the evidence that Kimathi offered later in court.

Under interrogation Kimathi had said nothing about surrender, had claimed a longer command of Mau Mau, and admitted to possessing both pistol and shotgun. This was, in effect, a threefold confession of guilt—as that was construed by Kenya's Emergency laws. He had also, finally, attributed his colleagues' anger to reasons other than the peace offers he had made to the government. Miller had "taken instructions," as lawyers put it, from Kimathi before this interrogation and will have known the danger in which his client was placed. Miller had then visited Nyeri again, presumably for more discussion, on the three days before the trial. These days of preparation and then the four days of listening to the prosecution case had given Kimathi and his counsel ample time in which to convert a confession of guilt, made under interrogation, into a case for acquittal.[12] How far they believed this strategy would be effective is something else we cannot know, but Kimathi had apparently decided not to challenge the trial as a farce, a bewigged mask for colonial injustice.[13]

Moreover, Kimathi's defense had much truth in it and, since he knew enough English to correct the interpreter, we may assume that the trial transcript is a fair representation of his case. Mau Mau's forest leadership was certainly divided, as the police already knew and a wider public has known since the first Mau Mau memoirs appeared, in the 1960s.[14] At issue were questions of strategy and authority. All insurgencies are a gamble. Their strategic choices, none of them safe, cannot be negotiated between institutions; they have to be argued out face-to-face by leaders whose authority is daily subject to the harsh audit of events; disagreement is inevitable. Kimathi's defense focused on a strategic dispute, his peace efforts, not on challenges to his authority. But dissent over strategy is all the more likely, and likely to be bitter, when, in a contested cause like Mau Mau, new leaders arise and with arguable authority and untested ability demand that their followers be ready to die. The court had no interest in this side of the forest debate but for Mau Mau it was vital. At bottom the argument was about "moral economy," being the reciprocal connections between personal authority and collective action, social obligation and self-reliance.[15] These relationships matter. Insurgents disillusioned by the inequalities of the forest war became the colonial forces' most valuable assets in the hunt for Kimathi.

Kenya's African politics had long been concerned with the same profound, intertwined issues of strategy and moral economy. Mau Mau was not unique in its strategic debates; its moral dilemmas were nothing new. Kimathi was not the first leader to risk assassination from within.

Strategy and Moral Economy

Bethwell Ogot, doyen of Kenyan historians, long ago showed how Mau Mau's *nyimbo,* its "hymns," tried and failed to reconcile moral economy and strategy, solidarity and action.[16] With their diverse imaginations of history, religion, and politics, the nyimbo (sing., *rwimbo*) called up different coalitions for divergent ends. Their political demands were secular and related to nationals, fellow Kenyans. But their pleas for the return of the land "stolen" by white settlers used images that were both biblical and specifically, ancestrally, Gikuyu. Such tensions are to be expected. As another senior historian of Kenya, Tom Spear, has put it, all human societies know many "levels of intimacy": gender, age, ethnicity, class, caste, schooling, religion, and so on.[17] Even British officials at the time had to recognize this inconvenient truth. In order to explain why some other Kenyans joined the supposedly all-Gikuyu Mau Mau, the colonial government put the blame not on its own failings but on Gikuyu cunning: on their "indoctrination," "viral infection," "contamination," "contagion," "canker," and "underground machination." But some officials broke ranks to report that workers from western Kenya, none of them Gikuyu, saw Mau Mau as "an African national movement."[18] Moral uncertainty was not peculiar to Africans; the British knew strategic ambiguities of their own.

Such moral and strategic changes of view and direction provide us with a useful frame for analyzing the history of colonial Kenya's African politics—what we need in order to understand Kimathi's defense. Mau Mau's debates, Kimathi's dangers, his lawful excuse, are an extreme example of political dilemmas repeatedly encountered, not a different story.

In summary, in the seventy short years of British rule, African political activity swung in social scale, between small and large; in political focus, between regional and national; and in method, legal and violent. The possibility of imagining ever wider "levels of intimacy" or political solidarity underlay this oscillation. At the start, in the 1890s, there could be no Kenyan resistance to conquest; the British had not yet imposed a "Kenya" on the land. Ethnic solidarity was equally unknown; "tribal" consciousness had not yet been sharpened by alien rule, biblical literacy, or nationalism. Some Gikuyu clans, accordingly, helped the British and their Maasai allies "punish" others; Luyia (not yet so named) and Luo settlements fought piecemeal; not all Nandi or Turkana joined in their own wars of resistance. Twenty years later the experience of migrant labor and Nairobi's town life brought together a multiethnic, even transcolonial, level of intimacy in the East Africa Association, bloodily suppressed by panicked police in 1922.[19] Twenty years of growing ethnic consciousness then followed. This has proved to be a more lasting enlargement, if also segmentation, of African moral imaginations, sparked among other things by what they were learning of world history.

Mission-taught literacy, *msoma* in many vernaculars, was in large part responsible. Kimathi was not the first to think the Israelites had shown that tribal history could teach global lessons.[20] The interwar years saw some of Kenya's ethnic groups reach out for a practical equivalent, namely, imperial citizenship. Two local examples encouraged them: the kingdom of Buganda, related by treaty with the British Crown, and East Africa's

Indians, able to exploit the anxieties of their imperial protector, the viceroy over the water, in Delhi.[21]

After the Second World War the Kenya African Union (KAU) fostered interethnic alliance, not cultural unity, thanks to a principled respect for each group's struggle to achieve *maendeleo,* or progress; local ethnic equality was now a more urgent aim than imperial citizenship. All ethnic groups were thought to deserve what a monolithic Kenyan nationalism might deny them—their right to self-determination, a reimagination of the stateless moral economy, well understood by all Kenyans, that prized the self-mastery of the male householder. But a particular moral agony divided the Gikuyu. A few, KAU activists among them, had done well out of British rule, but the many had suffered more grievously than other Kenyans. "Big men," both black elders in the increasingly crowded "reserves" and settler farmers in the newly prosperous White Highlands, had begun to prefer property to clients; both cut down their tenants' rights. The poor, betrayed by these once supportive patrons, lost hope of married adulthood. This social differentiation, a humiliation for many, blew the KAU's multiethnicity apart. Moral economy had not been so greatly outraged elsewhere; other peoples shared neither this Gikuyu despair nor, therefore, their militancy.[22] The Emergency, or Mau Mau war, then sharpened this interethnic divergence; British counterinsurgency split Gikuyu still more clearly into rival vanguard groups—Mau Mau subversives and "loyalist" security forces.[23] The crucible of war then taught Gikuyu, better than others, both how to press demands and how to use the state, whether to reform, repress, or attempt the two together.[24] This ethnic exceptionalism, finally, made it hard to imagine a common nationhood.[25]

This potted history suggests that strategy is argued within moral communities. What these are and how history has formed them are best explained by a Gikuyu proverb: "those without previous dealings with each other have no cause to quarrel."[26] People argue most with their nearest, those whom they most need to trust, who share a moral economy—that web of reputational relations forever torn between self-mastery and neighborly duty. Moral communities set boundaries to both. Here lies scholarly controversy.[27] How far did colonial rule deliberately stimulate the divisive ethnic identities that have often become the most pressing of Africa's moral communities? It is a large issue. For us the proverb is persuasive enough. For Kenya's modern ethnicities emerged from out of migrant peoples who for centuries before colonial rule had been loosely knit in themselves and closely interrelated with others. Yet material fixities underlay this social fluidity. Each hybrid people had to argue out the tolerably unequal terms of moral economy that enabled them to live in their particular environment: forest, hill, desert, or prairied plain. These ecological ethnicities then became still more vigorous debating societies under British rule, with new "dealings" to discuss. Alien rule and its African roots, mission literacy (especially for daughters), migrant labor, and rural capitalism all tested the conventional civic virtues of household duty and mutual reciprocity. Argument raised self-consciousness. The boundaries of these ethnic moral economies, moral ethnicities, tended to be confirmed rather than created by the "tribal" administrative districts of colonial rule.

Moral debate also raised a strategic question: might political recognition resolve internal difference? That was the issue of the 1920s, especially, again, for Gikuyu. Police firepower had killed Nairobi's multiethnic energy in the "Thuku troubles" of 1922, but in 1923 the British appeared to repent, with their "Devonshire declaration" that Kenya was primarily an African, not a white man's, country. London made this statement to calm conflict between Kenya's British and Indian immigrants, not to appease African unrest but what struck one Johnstone Kenyatta was that political concession had followed violent repression, a seemingly causal sequence he never forgot.[28] It encouraged Gikuyu "readers," Christian *athomi,* who drank tea rather than beer, to work for imperial recognition by pursuing "progress," a collective means to win the civic virtue previously earned by the costly public energy shown by prosperous, polygamous households. In 1930, with this modern ethnic patriotism at his back and Britain's democratic history before him, Kenyatta called on the colonial office to promote "by constitutional means the interests of the Gikuyu Community and their rights and liberties as citizens of the British Empire."[29] Like Kimathi years later, his representative role was soon undermined by argument behind his back.

Household and Paperwork

Gikuyu dispute came to a head in the "female circumcision crisis" of 1929, in which political strategy sprang from intimate moral economy. Men faced twin threats to their landed authority. Nairobi's carnal temptations might seduce wives and daughters; new white settlement, as rumored, might take more land. Men's chief defense against the giddiness of women was the same women's pride in the painful surgery of clitoridectomy, or (today) genital mutilation, that they endured in initiation ceremonies hosted by men of property. Yet the British were pressing Gikuyu to modify the operation; some missionaries wished to ban it altogether for Christian daughters. To the discomfort of its secretary, Kenyatta, away in London, and possibly against his instincts, the Kikuyu Central Association (KCA) angrily defended the custom as the guarantee of social order.[30] But some athomi now thought it barbarous; missionaries would not otherwise have dared such a radical bodily reform. Had Gikuyu opinion not been divided there would have been no crisis.[31]

Each side had a different history in mind.[32] KCA's conservatives relied, implicitly, on a patchwork dynastic past in which Gikuyu lineages had labored separately to civilize the land, a constant test. Christian subversives called on a parallel, pan-Gikuyu history of recursive change. Every thirty years or so in the past eligible sons had bought out their fathers' juridical powers in order to heal the land of their accumulated envy. Successive generations were later named after the changes they had seen or pioneered. "Readers" concluded that this tradition of invention gave their own generation authority to change the future, too. In 1929, after a Christian girl was cut against her will and the law took little notice, some protested that "we Kikuyu ourselves," not the Europeans, had now ruled against female circumcision: "We are at the beginning of a great building up of new customs and the forming of Christianity, the same as those before us made ordinances for the generations after them."[33]

The defenders of clitoridectomy called themselves *karing'a,* true Gikuyu. They ridiculed their opponents as *kirore,* after the thumbprint each had put to a petition calling for readers' daughters to be protected. True Gikuyu were self-reliant household heads; thumbprinters usurped this domestic autonomy with registers and rules, with paper. But karing'a soon had to adopt similar office procedures in order to compete with kirore, and indeed outdid the mission schools in giving the English-language tuition that made the case for imperial citizenship.[34] This tension between household reputation and bureaucratic order, rival bases of authority, was another foretaste of Kimathi's troubles.

The postwar KAU suffered the same tension at the national level. Returning from England two years after its foundation, to become the union's third successive Gikuyu president, Jomo Kenyatta (as he had become) still believed that ethnic self-help under propertied elders was a moral precondition of political responsibility.[35] As if to protect rural patriarchy from urban, panethnic, bureaucracy, he neglected the KAU's head office. KAU officials, all part-timers, could neither sustain the party newspaper nor pay the rent nor yet get many to renew their membership.[36] But Kenyatta was of two minds, for reasons (again) of both strategy and moral economy. He had to ask himself if industrious African progress, unsupported by political pressure, would be enough to make the British listen. Given Kenya's white supremacy and African anxieties, were either meritorious effort or sustained protest even imaginable?

Kenyatta would need Britain's imperial support if the colonial government were ever to reward black self-help, since that would be resisted by white settlers, whose profitable management of the war economy had consolidated their local power. This hope was not groundless. Kenyatta thought he had his precedent, the rifle fire of 1922 that he believed had shamed the imperial trustee of 1923. He also had friends in Britain's postwar Labour government. So he asked his KAU meetings: were there twenty Kenyattas ready to die? Could they withstand the kicking of the imperial lion (or donkey) if he held its head? Apparently without a nod to Thomas Jefferson, he told them that such martyr blood would nourish the tree of freedom; the British already had a guilty conscience.[37] There is no evidence that he ever called for armed revolt; an unarmed crowd had provoked the guns of 1922—and, so he thought, imperial unease. Victim solidarity in the face of colonial provocation could work again. Kenyatta was not alone in this strategic hope. The Luyia journalist Wycliffe Awori deplored the lack of any popular protest when the leader of a dockworkers' strike was sentenced to internal exile; if leaders were to take similar risks in the future "the common man" must become their "strong fortress."[38]

But was a strong fortress possible at a time of social disquiet? Patriotic men throughout East Africa felt that their moral economies, moral ethnicities founded on domestic discipline, were under threat. Big men, once supportive patrons of scarce labor on ample acres, were struggling to become capitalists in an era of rising population on limited land; their deserted clients despaired of marriage and self-mastery. Young men's migrant labor and female enterprise in trade, school, and urban property reinforced many men's sense of social decay; the seeming growth in sexual license and marital discord was all the more shameful when Christian revivalists publicly confessed their sins.[39]

Dedan Kimathi was born into this climate of intimate unease in Nyeri District, northern Gikuyuland.[40] Orphaned by his father's death and at risk of scorn by being circumcised not with his age-mates but in a dispensary, he attended a succession of schools, both Scottish mission and independent, between spells of work in varied capacities. After this disrupted youth, probably no more frustrating than for many others, one can see why, in his first public role as vice-secretary of a KAU branch in the White Highlands, his agenda included an African "code of behaviour."[41] For what this might mean to a man with a rare ability to reflect on his social and political circumstances we have the memory of Charles Harris, who as a teenager in the 1940s knew Kimathi as his father's farm dairy clerk. The latter disappeared before the Emergency, leaving papers that Harris thought sketched out "a new order." Kimathi had listed over twenty requirements, including those commonly demanded by ethnic welfare associations all over East Africa, namely, bans on prostitution, male and female, and on drinking bottled beer.[42]

The first Gikuyu-language novel, *Marriage Procedures*, by Kimathi's near age-mate Gakaara wa Wanjau, epitomized these anxious times. Its Christian heroine hanged herself over her father's gateway, his *riigi*, the symbol of household autonomy, because her lover, returned from the war, could not afford her father's extortionate bridewealth demands. An elder's greed had cursed young hopes of adult responsibility.[43] On all sides, then, there were calls to repair broken moral economies of social obligation, for reasons deeper than building a political fortress.

A fortress was needed nonetheless, and Gikuyu needed it most; they had known too many frustrations and defections. A conservative establishment of aging KCA men, chiefs, and lineage elders took the lead in trying to turn a fractious moral ethnicity into a reliable political base. The prime mover was senior chief Koinange, polygamous patron of the Gikuyu Anglican Church, who refused to cut his daughters, a pioneer of ox-plow and piped water, father of the first Gikuyu university graduate, and in 1948 Kenyatta's third father-in-law.[44] As in seventeenth-century England, with its "culture of subscription and oath-taking" ruled by propertied men,[45] so too the Gikuyu required men to confirm their loyalty to any joint enterprise with a livestock fee and an oath sworn in the presence of spiritual forces, watchful ancestors among them. The elders who took this *mbari*, or lineage oath, were known landowners, the sort of men who without much paperwork could swear to a greater solidarity than Gikuyu had ever known and yet retain self-mastery.[46]

A seemingly inexorable escalation of conflict undid this politics of notables, this strategy for disciplining popular action. It is a tale often told.[47] First, many natural leaders were discredited; juniors told elders to "keep silent."[48] Big men who failed to sponsor their clients' manhood had forfeited deference. Most made an exception of Kenyatta; his oratory was an uplifting patronage in words. The youthful poor were not the only ones to fear that adult self-mastery, *wiathi*, was now out of reach. Urban workers suffered rapid inflation; mechanization prompted white farmers to extinguish the tenancy rights of their workers, their "squatters," over one-quarter of the Gikuyu people; the stiff tenurial rules on new peasant settlement schemes shattered household self-determination.[49] The KAU's moderate nationalists exercised as little persuasive power as elders; a government investing in fresh white settlement paid them little attention. Gikuyu began to build local solidarities with oaths of unity that promised defense against despair. As usual, opinion divided; many elders thought that such heavy legal responsibility should not be laid on weak women and unmarried, untested men. In the next stumble toward war, the government soothed settler fears by banning these oaths and the movement gathering behind them, a determined new leadership that emerged within the KAU. Some of them contemplated violence: trade unionists familiar with the criminals of outcast Nairobi, traders, lorry owners, taxi drivers, office clerks. The secrecy they needed meant intimidating or eliminating any who refused an oath or threatened to tell. A spiral of state repression and the militants' need for silence, each abetting the other, wound its way to war.

The conflict flared in 1952, nominally between black and white, but Gikuyu were too divided to sustain that simple confrontation. True, most had sworn an oath of sexually disciplined unity that was believed capable of killing the disobedient. But many had done so late and defensively, in response to the British declaration of Emergency. Both the wealthy and landless joined in, the married and the young, Christians and unlettered, often from fear rather than consent. Social difference did not, therefore, enlist opposing lines of battle; rather, an erratic logic of violence unrolled. Friends and rivals in the enterprising, now incipiently capitalist, pursuit of self-mastery were thrown together or apart by the unpredictable demands of survival.[50] A torment in moral economy overwhelmed any strategy the insurgent organizers had had in mind—and some remember an intended massacre of whites.[51] Under further British pressure anticolonial resistance became African civil war, a mosaic of undecided loyalties that perturbed the British as much as they later alarmed Kimathi.

It was perhaps to counter this uncertainty that insurgents were such sticklers for paperwork; never was there a more bureaucratic subversion. Some members had burned their hated passbooks (sing., *kipande*); the movement forged their replacements. Activists also registered all who took a second, fighting (*mbatuni,* platoon) oath. A forest general's briefcase, never found, was said to hold the names of seventy-five hundred men under command; schools were raided for exercise books; Kimathi's diaries confirmed his responses to interrogation.[52] Two forest secretaries—Karari Njama, Kimathi's critical supporter, and Kahinga Wachanga, a bitter opponent—survived to write the two most informative war memoirs.[53] A managerial instinct for uniformity prompted the decision to omit from the movement's oaths any appeal to ancestral witnesses. These might well have cautioned landowners who knew their lineage of descent but could only divide Gikuyu at large.[54] Mythical ancestors or past generations were different; they unified—a reflection that raises the question of how the movement was known.

Militants quarried myth, memory, and moral economy for names. One of the commonest, Gikuyu na Muumbi, the ethnic Abraham and Sarah, came from myth out of mission literacy. In 1924, Marion Stevenson, a Scottish missionary, published a Gikuyu-language primer for use in schools. It told of a covenant between God, the Gikuyu people, and their fertile land. Her athomi readers, schoolteachers among them, named the ancestral covenanters as Gikuyu and his wife, Muumbi. So literacy served ethnic patriotism, so myth entered modernity.[55] Memory offered another name, *iregi,* a rebellious former generation. The basis of moral economy, "property and self-mastery" suggested a third, *ithaka na wiathi.* More simply, many called themselves *uiguano,* "unity"; *muingi,* "the people"; or *muhimu,* "important."[56]

But Mau Mau is the name that has stuck. Much ink has been spilled in its interpretation. There is little doubt that (however it originated)[57] it was a nickname first used by the movement's opponents to express regret as much as anger. Mau Mau is onomatopoeia, it mimics the ravenous guzzling of children made hungry by their parents. Most probably agreed that the government had failed to feed Gikuyu; but some seem to have felt that Gikuyu na Muumbi were nonetheless too impatient to eat their elders' authority. Kenyatta was among those who accepted this meaning.[58] How far he also thought it justified is a question. Called on by government to denounce Mau Mau, he denied knowing it but cursed it all the same. The muhimu committee warned him to watch his words if he valued his life; their younger enthusiasts, roused by his rhetorical vision of a self-reliant path to freedom, might feel betrayed.[59] But where then was the danger in cursing an unknown movement by its opponents' malicious nickname? However much their strategic aim forced them to recruit legal minors, did some within muhimu perhaps regret their greed for moral authority?

Parliament and Riigi

The British saved Kenyatta from possible danger—as much from angry settlers as from Mau Mau—by arresting him, with other supposed managers of the movement, on declaring a state of Emergency on 20 October 1952. Muhimu's undetected militants prepared more urgently for war. Again, others have told the Emergency's history; it need not be repeated here.[60] Moreover, after nearly four years of warfare Kimathi said nothing in court about the fighting; his defense lay in the bitterness of debate within Mau Mau, "a polity defined by dissent."[61] While the context was unprecedented in its brutality, the terms of debate were neither new nor revolutionary; they continued to reflect the dual experience of subjection to a global empire while also learning world history. Gikuyu-language portions of the Bible first appeared in 1903, the complete New Testament in 1926, and the Old in 1951,[62] so Kimathi the "reader" was well aware of his global environment. His letter of October 1954 not only compared Mau Mau with other contemporary conflicts but also situated Gikuyu in history. The children of Israel, the world's prototype nation, were his model.[63] This global comparison under the eye of history continued to point, as in the 1920s, to the need for a domestic "code of behaviour," especially if future generations were to be as self-disciplined as their elders. The arguments that Kimathi put on trial were entirely conventional. That is why they destroyed Mau Mau's cohesion from within as surely as did counterinsurgent warfare from without.

Since Gikuyu shared a sense of social breakdown, decisions to join one side or another of the Mau Mau war depended, as stated, on the shock of events. The most devastating was the mass reflux of squatter families from the White Highlands to their former, now crowded, homes.[64] This remigration—at once a labor protest, an official policy, and the outcome of white farmer fears—inflamed intimately poisonous land disputes between Gikuyu and supplied recruits for militant leaders. In a parallel process officials prodded the knots of "resistance" clustered around colonial chiefs into self-defense units that became the "loyalist" Kikuyu Guard (KG).[65]

Loyalist is as contentious a name as Mau Mau. The KG were more loyal to economic self-mastery than to alien rule but saw the British as more protective than Mau Mau of this civic virtue. The names Gikuyu themselves adopted can be understood in that sense. Insurgents were *itungati,* senior but still unmarried warriors who served as Kenyatta's rearguard, his "strong fortress," as their grandfathers had protected cattle raids on their return journey. The KG were *kamatimu,* spear-carrying junior elders, entitled to marry after completing their warrior duty.[66] Itungati fought, therefore, to reopen a path to adulthood, kamatimu to discipline juniors. Some thought Mau Mau were *irungu,* a candidate generation expected to "straighten" society, as Kimathi desired and kirore had intended in the 1930s. Others called the Emergency *Maina*'s war, the battle of a generation who would already have been in power, no longer irungu, had the practice of generational transition not fallen away under colonial rule.[67] Itungati and kamatimu shared, then, a philosophy of history; more immediately, some also held material interests in common.

A striking example of shared interests linked Kimathi, notorious "terrorist," and senior chief Muhoya, a leading "loyalist." Their home area, North Tetu, in Nyeri District, had experienced a particularly divisive struggle for rural capitalism, known officially as progressive farming. In the 1940s an emerging gentry converted their lineage seniority into registered property, at the expense of the usage rights they owed to juniors and clients. A KCA man in his youth, Muhoya was a pioneer in this revolution in moral economy, blandly called land reform. He led in the private fencing of pasture for the grade cattle (crossbreeds between indigenous and imported European cattle) he and others bought from white neighbors. Under veterinary regulations he obliged less wealthy stockowners to take costly measures of disease control to protect the investments of the few; he also started a dairy cooperative and for a time employed Kimathi as clerk. While the latter is said to have run off with the dairy's funds he nonetheless retained a tacit truce with his chief throughout the Emergency. Kimathi had age-mates among Muhoya's sons and school friends among the chief's KGs, including one who tended his wound after capture. Such local understandings existed elsewhere. The British did not dare dismiss Muhoya, indeed used him as Kimathi's postman (Exhibit No. 25). While they sacked younger chiefs who pursued a similar neutrality, officials turned a blind eye to other senior chiefs who, like Muhoya, disloyally tried to keep a Gikuyu peace.[68]

Doubts about the allegiance of their Gikuyu allies also obliged the British to collude with those loyalists who fought dirty in a civil war that, forced upon them in large part by British policy, was bound to be a dirty one. As is better known now with the release of "migrated" records, white officials could and did act illegally—not merely looking the other way—to protect loyalists who abused their power for private gain or, often in revenge, mistreated, even murdered, Mau Mau suspects or captives.[69] In early 1955 the government tried to save itself further embarrassment by disbanding the KG under a double amnesty that absolved both Mau Mau and loyalists of past crimes. The Fort Hall (Murang'a) district commissioner warned his staff to continue to tread with care; loyalists might still change sides. "They had no particular common cause with us, but nevertheless fought loyally on our side." They should be treated "with tact, fairness and consideration. If any fall from grace they must of course be dealt with according to law . . . [but if] they are spurned or ill-used after all they have done, they will turn against us and leave us with no means of controlling the still Mau Mau–inclined masses."[70]

If the British did not trust all loyalists, no more could forest leaders rely on all itungati. Mau Mau had no prisons; rewards for loyalty lay in an increasingly unlikely future; physical punishment and death were the only available sanctions. Kimathi's opponents called this dictatorship. But there was also endless and earnest discussion, recorded in insurgent memoirs.[71]

Mau Mau's public sphere shared with Gikuyu society at large its fear that poverty, land disputes, migrant labor, and now war, were all threats to civility. Itungati deplored the impossibility of marriage and parenthood—while depending for their supplies on mothers, wives, and sisters, a far from "passive wing." Meetings called to decide military strategy soon turned to worry about this amputated moral economy. Kimathi's peace feelers were motivated partly by a deep concern that war was bad not only for personal character but also for social relations, even for interracial understanding.[72] More immediately, rules of faithful cohabitation between male and female itungati were enacted to protect comradely trust from the corrosion of sexual competition. Kimathi, however, was said to flout his own rules by enjoying the company of a succession of women.

Debate about the production of comradeship inevitably raised questions of meaning and belief, both as taught by history. Most *mbuci,* or "bushes" (what the British called gangs), offered daily prayers to a God who was both the Gikuyu Ngai and Israel's Jehovah; missionaries had long preached this equivalence between Gikuyu and biblical Old Testaments. Some fighters compared their warfare with the Exodus ordeal that had once tested the Israelites; the forest was a "course," a proving ground, like the Sinai desert. A new rwimbo portrayed Kimathi as Moses, ascending the mountain alone. Some said the British, modern Philistines, had sent the giant Goliath against them.[73] In June 1953, Karari Njama, then secretary to the unlettered Stanley Mathenge, read aloud from the book of *Lamentations.* His itungati audience agreed that they shared the slavery Israel had suffered in Babylon. Njama reassured them: "Then don't be worried of what has become of us, saying that this is strange news you had never seen or heard of before. You have already heard it from the Israelites. It has happened to many other races and nations. It is History and History repeats itself. It is our turn now. All you have to do is persevere and fight bravely."[74]

In his letter of October 1954, Kimathi took a similar text as an inspiration to Gikuyu and a warning for the British: "In reading the history of the Israelites we also read the history of the Gikuyu. For there is one God for black and white and he rules the evil and the righteous together, for God is the ruler who is great. He always gives away the kingdom of the one who seeks to suppress."[75] One can only speculate, for lack of private papers, but it is tempting to imagine that Kimathi read into his Bible not only Gikuyu history but also his own, a onetime son of the Scottish mission. The Scots had a list of approved baptismal names, Dedan among them, and urged adherents to learn about their namesakes.[76] The biblical Dedan was both a man, of the lineage of Noah or Abraham and, later, a clan. This clan, with other "young lions," defeated the tyrant King Gog, who had devastated the land at a time when Israel had offended their God with their uncleanness (*thahu*) and transgressions (*kwagarara watho*).[77] In common with others, Kimathi the dairy clerk had once asked himself if Gikuyu were unclean. So were the British not only Philistines but also the avenging men of Gog, and in due course would their oppressions, like Gog's, cause their kingdom to be given away? These are questions impossible to answer, but would Kimathi have carried his Bible, as he did, and not have read it and wondered?

In July or August 1953 the onetime teacher Kimathi usurped the leadership of the ex-soldier Stanley Mathenge, first overall commander in the Nyandarua forest. Karari Njama, secretary now to Kimathi, was also a teacher. Such men, a second generation of readers, athomi, called the forest war to order on paper by devising a hierarchy of command, set over named units in battle formation.[78] They embodied this organization in the "Kenya Parliament," for which an imposing bamboo meeting hall was built high in the forest.[79] Literacy was essential for communication by courier, with trees serving as postboxes; it also countered the British propaganda that Mau Mau was a bestial reversion to a supposedly barbarous past. But, as in both the 1929 "female circumcision crisis" and in the tension between the landed network of mbari and muhimu's nominal roll, the authority of paperwork could be questioned.

Mathenge, with the charisma of one who had seen Jerusalem when in the British army, led the opposition to Kimathi's Parliament.[80] His dissenting mbuci leaders thought of themselves as the less educated but still needed paper—and a secretary in Kahinga Wachanga. The name they gave themselves said everything. It epitomized their constitutional opposition to written orders from officious superiors. They were the Kenya Riigi, a group that took its name from the outer gate that none but the householder should close. It secured domestic civility against the wild, protected self-mastery and defended, now, against the arrogance of paper.

The Riigi certainly threatened Kimathi; Wachanga called him a dictator. Riigi resented the insolence with which educated men presumed to instruct mbuci commanders. Parliament's paper stole the authority of face-to-face leadership, hard earned in the sharing of privation and danger. Readers were also cowards; Kimathi was said never to have fought in battle. Their Christianity, too, made literates despise the Gikuyu traditions that inspired the rank and file. Finally, when they looked to the future for which all were fighting, Riigi believed the educated would enjoy privileges and powers denied to the unlettered itungati by whose blood they would have been bought. According to Karari Njama, Parliament possessed a comprehensive rebuttal of these householder protests. In the modern world, first, the pen was mightier than the sword. Second, ideas set down on paper outlived the writer's death and so outweighed personality. In any case, third, personality tended to divide, ideas had the power to unite. Finally, some structure of command was essential. Riigi might think they were protecting the authority owed to each mbuci leader. Such householder sovereignty may once have been a virtue in the struggle against nature, but today it crippled collective resistance to unjust power.[81]

Kimathi's Parliament followed the logic of state building, Mathenge's Riigi spoke up for moral economy. This fundamental disagreement clearly gave Kimathi good reason to go armed, his supposedly lawful excuse. The conflict between Riigi and Parliament took at least three forms fatal to his leadership and, in the end, his life. Riigi men, first, were quicker than Kimathi to take up British offers of surrender talks, an initiative that infuriated him and intensified mutual suspicion between leaders.[82] Second, Superintendent Henderson got his best intelligence in his hunt for Kimathi from Riigi deserters, one of whom had been flogged for sleeping with a woman. Finally, on their capture or surrender in the later stages of the war many itungati decided to turn their coat and return into the trees as "pseudogangsters" under British command. These were the men who, increasingly on their own initiative, closed the net on Kimathi. Resentment of the forest leadership was among their motives. Mau Mau was demoralized by the acrimonious debates that Kimathi put on trial—but not, it must be remembered, before the movement had suffered casualties heavier than any regular army could have sustained. There were probably up to twenty thousand forest insurgents at the height of Mau Mau's strength in early 1954; by late 1956, the time of Kimathi's trial, they had lost nearly seventeen thousand dead, captured, and surrendered, most of them killed in action.[83]

Mau Mau's forest debates echoed those of the Gikuyu as a whole, in pitting the daily diplomacy of sovereign households against the unbending arrogance of institutional rules. Nor were these Gikuyu anxieties alone. The disputed conduct of their forest insurgency, however unique in its particular context in colonial history, raises questions of freedom, order, and authority of concern to us all.

Thirty years ago, in the late 1980s, Ngũgĩ wa Thiong'o asked, from his Swedish exile, "Why is history subversive?" It was a good question to pose in his foreword to Maina wa Kinyatti's edition of *The Dedan Kimathi Papers.*[84] Ngũgĩ's answer was that history tells, or should tell, both of humanity's common struggle against nature and of our internal battles to secure a just reward for all those who sweat at that task. He went on to argue that these struggles are what propel progressive social change. Most historians would agree. That is one reason why history is subversive, why it terrifies tyrants, why they try to rewrite it as a praise-song in which their sovereign will, not social struggle, is the motor of improvement. It was why, so Ngũgĩ concluded, Kenya's British rulers had suppressed the history of Mau Mau's "national struggle." They had praised, instead, the men whose "loyalist collaboration" with Britain had enabled them to become the rulers of a supposedly independent but in reality neo-colonial Kenya.

Yes, historians must always be subversive, and for another reason, too. We must always be critical of our sources, whether written or oral. They each tell their own, self-interested, story of the past; we must never take them at their word. But we must be self-critical as well, wary of our own stories since history, as Bethwell Ogot once advised us, is nothing if not a discipline of context.[85] But two contexts affect the way we write history and they tend to conflict. On one hand there is our own story: our present-day context cannot help but influence the historian's choice of the problems she or he wants to research, which witnesses to summon, and what questions to ask them. The other context is the past itself, that foreign country where they act and think differently from in the historian's own day. In the first context, we historians run the risk of creating a past that is interesting or useful to us today. But the past we thereby neglect or suppress—however unwittingly—may well have been the more important for those who lived it. And it is more complicated than that since there are always many such silenced pasts, each with their own discordant voices, like the discords of today, divided by age, class, gender, "race," and so on.

Ngũgĩ's context was his release from prison. He had been jailed by President Daniel arap Moi for writing treasonous books and plays; they had accused Kenya's criminal present of betraying the country's heroic past. As a student of Shakespeare, Ngũgĩ imagined the tyrant Moi kept sleepless by his fear of "the unavenged father's ghost of Kimathi's struggle and his Kenya Land Freedom Army." The memory of Mau Mau was certainly subversive in the context of the 1980s. But memory can serve contradictory purposes, in response to the changing context of the present day.[86] Under Moi the opponents of autocracy could look to Mau Mau for inspiration, as Prince Hamlet had looked to his father's ghost. More recently that same memory has been recast, to act in an opposing role, that of the sacrificial support, the historical justification, for what many see as the self-serving regime in power.[87] That is the problem with today's context for searching the past. Tomorrow's today will inevitably be different. Its history may have to differ too.

Yet, to insist, the foreign country of the past had its own lives, not always the same ones we find interesting or useful, each with their own anxieties and conflicts, endured and disputed with reference to still earlier remembered pasts. Under the stern eye of their own remembered history, Kimathi's forest fighters were obsessed with the seeming impossibility of achieving the responsible adulthood that their ancestors required of them. And how, in their turn, could they the childless be remembered? Fearing to die unmarried, reputation was the only descendant they could hope to generate. But the reputation that mattered most was the one that seemed beyond reach, that of propertied self-mastery, summed up as ithaka na wiathi, their unattainable self-description. It was the conventional ambition, shared between itungati and kamatimu. It was what both fought for, intimates but enemies; that was what made the war so brutal, so tragic. No civil war has ever simply aligned the honest, earnest, champions of the people against the crooked, heartless, servants of despotism. Opponents often turn out to be twins. If we are to enter a past country in its own context, with its own tragic sense of unanswerable questions then we have to subvert subversive history too.

In this reflection I again follow Ogot, who criticized the unanimity that the historian Michelet imposed on France's eighteenth-century revolutionaries. "This assumed unanimity," Ogot thought, was "confusing and unhelpful to the historian who seeks to understand the nature of the French Revolution. Such a historian must ask how unanimous the struggle was. Were there no cross-currents?"[88] If we want to understand the past for its own sake rather than use it for ours then that is one of the first questions any historian must ask.

Notes

While indebted to colleagues David Anderson, Donald Fraser, Ben Knighton, Godfrey Muriuki, Derek Peterson, and Richard Waller, and to two who were in Kenya at the time, Isabel Nanton (a Laikipia farmer's daughter) and Ian Parker (district officer, Kikuyu Guard, 1954–56), I alone remain responsible for what follows.

1. Anderson, *Histories of the Hanged.*

2. For reasons to question this evidence, see the foreword by Mĩcere Gĩthae Mũgo and Ngũgĩ wa Thiong'o, and Anderson's contribution to this volume.

3. Henderson, *Hunt,* 30–31; Wachanga, *Swords,* 25, 26–27; Gucu Gikoyo, *We Fought for Freedom: Tulipigania Uhuru* (Nairobi: East African Publishing House, 1979) is the memoir of a Mau Mau "enforcer"; for awe, see Karii Mubenge's diary, in Ian Parker, *The Last Colonial Regiment: The History of the Kenya Regiment (T.F.)* (Milton Brodie: Librario, 2009), 294–96.

4. See Exhibits Nos. B1 and D1, transcribed as Documents 12 and 14, respectively, in this volume.

5. For this aspect of the defense, see Anderson's contribution to this volume.

6. See Exhibit No. 22A, as translated by Derek Peterson and Joseph Kariuki Muriithi, reproduced as Document 8; and Exhibit No. 23, transcribed as Document 9 in this volume.

7. Exhibit No. 23, Document 9 in this volume.

8. An interestingly archaic phrase, recalling the 1890s, when officials wrote of Africans "coming in" (from the unruled bush) to submit to British (civilizing) rule.

9. See also Kimathi to Humphrey Slade, 10 March 1954, in David Lovatt Smith, *Kenya, the Kikuyu and Mau Mau* (Herstmonceux: Mawenzi Books, 2005), 309–13.

10. Thanks to Ian Parker for information from the archive of the (almost entirely white) Kenya Regiment.

11. For the latter, see Anderson's contribution to this volume.

12. Registrar of the Supreme Court of Kenya, Payment slip for Miller's travel expenses, 19 December 1956, Archives of the Institute of Commonwealth Studies, Senate House Library, Ralph Millner papers, ICS 165/3/2.

13. For other views on the trial, see Ngũgĩ and Mũgo's foreword and Githuku's contribution to this volume.

14. Clough, *Mau Mau Memoirs*, 13, 160–66.

15. Johanna Siméant, "Three Bodies of Moral Economy: The Diffusion of a Concept," *Journal of Global Ethics* 11, no. 2 (2015): 163–75.

16. Bethwell A. Ogot, "Politics, Culture and Music in Central Kenya: A Study of Mau Mau Hymns, 1951–1956," in *The Challenges of History and Leadership in Africa: The Essays of Bethwell Allan Ogot*, ed. Toyin Falola and Atieno Odhiambo (Trenton, NJ: Africa World Press, 2002), 113–28.

17. Thomas T. Spear, *The Kaya Complex: A History of the Mijikenda Peoples of the Kenya Coast to 1900* (Nairobi: Kenya Literature Bureau, 1978), 5.

18. Colonial Office, *Historical Survey of the Origins and Growth of Mau Mau* (Cmnd. 1030, 1960), 202–17.

19. Ethan R. Sanders, "The African Association and the Growth and Movement of Political Thought in Mid-Twentieth Century East Africa" (PhD diss., University of Cambridge, 2012), 49–58.

20. Exhibit No. 22A, Document 8 in this volume. Cf. Adrian Hastings, *The Construction of Nationhood: Ethnicity, Religion and Nationalism* (Cambridge: Cambridge University Press, 1997).

21. Sana Aiyar, *Indians in Kenya: The Politics of Diaspora* (Cambridge MA: Harvard University Press, 2015).

22. John Lonsdale, "KAU's Cultures: Imaginations of Community and Constructions of Leadership in Kenya after the Second World War," *Journal of African Cultural Studies* 13, no. 1 (2000): 107–24; see also Githuku's contribution to this volume.

23. Branch, *Defeating Mau Mau*.

24. Nicholas K. Githuku, *Mau Mau Crucible of War: Statehood, National Identity, and Politics of Postcolonial Kenya* (Lanham, MD: Lexington Books, 2016).

25. Rosberg and Nottingham, *Myth of "Mau Mau,"* 348–54.

26. Lonsdale, "Moral Economy," 265–504, quote from 463.

27. Richard Waller, "Ethnicity and Identity," in *The Oxford Handbook of Modern African History*, ed. John Parker and Richard Reid (Oxford: Oxford University Press, 2013), 94–113; Jonathan Glassman, "Ethnicity and Race in African Thought," in *The Blackwell Companion to African History*, ed. Charles Ambler, William Worger, et al. (Oxford: Blackwell, 2016).

28. Robert M. Maxon, *Struggle for Kenya: The Loss and Reassertion of Imperial Initiative, 1912–1923* (Cranbury, NJ: Associated University Presses, 1993); John Lonsdale, "Ornamental Constitutionalism in Africa: Kenyatta and the

Two Queens," *Journal of Imperial and Commonwealth History* 34, no. 1 (2006): 87–103.

29. Kenyatta to Passfield, 15 April 1930, *Correspondence between the Kikuyu Central Association and the Colonial Office*, KCA, Nairobi, 1930.

30. Joseph Kang'ethe, KCA president, to Senior Commissioner, Nyeri, 29 August 1929, in Church of Scotland, *Memorandum Prepared by the Kikuyu Mission Council on Female Circumcision* (Kikuyu, 1931), 41.

31. Jocelyn Murray, "The Kikuyu Female Circumcision Controversy, with Special Reference to the Church Missionary Society's 'Sphere of Influence'" (PhD diss., University of California at Los Angeles, 1974); Tabitha Kanogo, *African Womanhood in Colonial Kenya 1900–50* (Athens: Ohio University Press, 2005), 73–103; Bodil Folke Frederiksen, "Jomo Kenyatta, Marie Bonaparte and Bronislaw Malinowski on Clitoridectomy and Female Sexuality," *History Workshop Journal* 65 (2008): 23–48.

32. John Lonsdale, "Contests of Time: Kikuyu Historiographies Old and New," in *A Place in the World: New Local Historiographies from Africa and South-Asia*, ed. Axel Harneit-Sievers (Leiden: Brill, 2002), 201–54.

33. Church of Scotland, *Memorandum*, app. 4.

34. Peterson, *Creative Writing*, ch. 6.

35. Muoria-Sal et al., *Writing for Kenya*, 273–379; Jeremy Murray-Brown, *Kenyatta* (London: Allen and Unwin, 1972), 234–35.

36. John Spencer, *KAU: The Kenya African Union* (London: KPI, 1985), 173, 180–82, 221.

37. Director of Intelligence and Security to Member for Law and Order, 3 July 1947, KNA, Secretariat 1/12/8; Wachanga, *Swords*, 14; Spencer, *KAU*, 174; Eliud Mutonyi, "Mau Mau Chairman" (typescript, circa 1970, privately held), 83, 95; for the imperial donkey attributed to Kimathi, see Lotte Hughes's contribution to this volume, note 110.

38. "Where Are Our Gandhis and Nehrus in Kenya?" *Radio Posta*, 20 February 1948, KNA, MAA 8/105.

39. Derek Peterson, *Ethnic Patriotism and the East African Revival: A History of Dissent, c. 1935–1972* (Cambridge: Cambridge University Press, 2012).

40. Kanogo, *Dedan Kimathi;* Julie MacArthur, introduction to this volume.

41. See Document 5, interrogation report, 31 October 1956, in this volume.

42. Parker, *Last Colonial Regiment*, 150–52; Charles Harris, e-mail, January 2016. For more on Kimathi's possible ruminations, see Githuku's contribution to this volume.

43. Gakaara wa Wanjaũ, *Uhoro wa Ugurani* (1946), translated in Cristiana Pugliese, *Author, Publisher and Gĩkũyũ Nationalist: The Life and Writings of Gakaara wa Wanjaũ* (Bayreuth: African Studies Centre, 1995), 150–62.

44. Marshall S. Clough, *Fighting Two Sides: Kenyan Chiefs and Politicians, 1918–1940* (Niwot: University Press of Colorado, 1990).

45. Laura Stewart, "Why Were There No Levellers in Scotland?" *History Today* 65, no. 9 (2015): 33–39.

46. Rosberg and Nottingham, *Myth of "Mau Mau,"* 263–64; Spencer, *KAU*, 203–10; Greet Kershaw, *Mau Mau from Below* (Athens: Ohio University Press, 1997), 187–88, 194–95, 199–200, 206, 316.

47. In addition to the three works in the previous note, see David Throup, *Economic and Social Origins of Mau Mau, 1945–1953* (Athens: Ohio University Press, 1987); Berman, *Control and Crisis*, 256–346; Anderson, *Histories of the Hanged*, 9–118; Branch, *Defeating Mau Mau*, 1–93.

48. L. S. B. Leakey, *Defeating Mau Mau* (London: Methuen, 1954), 61; Maina wa Kinyatti, ed., *Thunder from the Mountains: Mau Mau Patriotic Songs* (London: Zed, 1980), 19.

49. For the Olenguruone settlement scheme and the squatters' plight, see also Simon Gikandi's contribution to this volume.

50. For rural capitalism, see Mutonyi, "Mau Mau Chairman"; Apollo Njonjo, "The Africanization of the 'White Highlands': A Study in Agrarian Class Struggles in Kenya, 1950–74" (PhD diss., Princeton University, 1977). For the logic of violence, see Lonsdale, "Moral Economy," 295, 401–5; and, esp., Branch, *Defeating Mau Mau*.

51. Renison Githige, "The Religious Factor in Mau Mau with Particular Reference to Mau Mau Oaths" (MA diss., University of Nairobi, 1978), 44–45.

52. Wachanga, *Swords*, xxxviii, 177; Osborne, *General China*, 174.

53. Barnett and Njama, *Mau Mau from Within;* Wachanga, *Swords*.

54. Githige, "Religious Factor," 140.

55. Peterson, *Creative Writing*, 97–98; Rosberg and Nottingham, *Myth of "Mau Mau,"* 259.

56. Itote, *"Mau Mau" General*, 55; Githige, "Religious Factor," 45–46, 61; Barnett and Njama, *Mau Mau from Within*, 54–55; Mutonyi, "Mau Mau Chairman," 75–79.

57. By e-mail Ben Knighton has sown fruitful doubt on this matter.

58. Mutonyi, "Mau Mau Chairman," 79; Barnett and Njama, *Mau Mau from Within*, 53–54; Ngugi Kabiro, *Man in the Middle: The Story of Ngugi Kabiro* (Richmond, BC: LSM Press, 1973) 32–33; Kershaw, *Mau Mau from Below*, 83, 208.

59. Kariuki, *"Mau Mau" Detainee*, 23; Bildad Kaggia, *Roots of Freedom 1921–1963* (Nairobi: East African Publishing House, 1975), 114; Mutonyi, "Mau Mau Chairman," 96.

60. R. W. Heather, "Counterinsurgency and Intelligence in Kenya, 1952–56" (PhD diss., University of Cambridge, 1993); Anderson, *Histories of the*

Hanged; Bennett, *Fighting the Mau Mau;* Branch, *Defeating Mau Mau;* Parker, *Last Colonial Regiment,* 135–346.

61. I here adopt Simon Gikandi's characterization; see his contribution to this volume.

62. David B. Barrett, *Schism and Renewal in Africa: An Analysis of Six Thousand Contemporary Religious Movements* (Nairobi: Oxford University Press, 1968), 308. A KiSwahili (Kiunguja) Bible, readable by literate Gikuyu, appeared in the 1890s.

63. Exhibit No. 22A.

64. Kanogo, *Squatters,* 138–9; Frank Furedi, *The Mau Mau War in Perspective* (Athens: Ohio University Press, 1989), 115–25; Parker, *Last Colonial Regiment,* 173.

65. Branch, *Defeating Mau Mau,* 66–88. For an official's view, see S. H. Fazan, *Colonial Kenya Observed: British Rule, Mau Mau and the Wind of Change,* ed. John Lonsdale (London: I. B. Tauris, 2015), 199–201, 204–9, 213–15, 220–22, 420. Fazan drew on Jock Rutherford, *A History of the Kikuyu Guard,* ed. John Pinney (1957; repr., Herstmonceux: Mawenzi Books, 2003).

66. For itungati, see L. S. B. Leakey, *The Southern Kikuyu before 1903,* 3 vols. (London: Academic Press, 1977), 3:1051. For contrasting views on kamatimu, see Jomo Kenyatta, *Facing Mount Kenya: The Tribal Life of the Gikuyu* (London: Secker and Warburg, 1938), 108; Kariuki, *"Mau Mau" Detainee,* 37–38.

67. Githige, "Religious Factor," 49–50, 53–56, 175; Peterson, "Writing in Revolution," 88.

68. Elspeth Huxley, *A New Earth: An Experiment in Colonialism* (London: Chatto and Windus, 1960), 231–38, Muhoya photographed facing p. 225; M. P. K. Sorrenson, *Land Reform in the Kikuyu Country: A Study in Government Policy* (Nairobi: Oxford University Press, 1967), 135–36; Lonsdale, "Moral Economy," 434–35; Branch, *Defeating Mau Mau,* 62–66, 118; Peterson, *Ethnic Patriotism,* 221–23; Donald Fraser, "The Rise and Fall of the British Veterinary Profession in the Agrarian Development of Kenya, 1937–1967" (PhD diss., University of Cambridge, 2015), 218–23; MacArthur, introduction to this volume.

69. Anderson, *Histories of the Hanged,* 289–327; Anderson, "British Abuse and Torture in Kenya's Counter-insurgency, 1952–1960," *Small Wars and Insurgencies* 23, nos. 4–5 (2012): 700–719; Anderson, "Guilty Secrets."

70. John Pinney, "Message from the District Emergency Committee to All Working in the Fort Hall District," n.d., Fort Hall Intelligence Report File for Kangema Guard Post, March 1954 to January 1956, courtesy of Ian Parker.

71. For sources, see Lonsdale, "Authority." Also see Gikandi's and Githuku's contributions to this volume. For similar discourses in detention camps, see Peterson, *Ethnic Patriotism,* 217–48.

72. Also see Githuku's contribution to this volume.

73. Kariuki, *"Mau Mau" Detainee,* 119, 121; Wachanga, *Swords,* 42, 77; Gikoyo, *We Fought,* 86–88.

74. Barnett and Njama, *Mau Mau from Within,* 184–85, 187.

75. Exhibit No. 22A, Document 8 in this volume.

76. Peterson, *Creative Writing,* 146–47; Peterson, pers. comm.

77. Genesis/*Kiambiriria* 10:7; I Chronicles/1 *Maundu ma Matuku ma Tene* 1:9, 32; Ezekiel/*Ezekieli* 27:20, 38:13, and chapter 39. Thanks to Nick Githuku for correcting my Gikuyu.

78. General China's order of battle was still more elaborate. Osborne, *General China,* 148–78.

79. For photographs, see Parker, *Last Colonial Regiment,* 298.

80. Wachanga, *Swords,* 24–31.

81. For these arguments at greater length, see Lonsdale, "Authority."

82. Kimathi to Slade, 6 March (or April) 1954, in Lovatt Smith, *Kenya, Kikuyu and Mau Mau,* 314–15. For the irony that Kimathi's 1953 peace feelers had helped to initiate British surrender policy, see Bennett, *Fighting the Mau Mau,* 133–43; Kanogo, *Dedan Kimathi,* 24; MacArthur, introduction, and Anderson's contribution to this volume.

83. Henderson, *Hunt,* 61–73, 167–72; Parker, *Last Colonial Regiment,* 299–314, statistics in ibid., 150, 311.

84. Kinyatti, *Kenya's Freedom Struggle*, xiii–xiv.

85. Bethwell A. Ogot, "Africa: The Agenda of Historical Research and Writing," in Ogot, *Challenges of History,* 467–84.

86. Which is why all historical actors or past events might be called floating signifiers. For discussion, see Gikandi's contribution to this volume.

87. Clough, "Contest for Memory;" Ogude, "Nation and Narration," 268–83; Coombes, Hughes, and Karega-Munene, *Managing Heritage.* Also see Gikandi's, Githuku's, and Hughes's contributions to this volume.

88. Bethwell A. Ogot, "Revolt of the Elders,"134.

3

The Unfolding of Britain and Kenya's Complex Tango

An Uneasy Return to a Critical Past and Its Implications

Nicholas Kariuki Githuku

Hidden Histories Unearthed, New Questions

It is not an exaggeration to describe as dramatic the cocktail of events and newsworthy developments reminiscent of the shared but uneasy history between Britain and Kenya. Some of these include the emphatic rehabilitation and reinstatement of the Mau Mau moment in Kenya's national history during the administration of its third president, Mwai Kibaki, which eventually culminated in the erection and official unveiling, in 2006 in the heart of Nairobi, of a statue honoring the embodiment of the struggle for independence, Dedan Kimathi Waciuri. This followed the publication of two seminal works touching on the criminal nature of British counterinsurgency in the 1950s by Caroline Elkins and David Anderson; and the triumphal high-profile case against the British government by a group of Mau Mau veterans who won the legal suit in London in June 2013.[1]

But even more fascinating was the unveiling, on 12 September 2015, of a monument funded by the British government honoring Kenyans killed, tortured, and ill-treated by British forces during the Mau Mau war in the 1950s. This particular event was presided over by the British high commissioner, Christian Turner. This particular project was part of the 2013 out-of-court settlement by the British government to pay £20 million ($30 million) in compensation to Mau Mau veterans.[2] Quite predictably, new litigation against the British government, by more than forty thousand Kenyans alleging physical abuse or mistreatment during the insurgency against colonial rule in the 1950s, was lodged in January 2016.[3]

All these critical developments are testament to the unrelenting power of the past, its riveting grip on human agents who lived it, and the resiliency and gravity of memory as well as its hypnotic relevance in the present, and, therefore, its embedded capacity to not only spark imagination of the possible but also to inspire both legal and political action. This lively demonstration of, and reflection on, how this particular past deeply affected specific individuals, families, and society at large and the development of the state is instructive. Britain and Kenya are, of necessity, embroiled in an uneasy tango with a critical past; and that gargantuan task calls for honest, memory-thrashing work.[4]

Such memory work is never simple. Yet it is not the only thing that needs urgent attention or a coming to terms with Britain's and Kenya's past. While the need for a far-reaching engagement with this important specific past is vital, it is crucial to go beyond legal suits and commemorations. The long-awaited and broader expectation of the rectification of historical injustices and reinstitution of social justice, is a critical matter that lies at the heart of the popular quest for statehood and the nation-building imperative. This is a critical task that requires many hands at the helm, including scholars from various disciplines and, importantly, political leaders in London and in Nairobi. Such is the seriousness of this unfolding complex historical entanglement of Britain and Kenya evident in these dramatic spills of the past into the present. Yet the best and most critical of these spills of the past into the present has waited to enter last into this crucial breaking of hitherto hidden histories into the present: the recovery of the court transcripts of the trial of freedom fighter Dedan Kimathi, and affiliated documents, including two appeals to the court of appeals for eastern Africa and to the privy council filed by Frederick Henry Miller, lead counsel for the defense. This archival find thrusts this important historical figure right to the center of British imperial history in Kenya.

Once more, the fortuitous discovery of this hitherto "inexistent" crucial document pierces the deliberate official silence of many years, and adds to the delicately sprouting but determined shoot of revealing hidden histories now thrust into the open. But even more crucial is the implication of this recovery to many questioning readers, analysts, the general public, and even to British-Kenya relations. This chapter is a reflection on the relevance of these files to questions of anticolonialism, loyalism, decolonization, and the (re)construction of postcolonial nationalism and statehood.

To this end, my reflections revolve around the following broad questions: what has, until now, been Kimathi's place in people's memory and how have people chosen to remember him (especially former fighters, then foes and contemporary admirers)? Where does he stand as a symbol of nationalism and as a rallying political object in the postcolonial process and project of nation and state building? Has or does the aura and political symbolism that has grown around Kimathi's militant image of defiance still continue to inspire political dissent in the postcolony? What are the implications of the discovery of the transcripts of Kimathi's trial and court appeals with regard to all the preceding questions. In other words, how will it affect how Kimathi is remembered? How will it affect Kimathi's political symbolism? Finally, how will it impact his militant image? Will it serve to fortify and solidify his selfless heroism for having paid the ultimate price and, hence, further his political symbolism that could, once again, rekindle the dwindling spirit of nationalism badly needed for national integration and state building? Will it confirm his unfailing mettle, even at the most trying moment of his trial, with the gallows hanging over his head? Even in his absence, and with his remains missing, do these documents serve to disinter and resurrect Kimathi, thus reigniting him as a distant but fiery figment in people's memory, an ever-burning flame of courage under fire and trial—the true Dedan Kimathi revealed as a man, a veritable statesman, who fought not only with guns but also prophetic, diplomatic words heavily laden with profound gems of Gikuyu wisdom and full of disarming cunning that was distrusted and feared by the colonial establishment?

In attempting a rough estimation of the real Kimathi, this reflection relies on theoretical tools spawned by Foucauldian analysis of the relation between power, resistance, and government. That is, the appreciation that power (or government legitimacy) and resistance seem inescapably and dialectically linked and, further, that both occur through the discursive expressions of existing conditions of existence that are socially framed.[5] Moreover, both depend on various technologies of the self or avenues of self-expression of politically aware, socially conscious, and practical people.[6] Subsequently, there exists a market of competing narratives of the self, and only in rare moments is such diversity represented or resisted in the name of some great unifying narrative or theme. This chapter presents Kimathi as a resistant subject who, in such a rare moment—in the context of the 1950s conflict—emerged as a "privileged identity" posited as a historical subject.[7] Put differently, a political actor who, through various identity-shaping disciplines and technologies of the self, achieved a posited identity that overcame individual isolation or inertia; an individual who understood power relations and how they affected his existence and that of others; one who was propelled by this knowledge to pursue possibilities of what he could be in the process of which he was also able to organize others against colonial authorities; and, lastly, one who attempted, with relative success, to tap into the rich loam of African dissent and real grievances.[8]

In spite of evidence showing that he was a man like any other, vulnerable, suffering personal weakness, and even, perhaps, having moments of self-doubt, in light of his celebration in the erection of the Kimathi statue and that of Mau Mau at Uhuru Park; in light of his constant disinterment in popular culture; in light of the "legal illegality" of colonialism, and therefore, the trial itself, and the burning embers of anticolonialism that are still alight; in light of the victorious litigation between 2009 and June 2013 by three Mau Mau veterans, and the newly lodged suit; and in light of the natural inclination and people's constant need for heroes, and the reliance by nations on national myths for nation- and state-building purposes, Kimathi's place in people's memory, and Kenya's history, remains intact. And, further, and following from the historical context of the "illegality" of colonialism, that the whole judicial process was a *mistrial.* Ultimately, instead of simply appreciating, literally, the black-and-white facts or demerits of the case against Kimathi, I seek, in the conclusion of this reflection and with the benefit of hindsight, to argue that what's important is what was *not* on trial in this colonial judicial process.

Indeed, it is here that one must not only end but also, most naturally, start critically engaging ruminations of the main documents related to the trial of Kimathi. From the outset, one is struck by the rather dated and in-the-heat-of-the-moment nature of the imperial judicial process. The entire trial and its findings were very much the product of the chaotic, emotionally charged, and racially volatile political situation of the Emergency period. Put more appropriately, Kimathi's conviction was by none other than a court of Emergency assize constituted under the Kenyan Emergency Regulations of 1953. In retrospect, there was never going to be a fair hearing. Just like the accused in the Rivonia trial in apartheid South Africa, Kimathi's guilt was never in doubt. Just as the accused in the infamous trial in South Africa, who were unlikely to have been found innocent under the Sabotage Act, Kimathi was not coming out unscathed, and acquittal was completely inconceivable under the Kenyan Emergency Regulations.[9]

The trial resembled George Orwell's "Shooting an Elephant" predicament.[10] In the politically charged environment surrounding it, the court had to satisfy public opinion eagerly following the trial in the colony, Britain, and around the world. In its final ruling, the court had to be seen to adhere to an unwritten transcript of the managing elite that generally confirmed ideas behind British rule and the claims colonial authorities made to legitimacy. The trial itself, therefore, was part of a wider exercise of power in which the judge was expected to venerate the law and thus affirm claim to legality and imperial high-mindedness.[11] Kimathi, the hotheaded elephant that had gone on rampage against the colonial order, had to be put down.[12] After all, it is well known that the court is not an organism dissociated from the times in which it exists. Kimathi was tried in a court that did not deliver its opinions in a legal vacuum. Colonial judges and prosecutors were not abstract oracles but rather men whose views were necessarily, though by no conscious intent, affected by inheritance, education, and environment, and by the impact of history, of the British imperial past, and of the Mau Mau moment that unfolded before their eyes.[13] It follows that one of the most prominent implications of the release of these archival materials to the public will be a bitter castigation of the British colonial brand of justice unfairly meted out against Kimathi. This expected reaction is not simply emotional or simply a demonstration of anticolonial patriotism or nationalism.

Rather it is an issue that strikes at the crucial intersection between law, morality, and natural law. Extended scrutiny of the sticky relationship between law and morality lies outside the purview of this reflection. Legal and moral norms vary from place to place and, most crucially in this case, from one historical period to another. Indeed, this is a persistent theme in the philosophy of law: the search for unchanging norms that are universally valid.[14] Underneath the thin veneer of consensus on legal principles, there is often a struggle of interest going on. The law can be seen as an ideological weapon in the hands of those who possess the power to use it for their own ends.[15] Contending sectional—sometimes ethnic, religious, or racial, and socioeconomic and even national—interests have ensured that the quest for fully fledged positive law continues to be a distant mirage, and, with this, assured the continued ephemeral nature of law, whether constitutional, property, contract, or criminal.

Put differently, the legal validity or legitimacy of laws is contestable owing to its sociological construction. There is perhaps no better illustration of such brevity or limitation of legal traction and moral relativism than the colonial system of justice that summarily sentenced Kimathi to death.[16] The recovery of the Kimathi trial transcripts further complicates the historical entanglement between Kenya and Britain and opens the question of how law often is the handmaiden of power. Whatever polity and in any era, law is, more often than not, a "system of enforceable rules governing social relations and legislated by a political system," which can be a stumbling block. That the law is connected to the system of political ideas means that law and politics seem inextricably linked. It is demoralizing but it is the reality; the life and heart of the law is never logic. Rather, it is experience. In general, and in the Kimathi case in particular, the felt necessities of the time, the prevalent moral and political theories, institutions of public policy, avowed or unconscious, even the prejudices that judges shared with their fellow men, had a lot to do with the determination of which colonial laws he was tried against, the court's procedure, and its findings.[17] Nothing could be more discomfiting, especially when considering the imperial social and political construction of illegality.

The Legal Illegality of Empire: Casting the Kimathi Trial in Broader Legal Perspective

Without a doubt, especially given the historical significance and centrality of Kimathi in the struggle for independence, there is a real possibility that the publication of this archival find could fling open the door to a grim and an uneasy past and bring into question not merely the skewed sense of British colonial justice but also the entire imperially inaugurated order and related issues of social and historical injustice.[18] After all, the subjugation, domination, and social control of Africans, and the exercise of power in the allocation of resources and services under the colonial order, was through a flimsy and dubitable cloak of legality. Throughout human history, when the legal process establishes a right of one particular person, group, or institution, it simultaneously imposes a restraint on those whose preferences impinge on the right established.[19] In this particular case, in the name of the law, the rights of white settlers were assured and their privilege entrenched even while the just and legitimate aspirations of millions of Africans were delegitimized, repressed, and extinguished without contemplation, with arbitrariness disguised as legality.[20] Moreover, the colonial order was contrived through legal prestidigitation. From the outset, the imperial legitimacy of power was, therefore, contested, and most segments of the African population in Kenya understood that the colonial order had been possible only through the legal production of illegality.[21] It follows, then, that the legality of an act does not necessarily make it a just one.[22] Furthermore, it cannot be taken for granted that imperial subjects sensed that they were being directed by law as an arm of political ideology in ways that were not transparent to them; that, indeed, colonial law cloaked illegitimate power. The presence of the ideological in law subverts its very intentions and compromises its integrity. After all, "the ideal of law involves a set of institutions that regulate or restrain power with reference to norms of justice."[23]

Certainly the appreciation of these facts is what must have informed the special motion in democratic Athens called a *graphe paranomon,* which was the equivalent of a charge of unconstitutionality (although the city-state did not have a written constitution). Nonetheless, in Athens, laws that were attacked as *paranomon,* or contrary to fundamental law, were usually invalidated and their sponsors fined.[24] In this particular case, the unjust act was the conviction of Kimathi on two charges of the unlawful possession of a firearm and the unlawful possession of ammunition contrary to the British imperially constructed paranomon, the Emergency Regulations of 1953, under which it was found that he threatened public safety and order.[25] As duly noted, this was in contravention of a colonial order that rested on the rickety stilts of the legal production and social construction of illegality, which is what had inspired the Mau Mau threat in the first place.

It is, in fact, curiously surprising that Kimathi's defense team never once argued, in entering its plea, as Mandela and Walter Sisulu, among other defendants, had in the Rivonia trial. Making a formal plea, the former had courageously stated that it was the government that should have been in the dock and not him. The latter had stated, "It is the government which is guilty, not me," adding, after being rebuked by Quartus de Wet, the presiding judge, who asked him to plead either guilty or not, "It is the government which is responsible for what is happening in this country."[26] In light of the foregoing, it is hereby posited that the oppressive colonial order resting, as it did, on the social and legal construction of illegality, was not on trial, which, in retrospect, casts a shadow of doubt on this case. In other words, it was a blatant miscarriage of justice.

As if this was not enough, as British colonial authorities were wont to do, Kimathi, the embodiment of anticolonialism, and by extension, a fighter against all that was evil in the heady, violent 1950s, was ignominiously executed and buried in an unmarked grave, his remains forever lost. With this physical, psychic, and existential erasure, it must also have been hoped that his memory was evermore expunged from the face of the earth. He was not only to be humiliated and dehumanized but also to be forgotten. As Ngũgĩ wa Thiong'o observes, this can be seen as part and parcel of, generally, a European, and, specifically, a British imperial, dismembering practice of power. As such, it was intended to pacify colonial subjects. Put differently, such physical, psychic, and existential erasure was a symbolic act and performance of power intended to produce docile African minds.[27] After all, the commutation of capital punishment was an integral aspect of colonial networks of power and violence. In addition, Kimathi's execution was a stark enactment of colonial power intended to reinforce an imperial order and impose the authority of the colonial state.[28] And this enactment of power over Kimathi as a colonial subject meant even more: this feared and hated "terrorist" was dismembered from memory, what he stood for now choked off, and the dangerous ideas and memories that he carried, buried.[29]

The man that colonialists wanted Kenya to forget became a byword for contempt and derision spoken only in hushed whispers. Kimathi, his image now besmirched, like that of many others whose lives were shamefully ended on the gallows and his memory all but wiped from the public eye, for at least half a century, was an ambiguous historical figure unlike self-styled but celebrated fathers of the nation. Even after independence, a street named after him was only a token honor. But the significant military role he had played in the fight for freedom stubbornly remained a part of the national metanarrative and subject of the school curriculum. For most people, he remained an unspoken hero.

But, as Simon Gikandi points out in this volume, there was a gradually spreading ripple of public acclaim emanating from Karunaini, Kimathi's birthplace, which naturally became the epicenter of the sustained memorialization of the man and what he stood for, despite years of neglect in the Kenyatta and Moi years. In the immediate neighborhood of Karunaini, numerous elementary and secondary schools are named after him. But the highest honor paid to him was by the Nyeri elite led by Mwai Kibaki, who in 1972 established the Dedan Kimathi University of Technology.[30] After ascending to the presidency, Kibaki took the memorialization of Kimathi a notch higher by commissioning the Kimathi statue that stands at the head of the street named after him at the center of the country's political and commercial capital, Nairobi.[31]

All this came at a time when Kenyans were witnessing a distantly related reincarnation of Mau Mau, the growing Mungiki movement among Gikuyu rural and urban youth.[32] This then is what explains why, in an intimate conversation, in 2006 with two close friends from my church in Nairobi, one concerned observer expressed fear that the Kimathi statue would send the "wrong" message in the country and signal "the return of his spirit." Whatever that might have meant, it was not far from the truth.[33] In my belated rejoinder to my friend's remark and, appropriately using biblical imagery, this recognition that came late in the day, was Kimathi's haunting blood bitterly crying out to be remembered, and for justice, from an unmarked grave. His voice joined at least a thousand others whose micronarratives are effectively detailed by Anderson's *Histories of the Hanged* and thus continue providing witness to British colonial political oppression, exploitation, injustice, and police and military brutality from their graves. This moment in Mau Mau history in general, and the commemoration of Kimathi in particular, marked the zenith of the retrieval from near oblivion of one of the most violent periods in Kenya's history that a few would rather not remember. That a small ripple could have reached such a national crescendo, and from the Nyeri region, which was particularly hard hit by the divisions and the violence that arose in the 1950s, and without the slightest demur from so-called loyalists, warrants an urgent revisit to what it meant to be a "rebel" or a "loyalist" in that decade. This, however, is an inquiry that lies beyond the scope of this chapter.[34] Nonetheless, it is important to cast Kimathi's political involvement and the war that he led in the light of Foucauldian analysis of resistance. Unlike many ordinary people of his time, lettered or unlettered, he understood the inner workings of power and exemplified vital political awareness that the British colonial authorities constantly failed, and were unwilling, to align their projects with those of the governed.[35] It is in this sense, therefore, that I posit that Kimathi, as a historical subject of great contemporary interest, may yet still emerge as "a privileged identity" around which flagging nationalism can again revolve.

Resistance Consciousness: Kimathi as a Privileged Identity

It is quite remarkable that a young peasant of Kimathi's humble background could have taken such a militant stance against the British becoming such a formidable imperial headache. This did not happen simply because he, as then alleged, was a demonic, bloodthirsty rebel or a deranged psychopath hell-bent on violence. This sort of offhanded criminalization and obvious dismissal has clouded a clear view of the man. It is crucial to examine the constitution and inner dynamics of resistance as exemplified by Kimathi, including the formation of his personal identity or how he "imagined himself as a leader of a new polity of citizens of an ordered, lawful, and progressive society."[36] In an attempt to shed light on this historical figure, I rely on Foucault's proposition that power and resistance are almost inescapably and dialectically linked. And the idea that resistance should be seen as the "efficacious influence" of those subordinate to power.[37]

Among many other useful insights of Foucauldian analysis of power and resistance are two important conceptions. One is that resistance, like legitimacy, is a kind of governance. Second, the idea that the process through which existing forms of government are addressed by the governed, referred to as "protogovernmentalization," is rooted in what people know. From the second notion follows the fact, usually taken for granted, that the power/knowledge nexus is central to understanding the inner dynamics or workings of power. The centrality of the power/knowledge nexus suggests that the conception of knowledge is the most promising fulcrum around which to articulate the relation of power, resistance, and government. Put differently, that both government and resistance work on and through knowledge, and that forms of social relations can be conceived of in terms of an ever-widening circle from self through individual freedom fighters, to "solidaristic others," and to "generalized others." Further, each of these may be thought of as constitutive aspects of the identity of a subject.[38] Following this Foucauldian-premised formula, I posit that we can identify at least four constitutive positions and inner dynamics of Kimathi's resistance, the first three of which were efficacious.

Kimathi's stature and resistance was achieved through an ever-widening circle of identity formation. The inner concentric circle of who he was consisted of his core self-identity shaped by personal experiences; a world of private thoughts and secret aspirations; and essential political values and beliefs. The second concentric circle of Kimathi's identity was defined by his relationships with, and organization of, like-minded key figures that he knew face-to-face (read: Mau Mau forest fighters). The third outer concentric circle of his identity was based on his understanding of, and appeal to, a solidaristic collective organization from which he drew upon the consciously organized resources of a social movement in pursuit of his individual agency. And, lastly, although this is where he floundered, was the outermost concentric circle consisting of his attempts to involve the organizational capacities of generalized agencies such as other global liberation movements and exemplars of revolution and their publications, and local and international media, which he read or knew only remotely, through their representations.[39]

In the first concentric circle of Kimathi's organization of resistance was a deep-seated resistance consciousness the spring of which was sufficient self-cognizance to enable him to act as a coherently organized individual or to exercise reflexive agency in power relations. Moreover, his inclination to join the nationalist movement; to become a member of the Kenya African Union (KAU), for which he served as the Ol Kalou branch secretary; and his subsequent involvement with the militant outgrowth of the Anake a Fortī (Young Men of the 1940s), "*Muhimu*," made up of ex-servicemen, urban gangs, and frustrated political activists from whose ranks he rose quickly to become a respected oath administrator and organizer, all must have stemmed from a solid base of intensive self-organization.[40] This sort of political activity demonstrates that Kimathi, as an individual, was organized enough to be able to seek to enroll, translate, interest, or oppose others in projects. This demonstrates his existence under conditions of well-framed knowledge that allowed uncurbed reflexivity. Kimathi well understood how power relations constituted his identity, which is what ignited reflexivity that propelled him to pursue possibilities of what he could be(come). This reflexive self-organization of himself as a "resistant subject" was based on framed knowledge about who he was and what he could or should be, which is what enabled him to take a stand against the established colonial order.

Kimathi lived at a crucial period of transition from African traditional ways to a racially hierarchical colonial modernity—at a time, therefore, when the very private experience of having a personal identity to discover, a personal destiny to fulfill, became a subversive political force of major proportions.[41] Moreover, he knew about and sought to exploit the deep, fertile soil of brewing African dissent and real grievances, and naturally, the latently explosive transcript of indignation hidden beneath it. Kimathi's ambition was to animate the collective cultural fantasy and dreams of violent revenge of subordinate but long-suffering Africans who, however, never gave their personal hidden transcripts expression, even among close friends and peers.[42] At the level of analytical understanding, this is what should matter to us most. It matters little, then, the idiosyncrasies attendant to the pursuit of his stand or whether that stand was an act of outrage or rebellion, or an existential gesture.[43] Equally, important as they are to our full understanding of the man, it matters little what ascriptions or variable representations and multiple interpretations his image attracted contemporaneously or thereafter.

Next, at the level of social organization, Kimathi was able to implicate other important players, some of whom he knew through face-to-face relations.[44] Put differently, he was able to draw upon resources of social organization greater than, or beyond, himself, such as ecologies of local community networks, and, by extension, the forged alliance of ethnic kinship and enlarged moral imagination of the Gikuyu.[45] This level can be said to have been reached when Kimathi took to the Nyandarua forest, where he rose to become one of the most important leaders of the Mau Mau rebellion. It is in the forest that he would found the Kenya Defence Council and Kenya's Parliament as attempts to bring order, hierarchy, and centralization to the scattered Mau Mau forces.[46] This could well have been the time when Kimathi, contemporaneously, started to attract and embody all manner of competing ascriptions and symbolize many of the contradictions represented by Mau Mau, Kenyan anticolonialism, and nationalism writ large.[47] It is while in the forest that a relatively well-prepared Kimathi, as a "resistant subject," a man of courage and practical power, launched his career proper—before, of course, taking the reins of state power. Having experienced, firsthand, misfortunes that he rightly attributed to the colonial structures of domination that resulted in systematic oppression, and having witnessed the wishes of the people, and judging himself to be a formidable man of will, Kimathi thought he knew how to come to their end, and, whispering to this friend, and arguing down that adversary, sought to mold society to his purpose. Looking upon people as wax for his hands, he started to take command of them as the wind does the clouds, as the mother does of the child, or the man that knows more of the man that knows less, in order to lead them, in glad surprise, to the very point they would be. And as a leader of men, he was, for a time, followed with acclamation.[48] But this stage also marked the beginning of his undoing.

After all, there are obstacles and limits to the construction of any collectivity, or people as a body. There is nothing automatic about the emergence of "a people." With him were people who, while sharing certain substantive values, consisted of multiple selves, people constituting their identities in a plurality of subject positions.[49] Although aspiring to forge the wishes of the people into a new polity of citizens, an ordered, lawful, and progressive society, as a leader of a loose coalition with divergent interests, Kimathi easily became a blank canvas upon which was inscribed various political demands and ends. In addition, he was a suspended hegemon in the making without firm or well-established authority, a floating signifier rather than a fixed one that was pinned down, ordering the form of debate, irrespective of the content. Not having achieved fixity that avails hegemonic power, his authority was subject to the harsh audit of his peers. It comes as no surprise then that Kimathi was less known for his prowess as a field general than for his motivational speeches and his legendary obsession with the output of bureaucratic prose, a discursive practice that is a constant site of struggle over power. In his power stratagem, he believed the pen was mightier than the sword. The power struggle was not just within the movement and its top leadership but also within the wider political frontiers of the colonial state.[50] Ultimately, this is what defused the violent forest struggle for land and freedom, arresting the momentum of Mau Mau's militant demand for independence. Competing loci of personal authority impaired collective action and blunted the first impulse of social obligation, muddling the core and shared substantive value between all Mau Maus as encapsulated by their central argument about "moral economy."[51]

Confrontations and divisions between forest fighters, and, specifically, challenges to Kimathi's authority, no doubt affected the stories that these opponents of colonial power wanted to tell Kenya and the world. Furthermore, this fragmentation of resistance lacked all vital centralization and a shared quantifiable strategic objective.[52] As a result, while initially successful in tapping into the energy, general mood of dissent, and resources of a movement that had discrete but wide support of the majority of people in Central Kenya, solidaristic organization there and elsewhere in the colony and beyond did not quite take root. In spite of his prowess at drawing on global exemplars of revolution and political thought, Kimathi's predicament was exacerbated by lack of success to connect with "generalized others" like such révolutionnaires elsewhere in the world and media organizations. In the long run, the colonial state caught up with this central figure whose personal resistance had become the keystone upon which the struggle to defeat tyranny, imperial hegemony, and regime of colonial "normalcy" or order rested. Once the influence of the person at the center of the Mau Mau rebellion was snuffed out, the back of the resistance was broken.[53] Thus ended the ambition of a man of courage and measured practical power to mold society to his purpose. But it is important to turn to the fulcrum on which this personal ambition and carefully cultivated identity turned: that is, various technologies of self-expression and, therefore, self-inscription and self-formation. Specifically, this refers to Kimathi's identity-shaping disciplines and discursive practices through which he sought to transform himself into a formidable man of will and a practical man of action and power, and which also enabled him to assume, as a personal mission, the alignment of ordinary people's everyday projects with authoritative images of the colonial social order.[54]

A Closed Double Riigi: All Crucial but Alienating Discursive Practices of Power

As Derek Peterson has observed, Kimathi's ensemble of representations and disciplines necessitating incessant writing, bureaucratic recording and record-keeping materials, typewriters, printing machines, and so forth were ways of imagining a counterstate.[55] More than being a hobby or obsession, it does seem that Kimathi understood the nature and inner workings of power—above all, that it is textual, semiotic, inherent in the very possibility of textuality, meaning, and signification in the social world. Moreover, his letter writing and record keeping can, and should, be seen as discursive resistance or discursive articulation of resistance that informed Kimathi's sense of self-identity and purpose.[56] His identity-shaping disciplines and discursive practices were a way of engaging with social reality, which cannot be known unequivocally but only through its representation in language. He was exercising discursive consciousness by putting things into words or giving verbal expression to the promptings of action.[57] His use of speeches, text, writing, cognition, and argumentation can, and should, be seen as reliance on language to represent possibilities, and to position possibilities, in relation to each other. In other words, he used language to define the possibilities of meaningful existence.[58] Although he was known to have written profusely, however, there is precious little that exists of Kimathi's records to shed light on his thinking, what he understood his cause to be, and his stand.[59] Nevertheless, it is worth making a gallant effort to reveal his thoughts.

For all his disrepute, Kimathi's sharpness, illustrated in his few surviving historical records, is not in doubt. Indeed, there hasn't been a more comprehensive testimony to the man's intellectual acuity until the recovery of transcripts of his trial. Although meant to argue for the prosecution, an expert witness, a medical doctor, stated that Kimathi was a "reasonably intelligent man, intelligent above the standard of a man of his education."[60] This rings true in the pages of his scant writing. His is a feeble and isolated prophetic voice crying out from the wilderness of colonial oppression, that of socioeconomic neglect of African reserves and exploitation. Nor was it a voice that was taken seriously. But what one deduces from the little writing available, and specifically that selectively adduced in the trial as evidence (Exhibits Nos. 22A, 23, and 24), is a person of more than average intelligence and a man wholly committed to a just cause, something that is echoed in Maina wa Kinyatti's *The Papers of Dedan Kimathi* the veracity, provenance, access, and translation of which, in academic circles unfortunately, is still much in doubt.[61]

Scattered throughout are gems of Gikuyu wisdom from a man moved to action, not out of flippant emotions but from the depths of the experience of colonial injustice and the pressing need for redress.[62] One gleans appeals to the colonial authorities to rely less on coercion or fear and more on truth; appeals for mutual trust, respect, and friendship, and mutuality in giving and acceptance; appeals for truth and justice; appeals for shared prosperity while appreciating that all people cannot be rich; appeals for the need for reconciliation; and appeals for peace and mutual coexistence and the hope that blacks and whites in Kenya be of one heart. One also finds, in these few pages, a stunning tenacity in the justifiability of the cause for which he was fighting. The reading of the three Kimathi letters also shows a clear understanding of his cause: Kimathi and others were fighting for the country and its people, for *wīathi* (self-mastery) and for truth and justice.

And, in this worthy struggle, surrender was out of the question.[63] It was something that could not get into the minds of intelligent people. Indeed, it was preferable to sell one's soul instead of having to surrender it. Surrender would also not bring about an end to the war.[64] It was also quite clear, in Kimathi's mind, who Mau Mau were, and it was not just a matter of white and black as the problems that beset Kenya affected both races. As such, justice could not be expected from the barrel of the gun. Mau Mau was the cry of a people suffering from poverty and exploitation. It was a vehicle to liberate Kenya, to regain the Kenyan soil that Europeans had occupied by force. The poor man was Mau Mau, and therefore bombs and other weapons could not finish the movement.[65] In fact, if the exploitation of the Africans did not stop, Kimathi said, it was to be expected that the war in Kenya would continue for a long time. Violent confrontation between the two sides could not bring about fairness or truth. Only peace could hold the Kenyan house together, as opposed to ruling Africans with the colonial whip in their faces.[66] There was need for reconciliation (*ũiguano*), and mending of the "paining" part of the colonial body politic, beyond the rift occasioned by the war.[67] The fight was not one of everlasting hatred but was, rather, a necessary but regrettable pause calling for the creation of a true and real brotherhood between white and black, so that the latter could be regarded as people, as capable and equal human beings.[68] All said, one may be forgiven for seeing in Kimathi a quite different kind of man from these letters. A Kimathi who was not a mastermind of evil and a militant man of action but rather an understanding diplomat in his own right, especially considering his constant appeals for peace.

Nonetheless, his cause and what he stood for, his thinking about the colonial order and his action(s) against it, and his appeals, were not taken as seriously as he would have wished. Indeed, because of it, his letter writing and record keeping, and the content therein, even proffers of peace, were met with a closed double *riigi* (door)—that of the colonial authorities on the one hand, and that of sections of the forest Mau Mau and their leadership on the other. Kimathi faced opposition from his fellow forest fighters over strategy revolving around his peace efforts as well as challenges to his authority.[69] This rift stemmed from literacy, which in the forest often became a dividing line, especially among the movement's leadership. While exercising identity-shaping disciplines and discursive practices, Kimathi elevated himself over his peers, whom he was often given to criticizing as unlettered. They, in turn, accused Kimathi of having been poisoned by Christianity and Western education.[70] It is not surprising that the modestly educated, like Kimathi, and the highly educated, like Karari Njama, were disturbed by traditional Gikuyu practices and superstitions, for instance, precolonial oath-taking elements, yet tolerated them for their utility.[71] In due time, those who clung to traditions and superstitions, deeming themselves to be authentic Gikuyus, retreated to the house of Gikuyu customs and closed the woven door (riigi) behind them. These Kimathi critics were weary of his bureaucratic Kenya Parliament with its incessant writing and record keeping and talks of making peace that they found untrustworthy. They accused Kimathi and other educated Protestant leaders of using their illiterate followers for their own selfish ends.[72]

On the other hand was the riigi of the colonial authorities. The colonial authorities, and the court, chose to look beyond Kimathi's motivations, what he stood for, and what he was fighting for. That mattered little. It is little wonder that Kimathi was tried within the narrow legal parameters of a court of Emergency assize. *Why* he was in possession of both an unlicensed revolver and six rounds of ammunition was not in question. His proffers of peace and appeals for redress of pressing African grievances; for the colonial authorities to rely less on coercion or fear, and more on truth; for mutual trust, respect and friendship, and mutuality in giving and acceptance; for shared prosperity while appreciating that all people cannot be rich; for the need for healing and reconciliation; for peace and mutual coexistence, and the expression of hope that blacks and whites in

Kenya be of one heart; and for justice and truth, came to naught. Indeed, what he represented, the truth of the weak spoken in the face of power, was inadmissible and unacceptable. Kimathi's insubordination against the constituted colonial order and its laws, and the insurrection that he had led, had breached the bounds of established rules of structured consensual interaction, including whatever conflict existed between the imperial authorities and their "lawful" African subjects. His war sought to reconfigure the socioeconomic formation of the state; the political order within it; and its power structure.[73] The violence and its envisioned objectives went beyond ordered conflict within the structured rules of interaction that colonial authorities oversaw.

What is more, Kimathi's truth and knowledge were at loggerheads with the ideas and beliefs that had (re)produced the colonial political, economic, and social structure. Structurally, what Kimathi stood for was dangerous to the systemic colonial structure and had to be rooted out and crushed.[74] What Kimathi stood for was, therefore, feared by, and undesirable for, the colonial authorities. He was the paragon of radical and revolutionary thought that demanded far-reaching reforms and fundamental decolonization. The door to this "dangerous" road had to be firmly shut, even if it meant granting flag and political independence to Kenya. Indeed, independence was one way of preventing this possibility: it was a safety valve that ensured that the madding crowd of have-nots could not at any time leap over the barriers and invade the pitch of sanitized politics of "law and order," as they had in 1952.

In death as in life, Kimathi represents the deep politics of moral ethnicity that continues to pit the haves and the have-nots that is, at once, a dynastic, factional, and generational game.[75] This, then, is what explains why he continues to be the revolutionary touchstone by which radical politicians such as J. M. Kariuki, writers acutely sensitive to social and political forces and relations of production, and socially conscious musicians, evaluate politics in Kenya. Kimathi remains, perhaps more than any other public figure in Kenya's history, the focal point of nationalism, the smoldering embers of which promise to glow brighter into an ever-shining dawn of the quest for popular statehood. It is important, therefore, to reflect, in closing, on how he has been valorized and disinterred in popular culture, the official silence of over half a century notwithstanding.

A Paragon of Radical Decolonization, Touchstone of Nationalism, and Subterranean Politics Disinterred

Written in the early 1970s, *The Trial of Dedan Kimathi,* a play by Ngũgĩ wa Thiong'o and Mĩcere Gĩthae Mũgo, was the first to recognize and give all due prominence to the role that Kimathi played in the struggle for independence. I have discussed this elsewhere:

> Thiong'o and Mũgo set out to write a revisionist play celebrating Mau Mau freedom fighters and, in so doing, admittedly, remake Kenya's history. Indeed, it was a deliberate attempt to excavate and expunge the ignominious, criminal depiction, trial and execution of Dedan Kimathi, and other freedom fighters, under an unjust and criminal colonial law. Thiong'o and Mũgo turn to theater as a medium of imaginative reconstruction of the past to inform and educate people about the existence of erstwhile colonial overlords disguised as "nationalists." Moreover, these writers transform the sphere of performance into a site of investigation of communal memory in order to reinstate the impeccable nature of the collective ethos of Africans. The end result is performative history: the performance of the play functions as a register of social memory through the deliberate (re)connection with the struggle of the 1950s. This play disinters and resurrects Dedan Kimathi as a revolutionary hero. It also powerfully and effectively portrays the injustices endured by ordinary Kenyans during the tumultuous decade of the 1950s.[76]

Indeed, more than imaginatively recreating the past—and in so doing, reflecting the collective will of Kenyan peasants and workers in their refusal to succumb to over sixty years of colonial torture and ruthless oppression—this play was written to give people courage and to urge them to an even higher level of resolve in their struggle for total liberation.[77] Ngũgĩ and Mũgo understood this work to be a continuation of the repertoire of political dissent epitomized by Kimathi as the embodiment of the country's anticolonial struggle. Both writers can, therefore, be seen as intellectual Mau Maus in this long lineage of dissent paying homage to the paragon of radical decolonization.

Likewise, Dan "Chizi" Aceda, a socially conscious musician, in his song "Guns and Arrows," from his 2010 breakout sophomore album,

Benganology, manages to evoke, indeed disinter, not only Dedan Kimathi but also Mekatilili wa Menza, a heroine of the early struggle against British imperialism in 1913 and 1914. In light of all that has gone wrong in the postcolony, Kimathi and Mekatilili, he sings, must be turning in their graves. Bearing the torch of dissent, Chizi's subliminal nationalism mourns the silencing of the voices of the people bereft of their dreams by the promise of warm and nutritious but empty democracy. In a tone reminiscent of Kimathi's passionate protestations for justice and truth, Chizi laments that people in Kenya have been served a democracy that does not fill their bellies; a democracy that does not deliver jobs; a democracy that does not give people a source of income; nor one that brings about peace and unity.[78] It is clear from this song, and numerous others produced by Chizi and other artists, that the struggle that Kimathi symbolizes is still on today.

But no one demonstrates this continuity more powerfully than the group Ukoo Flani Mau Mau's music video "*Angalia Saa*" (Look at the Times). The song is dedicated to all Kenyan heroes who struggled against British colonialism but have never been honored. To demonstrate both the continuity of the struggle for freedom and their admiration of their ideological forebears, the group visually plays with time and space in its audio and visual representations. Using song lyrics and video images, these time-warping artists present the past while simultaneously familiarizing the present. They assert that the postcolonial state is in stasis since everything remains the same as it was in colonial times. The song dramatizes the Mau Mau moment by overlapping old video clips of British military crackdowns and images of arrested Mau Mau suspects in screening and detention camps with clips of more recent political crises. Thus, these artists creatively merge the times, the Emergency period, and the present struggle in an unbroken continuity, transcending time and space. This time-warping visual effect is reinforced by using the central character in the music video, the "actorvist" Ndungi Githuku, who literally flees from the British military operations of the 1950s only to find himself in the middle of riotous Nairobi streets in the 2000s.[79]

But it is the end of the video that is most instructive in terms of evoking the memory of Kimathi as a symbol of nationalism and decolonization. It is here that the audience learns that Githuku is playing Kimathi. Lyrics to this effect are visually reinforced by the appearance of Githuku standing next to a painted portrait of Dedan Kimathi. Like the leader of the movement in the 1950s, he is arrested. In a powerful visual subtext, Githuku dramatizes the moment of Kimathi's capture immortalized in the photograph of him lying on a stretcher while a white man, alongside, displays the fighter's leopard skin jacket and cap. But, more powerful is the visual superimposition of the two bodies, Kimathi's and Githuku's.[80]

> The latter's image, faded perhaps to symbolize Kimathi's or the Mau Mau spirit of struggle, rises out of the former. This powerful imagery synchronizes the "distant" event in the past, which was the moment of both Kimathi's personal "defeat," and that of Mau Mau, with the triumphant resolve of the present. Both Kimathi and the Mau Mau struggle are symbolically liberated and disinterred in a heroic and victorious digital and, importantly, actual triumphant present. In this sense, this imagery is a transformative artistic gesture. The gesture presences this historical moment of apparent defeat while, simultaneously, familiarizing the audience with the present struggle by asking it to *Look at the Times*. It thus urges and demonstrates that times have not changed. It powerfully suggests that the struggle is still on and it is to be won.[81]

Such valorization is restorative and redemptive with regard to Kimathi's image. It (re)centers Kimathi within the core of calls for popular statehood, social justice, and mutuality. This signifies two closely related developments that deserve special mention, if anything, to interrogate what is now, more likely than not, going to be, with the recovery of the record of the Kimathi case court proceedings, under considerable ex post facto scrutiny: the unjust and criminal colonial law founded on the social and legal construction of illegality.

The Unjust and Illegitimate Colonial Paranomon Law(s) under Ex Post Facto Scrutiny

Glowing memorialization of Kimathi implies that he is increasingly being accepted as an hero of independence and the embodiment of anticolonialism and decolonization. This is happening beyond the limited boundaries of those who fought for, or were sympathetic to, the struggle for land and freedom, to embrace even erstwhile foes, if lack of any public opposition to this at the epicenter of public acclaim (Nyeri, a region where the 1950s divisions ran deep) is anything to go by. Perhaps, more than fifty years of independence has brought about clarity of perspective as people continue choosing sides and now truly see which "side" of Kenyan politics they are on. Moreover, the release of trial transcripts to the public will bring historical reality closer and, no doubt, open this colonial spectacle, and Kimathi's tragic fate, to scrutiny. In all likelihood, the result will be even more lionization of the man. Now, more than ever before, he is bound to forever remain in collective memory as "the man in the leopard skin coat and hat under the castor oil tree."[82]

Second, there is a possibility that we might yet witness increasing appropriation and deployment of the memory of the anticolonial struggle, and Kimathi's, in the task of nation and state building, even if half-heartedly at first. This is a possibility because of the amount of renewed interest that making the Kimathi trial and related documents available to the public will likely bring about. The public debate that arises from this haunting and stubborn past, if it does not degenerate into the politics of memory, will lead Kenyans to realize, more and more, that in their thought they argue the same issues, superficial ethnic boundaries notwithstanding.[83] Additionally, such a debate will, most assuredly, raise recriminations against what, in retrospect, will be perceived by Kenyans, as wrongful conviction of one of Kenya's freedom heroes, and that of many others, under an unjust and criminal colonial law.

At the same time, Kimathi, and others who fell during the struggle, will be extricated from blame—not a small matter but one that must occasion great contention. As intimated earlier, this debate should ultimately be prudently judged on the basis of the fact that the law upon which freedom fighters were convicted, was limited and contrary to fundamental law. Now under inverse historical scrutiny, given the clarity afforded the public by time and the benefit of hindsight, is the legal validity or legitimacy of, not only the particular legal provision used to convict Kimathi, but also colonial laws in general owing to their questionable sociological construction. Moreover, availability of this previously hidden archival information in the public domain will draw attention to the historical and political context. After all, it is obvious that, while the accused may have broken the colonial government's Emergency laws, the policies of that government—its racial oppression, intolerance of constitutional African opposition and even peaceful dissent, tyranny, ill-treatment, exploitation and denigration of black people, rule through force, and African poverty and absence of human dignity entrenched by legislation[84]—left Kimathi and forest fighters with no choice other than violent resistance. Yet, it is evident from the trial transcripts that this went unprobed. This politico-legal anomaly and oversight is open to question.

When, to what extent, and why did the colonial legal architecture flout natural and fundamental law thus severely constraining the freedom and well-being of imperial subjects who suffered subsequent legal disability? Considering the inherent legal defect of colonial laws, were freedom fighters obligated to obey the law? And, in hindsight, and in light of the foregoing questions, was the punishment meted out to them justified? One might even dare to suppose that penetrating legal arguments will find and extract a posthumous admission from Kenya's erstwhile imperial rulers that there was a gross miscarriage of justice. Might there also be a posthumous exoneration issued by the Kenyan state and from Britain as well?[85] Only time can tell. But time alone cannot make any reliable determination without an appreciable measure of moral probity in Kenyans' collective introspection and scrupulous examination of this regrettable past. These difficult questions call for a thorough, sobering, and critical view, and thrashing out of the shared past between Kenya and Britain with an appreciable measure of moral probity. The serious task of coming to terms with the past lies ahead of us all: intellectuals, the general public, or policy-makers. Sixty years later, the spirit of a man buried in an unmarked grave may yet, finally, rest with the assurance of passing through the open riigi and into both the mythology of the Kenyan state and its recorded history.

The Opened Door of Kenya's Mythology and Authentic History: A Eulogic Epilogue

The emerging image of Kimathi is that of a simple man who acted with courage when he experienced systematic colonial oppression. It is this courage that propelled him to take a daring stand and to fight as a David against an imperial Goliath for basic human rights and shared prosperity, dignity, truth, justice, mutual respect, and coexistence. In so doing, he exemplified Ralph Waldo Emerson's three qualities, which conspicuously attract the wonder and reverence of mankind. First, Kimathi demonstrated a purpose so sincere that it could not be sidetracked by any prospects of wealth or other personal advantage. It is this virtue that steeled his nerves as he waited for his end and must have enabled him to embrace self-sacrifice. It is such self-sacrifice that made renowned heroes of Greece and Rome such as Socrates, Aristides "the Just," Phocion, Quintus Curtius, and Regulus. Second, he was a man of practical power who sought to organize the wishes and thoughts of powerless peasants in carvings of wood and stone, brass and steel.[86]

Third, Kimathi excelled in courage, which, fertile and serene, no imperial terrors—neither bombs from the sky nor the gallows—could shake. His own truth and knowledge was the antidote of fear. Kimathi had the conviction that the imperial agents with whom he contended were not necessarily superior to him in strength, resources, and spirit. A self-made field marshal, his speeches motivated his *itungati* (troops of young "soldiers") reminding them that they were men and that their enemies were no more. It is this same sacred courage that steadied his pen as he scribbled his last letter, addressed to a Father Marino (from a Catholic mission in Nyeri).[87] From a stoic pen flowed words of a man who was persuaded that he had attempted to accomplish the cause that he was put in colonial Kenya by the Creator to do. Penning these last words, I wonder whether, as a professing Christian, Kimathi thought he was indestructible. Whether his only fear was facing his final judge, the Almighty, and not those who could kill the body but were unable to kill the soul or destroy his legacy. Otherwise, how could he have taken on the British unless he had the courage to believe he was more than a match for his antagonists then, and in the long sweep of history? Was death his final hope for escape from the imprisonment of an oppressive colonial architecture of legal strictures and exploitative policies; from the manacling of individual and collective wills; and from imperial spatial deletion and delimitation constraining the individual field and basis of action and, therefore, African agency?[88] And how could he have been impenitently "so busy and so happy preparing for heaven" on the very eve of his execution (by hanging by the neck until dead) unless he was consumed by the best and highest courages that are the beams of the Almighty?[89] Did he believe himself to have fought the good fight, to have run and finished the race and remained faithful to a just cause that had, for him, shone like the noonday sun?

We may never know the full answers to these questions. But one thing is without doubt: there was once a man in a leopard skin jacket and hat under a castor oil tree in the thick "tapestry of sickly wafting mist"[90] of the Nyandarua forest of the cold Aberdare ranges of Central Kenya. A man who consigned himself there because he loved the idea of a free country more than anything in the world, even his life. A man who, aiming for neither pelf nor comfort, ventured all to put, in one act of violent resistance, the invisible thought in his mind. A man who is in anybody's eyes and for all times will remain, a liberator, for he sought the ideal of self-mastery and freedom stemming from the restoration of alienated African lands. This man, Kimathi, must stand like a Hercules, an Achilles, a Rüstem, an Arthur, or a Cid in the mythology of the Kenyan state; and in its authentic history, like a Leonidas, a Scipio, a Caesar, a Richard Cœur de Lion, a Nelson, a Grand Condé, a Bertrand du Guesclin, a Doge Dandolo, a Napoleon, a Masséna, and a Ney.[91] But this is now a matter before the court of public opinion, which must decide this now reopened case: one between what Kimathi stood for and his stated cause, and that of Mau Mau, versus an obsolete and paranomon British colonial justice system.

Notes

1. These two masterful studies, Anderson's *Histories of the Hanged* and Elkins's *Britain's Gulag,* among a few others including that by Bennett, *Fighting the Mau Mau,* were vital for the manner in which they revealed hidden histories of Britain's imperial past in Kenya and the 1950s Mau Mau counterinsurgency in particular. These three revealing studies relied heavily on material that had for decades remained concealed in a secret archive deep in the Buckinghamshire countryside in Hanslope Park, sometimes referred to as "spook central." Elkins, Anderson and Bennett, therefore, were the first to pierce through the enshrouding in silent mystery of what exactly transpired during the Emergency in colonial Kenya. The bluff by a colonial official that some Mau Mau records would not be made available to the public, not even after fifty years, was thwarted. The sworn silence, and wish by some key colonial officials and some in London to keep mum about misdeeds, missteps, and, indeed, the cruel and heartless commission of evils while countering the militant Mau Mau, met its irreverent end at last. The sins that the Kenyan attorney general Griffiths-Jones had so wished, as indicated in a 1957 memorandum, to keep secret, were ultimately laid bare. For more on this, see Githuku, *Mau*

Mau Crucible, 96; Katie Engelhart, "40,000 Kenyans Accuse UK of Abuse in Second Mau Mau Case," *Guardian,* 29 October 2014.

2. Anne Soy, "Kenya Mau Mau Memorial Funded by UK Unveiled," BBC News—Nairobi, 12 September 2015.

3. Engelhart, "Second Mau Mau Case," *Guardian.*

4. The dark and eerie back room of memory of events in the past, whether private or collective, is one that we, as human beings—whoever and wherever we may be, academics, the general public, in institutions, in governments, or acting as nations—rarely want to venture into, and one, when we dare, we are scarcely able to deal with without succumbing to the temptation of moving things around. We find that we must rearrange memory to suit our present tastes; to allay fears that the past can visit upon the present; to avoid culpability or being held to account; and to redeem ourselves, reputations, and self-respect. In countries that have experienced intensely divisive conflict or gross violation of human rights and human dignity—such as Guatemala, which experienced a civil war that lasted slightly over three decades; Cambodia, which experienced one of the world's worst internal genocides in the 1970s; the long history of conflict in Northern Ireland; and apartheid in South Africa—has led to deep-seated social divisions usually accompanied by grief or a certain restlessness about the past. The ultimate result is the emergence of a memory of silence or fiery contestation about how the past ought to be remembered or interpreted. When errors of omission or embellishments of the past find their way into written history, what emerges is a multitude of arguments, counterarguments, and exculpatory narratives about the past derived from a formulaic rehearsal of old mantras or scripts which, with regard to un/critical reflections and/or versus repression of Nazi memory in Germany, gave rise to *Vergangenheitspolitik* (the politics of confronting the past) as opposed to a thorough, sobering, and critical view and a thrashing out of the past characterized by tackling difficult questions about it with an appreciable measure of moral probity (*Vergangenheitsbewältigung*). As the British imperial chickens come home to roost, this is the challenge that faces the disentangling and straightening out of history—both of Kenya itself that shared between Kenya and Britain.

5. Stewart Clegg, "Power and Authority, Resistance and Legitimacy," in *Power in Contemporary Politics: Theories, Practices, Globalizations,* ed. Henri Goverde, Philip G. Cerny, Mark Haugaard, and Howard H. Lentner (London: Sage, 2000), 81, 83, 90.

6. Michel Foucault, in his University of Vermont series of lectures, uses "technologies of the self" to refer to specific techniques that human beings use to understand themselves. Even more specifically, it refers to technologies that permit individuals to effect, by their own means or with the help of others, a certain number of operations on their own bodies and souls, thoughts, conduct, and way of being, in order to attain a certain state of happiness, purity,

wisdom, perfection, or immortality—in other words, internal work of the soul to know itself, which is also the principle upon which just political action can be founded. For more about this, see Michel Foucault, *Technologies of the Self: A Seminar with Michel Foucault,* ed. Luther H. Martin, Huck Gutman, and Patrick H. Hutton (Amherst: University of Massachusetts Press, 1998), 3–49. These technologies of the self, include, among other things, writing, taking notes about oneself and hence record keeping in the form of diaries and personal journals, speeches, and reading.

7. Clegg, "Power and Authority," 90.

8. Ibid., 80, 90. These differentiating personal leadership qualities and authority-creation techniques or discursive technologies of the self are fully explored in Nicholas Githuku, "'Collaborators' or 'Resistors,' 'Loyalists' versus 'Rebels': Problematizing a Colonial Binary Nomenclature through the Prism of Dedan Kimathi's Career" (unpublished).

9. Kenneth S. Broun, *Saving Nelson Mandela: The Rivonia Trial and the Fate of South Africa* (New York: Oxford University Press, 2012), 139.

10. James C. Scott recounts how, as a subinspector of police in the 1920s in colonial Burma, Orwell had to shoot an elephant that, being in heat, had broken its tether and ravaged a market, killing a man. By the time Orwell, rifle in hand, had caught up with the animal, the heat had passed and the elephant was peacefully grazing in the paddy fields. But Orwell felt compelled to kill it anyway now that there were more than two thousand colonial subjects who were watching what action he would take: would he walk away or shoot it and thus deliver a credible performance of mastery? He chose the latter to avoid being jeered, and, more important, to follow the established script. Scott, *Domination and the Arts of Resistance: Hidden Transcripts* (New Haven: Yale University Press, 2008), 10.

11. Ibid., 10–11. For a comprehensive reading of the interpenetration of the moral environment of the courtroom and that of the society in which the court is situated and, thus, the political atmosphere, see Peter Coss, ed., The Moral World of the Law (Cambridge: Cambridge University Press, 2000). As Lonsdale argues in reference to the Kenyatta trial, as in the 1952–53 trial, due process in the Kimathi trial was not without political blemish: politics definitely did break in and play a critical role in the judicial process despite the colonial state's insistence, spoken or unspoken, that politics had nothing to do with it. Lonsdale, "Kenyatta's Trial," this volume, 221, 232 and 238; see also Simon Gikandi, "Pan-Africanism and Cosmopolitanism: The Case of Jomo Kenyatta," English Studies in Africa 43, no. 1 (2000): 7. Thus, the public arena could not quite be held back. Opinions of the trial were inseparable from perceptions of the Emergency. In this instance, as in the Kenyatta trial, the law did appear to back the contested racially ordered social hierarchy, which weakened its legitimacy. See Chris Wickham, conclusion to Coss, *Moral World,* 246. Also see

G. Edward White, "The Evolution of Reasoned Elaboration: Jurisprudential Criticism and Social Change," *Virginia Law Review* 59, no. 2 (1973): 279–302.

12. The pun is not intended because the disregard for imperial subjects' lives by some Britons was legendary; according to Elizabeth Kolsky, colonial subjects were ranked with the beasts, a racial attitude that was forged in the crucible of chattel slavery. Kolsky, *Colonial Justice in British India* (Cambridge: Cambridge University Press, 2010), 16. From her remarkable examination of over 150 years of violent crimes against Indians, and in another study of similar cases in Kenya between 1905 and 1934 by Martin J. Wiener, *An Empire on Trial: Race, Murder, and Justice under British Rule, 1870–1935* (Cambridge: Cambridge University Press, 2009), 193–221, it is quite clear that imperial subjects, even those who never raised a finger in an attempt to regain their liberty or land, but especially those that did so, did not have the slightest chance; they were destroyed like wild beasts. More important, both studies show that in most cases, the law was complicit in condoning violent and abhorrent criminal acts by whites against imperial subjects, which raises serious doubts concerning the soundness and hence the legal validity of British colonial justice as a whole.

13. Charles Warren, *The Supreme Court in United States History,* 2 vols. (Boston: Little Brown, 1926), 1:2, as cited in A. Leon Higginbotham, Jr., *In the Matter of Color: Race and the American Legal Process: The Colonial Period* (New York: Oxford University Press, 1978), 14.

14. For more on problems of the philosophy of law, see Brian Leiter and Michael Sevel, "Philosophy of Law," *Encyclopedia Britannica* (Online): http://www.britannica.com/topic/philosophy-of-law. Also see Kenneth Einar Himma, "Philosophy of Law," in *Internet Encyclopedia of Philosophy,* http://www.iep.utm.edu/law-phil/#H2. According to Leiter and Sevel, sociological jurisprudence concerns itself with the effects of social phenomena on both the substantive and procedural aspects of law, as well as on the legislative, judicial, and other means of forming, operating, changing, and disrupting the legal order. Whereas Himma points out that normative jurisprudence involves normative, evaluative, and otherwise prescriptive questions about the law. A critical revisit to the Kimathi trial ought to examine it in light of three key issues related to sociological jurisprudence: (1) when and to what extent laws can restrict the freedom of citizens, (2) the nature of one's obligation to obey the law, and (3) the justification of punishment by law.

15. Vilhelm Aubert, ed., *Sociology of Law* (Baltimore: Penguin, 1969), 11, as cited by Higginbotham, *Matter of Color,* 13–14.

16. Kimathi's trial is not an isolated case and it will be most interesting to see how it figures in future comparative studies with other not so dissimilar cases within the context of imperial domination, including the Jomo Kenyatta Kapenguria and the Nelson Mandela Rivonia trials, together with

their respective comrades in the struggle against colonial political oppression, injustice, and economic exploitation.

17. Christine Sypnowich, "Law and Ideology," in *The Stanford Encyclopedia of Philosophy,* ed. Edward N. Zalta (Winter 2014), http://plato.stanford.edu/archives/win2014/entries/law-ideology; Oliver Wendell Holmes, *The Common Law* (Boston: Little, Brown, 1881), 1, as cited in Higginbotham, *Matter of Color,* 14.

18. This recovery of the Kimathi transcripts comes at an interesting time in the recent analytical development of historiographical accounts, particularly Mau Mau history writing, which has, as exemplified by Anderson's *Histories of the Hanged* and Elkins's *Britain's Gulag,* taken a sharp turn toward what Jean and John Comaroff have described as the "juridification of the past." Comaroff and Comaroff, *Theory from the South; Or, How Euro-America is Evolving toward Africa* (Boulder: Paradigm, 2012), 137). That is, the process in which the rights and wrongs of historical acts and facts, and the claims arising out of them, are subjected to determination either by legal procedures or by their simulacra.

19. Higginbotham, *Matter of Color*, 13.

20. Consider the penetrating and critical analysis by Jaume Asens and Gerardo Pisarello, "The Illegality of Power," 17 February 2012, http://criticallegalthinking.com/2012/02/17/the-illegality-of-power/. There is perhaps no better example of this fact than Higginbotham's detailed and authoritative study of how an entire legal apparatus and system was used by those in power to establish a solid legal tradition for the absolute enslavement of blacks. Higginbotham, *Matter of Color.*

21. Githuku, *Mau Mau Crucible,* 31, 32.

22. Asens and Pisarello, "Illegality of Power." Also see Githuku, *Mau Mau Crucible,* 49.

23. Sypnowich, "Law and Ideology."

24. See I. F. Stone, *The Trial of Socrates* (New York: Anchor, 1989), 245.

25. See the third assessment by Kibuthu Kihia.

26. Broun, *Saving Nelson Mandela,* 52. In light of this observation, Ngũgĩ wa Thiong'o and Mĩcere Gĩthae Mũgo's fictional Kimathi's statement from their play, *The Trial of Dedan Kimathi,* at the top of their foreword in this volume, is vindicated.

27. Ngũgĩ wa Thiong'o, *Something Torn and New: An African Renaissance* (New York: BasicCivitas Books, 2009), 3–4; reissued with new title, *Re-Membering Africa* (New York: BasicCivitas Books, 2010).

28. Stacey Hynd, "Killing the Condemned: The Practice and Process of Capital Punishment in British Africa, 1900–1950s," *Journal of African History* 49, no. 3 (2008): 403.

29. Ngũgĩ, *Something Torn,* 3–4.

30. Simon Gikandi's contribution to this volume.

31. For a scholarly analysis of the commissioning of this statue, see Coombes, "Monumental Histories."

32. For more about this sect see Grace N. Wamue, "The Politics of the Mungiki," *Wajibu: A Journal of Social and Religious Studies* 14 (1999): 15–16; Peter Mwangi Kagwanja, "Facing Mount Kenya or Facing Mecca? The Mungiki, Ethnic Violence and the Politics of the Moi Succession in Kenya, 1987–2002," *African Affairs* 102, no. 406 (2003): 25–49; Daniel Branch, *Kenya: Between Hope and Despair, 1963–2011* (New Haven, CT: Yale University Press, 2011), 236–42; Githuku, *Mau Mau Crucible,* 392–99; Ross Kemp, "A Kenya Special," documentary for SKY 1 TV, YouTube, published 1 December 2009; Ben Knighton, "Mungiki Madness," in *Religion and Politics in Kenya: Essays in Honor of a Meddlesome Priest,* ed. Knighton (New York: Palgrave Macmillan, 2009), 223–50; Jacob Rasmussen "Mungiki as Youth Movement: Revolution, Gender and Generational Politics in Nairobi, Kenya," *Young: Nordic Journal of Youth Research* 18, no. 3 (2010): 301–19; David Nderitu, "Mungiki: Wanjiku's Expression of Self," in *Wanjiku: A Kenyan Sociopolitical Discourse,* ed. Naomi L. Shitemi and Eunice K. Kamaara (Nairobi: Goethe-Institut Kenya/Native Intelligence, 2014).

33. The commissioning, erection, and unveiling of the Kimathi statue coincided with emboldened agitation accompanied by public political statements and criminal acts of violence by the Mungiki throughout 2007, when the group's violence was at an all-time high. This, I posit, was not a coincidence.

34. Githuku, "'Loyalists' versus 'Rebels,'" scrutinizes the rather superficial imperial political classification of "loyalists" and "rebels."

35. Clegg, "Power and Authority," 90–91.

36. See MacArthur, introduction to this volume.

37. Clegg, "Power and Authority," 81.

38. Ibid., 82, 83.

39. Ibid., 81, 83, 84, 86. According to Clegg, (self-)identity is contingent, provisional, achieved rather than given. Identity is always in process, always subject to reproduction or transformation through discursive practices that secure or refuse particular posited identities, something that Anthony Giddens aptly sums up thus: self-identity is not something that is just given, as a result of the continuities of the individual's action-system, but something that has to be routinely created and sustained in the reflexive activities of the individual. Self-identity is a reflexive achievement. Giddens, *Modernity and Self-Identity: Self and Society in the Late Modern Age* (Stanford: Stanford University Press, 1991), 52, 215.

40. Clegg, "Power and Authority," 83, 85, 86. See also MacArthur, introduction to this volume.

41. Theodore Roszak, *Person/Planet: The Creative Disintegration of Industrial Society* (London: Gollancz, 1979), xxviii, as cited in Giddens, *Modernity,* 209.

42. Scott, *Domination*, 7, 8, 9.

43. Clegg, "Power and Authority," 85, 86.

44. In making this assertion, it is assumed that Kimathi's followers were people he may have known or met as an ordinary villager in Karunaini; during his time as the secretary of KAU in Ol Kalou; and as a popular oath administrator and as fast-rising leader in the forest.

45. Clegg, "Power and Authority," 83, 86–88. Also see also Lonsdale's contribution to this volume.

46. See MacArthur, introduction to this volume.

47. Ibid.

48. Ralph Waldo Emerson, *The Works of Ralph Waldo Emerson*, 12 vols., Fireside Edition (Boston: 1909), vol. 7, *Society and Solitude*, accessed 2 April 2016, http://oll.libertyfund.org/titles/86.

49. Ernesto Laclau, *On Populist Reason* (London: Verso, 2005), 129, 171, 199–200, 206.

50. Clegg, "Power and Authority," 79, 80. See also MacArthur's introduction and Lonsdale's contribution to this volume.

51. See Lonsdale's contribution to this volume.

52. Clegg, "Power and Authority," 87; see also Lonsdale's contribution to this volume.

53. Clegg, "Power and Authority," 86.

54. Ibid., 82.

55. Peterson, "Writing in Revolution," 89–90.

56. Clegg, "Power and Authority," 80.

57. Anthony Giddens, *The Constitution of Society: Outline of the Theory of Structuration* (Berkeley: University of California Press, 1984), 45.

58. Clegg, "Power and Authority," 79–80.

59. Here it is important to draw parallels between the confiscation and thereafter, "loss" or destruction of captured Mau Mau archives of documents and letters most of them authored by Kimathi that were preserved in four sacks and, similarly, the shared fate of over a ton of Jomo Kenyatta's private papers and books. For this see Kinyatti, *Kenya's Freedom Struggle*, xviii; John Lonsdale, "Jomo Kenyatta, God and the Modern World," in *African Modernities: Entangled Meanings in Current Debate*, ed. Jan-Georg Deutsch, Peter Probst, and Heike Schmidt (Oxford: James Currey, 2002), 31–65. I contend that this intentional loss or willful destruction of such important documents is not simply suspect physical obliteration of historical record but also attempted discursive erasure of marginal African voices of popular and valid grievance and resistance.

60. For an appreciation of the modest education that Kimathi had received, see also MacArthur, introduction to this volume.

61. See ibid.

62. Unless indicated otherwise, this paragraph, and the next, contains and highlights relevant parts of the three letters produced in court in a bid to amplify Kimathi's stance and understanding of his cause as he saw it.

63. In the Kimathi letters produced in court—the shorter one, dated 20 March 1954 (Exhibit No. 23, transcribed as Document 9 in this volume), but especially that of 20 October 1954 (Exhibit No. 22A, transcribed as Document 8 in this volume), it is quite clear that the government's offer of amnesty following surrender was only the first step toward racial reconciliation as well as reaching a satisfactory solution for all underscored by truth and justice in light of longstanding African grievances. In the latter, Kimathi stated that there was no way of peacefully ending the African struggle. Might the manner in which Kimathi, and Mau Mau more broadly, were treated explain the consequent lineage of dissent in postcolonial Kenya? This is a question I have addressed extensively elsewhere.

64. As MacArthur noted (via personal e-mail), one of the interesting things about the trial's material discovery is how early talk of negotiation started, coupled, of course, with "surrender" and "amnesty." I agree with her that it is also a thorny issue and double-edged sword yet so little studied. It is no wonder that David Anderson's contribution in this volume identifies it as a theme of the history of the Mau Mau rebellion that needs more intellectual scrutiny. In *Mau Mau Crucible of War* (200–208), I have cast this topic of "surrender and amnesty" within the broader important question (one that engaged and divided members of the Legislative Council, especially Europeans), of what defeating Mau Mau and returning to "normalcy" really meant.

65. Dedan Kimathi, "An Open Letter to the British Authorities," in Kinyatti, *Kenya's Freedom Struggle*, 57, 63.

66. See Exhibit No. 22A, Document 8 in this volume.

67. See ibid. and Exhibit No. 23, Document 9 in this volume.

68. Kinyatti, *Kenya's Freedom Struggle*, 69. Similarly, Exhibit No. 23 contains an appeal from Kimathi for Africans and forest fighters to be regarded as (fellow) human beings.

69. See Lonsdale's contribution to this volume.

70. See MacArthur, introduction to this volume.

71. Clough, *Mau Mau Memoirs*, 99–102.

72. Peterson, *Creative Writing*, 207–8.

73. Githuku, *Mau Mau Crucible*, 6.

74. Mark Haugaard, "Power, Ideology and Legitimacy," in Goverde et al., *Power in Contemporary Politics*, 61, 62, 65.

75. Githuku, *Mau Mau Crucible*, 282–83. Also see Lonsdale, "Moral Economy," 466–68.

76. Githuku, *Mau Mau Crucible*, 263.

77. Ibid., 264.

78. Ibid., 430.

79. Ibid., 414, 417, 420.

80. Ibid., 420.

81. Ibid., 420–22.

82. The quote is from Njogi Ngatia, a Tribal Police constable who participated in the capture of Kimathi.

83. Lonsdale, "Moral Economy," 468.

84. Broun, *Saving Nelson Mandela*, 54, 70, 71, 73.

85. Some leading radical intellectuals, freedom fighters, and patriots in their own right do not consider this necessary, as it would serve to dignify and legitimize colonial law and "justice" and, indeed, the whole colonial enterprise that has, as Mĩcere Gĩthae Mũgo points out, come under searing criticism by, among others, Aimé Césaire in *Discourse on Colonialism*, trans. Joan Pinkham (New York: Monthly Review Press, 2001). With reference to my email exchanges (between 7 and 28 March 2016) with Mĩcere Gĩthae Mũgo, Maina Kinyatti, and Willy Mutunga, it is likely that the release of Kimathi's trial documents and this volume to coincide with the sixtieth anniversary of Kimathi's execution will witness even more radical demands including, in Mũgo's words: that the current British and Kenyan governments categorically denounce and dissociate themselves from a historical crime—specifically, the conviction and murder of Kimathi. Additionally, within this particular context, that a fresh official public apology be made to Kimathi's family, Kenya Land and Freedom Army ex-combatants, and the Kenyan people by both governments for condoning the crime over historical time by failing to officially condemn it; that both governments (definitely that of Kenya) reaffirm Kimathi as a Kenyan hero extraordinaire and think of an appropriate special medal to award him posthumously; and that, in consultation and collaboration with the family, Kimathi's remains be located, exhumed, and given a special public and hero's national burial. According to Mũgo, "An apology should be made to the family for the length of time it has taken to do this despite public requests and . . . many appeals by DK's family."

86. Emerson, "On Courage," in *Works*.

87. See "Final Letter from Kimathi to Father Marino," 17 February 1957, transcribed as Document 15 in this volume.

88. Githuku, *Mau Mau Crucible*, 13, 55, 75–79.

89. See "Final Letter from Kimathi to Father Marino"; also, Emerson, "On Courage."

90. Machua Koinange, "My Encounter with the Man Who Shot Dedan Kimathi," *Standard Digital*, 20 October 2013.

91. Emerson, "On Courage."

4

Dedan Kimathi

The Floating Signifier and the Missing Body

Simon Gikandi

If, as is commonly believed, the postcolonial Kenyan state needs forgetting as its will to truth, especially in the first decade of independence, it could be argued that it needs the figure of Dedan Kimathi to be located at the junction of forgetting and remembering.[1] Evidence of this is that even in the days when the Kenyatta government was eager to repress the recent anticolonial past, Kimathi's name circulates freely in the former "Mau Mau" zones in the Mount Kenya region, with schools, neighborhoods, and streets named after him. There is a Kimathi Estate in Nairobi with its own Kimathi primary school. There are Kimathi memorial secondary schools in various parts of Nyeri County. Karunaini, Kimathi's birthplace, is in a Kimathi sublocation. And in the 1970s, during a frenzy of institution building, the Nyeri elite, led by Mwai Kibaki, set up an Institute of Technology named after Kimathi, which later became a university chartered and sponsored by the Kenyan state. In the center of Nairobi, Hardage Street was renamed Kimathi Street, which joins Kenyatta Avenue (formerly Delamere Avenue) and Mama Ngina Street (Queen's Street). If the mandate of decolonization is that the Mau Mau movement be suppressed and forgotten so that the narrative of decolonization can be rewritten, the figure of Kimathi somehow resists repression and seems to sit outside the national doctrine of "forgive and forget."[2]

I therefore propose that Kimathi is neither the demonic figure of colonial discourse, nor the heroic subject of radical nationalism, but what the anthropologist Claude Lévi-Strauss famously called a "floating signifier," a term intended "to represent an undetermined quantity of signification," but is in "itself void of meaning and thus apt to receive any meaning."[3] Kimathi is a signifier with a value, but what this value represents is variable and open to multiple interpretations. I work under the influence of the poststructuralist lesson that there is no Kimathi except in the way he has been imagined and represented—to borrow a term from Jacques Derrida—*sous rature,* under erasure.[4] My search here is not for the real Kimathi but for the symbolic and the imaginary figure that both informs and haunts the national narrative from his grave.[5] I offer two readings of Kimathi: the symbolic figure that emerges out of the archive and the one imagined by creative writers. Somewhere in the cracks left by these two forms of discourses—the archival and the imaginative—we might recover Kimathi's quantity of signification and perhaps begin to understand what value he holds in debates about Kenyan pasts and presents.

Kimathi in the Symbolic Order

Jacques Lacan teaches us that the symbolic is a product of language and narrative. Conceived within the intelligible rules and constraints of language, a symbolic representation is premised on an acceptance of the rules of the Father, the rules that control desire and communication: "It is in the name of the father that we must recognize the support of the symbolic function which, from the dawn of history, has identified his person with the figure of the law."[6] Moreover, the symbolic function is what allows a subject to enter into the community of others—it is "the pact which links . . . subjects together in one action. The human action par excellence is originally founded on the existence of the world of the symbol, namely on laws and contracts."[7] Colonial discourse, for example, is keen to exclude Kimathi from the world of the Father (the law) and to delink him from the community that he claims to represent. The key lexicon in Ian Henderson's narrative of Kimathi is illegitimacy, deviation, and "a reputation for delinquency."[8] Conversely, the task of rewriting Kimathi as a nationalist hero depends on his insertion into a world of collective symbols and communal references intended to keep his spirit alive as part of the "continuing struggle of our people for democracy and social justice."[9]

There is no doubt that the Kimathi who emerges in retrospective accounts such as Karari Njama's *Mau Mau from Within* (1970), or in Kimathi's letters and speeches, is keenly attuned to his role in a community of symbols carefully cultivated through speech acts. In reference to the killing of some teachers by his forces, for example, Kimathi, who is an ardent advocate of education, speaks as the voice of a universal truth. He assumes that his listeners—and the people in general—share his views and that there is a concurrence between the speaker and his real and implied audience:

> "Of all the teachers who have been killed and schools which have been destroyed, very few [are due to] orders from me; in fact, none for the killing of teachers. But I have ordered the destruction of some schools for the demonstration of our objection to Beecher's Report [1949 Report on African Education], as you have learned from Gen. Kahiu-Itina raiding your school. The rest [of the raids] have been carried out by supporters and *komereras* (criminals) from mere bitterness to that harmful plan which has led to the closure of about 300 of our schools. The interpretation doesn't matter much, for one can interpret anything in any way he likes. If I were to speak to the people I would tell them the Government doesn't want us to be educated and that is why it has closed our schools; it wants us to continue witchcraft and superstition[,] for after closing the schools it has given us no substitute other than collective punishment without trials, and many innocent people are punished. Don't you think that the people would agree with me?" asked F. M. Kimathi proudly.[10]

Clearly, Kimathi is acutely aware of the work of speech acts in defining and channeling both personal and collective desires.

In short, the Kimathi who emerges out of the archives seems to understand his symbolic role as an avatar of a not-so-unusual combination of the nationalist, the traditionalist, and the Christian. A vivid example of this play of symbols can be found at the end of the historic meeting at Mwathe (August 1953). As reported by Njama, the scene opens with Kimathi cleansing his "household" with beer, invoking the power of God and his ancestors:

When he came out, he stood facing Mt. Kenya and poured some beer on the ground, saying: "God! We give thee only what we have, honey, animal (domestic) fat, cereals (a mixture of different kinds of millets)." Pouring a little of these on the ground, he said: "That is yours, our Father Gikuyu, and that is yours my father Waciuri."[11]

Attuned to the work of both an inherited and invented tradition, Kimathi is simultaneously a Gikuyu elder and a Christian, his dual roles prompted by a keen understanding of the limits of the old tradition and the temptations of the new ones.[12]

However, words are not enough to sustain the kind of symbology that Kimathi needs in order to assert his authority. At the end of the Mwathe meeting, then, Kimathi adopts what strikes Njama as a photographic pose: "Swinging his walking stick and standing alert as a person ready for his photo to be taken, Kimathi smiled as the crowd cheered him, wishing him the best luck on his journey as they dispersed."[13] Now, Kimathi is nothing less than a world image with all its symbolic associations and visible and invisible meanings:

Kimathi, aged 33, stood almost six feet, strong and healthy; his long self-woven hair hanging over a fair brown oval face; his big grey-white and brown eyes. protruding below black eyebrows separated by a wide short flat nose . . . his long neck shooting out of his wide shoulders, dressed in a suit of whitish-grey corduroy jumper coat, on which three army stars were fixed on both shoulders, and long trousers. Three writing pens were clipped on his top right hand jumper coat pocket, a heap of exercise books in his left hand, in which the ring finger had been cut off at the second joint, an automatic pistol hoisted at his leather waist belt, a metal bracelet on his right hand wrist.[14]

Even as a prisoner at his trial, Kimathi strikes a pose that reflects what Walter Benjamin would call an "aura."[15] The pose, however, also invites a set of difficult questions—what is the character of the person behind the pose? Is the photographic pose a projection of the self into public space or a form of concealment? Can we ever know who the real Kimathi is?

Here, it would be useful to recall that part of Kimathi's attraction to writers ranging from Henderson in 1958 to Sam Kahiga in the 1990s is the idea that he is an unknowable person. For Henderson and his policemen, the thrill of the hunt for Kimathi is that their quarry is "as elusive as a butterfly."[16] At the end of Kahiga's novel, *The Real Dedan Kimathi*, Major Theuri, one of Kimathi's aides, comes to realize that although he has spent many years close to the field marshal "and considered himself as one of the very few people who knew the real Kimathi, he knew nothing of the man."[17] Most attempts to write about Kimathi begin with an acknowledgment of the limits of the work of representation itself, a concession that in spite of the extensive archive he has left behind, the marshal remains unknown and unknowable. The corporeal absence of Kimathi—his death and missing body—made the task of representation even more daunting. If only Kimathi were alive today to tell his own story, says General China in *"Mau Mau" General*, "we would all be the wiser for it."[18]

But this wish begs two questions: What kind of story would Kimathi tell? And would this story lead us to a better understanding of his complicated life? My contention is that whatever story Kimathi might tell would take us no closer to understanding his life outside the mode of representation established by the genre of Mau Mau memoirs.[19] Locating himself within the theater of Kenyan nationalism, Kimathi—a former actor and director—would probably cast himself as what György Lukács famously described as the public character of modern drama, one in which "individual destinies" are represented in their exclusiveness so that they can give "*direct* expression to general destinies, destinies of whole nations, whole classes, indeed whole epochs."[20] Rather than focus on his subjective identity, Kimathi would probably locate himself in the collective drama of his epoch and use his life story to recall the experiences of a generation in a period of transition.

The story he would tell would probably stretch from the green fields of Karunaini and his education at the Scottish mission at Tumutumu; the unhappy move to the settled territories; life in the Nyandarua forest; the fateful day when a tribal policemen called Ndirangu shot and wounded him; and his interrogation by the police and eventual trial at the High Court in Nyeri. This could be Kimathi's story in some ways, but it would remain within the symbolic order because it would rehearse the shared experiences of the so-called generation of the 1940s. In fact, it would be very much like the story told by Waruhiu Itote (General China) in *"Mau Mau" General* (1967), Kiboi Muriithi in *War in the Forest* (1971), J. Wamweya in *Freedom Fighter* (1971), and H. K. Wachanga in *The Swords of Kirinyaga* (1975). If it were textualized, Kimathi's life story would have no identity or value outside the role assigned to him by a strange convergence of cultural forces—colonialism and the radical generation of the 1940s. In effect, Kimathi's coming into being as a radical would not make sense outside a common narrative of African disenchantment across a set of vectors—with the Christian mission, the colonial school, and the role of the father—shared by his generation.

To speculate further, the Kimathi who would emerge out of these narratives would fall neatly into the structure and tropes that have come to define African life writing in Kenya since the 1940s. We can assume that Kimathi, like other members of his generation, tries his hand at petty trade or takes up casual jobs. We know that he eventually makes his way to Ol Kalou, where he works as a clerk on a dairy or pig farm. And predictably, we know that Kimathi becomes radicalized when he comes face to face with other Gikuyu, Embu, and Meru subalterns, commonly known as squatters, in the so-called settled areas. Becoming a squatter is an important transition, the beginning of the road to radicalization.[21] And if squatters now appear to be the classical subalterns in colonial society, it is because of their uneven relationship to both the Gikuyu reserve and the White Highlands. They are a new kind of landless people, neither the traditional Gikuyu *ahoi* (tenants at will) under the protection of a landowning class nor people with the right to settlement in the White Highlands. But if squatters appear to be totally displaced, they are connected to the political economy of colonialism more than to the ordinary peasants in the reserve, and, driven by what Tabitha Kanogo has described as an "expansionist dynamic," they are eager to remake themselves outside the reserve and to reimagine themselves as new types of subjects—black settlers as it were.[22]

The Imaginary without an Image

If Kimathi's life is not extraordinary, why does he stand out as the great symbol of the anticolonial revolt in Kenya? And why does he attract the interest of creative writers? From a historical perspective, as the other essays in this volume vividly illustrate, Kimathi's symbolic power is enhanced by the enemies who demonize him and the followers who adore him. But I believe his control over the symbology of Mau Mau goes beyond his charisma or personality. What makes Kimathi stand outside the collective, symbolic economy of Mau Mau is that he is not there to fill the obvious gaps in his life story: Why was he expelled from Tumutumu mission school? What actually happened to him when he joined the army? How did he end up in the settled areas? When, how, and why did he end up in the forest? It is this incompleteness that makes Kimathi the ideal subject of tragic drama, of the imaginary reconstruction of history. Kimathi becomes a unique subject for drama because of what Susan Letzer Cole calls, in a different context, "the paradox of *embodied absence*."[23] In other words it is when we are confronted by gaps in Kimathi's story that the force of what Lacan calls the imaginary becomes crucial to understanding the poetics and politics of memory. For Lacan, the imaginary is necessitated by the discovery that the essential condition of the human subject is one of loss and separation. Confronted by a situation of loss, or what Lacan calls lack, the human subject comes to a realization that its needs and desires cannot be fulfilled and hence turns to create an image, a fantasy, that will function as a substitute for the real.[24]

Although Lacan is writing about the child coming to an identity of itself as an individual, his formulation can be applied to postcolonial subjects who discover that the dream of independence—the symbolic order, which should have been embodied by a figure like Kimathi—is difficult to realize. The difficulty of coming into being as a postcolonial subject in independent Kenya can be explained in two ways. First, like all subjects coming out of a violent history, Kenyans live under the fear that recalling the recent past will only remind them of the wrongs of history, its divisions, and its recent misfortunes.[25] Second, there is the difficulty of figuring a way to represent a figure like Kimathi outside the prison house of colonial discourse.

For if the postcolonial elite is the heir to colonial institutions, they cannot separate their new role, which is essentially that of governmentality, from an inherited anti-Mau Mau discourse. Matters are further complicated by the fact that even when the elite seems to desire forgetting as the condition of its newness, it still finds it difficult to shake off the past.

Indeed, one of the great ironies of Kenyan decolonization is what one may call a belated discourse of history in which colonial past and postcolonial futures meet each other at a discursive junction. Consider this: the Corfield Report, *The Origins and Growth of Mau Mau*, the official historical survey of the nationalist movement, is published in 1960, the year the State of Emergency ends; J. M. Kariuki's *"Mau Mau" Detainee*, considered to be the first account from inside the nationalist movement, is published in 1963. Corfield seems to want to lock the national narrative in a time that is passed; Kariuki wants to move the story forward, but he cannot do so without coming to terms with the past. The result is a discursive impasse.

Within this impasse, attempts to imagine Kimathi are caught between a recalcitrant colonial authority and postcolonial anxiety. Nationalists like Kariuki, who are eager to sustain Kimathi's memory, can only do so by recalling, not his heroism, but his arrest and subsequent hanging, now cast in what Nicole Loraux might call "a ceaseless song of lamentation, more specifically a song of lament."[26] At the Lodwar detention camp, news of Kimathi's arrest is met with a deep sense of loss: The detainees "mourned in silence, and those who could find a piece of cloth from old puttees, wore it on their shoulders in their grief, "Kariuki recalls.[27] From this moment onward Kariuki undertakes the task of turning Kimathi into a figure of mourning and commemoration:

> Dedan Kimathi was a brave and valiant fighter for freedom and a great leader of his people in the forest. . . . I have been told by a student who was once taught by him that he was at that time a very gentle, kindly man. In the forest his courage was legendary and my people are already talking of putting up a statue of him in Nairobi. Some of them refuse to believe even today that the Kenya Government hanged him: they still think he is alive. His wife, Mukami, and their children, suffered greatly in Nyeri after his execution, and I have done all I can to help the family since my release. The new Government must assist such people and all the others orphaned in the struggle.[28]

Significantly, the work of commemoration—which will later cost Kariuki his own life—is intimately tied to the fortunes or misfortunes of nationalist desire in its moment of dissipation. To put it another way, the figure of Kimathi will circulate in the popular imagination, but it will be wrenched away from commemorative historiography, turning the Mau Mau leader into "an imaginary without an image."[29]

Tragedy and the Figure of Mourning

This situation will change dramatically in 1974 when Kenneth Watene publishes *Dedan Kimathi,* a tragic drama whose motivations, intention, and value remain puzzling and controversial. The question of motivation seems to haunt Watene's work: why does the playwright who, like many members of his generation, had suffered under the State of Emergency provide us with a figure of Kimathi that rehearses the colonial version of the Mau Mau leader? Why does he rely on colonial sources such as Ian Henderson's book *The Hunt for Dedan Kimathi?* The most obvious responses to these questions would appear to be ideological rather than aesthetic—that Watene, either willfully or as a form of false consciousness, sets out to reproduce a settler-friendly image of Kimathi.[30]

My view is more charitable: rather than being a victim or beneficiary of colonialist ideologies, Watene, like his friend and classmate Sam Kahiga, is struggling to figure out what Mau Mau was all about and to locate Kimathi at the center of what had hitherto been an unspeakable history, a violent history that they had lived through as adolescents.[31] The more urgent question is this: why does Watene need to imagine Dedan Kimathi in 1974, ten years after independence and well after the publication of a series of fictions and memoirs that make Mau Mau more visible in public discourse? What is at issue in this recalling of the name of Kimathi when the business of the past seems to have been officially settled?

Answers to this question can best be gleaned from the views of two characters, forest fighters in the play, who see their primary duty as the protection of "the dignity of Kimathi" and the protection of "his name from destruction."[32] The forest fighters imagine a future in which the name of Kimathi will come to stand in for a heroic movement, a period when "the general mass of the people / Will give honor to the deserving / As is the wont of historical justice."[33] Whatever he does, Kimathi's reputation must be protected at all costs. But why and from whom does the name of Kimathi need to be protected? Why does his memory need to be secured for the future? Watene's play suggests that Kimathi's name needs to be protected, not from colonial slander, but from his own acts in the forest, which are going to be shown to have been most destructive. Indeed, by the time we get to this point in Watene's play, Kimathi's image is nothing less than a rehashing of Henderson's portrait of a paranoid murderer.

So, if Watene seeks to rescue Kimathi's reputation, it is precisely because he has already—and alarmingly—rehearsed him as the stereotypical *gitoi* (terrorist) of the colonial text. What might seem puzzling here is that Watene needs, counterintuitively, to preserve the Kimathi that is made available to him by colonial text even as he seeks to secure his reputation. But perhaps this is only a puzzle for those who read the play as a kind of commemorative historiography that ends up demonizing the absent figure it embodies onstage. What if Watene is not interested in Kimathi as a commemorative figure but simply wants to use him as the condition of possibility of tragic theater?[34] If Watene's starting point is not history but the idea of a tragic theater, then the Kimathi produced by colonial discourse, rather than the symbolic figure I discuss in the first part of this chapter, is ideal for this kind of theater. The Kimathi produced by colonial discourse in the works by Henderson and others is, like a Shakespearean tragic hero, defined by fatal flaws, constantly unable to live up to the mandate of his situation. Like Shakespeare's tragic heroes, Watene's Kimathi is a man haunted by the nightmares of friends turned into enemies, driven to insanity by "strange things" that he cannot define, and locked in a deep darkness that he has no capacity to grasp. Above all, Watene's Kimathi is a proud man driven by fear and lack of vision: "I used to see the future clearly. . . . But now I am dull and tremulous / And every step seems only to lead / To a fall, deep and everlasting."[35]

On the stage, this Kimathi is continuously diminished by his own words and those of his associates. To Wahu, his lover, he appears strange and afraid; to Rhino, his right-hand man, "There's something dark and ominous / That's been clouding his imagination."[36] Watene's desire to imagine a Kimathi whose actions and thoughts make him tragic, and yet one whose name will survive the scandals generated by the situation in which he finds himself, leads to two contradictory movements or moments: Kimathi is simultaneously represented as the weak and haunted figure imagined by Henderson and other colonial writers; but he is also the heroic subject who transcends his situation and imagines a future of dignity and freedom outside colonialism. If Watene relies on Henderson's book and not the other anticolonial texts available to him, most notably Njama, it is because the colonialist trope enables him to produce a tragic hero, the only figure that can generate the mourning that is needed if the nation is to come to terms with its past, or at least establish a new relationship to the dead.[37]

Like Lear on the heath, Kimathi's insights emerge when he is confronted by his own weakness and helplessness:

> The British hunt me down relentlessly
> To send me to the gallows.
> My mother has run amok
> And they torture my wife in the hope
> That she will lead them to arrest me.
> Those around me have grown faithless
> And those that have faith I cannot trust.
> My guardian spirits forsake me
> While my rituals lack their mystic power.
> My nights are thick with dark fears
> That sends me walking in my dreams.
> Lonely solitude overflows my cup
> And this whispering shroud of the forest
> Seems to conspire to betray me.
> What if I run off to a far country?
> What if I give up the pursuit of victory?
> Then I would outlive their malice,
> Return to an independent country
> And live in freedom and dignity.[38]

In this soliloquy, the contradictory moments that define Kimathi come together in unexpected ways: We have Kimathi bemoaning his fate ("The British hunt me down relentlessly / To send me to the gallows") and also imagining his possible return to "an independent country" where he can live "in freedom and dignity."

But whom does Kimathi address here? To the extent that this is a soliloquy, we could say that he is speaking to himself. Within the fiction of the stage, however, he is directly addressing an audience that already knows his fate and for whom the questions that he raises are about the present rather than the past. Moreover, within the moment of production of the play (1974), Kimathi is the embodied absence that asks some of the questions troubling the Kenyan audience: what is the meaning of freedom? What would it mean for one to live in an "independent country" in "freedom and dignity"? In mourning Kimathi—the absent one—the ideals for which he stood are articulated at the same time as their imminent and immanent betrayal is bemoaned:

> 1ST SCOUT (*in terror*): The sacred tree!
> The sacred tree!
> Kimathi has been arrested!
>
> RHINO: Our land!
> All Freedom![39]

The lesson of Watene's play is that the meaning of Kimathi's name in the present—and thus the fate of the narrative of postcoloniality—can only be learned from his failure.

The Performance of Ambivalence

The idea that it is only in his suffering and defeat that Kimathi can become a conduit for the aspirations and anxieties of Kenyans in the 1970s is not one that will satisfy the Kenyan Left, a group already engaged in what will turn out to be a deadly struggle with the postcolonial state. In *The Trial of Dedan Kimathi,* by Ngũgĩ wa Thiong'o and Mĩcere Gĩthae Mũgo, and produced at the Kenya National Theatre in 1976, we see a belated attempt to give Kimathi an affirmative character so that he can intervene in the politics of the present, move audiences beyond officially sanctioned amnesia, and perhaps chaperone social discontent toward revolutionary ends. *The Trial* sets out to undo Watene's ideology as it is represented in his dramaturgy, and to provide a systematic critique of the Kenyan state's version of history, especially what appears to be its willingness to privilege the interests of the pro-colonial forces over those of nationalism. The key to understanding the Ngũgĩ/Mũgo project, then, is to see how their deconstruction of Watene's dramaturgy goes hand in hand with their ideological critique of the Kenyan state. Ngũgĩ and Mũgo bemoan Watene's neocolonial project without mentioning his name; they cannot, however, escape its shadows.

Interesting points and counterpoints emerge here: if Watene's goal is to turn Kimathi into the tragic tope—the figure of suffering, betrayal, and lamentation—Ngũgĩ and Mũgo seek to detour the economy of suffering and mourning and instead dramatize the trial of the real, but elusive, Kimathi. If Watene's anxieties are dramaturgical, driven by the need to fit Kimathi into the idiom of Greek and Shakespearean tragedy, Ngũgĩ and Mũgo's anxieties are primarily historiographic; they want to use the dramatic stage as an extraterritorial space in which Kimathi, now freed from the colonial imaginary, can function as a symbol of the masses in "the only historically correct perspective."[40] Taking Kimathi's heroism for granted, Ngũgĩ and Mũgo do not seek to turn history into theater, but theatricality into history.[41]

It is hence significant that in *The Trial*, Kimathi's story is told in movements rather than acts and scenes. The first movement creates the historical canvas in which Kimathi will operate. In their stage directions, the authors insist that the play should take place in an atmosphere that is "tense and saturated with sadness," one in which "the barrier between formal and infinite time" is broken so that "past and future and present flow into one another."[42] Furthermore, for Ngũgĩ and Mũgo, the stage is not just an area confined to a specific setting, but an open space, one populated by sounds, mime, movement and even noise. It is in this open space that the drama of decolonization is played out by characters whose roles are largely symbolic. Thus, the woman who runs into a well-known colonial gauntlet is not just a courageous individual, but also "a mother, a fighter."[43] She is a familiar figure in the visual representations of Mau Mau women being "screened."

Ironically, like Watene before them, and Kahiga after them, Ngũgĩ and Mũgo rely heavily on the existing discourse on Kimathi, most prominently the work of Njama, which is also shadowed by Henderson. And because of this reliance on previous discourses, including colonial ones, *The Trial* cannot escape a familiar conundrum in narratives of decolonization: while Ngũgĩ and Mũgo seek to establish a "true" historical perspective, they can only do so through a rewriting of the already given narrative of Mau Mau, including an account of the "farcical 'trial' at Nyeri."[44] The authors' challenge, then, is to fall back on the already written narrative while marking their distance from the sources that they abhor—Henderson, Elspeth

Huxley, and Robert Ruark.[45] The authors' goal is to use performance to escape the historiographic trap; they seek to confront the event with the force of theatricality. Theatre, or performance, provides the space of dislocating the truth claims of colonial and postcolonial history. As dramatists, Ngũgĩ and Mũgo will seek to undo the colonial image of Kimathi by carefully deploying the technology of the international Avant-garde, more specifically the Brechtian epic theater, as a mode of undoing the ossified fact of history.[46] Onstage, colonial history will be subjected to radical acts of difference and *différance.*[47] A good example of this play of difference/ *différance* is the incorporation of Ian Henderson into *The Trial* as hunter, judge, and presumed executioner. For audiences familiar with Henderson and his role in the arrest and trial of Kimathi, his reappearance as the corporate, allegorical figure of colonialism past is has to be read as a paradoxical gesture of undoing colonial discourse. Renamed Shaw Henderson in the play, the discredited colonial agent comes to function as the ghost of the colonial past and the postcolonial present.[48]

Since Ngũgĩ and Mũgo are keen to rescue Kimathi from the prison house of colonial discourse—including what they considered to be the farcical trial in Nyeri—they need a dramaturgy that can rescue the nationalist hero from space, as much as time. In this respect, one of the most innovative devices in *The Trial* is the breakup of the unity of time and place associated with classical tragedy. The primary setting of the play is the courtroom in Nyeri, where Kimathi is tried, but this space doubles as a street, a camp in the forest, or even as a numinous historical space in which the drama of nationalism is played out. The dispersal of space enables Kimathi to escape the constricted prison house of colonial governmentality and the force of the law. In a sense, the Kimathi we see onstage always transcends spaces of confinement. Kimathi's transcendentalism enables him to function as a hero but not a tragic one. At the same time, however, it foregrounds the major tension in the play, the conflict between the authors' need to recuperate Kimathi as a figure of nationalist desire—someone the audience can easily identify with—and at the same time elevate him to a transcendental point where he can function as a world historical individual.[49]

Kimathi's transcendentalism is predicated on his ability to both occupy and dominate the stage without adopting the totality associated with the tragic figure. Indeed, in *The Trial,* minor characters—the Woman, the Boy, and the Girl—come to occupy an important role in the play as the shadow conscience of the hero. Representing ordinary people onstage, the minor characters call attention to Kimathi's ordinariness and his heroism:

WOMAN (*thoughtfully*): Listen. Kimathi is a genius in this struggle. It is therefore important to rescue him even at the cost of a few lives. The struggle must continue. . . . An unexpected surprise can do miracles. Once five fighters made a whole Homeguard post surrender. It's all a matter of timing.

BOY (*excited*): Trrrrrrrr! Trrrrrrrr!

GIRL: Trrrrrrrr! (*they mime a shoot-out. Then the Girl suddenly loses interest in the game. She turns to the Woman*): Who really is Dedan Kimathi?

WOMAN: Leader of the landless. Leader of them that toil.

BOY (*also catching the doubt in the Girl*): How do we really know that it is Kimathi that they have arrested and not another person?

GIRL: I myself do not believe it! Because Kimathi would have known of the arrest and escaped in time. I have heard of the story of how once he wrote a letter to the Governor. He said he would dine with the Governor at State House. The Governor collected all the police in Nairobi to come and capture Kimathi. But Kimathi went there. He was disguised as a European Inspector of Police. Later, he wrote another letter to the Governor: Thank you for your dinner last night. And it was signed: F/Marshal D.L.

BOY: I have also heard it said that he could turn himself into an aeroplane. And also that before an attack on a garrison, he himself would go and blow a bugle from the inside.

GIRL: That he could walk for a 100 miles on his belly—

BOY: That in the forest, he could laugh and no enemy would hear him.

GIRL: That he could mimic any noise of a bird and none could tell the difference.[50]

In the above exchange, the authors turn to the romance of Kimathi to undo the colonial mythology, but they do so with the awareness that a countermyth, even a positive one, is also a myth. The role of the Woman in the play, then, is to relocate Kimathi from the realm of the mythical to that of the human:

> WOMAN: . . . He, Great commander that he was, Great organizer that he was, Great fearless fighter that he was, he was human! (*almost savagely, bitterly*) Too human at times.[51]

Here, Kimathi's greatness is underscored, but also qualified; he is represented onstage as a hero, but not as a tragic hero. What is the difference? And why does it matter?

To answer this question, we need to recall an argument made by Jean-Pierre Vernant in "The Tragic Subject," an influential study on the origins of tragedy and tragic consciousness. Vernant's argument is that the tragic subject, tragic consciousness, and the tragic vision, were created in fifth-century BCE Athens as part of the search for "a new way for man to understand himself and take up his position in relation to the world, the gods, the other people, himself, and his own actions."[52] He then goes on to make the crucial point that when the creators of ancient tragedy turned to the past for theatrical materials, they were trying to recuperate, from the legends of the past, a truth that transcended "contemporary events and current political life":

> By refusing to place itself on the level of contemporary events and current political life, it acquired in Aristotle's eyes not less but more value, more truth than history. To present current events on stage would amount to no more than recounting what was happening. Producing a tragedy was a completely different undertaking. It was not a matter of inventing imaginary characters or devising a plot that took one's fancy. It meant using the names and destinies of universally known figures regarded as models, to construct a scenario, an arrangement of selected scenes in such a way as to show how and why such-and-such a character, being what he was, was likely, or even bound to take such-and-such an action that would lead to such-and-such a result.[53]

Onstage, it is hoped that the tragic figure—now connected to the legendary and universal—can help audiences cope with the disappointments of postcoloniality by distancing them from the authorized discourse of decolonization. Under this scheme, Watene's Kimathi works well as a tragic figure because he distances the audience from the pain of the postcolonial present and provides consolation through lamentation. In contrast, Ngũgĩ and Mũgo produce a Kimathi who is heroic but untragic. They imagine Kimathi as the kind of untragic hero who is "nothing but an exhibit of the contradictions which make up our society.[54] Although Kimathi embodies the tensions that define Kenyan society, he is most forceful when he acts as the catalytic conduit for the contradiction the authors consider immanent in neocolonial society, the forces embodied by the settler, the banker, the priest, and the politician. Kimathi's untragic heroism appears most vividly when he rebuffs the gifts offered to him by the agents of neocolonialism.

The best way of getting a measure of the heroic, then, is to see how subjects respond to the contradictions that they confront: Watene's Kimathi responds to his trials through lamentation; the Ngũgĩ/Mũgo version responds to them either through silence, or through a language that is choreographed to bring out his innate capacity to play the role assigned to him by history—that of "a poet, an orator, a politician."[55] In the circumstances, the most obvious mark of Kimathi's untragic heroism in *The Trial* is the absence of a discourse of lamentation and the constant attempts by the authors to undo Kimathi's emotive response to his own suffering.

Toward the end of the play, for example, we are presented with a scene where Kimathi, momentarily transported to the forest, is confronted with his younger brother's betrayal. Is he going to have his brother executed in the name of collective justice or will filial loyalty mitigate his actions? Kimathi's decision is made much more difficult by the arrival of a letter informing him of their mother's insanity:

KIMATHI: This was the letter
You brought me.
This was the terrible news . . .
Mother is now crazy
That she collects flowers
And keeps on singing

Calling on God
To spare Wambararia
To spare her youngest—[56]

Here, what should have been a classic opening to lamentation is halted by the Woman's intervention:

WOMAN: It pains the woman in me too!
Thinking of the past,
And the dear ones we left behind
Can weaken our resolve.
You are a leader of
A revolution
You must decide.
But remember
All the others
Have left their wives,
Their children,
Their mothers,
Behind.[57]

This confrontation points to the larger question that Ngũgĩ and Mũgo face as they struggle to represent Kimathi both as a historical figure and the embodiment of the future: How can Kimathi serve his symbolic role as the world historical individual, the character who provides "consciousness and great direction to a movement already present in society," if he does not have the individuality that would enable the audience to empathize with his cause, his struggles, and his doubts?[58] Can heroism without tragic consciousness speak to the demands of an age that lives under the shadow of an arrested decolonization and the pitfalls of national consciousness.[59] In what appears to be an attempt to reconcile the mandate of history with the desire to imagine an alternative future, *The Trial* ends with a staging of two conflicting demands: In the first instance, Kimathi is seen as an individual whose weakness or fatal flaw is his attachment to memories of his childhood and his family. In this context, Kimathi is tragic in the sense that he has made a choice that has led to the destruction of "Kindred blood / Blood of my blood."[60] In the second instance, however, Kimathi appears to repress his memories and overcome his personal loss—and hence the tragic consciousness—on the way to becoming the figure of legend, the one who embodies a justice that "is created / through a revolutionary struggle."[61]

In the end, it is significant that neither *The Trial of Dedan Kimathi* nor Watene's *Dedan Kimathi* lets the hero die onstage. By making sure that Kimathi's death does not take place in front of the audience ensures the survival of a legend and its mode of truth outside the narrative of history, very much like his missing body. In this case, then, instead of literary scholars insisting on the ideological differences between the two plays, it is perhaps more productive to read them as presenting two distinct responses to the crisis of the mid-1970s, a period that marks the end of the legitimacy of the Kenyatta government, a fact that is dramatized by another drama of the period—the assassination of J. M. Kariuki, in March 1975. For many writers and intellectuals, including Ngũgĩ, Kariuki's killing generates some of the most powerful sentiments on the failure of decolonization and is perhaps one of the major motivations behind the writing of *The Trial.*[62] And although Watene's play is written a year before the Kariuki assassination, it, too, is a dramatic response to the signs of the times.

My interest in this essay, then, is how the two plays, though different in ideology and form, exhume the figure of Kimathi as a medium for addressing the urgent need to rethink the terms of decolonization. Watene addresses this need by turning Kimathi into a tragic figure, the conduit for national mourning; Ngũgĩ and Mũgo reject the tragic form because it defeats the idealism inherent in the politics and poetics of decolonization. In both cases, however, the authors are compelled to work with the existing discourses on Kimathi and within the symbolic economy that I sketched out in the first half of this essay, which is, of course, how the Mau Mau figure enters the discourse of history. While it is not clear how the two plays relate to the actual trial in Nyeri, which is discussed elsewhere in this book, their power lies in the use of the imaginary to trouble the already existing narrative of the event. By insisting on the power of transcendental truth over the historical event, very much like the new "Mau Mau" monument at Uhuru Park in Nairobi (photo 10), both plays hold out the possibility of return and restitution. And there is nothing the postcolonial state seems to fear more than the haunting of the past or the proverbial return of the repressed.

Notes

1. This essay is written in memory of my uncle, Erastus Mwangi (Kagara) Karoki, who many years ago explained to me, a terrified child, what colonial terror was all about and what the dream of the independence yet to come meant.

2. This is the doctrine espoused by Prime Minister Kenyatta on the day of Kenyan independence: "Let us agree that we shall never refer to the past. Let us instead unite, in all our utterances and activities, in concern for the reconstruction of our country and the vitality of Kenya's future." Kenyatta, *Suffering without Bitterness: The Founding of the Kenya Nation* (Nairobi: East African Publishing House, 1968), 241.

3. Claude Lévi-Strauss, *Introduction to the Work of Marcel Mauss,* trans. Felicity Baker (London, Routledge and Kegan Paul, 1987), 63.

4. Gayatri Chakravorty Spivak, "Translator's preface to *Of Grammatology,* by Jacques Derrida, trans. Gayatri Chakravorty Spivak (Baltimore: Johns Hopkins University Press, 1977), 55.

5. The terminologies here are borrowed from Jacques Lacan's work. See Lacan, "Symbol and Language," in *The Language of the Self,* trans. Anthony Wilden (Baltimore: Johns Hopkins University Press, 1997), 29–51; Lacan, "The Signification of the Phallus," 271–80, and "The Mirror Stage as Formative of the Function of the I as Revealed in Psychoanalytic Experience," in *Écrits,* trans. Bruce Fink (New York: Norton, 2004), 3–9.

6. Lacan, *Écrits,* 67.

7. Jacques Lacan, *The Seminar of Jacques Lacan: Book 1: Freud's Papers on Technique 1953–1954,* ed. Jacques-Alain Miller, trans. John Forrester (New York: Norton, 1991), 230.

8. Henderson, *Hunt,* 23.

9. Kinyatti, *Mau Mau,* 93.

10. Barnett and Njama, *Mau Mau from Within,* 241. The subject of dispute here is the Beecher Report on African education, issued in 1949.

11. Ibid., 260.

12. Ibid., 261.

13. Ibid., 264.

14. Ibid., 265.

15. My association of the photograph with aura here seems to go against Walter Benjamin's claim that the mechanical reproduction of an image

eliminates the auratic element that defines its originality; but in a colonial situation the photograph, like the printed text, is presented as a mythical and mystical subject. Benjamin, "The Work of Art in the Age of Mechanical Reproduction," in *Illuminations: Essays and Reflections,* ed. Hannah Arendt, trans. Harry Zohn (New York: Schocken, 1968), 221.

16. Henderson, *Hunt,* 35.

17. Kahiga, *Dedan Kimathi,* 306.

18. Itote, *"Mau Mau" General,* 115.

19. See Clough, *Mau Mau Memoirs.*

20. Georg Lukács, *The Historical Novel,* trans. Hannah and Stanley Mitchell (Lincoln: University of Nebraska Press, 1983), 130.

21. For background to the squatter problem, see Furedi, *The Mau Mau War in Perspective;* Kanogo, *Squatters.*

22. Kanogo, *Squatters,* 10.

23. Susan Letzer Cole, *The Absent One: Mourning Ritual, Tragedy, and the Performance of Ambivalence* (College Park: Pennsylvania State University Press, 1985), 9; emphasis added.

24. When the subject realizes that its needs and desires cannot be fulfilled, argues Lacan, it seeks to create an image or fantasy that will function as the substitute for the real. Lacan, *Écrits,* ch. 5.

25. Nicole Loraux, *The Divided City: On Memory and Forgetting in Ancient Athens* (New York: Zone Books, 2006), 15.

26. Ibid., x, 27; Kariuki, *"Mau Mau" Detainee,* 121.

28. Kariuki, *"Mau Mau" Detainee,* 122.

29. Loraux, *Divided City,* 16.

30. Watene is not mentioned in the preface to Ngũgĩ and Mũgo's play, but there is no doubt that he is the source of their ire.

31. Watene and Sam Kahiga were classmates at Thika High School. But, more significantly, some of the earliest writings on Mau Mau were by its "children," including Ngũgĩ wa Thiong'o (*Weep Not, Child*), Charity Waciuma (*Daughter of Mumbi*), and Kahiga and his brother Leonard Kibera (*Potent Ash*).

32. Watene, *Dedan Kimathi,* 63.

33. Ibid., 63.

34. Apollo Obonyo Amoko, *Postcolonialism in the Wake of the Nairobi Revolution: Ngugi wa Thiong'o and the Idea of African Literature* (New York: Palgrave Macmillan, 2010).

35. Watene, *Dedan Kimathi,* 47.

36. Ibid., 61.

37. Olga Taxidou, *Tragedy, Modernity and Mourning* (Edinburgh: Edinburgh University Press, 2004), 163.

38. Watene, *Dedan Kimathi,* 67.

39. Ibid., 94.

40. Ngũgĩ and Mũgo, *Trial*, preface.

41. Samuel Weber, *Theatricality as Medium* (New York: Fordham University Press, 2004), 1–12.

42. Ngũgĩ and Mũgo, *Trial*, 2.

43. Ibid., 8.

44. Ibid., preface.

45. Ibid., preface.

46. Walter Benjamin, "What Is Epic Theater?," in *Illuminations: Essays and Reflections*, ed. Hannah Arendt, trans. Harry Zohn (New York: Schocken, 1968), 147–54.

47. Julia Kristeva, "Semiology and Grammatology," interview by Jacques Derrida, in *Positions*, trans. Alan Bass (Chicago: University of Chicago Press, 1981), 21.

48. Gichingiri Ndigirigi, *Ngũgĩ wa Thiong'o's Drama and the Kamiriithu Popular Theater Experiment* (Trenton, NJ: Africa World Press, 2007), 45–47.

49. Lukács, *Historical Novel*, 39–40.

50. Ngũgĩ and Mũgo, *Trial*, 61.

51. Ibid., 62.

52. Jean-Pierre Vernant, "The Tragic Subject: Historicity and Transhistoricity," in *Myth and Tragedy in Ancient Greece*, ed. Jean-Pierre Vernant and Pierre Vidal-Naquet, trans. Janet Lloyd (New York: Zone Books, 1998), 240.

53. Ibid., 245.

54. Benjamin, "Epic Theater," 149.

55. Ngũgĩ and Mũgo, *Trial*, 26.

56. Ibid., 77.

57. Ibid., 77.

58. Lukács, *Historical Novel*, 39.

59. Biodun Jeyifo, "The Nature of Things: Arrested Decolonization and Critical Theory," *Research in African Literatures* 21, no. 1, Critical Theory and African Literature (Spring 1990): 33–48; Frantz Fanon, *The Wretched of the Earth*, trans. Constance Farrington (New York: Grove, 1963).

60. Ngũgĩ and Mũgo, *Trial*, 76.

61. Ibid., 82.

62. The assassination of Kariuki, in March 1975, will be considered a turning point in the Kenyatta government's loss of legitimacy; the public outcry that follows is described by Ngũgĩ as the lamentation of a generation: "Where have all our hopes gone? They have been replaced by a general feeling that water, water everywhere is bitter." Ngũgĩ wa Thiong'o, "Born Again: Mau Mau Unchained," in *Writers in Politics* (London: Heinemann, 1981), 86.

5

Memorialization and Mau Mau

A Critical Review

Lotte Hughes

It was the face that launched a million T-shirts and street art portraits: that of a dreadlocked Dedan Kimathi in the dock. Haughty, defiant, looking down his nose direct to camera, this has become *the* iconographic image of the resistance leader, in contrast to the equally well known but less favored image of Kimathi lying half-naked on a stretcher, just after capture. Though both images are still in wide circulation, his fans (particularly Kenyan youth) appear to show a preference for the first image. Reasons for this may include the fact that the courtroom photograph was taken head-on at eye level, whereas the second was shot from above, thereby diminishing the subject. The latter image shows Kimathi supine, rendered helpless, injured, and handcuffed, whereas he sits upright with his upper body clothed in the first image, albeit still handcuffed.[1] In the dock, Kimathi's dreads stand out from his head in two bunches, forming a natural circular frame reminiscent of a bull's horns, a shape that lends itself to mass reproduction.[2] The composition of the second image makes it more difficult to copy and mass-reproduce; in some versions Kimathi's head is turned slightly to one side, and his hair has been piled on top of his head—the dreaded dreads are thereby rendered (deliberately?) less visible at this steep angle.[3]

In the courtroom photograph, taken presumably by an official British photographer, Kimathi (who understood the importance of managing publicity, and in 1953 had sent the British authorities a photograph of himself on learning that they did not have one) is critically gazing back at empire, represented by the body of the photographer.[4] The image is invariably accompanied today in popular artwork by the quote attributed to Kimathi, which is in fact believed to have been coined much earlier by others: "It is better to die on your feet than live on your knees."[5] It implies "no surrender." All this is grist for the mill of popular memorialization.

However, the rediscovered trial papers destabilize this reading of Kimathi. First, Kimathi's defense lawyer told the court that his client had been planning to surrender at the time of his capture and was only carrying a gun in self-defense because he feared being killed by fellow fighters. In Kimathi's own verbal testimony, "a large number" of his men had turned against him after he had written to the British government seeking peace. "This pistol was handed to me . . . to defend myself against those who wished to kill me, that is forest men . . . I mean Mau Mau." In other passages he tells the court, "I said to myself: 'It is better to come out [of the forest] either to be killed, or if I am lucky to get to the Government.' My intention was to surrender." And, "When I wrote the first letter [to the government] I had abandoned Mau Mau. I was on the Government's side."[6]

It will be interesting to see what impact these devastating revelations have on contemporary popular memorialization, *some* of which revolves around this dock image and accompanying quote. For hip-hop musicians, their young fans, and graffiti artists, for whom dreadlocks and Kimathi represent the ultimate in resistance (both anticolonial and present day), the answer is likely to be "very little."[7] It will be dismissed, maybe, as further proof that Kimathi was framed, that his statement was altered, or that he was incorrectly quoted in court.[8] Facts have little or no influence on memory and memorialization, which should become apparent as this chapter unfolds. Most important, the manipulation of these images by contemporary artists and rappers may be read as an example of the "reappropriation of the [imperial] archive as a system of knowledge," part of a larger "return to the archive [that] is informed by a quest for . . . utopian pasts and futures."[9]

Unlike other chapters in this volume, this one will not center so much on the figure of Dedan Kimathi as on the broader regime of memory around Mau Mau, contemporary and historical. Kimathi is not therefore as central to the debates that will be brought out here, but he and his memorial legacy must be considered as part of the wider discussion. Indeed, he and his literate comrades started it. In the forest, Kimathi already had one eye on the future memorialization of freedom struggle, hence his "obsession" with record keeping and writing everything down.[10] He was not alone in this, as Derek Peterson has described when discussing the efforts of Karari Njama, general secretary of the Kenya Land and Freedom Army, to pursue what Njama called "the pen battle [which] was as great as the rifle battle." Peterson writes, quoting Njama, "By memorializing Mau Mau's struggles, record books and letters to parliamentarians allowed forest fighters to hope that, indeed, they would 'receive happiness equal to the misery' they had suffered." He goes on: "Forest fighters were terrified of being forgotten. . . . The question of memory was the central concern of the famous Mwathe meeting of August 1953, convened in the Aberdare Forest to organize far-flung bands of forest fighters. Dedan Kimathi . . . lectured hundreds of attendees about accounting. Each Mau Mau camp was to keep ten record books. . . . Kimathi wanted memorial halls constructed after independence to house the registers. Mau Mau's bureaucracy was devoted to popular memory."[11]

Before turning to consideration of memory, its uses over time, and the nature of what is remembered, let us stay with the subject of forgetting—or rather, notions *about* forgetting. Some sections of the Kenyan media have long peddled a pernicious line on Mau Mau—the idea that it has been "forgotten." This could not be further from the truth. What journalists mean, influenced by obvious pressure from veterans and human rights groups in particular, is that demands by veterans and their families for greater recognition, land, and relief from poverty have (apart from the first) largely been ignored by successive postindependence governments. The veterans concerned are predominantly Gikuyu, and their narratives echo much earlier communal grievances, and reflect internal divisions, that date back at least as far as Gikuyu submissions to the Kenya Land Commission (1932–34), if not much earlier. Histories and memories of the conflict and movement have *not* been forgotten, though some narratives remain submerged, repressed, or heavily (sometimes self-) edited.[12] However, far less scholarly attention has been paid to discussion and analysis of the memory and memorialization of Mau Mau, compared to the extensive historiography. Reasons for these lacunae may include some historians' wariness of the notoriously slippery canon of memory, and disciplinary boundaries between history and memory studies, though these are becoming more porous.

At the time of writing, yet another example of the "forgetting" trope has appeared in the *Daily Nation*. Under the headline "Rewriting the Mau Mau Story," the reporter accuses retired British diplomats of "retroactively censoring" historical documents on Mau Mau held in UK archives, thereby destroying "evidence" that veterans require to bring future claims.[13] He ends by stating, "It won't be long until the last of the veterans dies. Perhaps the British government will breathe a sigh of relief when that happens. Perhaps the Kenyan government will no longer need to deal with the messy business that is the place of Mau Mau in the history of Kenya. Perhaps the legacy of these fighters who fought for a land they never gained will never be forgotten, because it was never remembered."[14]

Here I try to describe and periodize how and why memory practices and "regimes of memory,"[15] centered on Mau Mau, simultaneously feature "forgetting," occlusion, absences, contradictions, and often a surfeit of memory. Documents, memoirs, speeches, artworks, photographs, blogs, songs, spaces, absences, and so on have themselves become sites of contestation over Mau Mau memory and have produced their own histories—myths that swirled around the "lost" trial papers, the dramatic recreation of the trial by Ngũgĩ wa Thiong'o and Mĩcere Gĩthae Mũgo, and the mysterious appearance in Nairobi in 2003 of an aged Ethiopian peasant masquerading as long-lost fighter Stanley Mathenge are all key examples of attempts by various players to fill absences.[16] Finally, I describe how Mau Mau is represented (or not) in contemporary state and nonstate heritage initiatives in Kenya.[17]

The Manipulation of Memory

It may be said that the long struggle to manipulate memories of Mau Mau as a movement and conflict began in earnest at Lari, a small upland settlement in what is now Kiambu County, in late March 1953.[18] It was initiated by British government propagandists who used a variety of means to whip up anti–Mau Mau hysteria at home and abroad, following a particularly bloody double massacre.[19] Propaganda efforts predated these events by at least six months: "The struggle to shape Mau Mau memory in Kenya began even before independence. The British official description of the movement as atavistic, tribalist, racist, anti-Christian, and criminal, issued at the beginning of the Emergency in October 1952, set the tone for most European commentary on Mau Mau over the next eight years."[20] Mau Mau skillfully counterattacked in the propaganda war.[21] But six months into the Emergency, the Lari massacre gave British propagandists an opportunity to up their game—and snuff out news of the daring, highly successful Mau Mau raid on the Naivasha police station, which had taken place the same night.[22] The circulation of gory images of massacre victims was central to this effort; besides photographs used in leaflets and so on, footage of Lari was also taken to the Gikuyu reserves in a mobile cinema van.[23] The propaganda campaign was successful in not only influencing British public attitudes toward Mau Mau, via the British media and newsreels, but also in repelling many Kenyans, including Gikuyu "waverers."[24] As Daniel Branch describes it, "The massacre of loyalists at Lari . . . played a critical role in the consolidation of an [African] opposition to Mau Mau that in 1953 dared not speak its name."[25] Devout Christians were particularly revolted by this violence, and it was the photographs and film of mutilated bodies, especially of women and children, that burned into the public psyche. These images apparently showed only victims of the first massacre (though some scholars cast doubt upon this).[26] There was virtually no coverage of the second, for obvious reasons.[27]

Lari has been described variously as "the crucial turning point in the Mau Mau war," "the war's iconographic moment," and "a pivotal moment" in propaganda terms.[28] In *Petals of Blood*, Ngũgĩ wa Thiong'o called it "the storm-centre of Kenya's history."[29] He also wrote about it in his childhood memoir, since it happened close to his boyhood home.[30] Briefly, this is what happened at Lari on the twenty-sixth and twenty-seventh of March. Though often referred to in the singular as a "massacre," especially by Kenyans (including in the final report of the Truth, Justice and Reconciliation Commission),[31] there were in fact two massacres within hours of each other: the first, on the night of the twenty-sixth, involved an attack by several hundred Mau Mau (only a small fraction of them forest fighters) on their neighbors' homesteads, which resulted in an estimated seventy-four deaths. What lay behind the attack were long-simmering disputes over land, a contentious eviction, and widespread hatred of "loyalist" Chief Luka wa Kahangare; he and his family were virtually wiped out. All victims of the first massacre were carefully targeted government servants, clients of Luka and another chief, Makimei. The second massacre occurred between ten at night and dawn the following morning, in a retaliatory counterattack initiated by Home Guard, joined later by British forces and other Africans under British command. The reprisal was vicious and chaotic, with revenge taken in cold blood on anyone suspected of having Mau Mau sympathies. This attack resulted in an estimated 150 fatalities, though the figure could well be much higher.[32]

Lari was also a turning point for another reason: for the first time, as a result of the coverage and whispered dissemination of this awful news via the public grapevine, it was starkly apparent to Kenyans that Mau Mau had become a civil war. This unpalatable fact—which is still not accepted by everyone, including Mũgo and Ngũgĩ and in the foreword to this volume, because it is regarded as continuing British propaganda—has complicated and destabilized "memories" and "forgetting" ever since.[33] Scholars, and Kenyans (both academic and nonacademic), have long argued and continue to argue about who deserves commemoration. Just Mau Mau, or their opponents and victims, too?[34] This discussion links to a wider debate, which involves ethnic communities outside the former Central Province claiming they also fought for freedom at various times. I shall discuss this below, in The Amnesia Years and later sections.[35]

Remembering Lari

A selection of these photographs now adorns the walls of the Lari Memorial Peace Museum in Kimende, a grubby trading center on the main Nairobi-to-Nakuru highway just north of Limuru. Their purpose these days, according to those running this tiny nonstate museum, is to remind visitors (largely local schoolchildren and other Kenyans—this is not on the tourist trail) of the internecine violence that tore this community apart, which must be "remembered" in order to avoid repetition. The museum was founded in 2001 as part of the Kenyan peace museums movement, initiated in the late 1990s by then National Museums of Kenya (NMK) chief ethnographer Sultan Somjee.[36] Its management committee is made up of ex–Mau Mau and ex–Home Guard who collectively decided that something should be done to heal the social wounds that had festered ever since 1953, and that the healing had to start with them. Young curator Waihenya Njoroge, grandson of a Mau Mau fighter who admitted taking part in the first massacre and narrowly escaped the gallows, told me, "Our job is to bring healing, and do as Desmond Tutu said: 'There is no future without forgiveness.'"[37] In this regard, the Lari Memorial Peace Museum represents a unique reconciliation initiative that has gone further, in its own small way, than any state effort—and deserves greater official recognition. The museum carries out peace education in local schools, worked with fellow peace museums to reconcile warring communities after the 2008 post-election violence, and displays items of material culture symbolizing peace in different ethnic communities, promoting the idea that "traditional" peace cultures can be used to unite and reconcile modern-day Kenyans.[38]

Annie Coombes makes the important point that the museum's juxtaposition of photographs of massacre victims (many unnamed) and the handwritten list of names of both victims and perpetrators, displayed on a wall nearby, "effectively undoes the intention of the colonial archive" and involves "promiscuous recycling of British propaganda in order to narrate a tale of violence enacted by *both* sides of the divide."[39] The lists also restore some humanity to otherwise largely unidentified and unidentifiable victims.[40] Elsewhere, she has argued that the novel way in which the museum uses material culture, oral history, and memories of the Emergency "may represent a recognition of a more fragmentary lived experience of both the history of the struggle for independence and its aftermath," which is not to be found in state museums.[41]

I have dwelled at some length on Lari because it provides a highly instructive case study for understanding the complexity and ambiguity of contemporary memorialization of Mau Mau. Unfortunately, most Kenyans appear to be unaware of the existence of this museum and the peace and reconciliation work it and other peace museums do.[42]

The Amnesia Years

On coming to power, Jomo Kenyatta ushered in a period of state-orchestrated amnesia about Mau Mau, which served his political purposes.[43] The writing was already on the wall long before independence, as Ngũgĩ reminds us: "Some days later [after the assassination of Senior Chief Waruhiu, in October 1952] we heard that Kenyatta had addressed a mammoth rally in Kĩambu, denouncing Mau Mau with the expression "Let it disappear under the roots of the Mikongoe trees."[44] (British propagandists had also "sought to obliterate Mau Mau from public discourse in the colony and beyond," in a change of tack from 1955.)[45] The official mantra after independence was: "We all fought for freedom"—not just Gikuyu, Meru, Embu, and the few fighters drawn from other ethnic communities; Kenyans were asked to believe that every group had done its bit to achieve liberation. However, it was blindingly obvious, not least to war veterans, that many former "loyalists" were now reaping the rewards of uhuru with top jobs in government and the civil service, land, and other official favors, while ex-fighters and their families mostly languished in poverty. Such laments have been reiterated ever since, publicly and privately, as a core part of the expression of "Mau Mau memory"—which invariably centers on *blame.* Writing about what happens when identity politics meets the "memory boom," Jeffrey Olick, Vered Vinitzky-Seroussi, and Daniel Levy note, "Most often, these identities nursed a wound and harboured a grudge. The memory boom thus unleashed a culture of trauma and regret."[46] I will return to trauma narratives later.

A generous interpretation of the amnesia policy is that Kenyatta sought to unite the nation, inspire in citizens a sense of multiethnic nationhood, appease European settlers, and heal rifts in his own Gikuyu community. "Kenyatta had to say this [to forget Mau Mau] chiefly for political reasons, and especially because the existence of a people or group that fought and suffered more for Independence than anybody else is incompatible with the myth of Kenyan unity."[47] It was also a means of fending off veterans' unrealistic demands for compensation, free land, and jobs, and avoiding the expense of erecting public memorials to liberation "heroes." It was not until 2006–7 that the government of then president Mwai Kibaki embarked on a mausoleum-building spree, the latest chapter of which is a mausoleum for Kapenguria Six member Fred Kubai, completed in July 2015.[48]

Kershaw explains "forgetting" very differently, in Gikuyu cultural terms: "The independent government's attempt to wipe [Mau Mau] out of history was a proper Kikuyu response to a painful event," on a par with famine and other disasters that should not be referred to again.[49] Alternatively, it may be argued the new president sought to obscure the fact that he had never been a member of Mau Mau, let alone lost blood in the forests. Those who had, knew the truth. As one of my late informants, a former forest fighter, oath administrator, and detainee, angrily put it:

"Kenyatta was not a Mau Mau. Who could have become the first president of Kenya? Is it Kenyatta or Kimathi? Kimathi continued fighting for freedom up to the end of his life, but Kenyatta surrendered—he betrayed his people, even though he became president. If Kenyatta was a forest fighter, or had he been, he could have helped the forest fighters thereafter. But he did not. . . . Kenyatta was there to say [to the British], 'Kill Kimathi! Let him die!' Because he knew that he would [otherwise] have no chance of being president."[50]

Contrast this with the image of Kimathi, and his supposed relationship to Kenyatta,[51] painted by Ngũgĩ's adult friend Mzee Ngandi in the memoir *Dreams in a Time of War:* "It is Kĩmathi who will set Kenyatta free," the boy is led to understand by an old man whose fantastical stories enthrall him. They include stories about the Lari massacres, Kenyatta's trial, and Kimathi's alleged magical powers—he was said to have "once disguised himself as a white police officer and went to dine with the governor."[52] Ngũgĩ describes how this master storyteller mixed fact, fiction, and rumor in oral performance until "the real and the surreal were one," leading him to conclude: "Perhaps it is myth as much as fact that keeps dreams alive even in times of war." The same might be said of "memory," at all times. Fiction and memoirs have been hugely influential in shaping contemporary public memory of Mau Mau.[53]

However, Kenyatta did not entirely shun Mau Mau. Like his successor, Daniel arap Moi, he selectively rewarded or paid tribute to certain veterans while ignoring others. Clough divides the Kenyatta government's treatment of Mau Mau into two periods: 1963–66, when the regime took care to distance itself, and 1966–78, when it practiced selective "rapprochement with Mau Mau veterans and Mau Mau memories the regime could use for its purposes."[54] In the second phase, Kenyatta initiated some of the first acts of state commemoration—such as laying the cornerstone of the Dedan Kimathi Memorial Library near Nyeri in March 1971. He used the occasion to pay tribute to fighters and said the place where Kimathi had been captured, just eight hundred yards away, "should be clearly marked."[55]

Much of the amnesia rhetoric, combined with denunciation of Mau Mau, was expressed in Kenyatta's speeches. He later wrote that "Mau Mau was a disease which had been eradicated, and must never be remembered again," repeating what he had said at Githunguri in 1962 just after being released from detention.[56] On Kenyatta Day in 1964, he told the crowds "the foundations of our future must lie in the theme: Forgive and forget. There is no point then, and there is still less purpose today, in dwelling on the past, in stoking fires of revenge or animosity."[57] "Forgive and forget" became another key mantra, along with "Harambee!" (Let's pull together). The emphasis was now on hard work: Kenyans were sharply told not to expect free things, such as handouts of land to veterans. Past divisions were to be "forgotten" in order to forge a bright new nation. This has been explained by scholars as an understandable effort to "get one's history wrong in order to get one's national identity right."[58]

Below the radar, Kenyans continued to discuss, reminisce and argue about Mau Mau, regardless of official edicts. There was even a "sort of Mau Mau 'revival' in public life" in the early 1970s.[59] Above the radar, simultaneously with the rise of the Kenya People's Union, MPs including Paul Ngei, Bildad Kaggia, and J. M. Kariuki kept memories of Mau Mau alive, challenging the government to do more for veterans' welfare, reminding it of the values for which guerrillas had fought in the first place, and accusing the elite of neocolonialism. Clough terms it Kenya's second "crisis of memory," after the amnesia policy.[60] The challenge to government to ignore the past at its peril featured in a spate of published memoirs by veterans and others, from 1963 onward, as well as in the explosive fiction Ngũgĩ produced through the 1960s and 1970s, in which liberation struggle (and how it ought to be commemorated) was a constant theme. For example, the character Joseph, in *Petals of Blood,* hoped to see the birthplaces of Kimathi and J. M. Kariuki turned into "national shrines" and a theater built in memory of Kimathi.[61] Veterans' memoirs allowed for fresh interpretation of memory and history, and the fraught relationship between them, sparking controversy that continues to this day.[62] Naturally they focused on personal experience (a repeated refrain in veterans' calls for the history of Mau Mau to be rewritten by insiders), which "reflects a common desire to privilege memory over history in the belief that it is intrinsically authentic and true."[63] An obvious omission from this canon is the absence of "loyalist" memoirs, although Obadiah Kariuki's *A Bishop Facing Mount Kenya* (1985) may be construed as such.[64] Both in published memoirs and media stories, there is on the one hand a surfeit of veterans' "memories" and, on the other, an absence of alternatives or counternarratives.[65] This not only produces distortion but further silences and marginalizes those who might have different stories to tell.

Mau Mau Unbound: The Ban Ends

The then president Kibaki lifted the colonial ban on Mau Mau as an organization in 2003, shortly after NARC (the National Rainbow Coalition he then headed) came to power. This move triggered a host of memorialization-related activities and demands. First, it "prompted many Mau Mau veterans to restate their demands for the history of their role in the liberation struggle to be nationally acknowledged and for their heroes to gain official recognition."[66] Second, there were increased calls for the "true" history of Kenya to be rewritten from the veterans' viewpoint and for this to be included in school textbooks.[67] A surge of stories about destitute liberation heroes filled the media (not that they had ever gone away), with the government again accused of neglecting them, not least Oneko, last remaining member of the Kapenguria Six until his death, in 2007.[68] Given their advanced age, the plight of these grizzled veterans was now more poignant than ever. Many, including Oneko, declared they did not want a mausoleum or other type of memorial, and the bogus commemoration that represented, but to be helped in cash, now. The Kenya Human Rights Commission (KHRC) began working toward a reparations claim, framing this simultaneously as a memorialization and a human rights issue—recognition for liberation heroes and reparations for historical abuses were equally due, the commission argued. The then KHRC deputy director Steve Ouma Akoth, who played a key role in the initial campaign, together with Paul Muite and Willy Mutunga, explained the genesis of the campaign starting in 2003:

> We had four things in mind: (1) To expand the idea of freedom that had been developed in NARC's "velvet revolution"; (2) To revisit the myth that Mau Mau was a Kikuyu nationalist movement—our approach was that Mau Mau was part of the larger independence movement that had following and leadership beyond the Kikuyu; (3) Consistent with the emerging "era of human rights," it was time to extend our broader campaign against impunity; and (4) that it was time to "re-frame" the history of Kenya from a human rights prism. Such reframing required that "true heroes" like Dedan Kimathi and other Mau Mau's be recognised.[69]

It is important to identify where the initial push came from—war veterans, not human rights lawyers or activists. As is also the case in Zimbabwe and Eritrea, for example, war veterans have driven and continue to shape the production of a metanarrative of nation and patriotic history centered on liberation struggle, one that is rarely challenged by nonscholars.[70] The KHRC was besieged by lobbyists from competing veterans' groups.[71] Between 2003 and 2005 the KHRC developed these ideas, which were "further shaped" by three events: Makau Mutua was appointed chair of the task force set up to establish whether Kenya needed a Truth Commission; Caroline Elkins's *Britain's Gulag* was published to huge acclaim in Kenya, especially among Gikuyu, since it focused largely on their experience of the Emergency; and former colonial district-officer-turned-whistle-blower John Nottingham "agreed to assist in developing what could be claimed from a human rights perspective."[72] It was another six years (June 2009) before the campaign climaxed in the bringing of a reparations case in London's High Court, by the KHRC, the Mau Mau War Veterans' Association (MMWVA), and the British law firm Leigh Day. The case centered on human rights abuses suffered by five plaintiffs in detention during the Emergency and was ultimately settled out of court in June 2013.[73] (More on this later.)

It took some time for the government to respond to calls for heroes to be recognized and suitably anointed. A Taskforce on National Heroes and Heroines was finally launched in March 2007, under the chairmanship of Professor Vincent Simiyu, a historian at the University of Nairobi. Its main tasks were to canvass public opinion nationwide on who ought to be recognized as a hero or heroine, draw up criteria for their identification, and develop a National Heroes and Heroines Square. This latter plan was later modified, with the idea of a square replaced with a Heroes' Acre in Uhuru Gardens, Nairobi. This was in turn downsized to plans for a Heroes' Corner in Uhuru Park, which has not materialized. But in the park's Freedom Corner, the country's first Mau Mau memorial was officially unveiled on 12 September 2015 (photo 10). Thousands of veterans, many of them bused in from former Central Province, turned out in bespoke red-and-white T-shirts bearing the slogan "Shujaa wa Mau Mau" (Mau Mau heroes).[74] Beyond irony, the memorial was funded by the British government as part of the London reparations settlement. High Commissioner Christian Turner declared at the opening, "The memorial is a symbol of reconciliation between the UK, the Mau Mau and all those who suffered during the emergency period," a sentiment previously expressed by the KHRC on its website.[75] This is the first time to my knowledge that "all" victims have been acknowledged publicly. One of several plaques which form components of the memorial repeats this statement almost word for word, substituting "the British Government" for "the UK" and omitting the word "period." However, local media coverage does not appear to have mentioned the crucial word "all." If the slogans worn that day were anything to go by, veterans did not get the message either; in their eyes, the memorial commemorates their heroism rather than being a marker of reconciliation. Will non–Mau Mau regard the memorial as inclusive of them? I find this highly doubtful. A splinter group within the MMWVA immediately disowned the monument and called for it to be pulled down.[76] The monument is nonetheless a very significant addition to the postindependence memorial landscape of Nairobi, and one of the few that features subaltern figures, including a woman. The central figures are a male Mau Mau fighter receiving a basket of food from a female, their eyes deliberately averted from one another for wartime security reasons. With this monument, Mau Mau has thereby been inscribed more fully into the city's symbolic landscape than the lone statue of Kimathi (see below).[77]

To return to the Taskforce on National Heroes and Heroines, its final report (August 2007) was never published or made public.[78] Mau Mau featured quite prominently, but care was taken to suggest that Kenyans from all communities had contributed to the freedom struggle, a panethnic line that the KHRC has vigorously promoted (echoing Jomo, and Ngũgĩ too). The report declared, "All communities took part in the Mau Mau activities in different ways," and "the struggle for freedom by all Kenyans in their various communities, culminating in the armed struggle known as The Mau Mau War and the final attainment of independence was a macrocosm of national and community heroism."[79] It was not until 2010 that the government held the first Mashujaa Day, or Heroes' Day, which replaced the annual Kenyatta Day ceremonies on 20 October. Mau Mau veterans are central to this event, though from research evidence some are clearly being used to voice official sentiments they do not necessarily share.[80] A Kenya Heroes Act was passed in 2014, which established a National Heroes Council, whose functions include identifying and recommending national heroes for honors. Significantly, the act places Liberation Struggle first on its list of eleven criteria for the identification of heroes.[81] Though Mau Mau is not mentioned by name, it is central to this piece of legislation. Liberation fighters are also lauded as heroes in the preamble to the new (2010) constitution; again the words "Mau Mau" do not appear.[82] During ceremonies to mark fifty years of independence, war veterans were again placed center stage and officially presented as cornerstones of nationhood. The question is rarely asked, whose nationhood?

A grassroots campaign, which had begun in the early 1990s but climaxed unsuccessfully in January 2004, centered on calls for Kimathi's remains to be located in the grounds of Kamiti Prison, Nairobi, exhumed and reburied with due ceremony.[83] Kimathi had been buried in an unmarked mass grave, but no one knew exactly where. With the ban lifted, and KANU swept from power after forty years, the new government (elected in December 2002) declared its intention to find and rebury Kimathi in Heroes' Acre, not that it existed then or since. Noting the curious fact that "concern for Kimathi's remains did not arise for a long period after his death," Branch tells how a Free Kimathi Committee was formed in 2000 by veterans, human rights activists, and the Kimathi family.[84] It organized a large street demonstration in Nairobi on the forty-third anniversary of Kimathi's execution, on 18 February 1957. Protesters also used the occasion to chant anti-Moi slogans and accuse the regime of neocolonialism. These efforts came to nothing after the family, guided by people who claimed to know its whereabouts, failed to find the body. The search could not continue without state support, which was scaled down after January 2004. Branch sees the state's decision to commission a statue of Kimathi, erected opposite the Hilton Hotel in the center of Nairobi in February 2007, as very probably marking the official end of the search.

In a discussion of the commissioning of the statue, Coombes points out that moves to erect a monument to Kimathi had first been made in 1971, when the Nairobi city council considered rededicating the King George memorial to Kimathi; the plan was aborted.[85] She links the government's decision to start planning the statue in 2006 to elections the following December, which were to trigger the greatest bloodletting of the postindependence period. She also notes how "Kimathi's memory remained highly contentious throughout this period"; 2006 was marked by police crackdowns on members of the "Kimathi Movement." She concludes that the statue "is susceptible to multiple symbolic stagings by competing constituencies," which is both its strength and weakness, and that "it clearly lends itself to the reanimation of different versions of Kenya's past while at the same time being the focus point for the demonstration of demands about its political future."[86] This symbolism became acute in June 2014, when a young unemployed man claiming to be Kimathi's grandson, who said he shared the same name, chained himself to the statue in order to draw attention to the family's enduring poverty. The figure of the fighter, freed by the sculptor from his emasculating handcuffs in the classic "gotcha" image from 1956, was once again in chains.[87]

The Reparations Case

While hailed as a triumph by (some) veterans, and certainly by human rights activists and lawyers, the settlement of this case, in 2013, has led to several problems—not least, a growing compensation culture in Kenya in which publicized "memories" and "histories" of alleged human rights abuse and loss suffered during and since the 1950s are touted as commodities that have potential value in future legal claims. The case indirectly generated dozens of public-trauma narratives (largely from people aggrieved that they missed out in the London case, who failed to understand that they had to have been clients of Leigh Day to win compensation). These narratives may be regarded as counterproductive to unification and social healing—since they focus entirely on Mau Mau victims of the Emergency period, or their descendants, with no acknowledgment that others may have suffered too, not least at the hands of Mau Mau; they reinforce the exclusivity of the "Mau Mau story," and a predominantly Gikuyu one at that. Space precludes a longer discussion, but in memory terms I have argued elsewhere that the outpouring of narratives triggered by the legal case (*not* those of the plaintiffs, but personal stories unrelated to the actual case, published and broadcast primarily in the local media), their repetitive nature and mass circulation, are serving to skew public, media, and even some scholarly discourses about Mau Mau.[88] The interplay between repetition and recollection is a problematic one, as Patrick Hutton pointed out long ago, prompting the question: has the repetition of (unnuanced) trauma narratives in this context led to the construction of "false" memories or, at the very least, rather unreliable ones?[89] The case could be described as one of the "social cues" that has triggered the production of collective "remembering" in this group context—the realm of veterans' groups and their supporters.[90] Some narratives have not been produced by victims at all, but by spokespersons. Writing on the global proliferation of victimhood as a construct, Didier Fassin and Richard Rechtman note how "the voice that is generally heard is [increasingly] not that of the victims, but that of their self-appointed spokespeople."[91] One no longer has to have been a direct witness to suffering, or to have experienced it, in order to be a victim.

Using the media to fan the politics of recognition, different groups are competing for attention, employing a hierarchy of trauma in which their historical pain is portrayed as worse than that of others, and therefore more deserving of recompense—or simply a larger slice of the postindependence cake. Explicitly or implicitly, there is a localized "blame" thread running through many of these narratives (blame of Kenyans, especially "loyalists," rather than the British; also blame by one veterans' group of other veterans' groups), which is likely to make many fellow Kenyans feel uncomfortable. Moreover, the lawsuit outcome has reinforced the idea that Mau Mau veterans occupy the moral high ground—building on the notion that they single-handedly liberated Kenya from colonial rule. Many scholars refute this, and so does the History of Kenya exhibition at the Nairobi National Museum—though one would not know this from the space dedicated to liberation struggle.[92]

Mau Mau in State Heritage Spaces

To this day there is not a single museum dedicated to Mau Mau or liberation struggle anywhere in Kenya. Compared to the "struggle" heritage scene in South Africa, in particular, this seems extraordinary. Or maybe not: such are the huge sensitivities that still surround the conflict and its legacy, this is a nettle that state heritage managers have not wanted to grasp, for fear of upsetting certain people. However, in the early 1970s, the NMK created a pictorial exhibit at the Nairobi National Museum as part of Kenya's tenth independence anniversary celebrations. It was considered controversial even before it opened, several images were removed on government orders because they were deemed offensive to "one side or the other," and a much-reduced exhibit (photographs with no accompanying text) was mysteriously removed altogether in the mid-1990s.[93] Nothing more was done to address the heritage of liberation struggle until the NMK began planning a permanent History of Kenya exhibition in 2005, which includes a room dedicated to "Armed Struggle."[94] (Originally the NMK also planned a traveling exhibition on "Kenya independence struggles," which would have included earlier anticolonial rebellions; this was aborted.)[95] Historically, given its colonial rootedness in paleontology, archaeology, and the natural world, the institution appears to have felt much more comfortable with the far distant past and "non-controversial subjects."[96]

The Armed Struggle space includes cabinets displaying Kimathi's improbably outsized shorts, leather jacket, the uncropped photograph of him on a stretcher just after capture, his pistol, and a few letters (e.g., to General China); a display of homemade Mau Mau guns, which is from observation particularly popular with visiting schoolboys; a video made by NMK staff that plays continually in a loop, featuring interviews with war veterans;[97] a map of the detention camps; the bullet that lodged in General China's chest for thirty-four years; and photographs of Achieng' Oneko, Bildad Kaggia, and Paul Ngei (why not the entire Kapenguria Six?) with a caption describing them as "the militant leaders of the Mau Mau movement" rather than members of the militant wing of the Kenya African Union; and a photograph of the body of Senior Chief Waruhiu, with no explanation as to why Mau Mau murdered him, triggering the declaration of a State of Emergency, in October 1952. The interviewees in the video appear to be exclusively Gikuyu, which belies what NMK staff have previously said (for example, at exhibition-planning meetings I attended) about the need to broaden "the story of Mau Mau" to include people from other ethnic groups, in line with the KHRC campaign described earlier. The poisoned word "loyalism" barely appears in this particular space, other than in the (presumably colonial-era) caption "Loyalist guards keep watch over Mau Mau suspects at Langata camp," and a Home Guard's badge (unexplained). There are veiled references elsewhere (the exhibit on trade union struggle is particularly good, but from observation it is bypassed by many visitors; schoolchildren in particular are whisked past at great speed)—for example, mentions of "prominent chiefs" like Luka and "Africans who would see to it that the interests of the colonial government were protected." The role of Jomo Kenyatta in Mau Mau (if any) is not made at all clear; he barely features in this space.[98]

It is important to note two major differences between state and non-state museum displays on Mau Mau: guns are *not* on display at peace museums—though Agikuyu Peace Museum, Nyeri, has a corner devoted to liberation struggle, featuring a faded photocopied image of Kimathi.[99] Neither is there any tone of triumphalism in this latter space, whereas it is palpable in the History of Kenya exhibition.[100] The centrality of Gikuyu in the "Armed Struggle" space can partly be explained by the reported difficulty that exhibition developers had in finding tangible, displayable evidence of the role played by other communities in liberation struggle, and the influence of Gikuyu staff, who from observation relied heavily on Elkins's 2005 book, which centers almost exclusively on Gikuyu involvement in Mau Mau.[101] Elsewhere in the history exhibition, in a display on African responses to colonial conquest, there is a problematic binary opposition of "collaborators" versus "resisters," which reinforces a simplistic theme common in school textbooks. "In labeling one ethnic community 'bad' (for allegedly collaborating with the colonialists), and another 'good' (they resisted), a particular construction of moral ethnicity is permanently concretised."[102] This in itself is a powerful contributor to national memory making. Entire communities are forever condemned as traitors to the cause, with no nuanced attempt made to explain the challenges of survival in a time of war.

The Development of the Nyeri Museum and Other Initiatives

Kariuki Thuku, the late son of war veteran Paul Thuku Njembui (quoted earlier), first took me to see the abandoned Old African Courthouse at Ruring'u, near Nyeri town, in 2008. Not far away is the stadium where dreadlocked fighters famously laid down their arms, before Kenyatta and Kimathi's widow, Mukami, in December 1963. Built by the British in 1924, the courthouse was used for customary-law trials by and of Africans, and meetings of Local Native Councils. Despite being half ruined, Kariuki thought it would make a great museum—in part because he and his father were convinced Kimathi had been tried there, which of course he was not.[103] It appears he persuaded some NMK staff and others of this notion, too; if true, it would have added immensely to the building's appeal today as a potential Mau Mau heritage tourism site. Though a key figure in the peace museums movement, and founder in 1997 of the above-mentioned Agikuyu Peace Museum, Kariuki also had a passion for Mau Mau heritage and was trying to persuade the NMK to restore it and other war-related sites, such as the remains of emergency villages and caves used by fighters, one of which he took me to.[104] He was ignored; the NMK's then director of sites and monuments, Dr. Kibunjia Mzalendo, currently its director general, considered him a thorough nuisance.[105] I would not be surprised, however, if the NMK did not lift certain ideas from Kariuki. It later gazetted the building as Ruring'u Old African Courthouse, restored it, and decided to turn it into a museum; it is the first NMK museum to be established in the former Central Province. Oddly, when I last visited the site the NMK had allowed groups of war veterans to use other gazetted buildings in the grounds for their meetings; at the time these focused in large part on plans for the first reparations claim. From our conversations at the site, these elders clearly thought the museum was to be devoted to Mau Mau and expressed hopes that tourist revenue would come their way.[106]

The museum is now open but contains very little apart from some antique chairs from the original court, a temporary pictorial exhibit from Nairobi National Museum's Kenya@50 exhibition (created to mark fifty years of independence), and, more controversially, a broken stone plaque commemorating "the Kikuyu guard and other security forces and all loyal subjects of the Queen who died in the fight against terrorism, 1951–57."[107] Though NMK staff now flatly deny this, back in 2009 the site was being touted as a future Mau Mau museum, and rumor had it that the British High Commission was planning to fund it.[108] Local staff told me at various times that they were just waiting for the NMK to send them Mau Mau artifacts from Nairobi National Museum.[109] But I knew the NMK was having enough problems filling the History of Kenya exhibition space, let alone finding enough material Mau Mau heritage to fill a whole museum. To confuse matters, a separate nearby project spearheaded by veterans was by late 2012 being referred to as "the first Mau Mau museum in Nyeri" in a television news report; this showed veterans laying a cornerstone and invoking memories of Kimathi.[110] Also, in 2013 representatives of the Nyeri County Government talked in media reports of plans to establish a Mau Mau museum in the county, without specifying where; no progress appears to have been made since.[111] All this—particularly the refrains of veterans, which can be seen as chiming with the themes of subversive rap[112]—suggests that subaltern desire for concrete memorialization of both Kimathi and Mau Mau remains irrepressible but (outside Nairobi) has yet to be given material form by either national or county-level heritage managers—which is particularly odd in the movement's heartland of former Central Province. This may well be a victim of devolution, fallen in the chasm between draft national and county cultural-heritage legislation.[113] Moreover, the NMK has the professional know-how but lacks the cash; the county government has the funds but lacks the know-how.[114] The two have recently agreed to collaborate in the "mapping and gazetting of Mau Mau historical sites" in Nyeri County, which include preindependence native courts.[115]

NMK has also gazetted a number of other Mau Mau-related sites, such as the trench where Kimathi was shot and captured,[116] a fig tree in the Aberdare used as a post office, and caves allegedly used by fighters, but to my knowledge it has not developed these as heritage sites; as mentioned, it faces a financial crisis and cannot afford to do so. (The new agreement with Nyeri County Government could change matters.)[117] There was also the very curious case of an attempt in 2009 by an NMK "honorary warden" to gazette alleged Mau Mau caves and other heritage sites on the Soysambu estate of Lord and Lady Delamere; this came to nothing, but it embarrassed the then director general when he learned of it and annoyed the Delameres.[118] A more recent initiative is NMK's collaboration with scholars at Karatina University, Nyeri County, to excavate trenches and other war-related sites, including a "Kimathi trench," and to establish a "Mau Mau education centre."[119]

Commemoration of the Emergency period is hampered by an absence of materiality—no battlefields to match those of South Africa, heavily promoted in lucrative cultural tourism, or the street murals (largely) celebrating paramilitary heroes of the Troubles, which have become a huge heritage tourism draw in Belfast, to give but two examples from other parts of the world.[120] The Kenyan landscape simply does not feature much physical evidence of what happened. Trenches and the odd tree are a tame substitute, while mass graves and massacre sites are unlikely to appeal to either domestic or international tourists, besides those of a very "dark heritage" persuasion.[121] In the absence of other materiality, veterans have themselves become the embodiment of Mau Mau material culture in their matching branded garments, some sporting gray dreadlocks and brandishing Jomo-esque fly whisks. Hip-hop artists and other male youth can be seen as a younger version of this phenomenon, in their branded Kimathi T-shirts, though many have cut off their dreads in order to avoid police harassment for being suspected members of the outlawed Mungiki sect.[122]

Maloba has previously described how both left and right in Kenya have used Mau Mau for their own ends.[123] Now left, right, and factions in between (including veterans and their spokespeople) are attempting to use "memories" of the movement and conflict for a variety of new purposes. Since devolution, some county governments are seizing opportunities to use Mau Mau to brand counties and (attempt to) develop struggle-related heritage tourism, taking advantage of the ongoing crisis in national heritage management and lack of clarity with regard to draft legislation. Following the postelection violence and International Criminal Court indictments that netted the current president and his deputy, it may be argued that the political elite promoted Mau Mau partly in order to deflect Kenyans' attention from present-day abuses; it was used as a smokescreen. This constitutes *Deckerinnerung*, or the use of "one traumatic memory in order to cover up memories of another traumatic event that cannot be contemplated directly."[124] This chapter has discussed other examples.

A major problem is, and always was, the *usability* of Mau Mau memory and history, and its relationship to nation and nationhood. Clough has written, "Mau Mau is difficult to assimilate into the useable historical memory" for reasons that include its violence, ethnic composition, and regional nature, and the disparity between its original ideals and the sorry state of postindependence Kenya and citizens' betrayal by successive political elites.[125] Lonsdale has also discussed the usability of such memory, in the context of internecine violence and the "poisoned national memory of ethnic competition" to which Mau Mau has contributed.[126] At the end of the day, the exclusivity of a "story" that marginalizes or silences the majority of other Kenyans remains a major impediment to the usability of Mau Mau memory in public national history. Apart from two monuments and a puzzling "Armed Struggle" exhibit at the Nairobi National Museum, none of which is inclusive of all who were affected by the Emergency, we are left with the haunting image of Kimathi in the dock, silently accusing his accusers. It is just as well there is no surviving soundtrack in Kimathi's own words, describing his personal struggle within a struggle toward the end of his life, for that would bring nuance, complexity, and contradiction—which is more than Mau Mau memorialization can bear.

Notes

1. MacArthur, in the introduction to this volume, briefly discusses these images, opining that the stretcher image depicts Kimathi "as if a subdued animal or helpless infant." She reproduces the uncropped courtroom image in her online article "The Hunt for (the Trial of Dedan Kimathi)," *Africa Is a Country*, 24 March 2016. This image reveals that he was in fact draped in blankets from the waist down, which are not visible in the cropped image. She, too, notes that his bunched dreadlocks look like horns here (see photos 2 and 3). Here Kimathi has been stripped of the leopard-skin coat and hat, leather jerkin, and other clothes he was wearing when captured. A 1956 newsreel shows an unidentified white man standing next to him, holding the coat and hat above Kimathi, a disempowering gesture that could be read as mockery. "Mau Mau Chief Captured," England: British Pathé, 1956, http://www.britishpathe.com/video/mau-mau-chief-captured; https://www.youtube.com/watch?v=Q-nx8mr4Re8, both accessed 12 June 2017. The still of this uncropped image, which is much more rarely seen than the one cropped tight to his body, is displayed in the History of Kenya exhibition at the Nairobi National Museum, and reproduced as fig. 3 in Annie E. Coombes, "Photography against the Grain: Rethinking the Colonial Archive in Kenyan Museums," *World Art* 6, no. 1 (2016): 61–83. Coombes mentions the growing "cult value of Kimathi's image" in "Monumental Histories," 202–23; quote is 216. Also see Nicholas Githuku's contribution to this volume; Simon Gikandi's contribution to this volume discusses Kimathi's deliberate manipulation of imagery: "Now, Kimathi is nothing less than a world image with all its symbolic associations and visible and invisible meanings."

2. That is to say, the circular shape fits neatly within a square, which in turn fits easily on a T-shirt, poster, or the side of a matatu (minibus), for example—uses that MacArthur mentions in her introduction to this volume.

3. The trial transcript states, "The prisoner's hair was then wound on top of his head." Evidence of Ndirangu s/o Mau.

4. The identity of the photographer is not known. MacArthur, introduction to this volume, mentions this gifting of his photograph.

5. A version of this quotation is commonly attributed to Mexican revolutionary Emiliano Zapata (1879–1919). In their foreword to this volume, Mĩcere Gĩthae Mũgo and Ngũgĩ wa Thiong'o attribute slightly different words to Kimathi: "I would rather die on my feet than live on bended knees."

6. Testimony of Dedan Kimathi s/o Wachiuri.

7. For a discussion of hip-hop artists Ukoo Flani Mau Mau and other Kenyan rappers, their use of Mau Mau "memory," and images of Kimathi, see Caroline Mose, "Hip Hop Halisi: Continuities of Heroism on the African Political Landscape," and Mich Nyawalo, "Redefining the Struggle: Remembering the Mau Mau through Hip Hop Music," in *Hip Hop and Social Change in Africa: Ni wakati,* ed. Msia Kibona Clark and Mickie Mwanzia Koster (Lanham, MD: Lexington Books, 2014), 3–25, 72–92. Nyawalo explores how certain rappers have taken inspiration from Mau Mau freedom songs, "exalt[ed] . . . the memory of the nationally mythologized Mau Mau uprising . . . in their artistic performances," and used it when rapping about the predicament of marginalized youth (73). Also see Mwanzia Koster, "The Hip Hop Revolution in Kenya: Ukoo Flani Mau Mau, Youth Politics and Memory, 1990–2012," *Journal of Pan African Studies* 6, no. 3 (2013): 82–105. Mwanzia Koster describes Ukoo Flani Mau Mau as a "conglomerate" of many different groups rather than a single group (86). The name is used, according to her informants, to "carry on the anti-colonial Mau Mau struggle" (92). Interestingly, in the graffiti art shown in fig. 2 of that article, the artist appears to have amalgamated the stretcher and dock images to show Kimathi with his eyes looking to his right (as in some versions of the stretcher image) but with his moustache, goatee, and visible dreadlocks restored (the dock image). This may be read as an example of the "creative reworking of the colonial archive," which is thereby "effectively destabilize[d]." Coombes, "Photography against the Grain," 15. Coombes discusses other Kenyan examples.

8. Mũgo and Ngũgĩ, in their foreword to this volume, cast doubt on the veracity of the trial transcript and statements purportedly given to police by Kimathi, saying the latter is "most likely yet another colonial fabrication." But Kimathi's lawyer, Frederick Miller, told the court, "In my opinion that [police] statement was voluntarily made not as a result of any threat or inducement."

9. Ferdinand De Jong, "At Work in the Archive," introduction to special issue, *World Art* 6, no. 1 (2016): 6, 7. He discusses artists, authors, and others who are "interrupting established historical narratives of colonial domination" by examining the colonial archive, and subverting it.

10. Anderson, *Histories of the Hanged,* 249; MacArthur, introduction to this volume.

11. Peterson, "Writing in Revolution," 76, 89. Also see Osborne, "'Rooting Out,'" 92.

12. For a discussion of forgetting and remembering of Mau Mau, and most specifically Dedan Kimathi, that draws more fully than I do on literary sources, see Gikandi's contribution to this volume.

13. Regarding the discovery and release of Mau Mau documents held in UK archives, see Anderson's contribution to this volume.

14. Ngare Kariuki, "Rewriting the Mau Mau Story," *Daily Nation*, Living Supplement, 7 August 2015, 2–3.

15. This term appears to have been coined by Susannah Radstone and Katharine Hodgkin, eds., *Regimes of Memory* (London: Routledge, 2011).

16. For media coverage of the fake Mathenge, see, for example, "Kenya Flies Home Mau Mau 'Imposter,'" BBC News, 6 June 2003, accessed 16 October 2016, http://news.bbc.co.uk/1/hi/world/africa/2970096.stm. The episode inspired a short story by Parselelo Kantai, "Comrade Lemma and the Black Jerusalem Boys Band," *Kwani?* 2 (Nairobi: Kwani Trust, 2004): 208–23.

17. A fuller discussion would require more reference to the comparative international literature, especially on postconflict memory. For space reasons there are also other omissions, e.g. no mention of Mungiki, whose members portray themselves as "sons of Mau Mau" and purport to keep its memory alive, or a discussion of how Mau Mau is remembered outside Kenya, especially in Britain. It has notoriously "lived in British memory as a symbol of African savagery." Lonsdale, "Mau Mau's of the Mind," 393–421. More recently, Adam Foulds's epic poem *The Broken Word* (London: Jonathan Cape, 2008), centered on a fictitious young British man caught up in the Emergency, won the 2009 Costa Poetry Award.

18. For mention of the Lari massacres and trials, see Anderson's contribution to this volume.

19. Osborne, "Rooting Out," 78, 82–84.

20. Clough, "Contest for Memory," 254; Osborne, "Rooting Out."

21. Osborne, "Rooting Out," 78.

22. Anderson, *Histories of the Hanged*, 32–33. The Naivasha raid took place "almost simultaneously" with the first massacre, according to Yannick Veilleux-Lepage and Jan Fedorowicz, "The Mau Mau Revolt in Kenya, 1952–1956," in *A History of Counterinsurgency: From South Africa to Algeria, 1900 to 1954*, ed. Gregory Fremont-Barnes (Santa Barbara: Praeger, 2015), 189.

23. Osborne, "Rooting Out," 82–83. The film shown was *The Mark of the Mau Mau*, centered on the Githunguri trials of Lari accused, no director named (England: British Pathé, 1953), accessed 4 August 2015, http://www.britishpathe.com/video/the-mark-of-the-mau-mau-exclusive/query/Lari+massacre.

24. Osborne, "Rooting Out," 82. For British media coverage, see Joanna Lewis, "'Daddy Wouldn't Buy Me a Mau Mau': The British Popular Press and

the Demoralisation of Empire," in Atieno Odhiambo and Lonsdale, *Mau Mau and Nationhood,* 227–50.

25. Branch, *Defeating Mau Mau,* 58.

26. Coombes suggests that the photographs on display at Lari could also show victims of the second massacre, but does not provide evidence to substantiate this claim. Coombes, "Photography against the Grain," 14–17. Close examination of photographs of the Lari "massacre" held in file TNA:PRO, CO 1066/1, which I have obtained copies of, suggests a different story. Questions arising include: why would British government propagandists circulate grisly images of people killed and mutilated by their own side? Why are many of the bodies burnt (which by all accounts they were not in the second massacre), mutilated by pangas (machetes) (ditto), with no visible bullet wounds (guns were not used in the first massacre), and with village or homestead structures clearly visible in the background, when the second massacre reportedly largely took place in nearby forests?

27. Photographs of victims of the first Lari massacre, and one of suspects shot in the second, were published, for example, in *Mau Mau: A Pictorial Record* (Nairobi: The English Press, 1953). The single image of victims of the second massacre shows a neat lineup of male bodies laid on their backs, captioned "The Day after Lari . . . Mau Mau who met the 23rd" (a reference to the 23rd King's African Rifles). Its careful composition seems to deliberately suggest a "cleaner" orderliness of state-orchestrated killing with guns, as opposed to the "mess" left by Mau Mau pangas, but this second massacre was anything but clean or orderly.

28. Anderson, *Histories of the Hanged,* 177; Osborne, "Rooting Out," 82.

29. Ngũgĩ wa Thiong'o, *Petals of Blood* (London: Heinemann, 1977, 1986 ed. cited), 100.

30. Ngũgĩ wa Thiong'o, *Dreams in a Time of War: A Childhood Memoir* (London: Harvill Secker, 2010), 281–84.

31. The TJRC's public hearings across Kenya between 2009 and 2011 covered a wide range of historical abuses. The TJRC's mandate ran from independence, in December 1963, to February 2008, hence earlier abuses related to Mau Mau could not be considered. However, its final report devoted a surprisingly large amount of space to Mau Mau–era abuses (for instance, there are seven pages on the Lari "massacre"); despite the use of the singular in the section title, the report does mention the second wave of killings. TJRC, "Lari Massacre: The Night of the Long Knives," in *Final Report of the Truth, Justice and Reconciliation Commission* (Nairobi: TJRC, May 2013), vol. 11A, chap. 4, 164–71.

32. The fullest discussion of these events is in Anderson, *Histories of the Hanged,* chap. 4, 119–80. Also see Branch, *Defeating Mau Mau,* 57.

33. Mũgo and Ngũgĩ, in the foreword to this volume, condemn "a scholarship that tries to diminish the armed wing of the entire anticolonial liberation by describing the struggle that Kĩmathi led as a civil war."

34. See, for example, Lewis, "Nasty, Brutish and in Shorts?," 201–23. She writes: "Anderson wants all victims memorialized, including those Africans who fought *against* Mau Mau . . . In Elkins' [2005] history only the Mau Mau deserve memorialization (and reparation)" (204, emphasis in original). See also Anderson, *Histories of the Hanged,* 343–44; Anderson and Lane, "Unburied Victims."

35. See, for example, Lotte Hughes, "'Truth Be Told': Some Problems with Historical Revisionism in Kenya," *African Studies* 70, no. 2 (2011): 182–201; Coombes, "Monumental Histories." For work on Mekatilili, the early-twentieth-century Giriama rebel, and Nandi prophet Koitalel arap Samoei, see respectively Neil Carrier and Celia Nyamweru, "Reinventing Africa's National Heroes: The Case of Mekatilili, a Kenyan Popular Heroine," *African Affairs* 115, no. 461 (2016): 599–620; Chloé Josse-Durand, "Building Local Memories, Pluralizing the National Narrative: Community Museums and the Political Use of Heritage and Memory in Kenya and Ethiopia" (PhD diss., Institut d'Études Politiques de Bordeaux, 2016).

36. A study of these peace museums was carried out as part of the AHRC-funded research project Managing Heritage, Building Peace: Museums, Memorialization and the Uses of Memory in Kenya (2008–11), led by me, whose main written output was Coombes, Hughes, and Karega-Munene, *Managing Heritage.*

37. I conducted interviews, with contributions from curator Waihenya Njoroge, with two members of the museum's management board, ex–Home Guard Douglas Wainana and Waihenya's grandfather, ex–Mau Mau Joseph Kaboro Tumbo, at the Lari Memorial Peace Museum, Kimende, Kenya, 10 July 2006. Both are now deceased. Some of this material was used in Rodney Harrison and Lotte Hughes, "Heritage, Colonialism and Postcolonialism," in *Understanding the Politics of Heritage,* ed. Harrison (Manchester: Manchester University Press in association with the Open University, 2010), 257. Coombes interviewed these and other elders associated with the museum at a later date, for the Managing Heritage, Building Peace research project on which I was principal investigator, Coombes co-investigator, and Karega-Munene lead consultant.

38. Annie E. Coombes, "Object Lessons: Learning from the Lari Massacre(s)," in *Managing Heritage,* Coombes, Hughes, and Karega-Munene, 53–98, and other chapters in that volume; Coombes, "Photography against the Grain"; Harrison and Hughes, "Heritage"; Lotte Hughes and Karega-Munene, "Cultures of Peace in Community Museums," *Awaaz* (Nairobi) 28 January 2013, accessed 1 October 2015, http://www.awaazmagazine.com/previous/index.php/archives/item/439-cultures-of-peace-in-community-museums.

39. See note 26 above. I do not agree with her broader argument that the photographs may show victims of both massacres; no evidence is given.

40. Coombes, "Photography against the Grain," 17, 10–12.

41. Coombes, "Object Lessons," 54.

42. Ogot briefly mentioned the Lari Memorial Peace Museum in his double review of David Anderson, *Histories of the Hanged,* and Caroline Elkins, *Britain's Gulag.* He noted its reconciliation work "appears to be the way forward towards healing the deep wounds created by the Mau Mau war within Kikuyu society." Ogot, "Britain's Gulag," 503.

43. For example, Robert Buijtenhuis, *Mau Mau: Twenty Years After: The Myth and the Survivors* (The Hague: Mouton, 1973); Hélène Charton, "Jomo Kenyatta et les méandres de la mémoire de l'indépendance du Kenya," *Vingtième siècle* 118, no. 2 (2013): 45–59; Clough, *Mau Mau Memoirs;* Clough, "Contest for Memory"; Lonsdale and Odhiambo, introduction to *Mau Mau and Nationhood;* Coombes, Hughes, and Karega-Munene, *Managing Heritage*; Hughes, "'Truth Be Told'"; Coombes, "Monumental Histories"; and, to a lesser extent, Greet Kershaw, "Mau Mau from Below: Fieldwork and Experience, 1955–57 and 1962," *Canadian Journal of African Studies* 25, no. 2 (1991): 274–97; Ogot, "Britain's Gulag"; Kinyatti, *Kenya's Freedom Struggle,* 119. See also Simon Gikandi's contribution to this volume, in which he discusses the repression of memory.

44. Ngũgĩ, *Dreams,* 154. This speech was in fact given on 24 August 1952 at Kiambu cricket ground. My thanks to John Lonsdale for this information.

45. Osborne, "Rooting Out," 78, 93–97.

46. Jeffrey K. Olick, Vered Vinitzky-Seroussi, and Daniel Levy, introduction to *The Collective Memory Reader,* ed. Olick, Vinitzky-Seroussi, and Levy (Oxford: Oxford University Press, 2011), 3–62. They argue that the global "memory boom" began in the late 1970s and coincided with the proliferation of identity politics and "the decline of utopian visions," 3.

47. Buijtenhuis, *Twenty Years After,* 52.

48. Annie E. Coombes, "Monuments and Memories: Public Commemorative Strategies in Contemporary Kenya," in Coombes, Hughes, and Karega-Munene, *Managing Heritage.* Earlier mausolea were built to honor fellow Kapenguria Six members Jomo Kenyatta, Paul Ngei, Bildad Kaggia, and Achieng' Oneko, as well as Tom Mboya. The Kubai mausoleum took nearly five years to build. My thanks to Wycliffe Oloo of NMK for information. Wycliffe Oloo, e-mail message to author, August 2015.

49. Kershaw, "Mau Mau," 293.

50. Paul Thuku Njembui, interview by Lotte Hughes, World Social Forum, Nairobi, 25 January 2007. Then aged about eighty, he spoke some English, picked up during his seven years in detention camps. This was the first of many interviews and conversations with Thuku, mostly when I stayed at

his home, in Kinayu village, Karima Forest, Othaya District. He had earlier been a key informant of Derek Peterson's. Thuku died in 2014. He claimed to have sheltered Dedan Kimathi in his home in 1952. By saying "Kenyatta was there," Thuku implies that the British sought his advice about what to do with Kimathi, which is obviously a mythical construct. Thuku headed the board of the Agikuyu Community Peace Museum, Nyeri, established by his late son Kariuki. See Lotte Hughes, "Sacred Spaces, Political Places: The Struggle for a Sacred Forest," in Coombes, Hughes, and Karega-Munene, *Managing Heritage*. Unlike the Lari Memorial Peace Museum, the board then consisted solely of ex–Mau Mau. Since Kariuki and his father died the museum has been taken over by Kariuki's widow, Lydia, who has distanced herself from other Kenyan peace museums; it is not clear if it still has a board.

51. An illustration of how confused some Kenyans still are about the relationship (if any) between Kimathi and Kenyatta, is this request, in response to a picture story about the unveiling of Kimathi's statue and war veterans mingling with young fans of Mau Mau, by "Njuguna," asking for the photos "plus any vedio [*sic*] of dedan kemathi [*sic*] with mzee jomo" posted online 19 November 2003. See "If you didn't know, we all street!" https://wanyex.wordpress.com/photo-gallery/. No date given but the statue was unveiled on 18 February 2007. In Kimathi's interrogation report (see Document 5 in this volume), he told his interrogators he had attended a public KAU meeting at Thomson's Falls, where he was then branch secretary, on 26 June 1952, at which Kenyatta spoke. "Subject stated that he had only seen JOMO once before and he never had private conversations with him or with other political leaders." Also, Kimathi and eighty KAU leaders were with Kenyatta in Nairobi in October or November 1951. My thanks to Julie MacArthur and Ben Knighton for this information.

52. Ngũgĩ, *Dreams,* 195.

53. For more on the role of literature in shaping memories of Mau Mau, and also Kimathi's relationship to what is "literary," see Gikandi's contribution to this volume.

54. Clough, *Mau Mau Memoirs,* 250.

55. Buijtenhuis, *Twenty Years After,* 64. Other rapprochement with veterans included hosting former generals at his home in August 1963, inviting veterans to the independence day celebrations, and in the company of Kimathi's widow, Mukami, welcoming forest fighters to lay down their arms in a ceremony at Ruring'u Stadium, Nyeri, four days after independence, on 16 December 1963. Clough, "Contest for Memory," 255. Echoing Mau Mau ritual, Kenyatta sanctioned mass oathing to bind the House of Mumbi at his home in 1969. Ben Knighton, "Going for Cai at Gatũndũ, 1968–9: Reversion to a Gĩkũyũ Ethnic Past or Building a Kenyan National Future?," in *Our Turn to Eat: Politics in Kenya since 1950,* ed. Nic Cheeseman and Daniel Branch

(Berlin: LIT Verlag, 2010), 107–28. For references to recent commemorative activities in this volume, see the introductory note by Willy Mutunga and Gikandi's contribution to this volume.

56. Kenyatta, *Suffering without Bitterness*, 189.

57. Ibid., xv.

58. Ali A. Mazrui, "Between Cultural Nostalgia and Cultural Amnesia: African Museums and the Archival Memory," *Kenya Past and Present* 35 (Nairobi: Kenya Museum Society, 2005): 30, citing French philosopher Ernest Renan; Mazrui, "On Heroes," 23.

59. Buijtenhuis, *Twenty Years After*, 62. The monthly *Kenya Mirror* produced a special issue on Mau Mau at the end of 1971.

60. Clough, "Contest for Memory," 257.

61. Ngũgĩ, *Petals*, 339–40.

62. A section on memoirs has been cut for space reasons. The most comprehensive discussion of this canon is Clough, *Mau Mau Memoirs*. Also see Luise White, "Separating the Men from the Boys: Constructions of Gender, Sexuality and Terrorism in Central Kenya, 1939–1959," *International Journal of African Historical Studies* 23, no. 1 (1990): 1–25. For an analysis of women's memoirs, see Cora Ann Presley, *Kikuyu Women, the Mau Mau Rebellion, and Social Change in Kenya* (Boulder: Westview, 1992).

63. Hughes, "'Truth Be Told,'" 188, citing Radstone and Hodgkin, *Regimes*, 2. It is beyond the scope of this chapter to cover European memoirs about Mau Mau and the Emergency, but they notably include Henderson, *Hunt*, an account of the hunt for Kimathi by the Special Branch policeman who captured him.

64. My thanks to Dan Branch for drawing this to my attention. He points out that politicians' memoirs tend to gloss over the 1950s; for instance, Kenneth Matiba's autobiography *Aiming High: The Story of My Life* (Nairobi: People Ltd., 2000). Daniel Branch, e-mail message to author, September 2015.

65. The few exceptions include local press stories about the Lari "massacre" in annual commemoration coverage, which include interviews with surviving "loyalist" victims, for instance, N. Gicheha, "The Night of the Long Knives: Slain Colonial Chief's Widows Recall Lari Massacre," *Star*, 25 March 2011.

66. Coombes and Hughes, introduction to *Managing Heritage*, 2.

67. Hughes, "'Truth Be Told,'" 188–91.

68. Coombes, "Monumental Histories," 203.

69. Steve Ouma Akoth, e-mail messages to author, 2–8 September 2015. My thanks to Steve for information and insights. Also see, for example, "Support the Mau Mau Reparations Campaign," *Pambazuka News*, issue 422, no. 3 (May 2009), accessed August 2015, http://pambazuka.org/en/category/features/54582.

70. Terence Ranger, "Nationalist Historiography, Patriotic History and the History of the Nation: The Struggle over the Past in Zimbabwe," *Journal of*

Southern African Studies 30, no. 2 (2004): 215–34; Peter R. Schmidt, "Postcolonial Silencing, Intellectuals, and the State: Views from Eritrea," *African Affairs* 109, no. 435 (April 2010): 293–313.

71. Confirmed by Steve Ouma Akoth, and also in earlier conversations I have had with former KHRC director Muthoni Wanyeki. Akoth told me, "We were sometimes accused by other groups [besides the Mau Mau War Veterans' Association] of bias." Akoth, ibid.

72. Akoth, Ibid.

73. *Mutua and Others v. The Foreign and Commonwealth Office* (2013). The number of plaintiffs was later reduced to three, one died, and another withdrew. Britain paid £19.9 million to 5,228 claimants, all clients of Leigh Day. A second claim, by Kimathi's widow, Eloise Mukami Kimathi, and others, has been brought to court by another British law firm, Tandem Law.

74. Nancy Muigei (then political officer/human rights, British High Commission, Nairobi), e-mail messages to author, August 2015.

75. Eunice Kilonzo, "Veterans and Families Turn Up to Witness the Unveiling of Memorial," *Daily Nation*, 12 September 2015, accessed 1 October 2015, http://www.nation.co.ke/news/Veterans-and-families-turn-up/-/1056/2868192/-/26741kz/-/index.html. Initially the KHRC reported that the memorial "is to promote reconciliation and commemorate all those who suffered on all sides during the Emergency period," Something similar, but broader, was given in a KHRC Statement, 24 July 2014. The memorial, it said, "is designed as a memorialization feature for the remembrance of all victims of torture and ill treatment during the colonial era," accessed 12 June 2017, http://www.khrc.or.ke/2015-03-04-10-37-01/press-releases/389-khrc-statement-on-ground-breaking-ceremony-for-the-memorial-to-victims-of-torture-and-ill-treatment-during-the-colonial-era-1952-1963.html.

76. Lydiah Nyawira, "Mau Mau Veterans Disown Freedom Monument," *Standard*, 25 September 2015, 21. I also discuss this memorial in "Mau Mau: The Divisive Heritage of Liberation Struggle in Kenya," in *Heritage and Peacebuilding*, ed. Peter Davis, Daniel Laven, and Diana Walters (Woodbridge, Suffolk, UK: Boydell and Brewer, 2016). Also see Nicholas Githuku, this volume, who sees the significance of the monument in different terms.

77. This terminology is taken from Laragh Larsen, "Power, Politics and Public Monuments in Nairobi, Kenya," *Open Democracy*, 8 April 2013, accessed 15 September 2016, https://www.opendemocracy.net/laragh-larsen/power-politics-and-public-monuments-in-nairobi-kenya. For her earlier work on the changing monumental landscape of Nairobi, see Larsen, "Notions of Nation in Nairobi's Nyayo-Era Monuments," *African Studies* 70, no. 2 (2011): 264–83. Here Larsen describes the Moi-era National Monument in Uhuru Gardens, whose "*Harambee* sculpture" depicts three men and one woman raising the Kenyan flag. She notes that "the inclusion of a woman in the

raising of the Kenyan flag is significant, highlighting the ideal that all Kenyans, men and women, have a role to play in the nation-building process" (271). The "Wanjiku" peasant woman depicted in the Mau Mau Memorial may be seen as continuing that tradition, though she is secretly bringing food to starving forest fighters, rather than raising a flag amid public pomp and ceremony.

78. Coombes, "Monuments and Memories," 145; Hughes, "'Truth Be Told,'" 183.

79. "Report of the Taskforce for Country-wide Data Collection on Criteria and Modalities of Honouring National Heroes and Heroines" (Nairobi: Taskforce on National Heroes and Heroines, August 2007, unpublished), 12, vii, copy obtained from Kenyan contacts. Also see Hughes, "'Truth Be Told.'" I asked former KHRC deputy director Steve Ouma Akoth when and from whom the KHRC originally got the idea that Mau Mau was a panethnic movement: he replied, "This was our own revisionist idea as human rights activists. I do know that it is historically inaccurate." Akoth, e-mail message to author, 8 September 2015. Ngũgĩ began promoting this idea a long time ago, in concert with scholar Maina wa Kinyatti. For instance, in his foreword to Kinyatti, *Kenya's Freedom Struggle*, he claimed Mau Mau had been supported by "millions of workers and peasants of all nationalities in Kenya" (xvi).

80. A Kimeru veteran who has been officially decorated as a hero told me how he was bounced into giving a speech (written by a Kenyan scholar who shall remain nameless) at the 2014 event. He did not appear to fully understand the speech and indicated that he knew he was being used on this occasion by politicians and others. Lotte Hughes, "Claims, Victimhood, Reluctant Heroes, and Other Problematic Legacies of Mau Mau," paper presented at Legacies of Struggle in Southern and Eastern Africa workshop, British Institute in Eastern Africa, Nairobi, 18–20 March 2015.

81. The other criteria are, in order of listing: spiritual leadership; indigenous knowledge; cultural practices and values; arts; sports; scholarship, professionalism, research; peace making; statesmanship; entrepreneurship and industry; and philanthropy.

82. Preamble to the Constitution of Kenya (2010); Hughes, "'Truth Be Told.'"

83. Branch, "Search," 301–20.

84. The quote is from ibid., 301.

85. Coombes, "Monumental Histories," 211.

86. Ibid., 213, 219. Members of the Kimathi Movement tried to celebrate Kimathi Day in Nyeri on 18 February 2006, but were arrested and jailed. "Locals had apparently celebrated Kimathi Day without incident since 2003 and were distressed by this turn of events, accusing the Kibaki government of sidelining former freedom fighters" (213).

87. Judie Kaberia, "Dedan Kimathi's Grandson Chains Himself to the Monument," *Capital News,* 8 June 2014, 13 June 2017, http://www.capitalfm.co.ke/news/2014/06/dedan-kimathis-grandson-chains-himself-to-monument/.

88. Hughes, "Claims, Victimhood."

89. Patrick Hutton, "History as an Art of Memory," in Olick, Vinitzky-Seroussi, and Levy, *Collective Memory Reader,* 411–15.

90. Discussing the work of Maurice Halbwachs, the French philosopher credited with inventing the idea of collective memory, Olick, Vinitzky-Seroussi, and Levy state, "All individual remembering . . . takes place with social materials, within social contexts, and in response to social cues," *Collective Memory Reader,* 18.

91. Didier Fassin and Richard Rechtman, *The Empire of Trauma: An Inquiry into the Condition of Victimhood,* trans. Rachel Gomme (Princeton: Princeton University Press, 2009), 193.

92. Other displays in the exhibition describe how independence was brought about in a variety of ways, including via political and trade union struggle, placing less emphasis on violent means.

93. Karega-Munene, "Museums in Kenya: Spaces for Selecting, Ordering and Erasing Memories of Identity and Nationhood," *African Studies* 70, no. 2 (August 2011): 235.

94. Hughes, "'Truth Be Told'"; Lotte Hughes, "The Production and Transmission of National History: Some Problems and Challenges," in Coombes, Hughes, and Karega-Munene, *Managing Heritage.*

95. Hughes, "Production and Transmission," 204–5. I took part in a planning meeting for this proposed exhibition, chaired by Caroline Elkins, at Nairobi National Museum in May 2010. So far as I know the plans were not taken forward.

96. Karega-Munene, "Towards Recognition of the Right to a Cultural Past in the Twenty-first Century: An Example from East Africa," in *Postcolonial Archaeologies in Africa,* ed. Peter R. Schmidt (Santa Fe: School for Advanced Research, 2009), 80.

97. *Mau Mau: The Unsung Heroes,* video. Executive Producers Dr. Idle Farah (then NMK director general) and Connie Maina (Nairobi: NMK, 2010).

98. I have not visited this exhibition recently; changes may have been made since these observations were made, in 2011.

99. Coombes, "Object Lessons," 79–82.

100. On display is a long poem called "The War," written by former curator Francis Muritu. It includes the Gikuyu proverb "War is not porridge," to which he has added "but a smelly food for fools." He explained this to me as "them that think war is porridge, as in something that you take everyday [*sic*] to fill your stomach and nourish you, it isn't; war kills, leaves people with nothing but 'chronic wounds' that refuse to go throughout your life." Francis Muritu, e-mail message to author, July 2015.

101. Hughes, "Production and Transmission," 204. The NMK had no collection of historical objects it could use for this exhibition. A public appeal for donated items was unsuccessful, I was told; people wanted to be paid for them, and NMK could not afford to do so.

102. Ibid., 211.

103. Paul Thuku told me the "fact" that Kimathi had been tried in this building had "remained in the dark until Kariuki saw the book with the judgment handed by the judge called John somebody." He believed it was the only copy in the country. "But when it was known that Kariuki had the book in his possession, the police started looking for him and he was given refuge by Paul Muite and Wangari Maathai." Paul Thuku Njembui, interview by Lotte Hughes, February 2009, Kinaya village, Karima Forest, Othaya District.

104. For a discussion of Kariuki's creation of the Agikuyu Community Peace Museum and later career, see Hughes, "Sacred Spaces." The cave he took me to was part of the Kariba Mau Mau Caves on the Ruui Ruiru River, Ngaine Location, Mathira West District, July 2006. Kariuki also shared with me a well-researched proposal for creating a replica emergency village—"Forgotten Relic: A Kenyan Emergency Era Village" (no date, but likely to have been 2007/8). He constantly lobbied NMK and may well have shared this idea with them, too. He wrote in the proposal: "Why does Kenya need a replica of a colonial emergency era village now? The 1953–1961 colonial villages shall remain a strong historical heritage of our collective memory and history that we cannot afford to lose. . . . So much of our Mau Mau memories resides [*sic*] in the experiences lived out inside [these villages]." He saw their potential in what he called "democracy-based tourism."

105. Hughes, "Sacred Spaces," 132n45.

106. I have spoken on several occasions to veterans at this site, including 27 August 2009. Nicholas Githuku, contributor to this volume, also spoke to veterans there when assisting me with research for the project Managing Heritage, Building Peace.

107. The chairs and some other exhibits can be seen on the Nyeri Museum Facebook page. The plaque was originally on a street in the middle of Nyeri town, where it was vandalized. It was brought into the courthouse partly for safekeeping. My thanks to Julie MacArthur for information. The museum's collection may have changed since she visited.

108. I was previously told by NMK staff that it was to be called the Mau Mau Museum. But NMK contacts now say this was never the case and that its official name is Ruring'u Old African Court; this is contradicted by its "Nyeri Museum" Facebook page. Information from sources contacted in 2016 who do not wish to be named; also earlier information supplied by Kiprop Lagat, conversation with author, 24 February, 9 September 2009; Hassan Wario Arero (then NMK director of sites and monuments, now cabinet

secretary in the Ministry of Sports, Culture and the Arts), conversation with author, July 2010.

109. The honorary NMK warden for that region, son of a war veteran from Karima Forest, where my informant Paul Thuku Njembui also lived, told me in 2009 that he was collecting Mau Mau artifacts for the Old Courthouse Museum, but doubted it would open on time. Like Paul and Kariuki Thuku, he wrongly believed Kimathi had faced trial in this building rather than at Nyeri Supreme Court. Mureithi Kibaaba, conversation with author, 27 August 2009.

110. KTN News, "First Mau Mau Museum in Nyeri," 12 December 2012, accessed 1 October 2015, https://www.youtube.com/watch?v=4W-ucZwuDG8.

Veterans filmed included one who said, "He [Kimathi] would tell us he will hold the donkey's mouth [a reference to the colonialists] and you [Gikuyu] people will hold its legs, because we shall fight the Europeans for them to leave our country." My thanks to Gordon Omenya and Betty Karanja for translation (24, 25 September 2015). References made to a proposed museum were to a separate two-acre site opposite the courthouse. I was told by an NMK staffer who wishes to remain anonymous that this is a "purely Mau Mau project with [NMK's] input only being advisory or technical as required."

111. Muthini Stephen, "Nyeri Plans Mau Mau Museum to Attract Tourists," *Business Daily,* 17 November 2013, accessed 10 June 2015, http://www.businessdailyafrica.com/Corporate-News/Nyeri-plans-Mau-Mau-museum-to-attract-tourists/-/539550/2119158/-/6f7023z/-/index.html. This article quotes county governor Nderitu Gachagua as saying some of the museum's revenue would go to support veterans. Since devolution to forty-seven county governments in 2013, control of regional museums has passed from the NMK to counties. However, in this case the building was already gazetted as a monument, rather than a museum, and therefore remains in NMK control.

112. On the significance of rap lyrics inspired by freedom songs, See Nyawalo, "Redefining the Struggle."

113. Some county governments are drafting their own cultural heritage legislation, but I do not know if this applies to Nyeri County.

114. Fred Oluoch, "Heritage at Risk: National Museums of Kenya in Financial Crisis, *East African,* 20 March 2015, accessed 9 September 2015, http://www.theeastafrican.co.ke/magazine/Heritage-at-risk-National-Museums-of-Kenya-in-financial-crisis/-/434746/2659530/-/r7yy3sz/-/index.html.

115. Nicolas Komu, "National Museums to Map Mau Mau Sites," *Daily Nation*, 24 May 2017, 10. This story states the NMK and Nyeri County Government have entered into an agreement to map Mau Mau sites including detention camps, native courts, war museums, caves and fig trees used as "post offices" by fighters.

116. See MacArthur, introduction to this volume.

117. Mau Mau caves had long been on the radar of provincial and district cultural officers, who saw them as potential heritage tourism sites. (Following devolution, these posts no longer exist; county cultural officers have taken over their duties.) I discussed caves near Nyeri with the then district cultural officer on a visit to his office in February 2009.

118. I learned this directly from Lady Delamere, who asked if I could help. She told me this warden and another person (the director of a nearby tourist lodge) had trespassed on the farm, making what appeared to have been a reconnaissance mission, while the Delameres were in Nairobi at their son Tom's murder trial. (Tom Cholmondeley has since died.) They later received a letter on NMK letterhead stating that NMK proposed to gazette caves and other heritage sites on the estate, adding a thinly veiled threat that the land would be appropriated if the Delameres refused. I have seen the letter. I later heard from contacts that it was not authorized by the then NMK director general, Dr. Idle Farah, who was very annoyed when he found out. The episode may be described as an extraordinary example of overzealousness by this untrained warden, who has been responsible for identifying many of the Mau Mau heritage sites in the Central Region that the NMK has subsequently gazetted. (The Central Region is an NMK area of operation, not to be confused with the former Central Province.)

119. Emmanuel Ndiema and John M. Mwaruvie, "Excavation and Rehabilitation of Mau Mau Trench at Karatina University: Preliminary Findings," paper presented at Legacies of Struggle in Southern and Eastern Africa workshop, British Institute in Eastern Africa, Nairobi, 18–20 March 2015. Trenches are gazetted as national monuments. They were dug around Emergency-era villages where Gikuyu people were incarcerated in an attempt to cut off supply lines to forest fighters. Karatina University, accessed 3 October 2015, http://www.karatinauniversity.ac.ke/index.php?option=com_content&view=article&id=116:excavation-rehabilitation-and-restoration-of-mau-mau-trench&catid=23:latest-events&Itemid=207.

120. For an example of South African battlefield tourism promotion, see Cedarberg Africa, Personal Safari Planning, accessed 5 October 2015, https://www.cedarberg-travel.com/destinations/south-africa/kwazulu-natal-holidays/natal-battlefields-zulu-battlefields?gclid=CK6C8-eHq8gCFUSe2wody-APDg#search-results1. I took a guided tour of Belfast street murals and graffiti art in October 2016. The massing of black cabs, which seem to have cornered the market in this type of heritage tourism, around the murals reminded me of tourist minibuses in the Masai Mara Game Reserve, thronging around a lion or cheetah. For every image of a dead republican hero, there is one of a "Loyalist," sometimes murdered by one of their own. If Kenyans were to try to emulate this, in commemorating victims of the Emergency, they would have to broaden the iconography beyond images of Kimathi.

121. Anderson and Lane, "Unburied Victims"; Ephraim Wahome, "Practical Challenges in the Conservation of Tangible Mau Mau Legacy in Kenya," paper presented at Legacies of Struggle in Southern and Eastern Africa workshop, British Institute in Eastern Africa, Nairobi, 18–20 March 2015.

122. Mose, "Hip Hop Halisi," 4.

123. Maloba, *Mau Mau and Kenya,* 169–80.

124. Ana Douglass and Thomas A. Vogler, introduction to *Witness and Memory. The Discourse of Trauma,* ed. Douglass and Vogler (New York: Routledge, 2003), 53.

125. Clough, *Mau Mau Memoirs,* 3–4.

126. John Lonsdale, "Mau Mau Nation or Immigrant Nation? The Politics of Memory in Kenya," unpublished 2011 paper shared with me.

Appendix

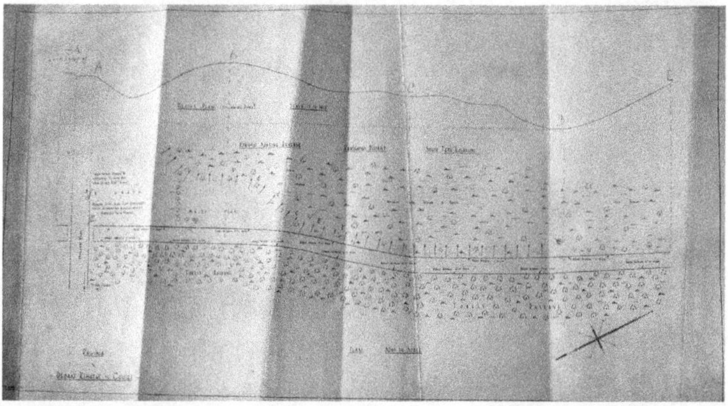

FIGURE A.1 Exhibit No. 1, plan of capture scene. *Supreme Court of Kenya, Kimathi File.*

FIGURE A.2 Exhibit No. 6, pistol. *National Museums of Kenya.*

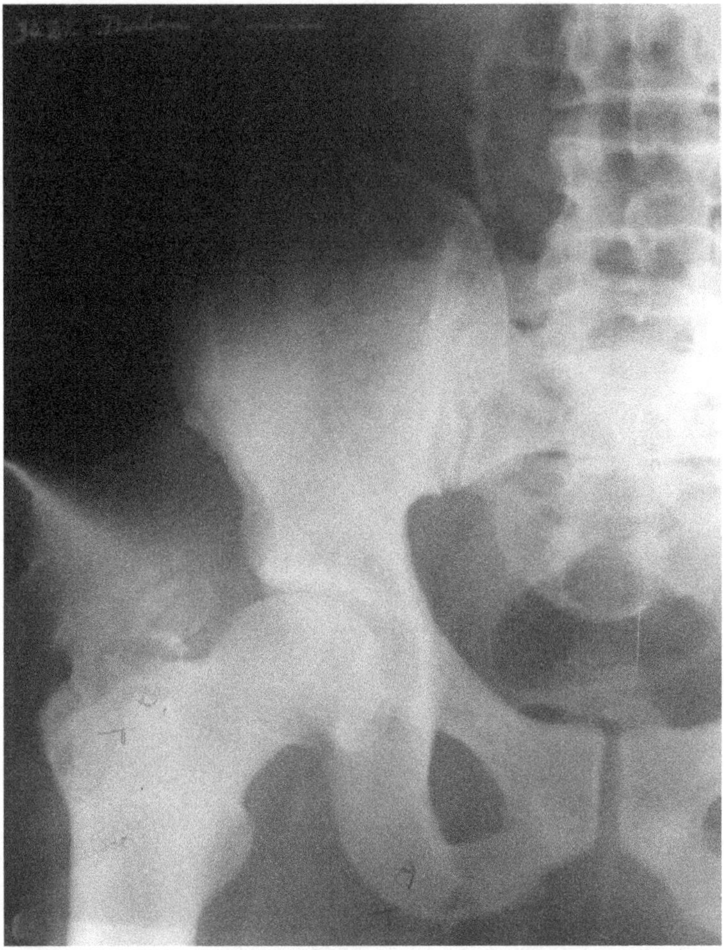

FIGURE A.3 Exhibit No. A, X-ray photograph of Kimathi's bullet wound to the thigh. *Supreme Court of Kenya, Kimathi File.*

FIGURE A.4 Exhibit No. 21, photo of Dedan Kimathi, June 1953. *Supreme Court of Kenya, Kimathi File.*

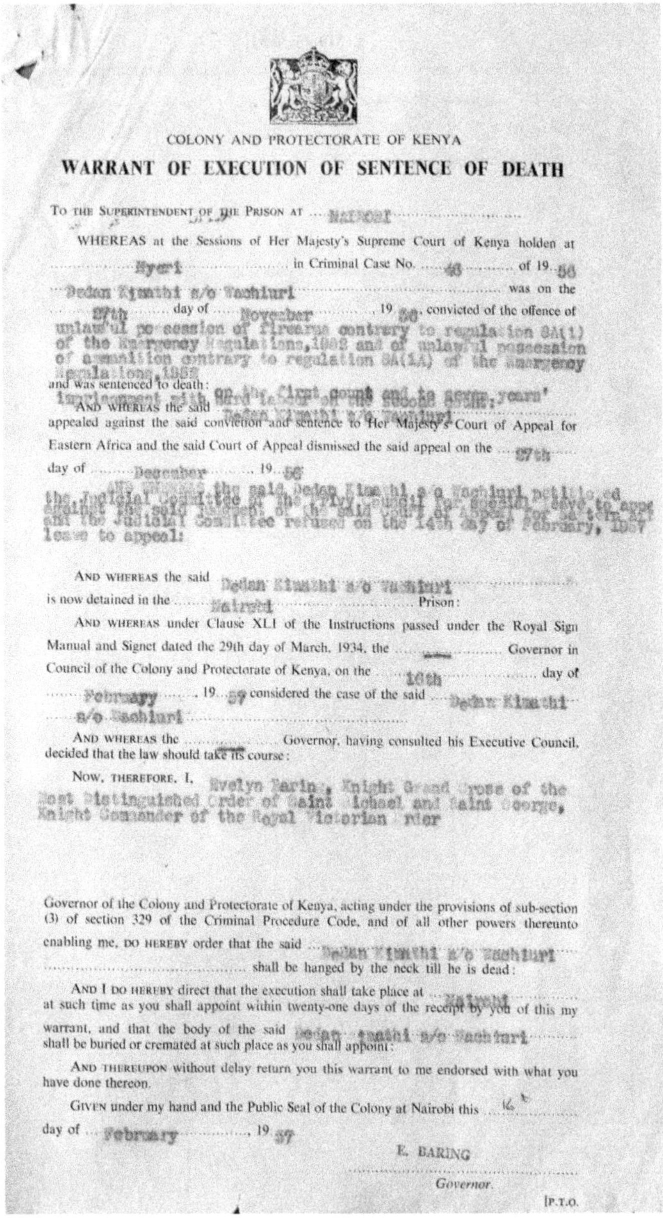

COLONY AND PROTECTORATE OF KENYA

WARRANT OF EXECUTION OF SENTENCE OF DEATH

To the Superintendent of the Prison at ..... Nairobi .....

WHEREAS at the Sessions of Her Majesty's Supreme Court of Kenya holden at ..... Nyeri ..... in Criminal Case No. ..... 46 ..... of 19..56 ..... Dedan Kimathi s/o Wachiuri ..... was on the ..... 27th ..... day of ..... November ....., 19..56. convicted of the offence of unlawful possession of firearms contrary to regulation 8A(1) of the Emergency Regulations,1952 and of unlawful possession of ammunition contrary to regulation 8A(1A) of the Emergency Regulations,1952

and was sentenced to death: imprisonment with hard labour on the first count and to seven years' imprisonment with hard labour on the second count;

And whereas the said ..... Dedan Kimathi s/o Wachiuri ..... appealed against the said conviction and sentence to Her Majesty's Court of Appeal for Eastern Africa and the said Court of Appeal dismissed the said appeal on the ..... 27th ..... day of ..... December ....., 19..56

AND WHEREAS the said Dedan Kimathi s/o Wachiuri petitioned the Judicial Committee of the Privy Council for special leave to appeal against the said judgment of the said Court of Appeal for Eastern Africa and the Judicial Committee refused on the 14th day of February, 1957 leave to appeal:

And whereas the said ..... Dedan Kimathi s/o Wachiuri ..... is now detained in the ..... Nairobi ..... Prison:

And whereas under Clause XLI of the Instructions passed under the Royal Sign Manual and Signet dated the 29th day of March, 1934, the ..... Governor in Council of the Colony and Protectorate of Kenya, on the ..... 16th ..... day of ..... February ....., 19..57 considered the case of the said ..... Dedan Kimathi s/o Wachiuri .....

And whereas the ..... Governor, having consulted his Executive Council, decided that the law should take its course:

Now, therefore, I, Evelyn Baring, Knight Grand Cross of the Most Distinguished Order of Saint Michael and Saint George, Knight Commander of the Royal Victorian Order

Governor of the Colony and Protectorate of Kenya, acting under the provisions of sub-section (3) of section 329 of the Criminal Procedure Code, and of all other powers thereunto enabling me, do hereby order that the said ..... Dedan Kimathi s/o Wachiuri ..... shall be hanged by the neck till he is dead:

And I do hereby direct that the execution shall take place at ..... Nairobi ..... at such time as you shall appoint within twenty-one days of the receipt by you of this my warrant, and that the body of the said ..... Dedan Kimathi s/o Wachiuri ..... shall be buried or cremated at such place as you shall appoint:

And thereupon without delay return you this warrant to me endorsed with what you have done thereon.

Given under my hand and the Public Seal of the Colony at Nairobi this ..... 16th ..... day of ..... February ....., 19..57

E. BARING

.....

Governor.

[P.T.O.

FIGURE A.5A–B Warrant of execution of sentence of death, 18 February 1957. *Supreme Court of Kenya, Kimathi File.*

ENDORSEMENT

I have the honour to inform you that I carried out the sentence of death upon DEDAN KIMATHI S/O WACHIURI. in the Prison at NAIROBI at 6. a.m. this 18th. day of February, 1957

[signature]
Superintendent of the Prison.

I hereby certify that I was present at the execution of DEDAN KIMATHI S/O WACHIURI. at about 6 a.m. this morning and .... after the execution I examined the body of the deceased man and found life to be extinct. Death was caused by HANGING and was * INSTANTANEOUS.

Dated at NAIROBI this 18th. day of February, 1957.

K. E. ROBERTSON
Medical Officer.

* Instantaneous.

copy to-
The Hon. Chief Secretary, Nairobi.
The Registrar Supreme Court of Kenya, Nairobi.
The Commissioner of Prisons, Nairobi.

G.P.K. 1586—5,000—7/54

Bibliography

Aiyar, Sana. *Indians in Kenya: The Politics of Diaspora.* Cambridge, MA: Harvard University Press, 2015.

Alam, S. M. Shamsul. *Rethinking the Mau Mau in Colonial Kenya.* New York: Palgrave Macmillan, 2007.

Amoko, Apollo Obonyo. *Postcolonialism in the Wake of the Nairobi Revolution: Ngugi wa Thiong'o and the Idea of African Literature.* New York: Palgrave Macmillan, 2010.

Anderson, David M. "British Abuse and Torture in Kenya's Counter-insurgency, 1952–1960." *Small Wars and Insurgencies* 23, nos. 4–5 (2012): 700–719.

———. "Exit from Empire: Counter-insurgency and Decolonization in Kenya, 1952–63." In *At the End of Military Intervention: Historical, Theoretical, and Applied Approaches to Transition, Handover, and Withdrawal,* edited by Robert Johnson and Timothy Clack, 107–36. Oxford: Oxford University Press, 2015.

———. "Guilty Secrets: Deceit, Denial, and the Discovery of Kenya's 'Migrated Archive.'" *History Workshop Journal* 80, no. 1 (Autumn 2015): 142–60.

———. *Histories of the Hanged: Britain's Dirty War in Kenya and the End of Empire.* London: Weidenfeld and Nicolson, 2005.

———. "Mau Mau in the High Court and the 'Lost' British Empire Archives: Colonial Conspiracy, or Bureaucratic Bungle?" *Journal of Imperial and Commonwealth History* 39, no. 5 (2011): 699–716.

Anderson, David M., and Paul J. Lane. "The Unburied Victims of Kenya's Mau Mau Rebellion: Where and When Does the Violence End?" In *Human Remains in Society: Curation and Exhibition in the Aftermath of Genocide and Mass-Violence,* edited by Jean-Marc Dreyfus and Élisabeth Anstett, 14–37. Manchester: Manchester University Press, 2017.

Asens, Jaume, and Gerardo Pisarello. "The Illegality of Power." *Critical Legal Thinking,* 17 February 2012. http://criticallegalthinking.com/2012/02/17/the-illegality-of-power/.

Atieno Odhiambo, E. S. "The Production of History in Kenya: The Mau Mau Debate." *Canadian Journal of African Studies* 25, no. 2 (1991): 300–307.

Atieno Odhiambo, E. S., and John Lonsdale, eds. *Mau Mau and Nationhood: Arms, Authority, and Narration.* Athens: Ohio University Press, 2003.

Aubert, Vilhelm, ed. *Sociology of Law.* Baltimore: Penguin, 1969.

Barnett, Donald L., and Karari Njama. *Mau Mau from Within: Autobiography and Analysis of Kenya's Peasant Revolt.* New York: Monthly Review Press, 1966.

Barrett, David B. *Schism and Renewal in Africa: An Analysis of Six Thousand Contemporary Religious Movements.* Nairobi: Oxford University Press, 1968.

Baskind, Roy, and Gretchen L. Birbeck. "Epilepsy-Associated Stigma in Sub-Saharan Africa: The Social Landscape of a Disease." *Epilepsy and Behavior* 7, no. 1 (2005): 68–73.

Benjamin, Walter. "What Is Epic Theater?" In *Illuminations: Essays and Reflections,* edited by Hannah Arendt. Translated by Harry Zohn, 147–54. New York: Schocken, 1968.

———. "The Work of Art in the Age of Mechanical Reproduction." In Arendt, *Illuminations,* 217–54.

Bennett, Huw. *Fighting the Mau Mau: The British Army and Counter-insurgency in the Kenya Emergency.* Cambridge: Cambridge University Press, 2013.

Berman, Bruce. *Control and Crisis in Colonial Kenya: The Dialectic of Domination.* Athens: Ohio University Press, 1990.

———. "Nationalism, Ethnicity, and Modernity: The Paradox of Mau Mau." *Canadian Journal of African Studies* 25, no. 2 (1991): 181–206.

Branch, Daniel. *Defeating Mau Mau, Creating Kenya: Counterinsurgency, Civil War, and Decolonization.* Cambridge: Cambridge University Press, 2009.

———. *Kenya: Between Hope and Despair, 1963–2011.* New Haven: Yale University Press, 2011.

———. "The Search for the Remains of Dedan Kimathi: The Politics of Death and Memorialization in Post-Colonial Kenya." *Past and Present,* suppl. 5 (2010): 301–20.

Broun, Kenneth S. *Saving Nelson Mandela: The Rivonia Trial and the Fate of South Africa.* New York: Oxford University Press, 2012.

Buijtenhuijs, Robert. *Mau Mau: Twenty Years After: The Myth and the Survivors.* The Hague: Mouton, 1973.

Carothers J. C. *The Psychology of Mau Mau.* Nairobi: Government Printer, 1954.

Césaire, Aimé. *Discourse on Colonialism.* Translated by Joan Pinkham. New York: Monthly Review Press, 2001.

Carrier, Neil, and Celia Nyamweru. "Reinventing Africa's National Heroes: The Case of Mekatilili, a Kenyan Popular Heroine." *African Affairs* 115, no. 461 (2016): 599–620.

Charton, Hélène. "Jomo Kenyatta et les méandres de la mémoire de l'indépendance du Kenya." *Vingtième siècle* 118, no. 2 (2013): 45–59.

Clark, Msia Kibona, and Mickie Mwanzia Koster, eds. *Hip Hop and Social Change in Africa: Ni wakati.* Lanham, MD: Lexington Books, 2014.

Clayton, Anthony. *Counter-insurgency in Kenya: A Study of Military Operations against Mau Mau*. Nairobi: Transafrica, 1976.

Clegg, Stewart. "Power and Authority, Resistance and Legitimacy." In Goverde et al., *Power in Contemporary Politics*, 77–92.

Clough, Marshall S. *Fighting Two Sides: Kenyan Chiefs and Politicians, 1918–1940*. Niwot: University Press of Colorado, 1990.

———. "Mau Mau and the Contest for Memory." In Atieno Odhiambo and Lonsdale, *Mau Mau and Nationhood*, 252–67.

———. *Mau Mau Memoirs: History, Memory, and Politics*. Boulder: Lynne Rienner, 1998.

Cohen, David William. *The Combing of History*. Chicago: University of Chicago Press, 1994.

Cole, Susan Letzer. *The Absent One: Mourning Ritual, Tragedy, and the Performance of Ambivalence*. College Park: Pennsylvania State University Press, 1985.

Comaroff, Jean, and John Comaroff. *Theory from the South; Or, How Euro-America is Evolving toward Africa*. Boulder: Paradigm, 2012.

Coombes, Annie E. "Monumental Histories: Commemorating Mau Mau with the Statue of Dedan Kimathi." *African Studies* 70, no. 2 (2011): 202–23.

———. "Monuments and Memories: Public Commemorative Strategies in Contemporary Kenya." In Coombes, Hughes, and Karega-Munene, *Managing Heritage*.

———. "Object Lessons: Learning from the Lari Massacre(s)." In Coombes, Hughes, and Karega-Munene, *Managing Heritage*, 53–98.

———. "Photography against the Grain: Rethinking the Colonial Archive in Kenyan Museums." *World Art* 6, no. 1 (2016): 61–83.

Coombes, Annie, Lotte Hughes, and Karega-Munene. *Managing Heritage, Making Peace: History, Identity and Memory in Contemporary Kenya*. London: I. B. Tauris, 2014.

Cooper, Frederick. "Mau Mau and the Discourses of Decolonization." Review of *Squatters and the Roots of Mau Mau*, by Tabitha Kanogo, and *Economic and Social Origins of Mau Mau*, by David W. Throup. *Journal of African History* 29, no. 2 (1988): 313–20.

Coss, Peter, ed. *The Moral World of the Law*. Cambridge: Cambridge University Press, 2000.

De Jong, Ferdinand. "At Work in the Archive." Introduction to special issue. *World Art* 6, no. 1 (2016): 3–17.

Douglass, Ana, and Thomas A. Vogler. Introduction to *Witness and Memory: The Discourse of Trauma*, edited by Douglass and Vogler, 1–54. New York: Routledge, 2003.

Duffy, Aoife. "Legacies of British Colonial Violence: Viewing Kenyan Detention Camps through the Hanslope Disclosure." *Law and History Review* 33, no. 3 (August 2015): 489–542.

Durrani, Shiraz. *Kĩmathi: Mau Mau's First Prime Minister of Kenya*. London: Vita Books, 1986.

Elkins, Caroline. "Alchemy of Evidence: Mau Mau, the British Empire, and the High Court of Justice." *Journal of Imperial and Commonwealth History* 39, no. 5 (December 2011): 731–48.

———. *Britain's Gulag: The Brutal End of Empire in Kenya*. London: Pimlico, 2005.

———. "Detention, Rehabilitation, and the Destruction of Kikuyu Society." In Atieno Odhiambo and Lonsdale, *Mau Mau and Nationhood,* 191–226.

Emerson, Ralph Waldo. *The Works of Ralph Waldo Emerson.* 12 vols. Fireside Edition. Boston: 1909. Vol. 7, *Society and Solitude,* http://oll.libertyfund.org/titles/86.

Fanon, Frantz. *The Wretched of the Earth.* Translated by Constance Farrington. New York: Grove, 1963.

Fassin, Didier, and Richard Rechtman. *The Empire of Trauma: An Inquiry into the Condition of Victimhood.* Translated by Rachel Gomme. Princeton: Princeton University Press, 2009.

Fazan, S. H. *Colonial Kenya Observed: British Rule, Mau Mau and the Wind of Change.* Edited by John Lonsdale. London: I. B. Tauris, 2015.

Foucault, Michel. *Technologies of the Self: A Seminar with Michel Foucault.* Edited by Luther H. Martin, Huck Gutman, and Patrick H. Hutton. Amherst: University of Massachusetts Press, 1998.

Foulds, Adam. *The Broken Word.* London: Jonathan Cape, 2008.

Franklin, Derek Peter. *A Pied Cloak: Memoirs of a Colonial Police (Special Branch) Officer.* London: Janus, 1996.

Fraser, Donald. "The Rise and Fall of the British Veterinary Profession in the Agrarian Development of Kenya, 1937–1967." PhD diss., University of Cambridge, 2015.

Frederiksen, Bodil Folke. "Jomo Kenyatta, Marie Bonaparte and Bronislaw Malinowski on Clitoridectomy and Female Sexuality." *History Workshop Journal* 65 (2008): 23–48.

French, David. *The British Way in Counter-insurgency, 1945–1967.* Oxford: Oxford University Press, 2011.

Furedi, Frank. *The Mau Mau War in Perspective.* Athens: Ohio University Press, 1989.

Giddens, Anthony. *The Constitution of Society: Outline of the Theory of Structuration.* Berkeley: University of California Press, 1984.

———. *Modernity and Self-Identity: Self and Society in the Late Modern Age.* Stanford: Stanford University Press, 1991.

Giffard, Hardinge Stanley. *The Laws of England.* 23 vols. London: Butterworth and Co., 1955.

Gikandi, Simon. "Pan-Africanism and Cosmopolitanism: The Case of Jomo Kenyatta." *English Studies in Africa* 43, no. 1 (2000): 3–27.

Gikoyo, Gucu. *We Fought for Freedom: Tulipigania Uhuru.* Nairobi: East African Publishing House, 1979.
Githige, Renison. "The Religious Factor in Mau Mau with Particular Reference to Mau Mau Oaths." MA diss., University of Nairobi, 1978.
Githuku, Nicholas K. *Mau Mau Crucible of War: Statehood, National Identity, and Politics of Postcolonial Kenya*. Lanham, MD: Lexington Books, 2016.
Glassman, Jonathan. "Ethnicity and Race in African Thought." In *The Blackwell Companion to African History,* edited by Charles Ambler, Dmitri van den Bersselaar, and William Worger. Oxford: Blackwell, 2016.
Goverde, Henri, Philip G. Cerny, Mark Haugaard, and Howard H. Lentner, eds. *Power in Contemporary Politics: Theories, Practices, Globalizations,* 77–92. London: Sage, 2000.
Gray, John. "Opinions of Assessors in Criminal Trials in East Africa as to Native Custom." *Journal of African Law* 2, no. 1 (1958): 5–18.
Harrison, Rodney, and Lotte Hughes. "Heritage, Colonialism and Postcolonialism." In *Understanding the Politics of Heritage,* edited by Harrison, 234–69. Manchester: Manchester University Press in association with the Open University, 2010.
Hastings, Adrian. *The Construction of Nationhood: Ethnicity, Religion and Nationalism.* Cambridge: Cambridge University Press, 1997.
Haugaard, Mark. "Power, Ideology and Legitimacy." In Goverde et al., *Power in Contemporary Politics,* 59–76.
Heather, R. W. "Counterinsurgency and Intelligence in Kenya, 1952–56." PhD diss., University of Cambridge, 1993.
Henderson, Ian. *The Hunt for Kimathi.* With Philip Goodhart. London: Hamish Hamilton, 1958.
Higginbotham, A. Leon, Jr. *In the Matter of Color: Race and the American Legal Process: The Colonial Period.* New York: Oxford University Press, 1978.
Holmes, Oliver Wendell. *The Common Law.* Boston: Little, Brown, 1881.
Hughes, Lotte. "Claims, Victimhood, Reluctant Heroes, and Other Problematic Legacies of Mau Mau." Paper presented at Legacies of Struggle in Southern and Eastern Africa workshop, British Institute in Eastern Africa, Nairobi, 18–20 March 2015.
———. "Mau Mau: The Divisive Heritage of Liberation Struggle in Kenya." In *Heritage and Peacebuilding,* edited by Peter Davis, Daniel Laven and Diana Walters. Woodbridge, Suffolk: Boydell and Brewer, 2016.
———. "The Production and Transmission of National History: Some Problems and Challenges." In Coombes, Hughes, and Karega-Munene, *Managing Heritage,* 179–215.
———. "Sacred Spaces, Political Places: The Struggle for a Sacred Forest." In Coombes, Hughes, and Karega-Munene, *Managing Heritage,* 99–138.
———. "'Truth Be Told': Some Problems with Historical Revisionism in Kenya." *African Studies* 70, no. 2 (2011): 182–201.

Hughes, Lotte, and Karega-Munene. "Cultures of Peace in Community Museums." *Awaaz* (Nairobi), January 28, 2013. http://www.awaazmagazine.com/previous/index.php/archives/item/439-cultures-of-peace-in-community-museums.

Hutton, Patrick. "History as an Art of Memory." In Olick, Vinitzky-Seroussi, and Levy, *Collective Memory Reader*, 411–15.

Huxley, Elspeth. *A New Earth: An Experiment in Colonialism*. London: Chatto and Windus, 1960.

Hynd, Stacey. "Killing the Condemned: The Practice and Process of Capital Punishment in British Africa, 1900–1950s." *Journal of African History* 49, no. 3 (2008): 403–18.

Iliffe, John. *Honour in African History*. Cambridge: Cambridge University Press, 2005.

Itote, Waruhiu [General China]. *"Mau Mau" General*. Nairobi: East African Publishing House, 1967.

———. *Mau Mau in Action*. Nairobi: Transafrica, 1979.

Jearey, J. H. "Trial by Jury and Trial with the Aid of Assessors in the Superior Courts of British African Territories: Part II." *Journal of African Law* 5, no. 1 (1961): 36–47.

———. "Trial by Jury and Trial with the Aid of Assessors in the Superior Courts of British African Territories: Part III." *Journal of African Law* 5, no. 2 (1961): 82–98.

Jeyifo, Biodun. "The Nature of Things: Arrested Decolonization and Critical Theory." *Research in African Literatures* 21, no. 1, Critical Theory and African Literature (Spring 1990): 33–48.

Jilek-Aall, Louise. "*Morbus Sacer* in Africa: Some Religious Aspects of Epilepsy in Traditional Cultures." *Epilepsia* 40, no. 3 (1999): 382–86.

Josse-Durand, Chloé. "Building Local Memories, Pluralizing the National Narrative: Community Museums and the Political Use of Heritage and Memory in Kenya and Ethiopia." PhD diss., Institut d'Études Politiques de Bordeaux, France, 2016.

Kabiro, Ngugi. *Man in the Middle: The Story of Ngugi Kabiro*. Richmond, BC: LSM Press, 1973.

Kaggia, Bildad. *Roots of Freedom 1921–1963*. Nairobi: East African Publishing House, 1975.

Kagwanja, Peter Mwangi. "Facing Mount Kenya or Facing Mecca? The Mungiki, Ethnic Violence and the Politics of the Moi Succession in Kenya, 1987–2002." *African Affairs* 102, no. 406 (2003): 25–49.

Kahiga, Sam. *Dedan Kimathi: The Real Story*. Nairobi: Longman Kenya, 1990.

Kanogo, Tabitha. *African Womanhood in Colonial Kenya, 1900–1950*. Athens: Ohio University Press, 2005.

———. *Dedan Kimathi: A Biography*. Nairobi: East African Educational Publishers, 1992.

———. *Squatters and the Roots of Mau Mau, 1905–1963*. Athens: Ohio University Press, 1987.

Kantai, Parselelo. "Comrade Lemma and the Black Jerusalem Boys Band." *Kwani?* 2 (Nairobi: Kwani Trust, 2004): 208–23.

Karega-Munene. "Museums in Kenya: Spaces for Selecting, Ordering and Erasing Memories of Identity and Nationhood." *African Studies* 70, no. 2 (August 2011): 224–45.

———. "Towards Recognition of the Right to a Cultural Past in the Twenty-first Century: An Example from East Africa." In *Postcolonial Archaeologies in Africa*, edited by Peter R. Schmidt. Santa Fe: School for Advanced Research, 2009.

Karimi, Joseph. *Dedan Kimathi: The Whole Story*. Nairobi: Jomo Kenyatta Foundation, 2013.

Kariuki, Josiah Mwangi. *"Mau Mau" Detainee: The Account by a Kenya African of His Experiences in Detention Camps, 1953–1960*. London: Oxford University Press, 1963.

Keane, Adrian, and Paul McKeown, eds. *The Modern Law of Evidence*. Oxford: Oxford University Press, 2014.

Kenyatta, Jomo. *Facing Mount Kenya: The Tribal Life of the Gikuyu*. London: Secker and Warburg, 1938.

———. *Suffering without Bitterness: The Founding of the Kenya Nation*. Nairobi: East African Publishing House, 1968.

Kershaw, Greet. *Mau Mau from Below*. Athens: Ohio University Press, 1997.

———. "Mau Mau from Below: Fieldwork and Experience, 1955–57 and 1962." *Canadian Journal of African Studies* 25, no. 2 (1991): 274–97.

Kibera, Leonard, and Samuel Kahiga. *Potent Ash: Short Stories*. Nairobi: East African Publishing House, 1968.

Kinyatti, Maina wa. *History of Resistance in Kenya, 1884–2002*. Nairobi: Mau Mau Research Centre, 2008.

———. *Kenya's Freedom Struggle: The Dedan Kimathi Papers*. London: Zed, 1987.

———. *Mau Mau: A Revolution Betrayed*. New York: Mau Mau Research Centre, 1991.

———, ed. *Thunder from the Mountains: Mau Mau Patriotic Songs*. London: Zed, 1980.

Knighton, Ben. "Going for Cai at Gatũndũ, 1968–9: Reversion to a Gĩkũyũ Ethnic Past or Building a Kenyan National Future?" In *Our Turn to Eat: Politics in Kenya since 1950*, edited by Nic Cheeseman and Daniel Branch, 107–28. Berlin: LIT Verlag, 2010.

———. "Mungiki Madness." In *Religion and Politics in Kenya: Essays in Honor of a Meddlesome Priest*, edited by Knighton, 223–50. New York: Palgrave Macmillan, 2009.

Kolsky, Elizabeth. *Colonial Justice in British India*. Cambridge: Cambridge University Press, 2010.

Koster, Mickie Mwanzia. "The Hip Hop Revolution in Kenya: Ukoo Flani Mau Mau, Youth Politics and Memory, 1990–2012." *Journal of Pan African Studies* 6, no. 3 (2013): 82–105.

———. *The Power of the Oath: Mau Mau Nationalism in Kenya, 1952–1960.* Rochester: University of Rochester Press, 2016.

Kristeva, Julia. "Semiology and Grammatology." Interview by Jacques Derrida. In *Positions.* Translated by Alan Bass. Chicago: University of Chicago Press, 1981.

Lacan, Jacques. *Écrits.* Translated by Bruce Fink. New York: Norton, 2007.

———. *The Language of the Self.* Translated by Anthony Wilden. Baltimore: Johns Hopkins University Press, 1981.

———. *The Seminar of Jacques Lacan: Book 1: Freud's Papers on Technique 1953–1954.* Edited by Jacques-Alain Miller. Translated by John Forrester. New York: Norton, 1997.

Laclau, Ernesto. *On Populist Reason.* London: Verso, 2005.

Leakey, L. S. B. *Defeating Mau Mau.* London: Methuen, 1954.

———. *The Southern Kikuyu before 1903.* 3 vols. London: Academic Press, 1977.

Leiter, Brian, and Michael Sevel. "Philosophy of Law." *Encyclopædia Britannica* (Online). http://www.britannica.com/topic/philosophy-of-law.

Lévi-Strauss, Claude. *Introduction to the Work of Marcel Mauss.* Translated by Felicity Baker. London: Routledge and Kegan Paul, 1987.

Lewis, Joanna. "'Daddy Wouldn't Buy Me a Mau Mau': The British Popular Press and the Demoralisation of Empire." In Atieno Odhiambo and Lonsdale, *Mau Mau and Nationhood,* 227–50.

———. "Nasty, Brutish and in Shorts? British Colonial Rule, Violence and the Historians of Mau Mau." *Round Table* 96, no. 389 (April 2007): 201–23.

Lonsdale, John. "Authority, Gender and Violence: The War within Mau Mau's Fight for Freedom." In Atieno Odhiambo and Lonsdale, *Mau Mau and Nationhood,* 46–75.

———. "Britain's Mau Mau." In *Penultimate Adventures with Britannia: Personalities, Politics and Culture in Britain,* edited by William Roger Louis, 259–73. London: I. B. Tauris, 2008.

———. "Contests of Time: Kikuyu Historiographies Old and New." In *A Place in the World: New Local Historiographies from Africa and South-Asia,* edited by Axel Harneit-Sievers, 201–54. Leiden: Brill, 2002.

———. "Jomo Kenyatta, God and the Modern World." In *African Modernities: Entangled Meanings in Current Debate,* edited by Jan-Georg Deutsch, Peter Probst, and Heike Schmidt, 31–60. Oxford: James Currey, 2002.

———. "KAU's Cultures: Imaginations of Community and Constructions of Leadership in Kenya after the Second World War." *Journal of African Cultural Studies* 13, no. 1 (2000): 107–24.

———. "Kenyatta's Trials: Breaking and Making an African Nationalist." In Coss, *Moral World,* 196–239.
———. "Mau Maus of the Mind: Making Mau Mau and Remaking Kenya." *Journal of African History* 31, no. 3 (November 1990): 393–421.
———. "The Moral Economy of Mau Mau: Wealth, Poverty and Civic Virtue in Kikuyu Political Thought." In *Unhappy Valley: Conflict in Kenya and Africa,* vol. 2, *Violence and Ethnicity,* edited by Bruce Berman and John Lonsdale, 315–504. Athens: Ohio University Press, 1992.
———. "Ornamental Constitutionalism in Africa: Kenyatta and the Two Queens." *Journal of Imperial and Commonwealth History* 34, no. 1 (2006): 87–103.
Loraux, Nicole. *The Divided City: On Memory and Forgetting in Ancient Athens.* New York: Zone Books, 2006.
Lovatt Smith, David. *Kenya, the Kikuyu and Mau Mau.* Herstmonceux: Mawenzi Books, 2005.
Lukács, Georg. *The Historical Novel.* Translated by Hannah and Stanley Mitchell. Lincoln: University of Nebraska Press, 1983.
Luongo, Katherine. *Witchcraft and Colonial Rule in Kenya, 1900–1955.* Cambridge: Cambridge University Press, 2011.
MacArthur, Julie. "Rebel Litigants: The Lost Trials of Elijah Masinde and Dedan Kimathi." Dedan Kimathi University of Technology, Conference Proceedings, July 2014.
Mahone, Sloan. "The Psychology of Rebellion: Colonial Medical Responses to Dissent in British East Africa." *Journal of African History* 47, no. 2 (2006): 241–58.
———. "The Psychology of the Tropics: Conceptions of Tropical Danger and Lunacy in British East Africa." PhD thesis, University of Oxford, 2004.
Mahone, Sloan, and Megan Vaughan, eds. *Psychiatry and Empire.* New York: Palgrave Macmillan, 2007.
Maloba, Wunyabari O. *Mau Mau and Kenya: An Analysis of a Peasant Revolt.* Bloomington: Indiana University Press, 1993.
Matiba, Kenneth. *Aiming High: The Story of My Life.* Nairobi: People Ltd., 2000.
Maxon, Robert M. *Struggle for Kenya: The Loss and Reassertion of Imperial Initiative, 1912–1923.* Cranbury, NJ: Associated University Presses, 1993.
Mazrui, Ali A. "Between Cultural Nostalgia and Cultural Amnesia: African Museums and the Archival Memory." *Kenya Past and Present* 35 (Nairobi: Kenya Museum Society, 2005): 87–98.
———. "On Heroes and Uhuru-Worship." *Transition* 3, no. 11 (November 1963): 23–28.
———, ed. *The Warrior Tradition in Modern Africa* (Leiden: Brill, 1977)
Mose, Caroline. "Hip Hop Halisi: Continuities of Heroism on the African Political Landscape." In Clark and Mwanzia Koster, *Hip Hop,* 3–25.

Muoria-Sal, Wangari, Bodil Folke Frederiksen, John Lonsdale, and Derek Peterson, eds. *Writing for Kenya: The Life and Works of Henry Muoria.* Leiden: Brill, 2009.
Muriithi, J. Kiboi. *War in the Forest: The Personal Story of J. Kiboi Muriithi as Told to Peter N. Ndoria.* Nairobi: East African Publishing House, 1971.
Murray, Jocelyn. "The Kikuyu Female Circumcision Controversy, with Special Reference to the Church Missionary Society's 'Sphere of Influence.'" PhD diss., University of California at Los Angeles, 1974.
Murray-Brown, Jeremy. *Kenyatta.* London: Allen and Unwin, 1972.
Mutonyi, Eliud. "Mau Mau Chairman." Typescript, circa 1970, privately held.
Nderitu, David. "Mungiki: Wanjiku's Expression of Self." In *Wanjiku: A Kenyan Sociopolitical Discourse,* edited by Naomi L. Shitemi and Eunice K. Kamaara. Nairobi: Goethe-Institut Kenya/Native Intelligence, 2014.
Nderitũ, Wairimũ. *Mũkami Kĩmathi: Mau Mau Freedom Fighter.* Nairobi: Mdahalo Bridging Divides, 2017.
Ndigirigi, Gichingiri. *Ngũgĩ wa Thiong'o's Drama and the Kamiriithu Popular Theater Experiment.* Trenton, NJ: Africa World Press, 2007.
Njeng'ere, David. *Dedan Kimathi: Leader of Mau Mau.* Nairobi: Sasa Sema Publications, 2003.
Njonjo, Apollo. "The Africanization of the 'White Highlands': A Study in Agrarian Class Struggles in Kenya, 1950–74." PhD diss., Princeton University, 1977.
Nyawalo, Mich. "Redefining the Struggle: Remembering the Mau Mau through Hip Hop Music." In Clark and Mwanzia Koster, *Hip Hop,* 72–92.
Ochieng', William R. "Dedan Kimathi: The Real Story." *Maseno Journal of Education, Arts and Science* 1, no. 1 (1992): 132–34.
Ogot, Bethwell A. "Africa: The Agenda of Historical Research and Writing." In Ogot, *Challenges of History,* 467–84.
———. "Britain's Gulag." Review of *Histories of the Hanged: Britain's Dirty War in Kenya and the End of Empire,* by David M. Anderson, and *Britain's Gulag: The Brutal End of Empire in Kenya,* by Caroline Elkins. *Journal of African History* 46, no. 3 (2005): 493–505.
———. *The Challenges of History and Leadership in Africa: The Essays of Bethwell Alan Ogot.* Edited by Toyin Falola and E. S. Atieno Odhiambo. Trenton, NJ: Africa World Press, 2002.
———. "Mau Mau and Nationhood: The Untold Story." In Atieno Odhiambo and Lonsdale, *Mau Mau and Nationhood,* 8–36.
———. "Politics, Culture and Music in Central Kenya: A Study of Mau Mau Hymns, 1951–1956." In Ogot, *Challenges of History,* 113–28.
———. "Revolt of the Elders: An Anatomy of the Loyalist Crowd in the Mau Mau Uprising, 1952–1956." In *Politics and Nationalism in Colonial Kenya,* edited by Ogot, *Hadith 4,* 134–48. Nairobi: East African Publishing House, 1972.

Ogude, James. "The Nation and Narration: 'The Truths of the Nation' and the Changing Image of Mau Mau in Kenyan Literature." In Atieno Odhiambo and Lonsdale, *Mau Mau and Nationhood,* 268–83.

Okunoye, Oyeniyi. "Dramatizing Postcoloniality: Nationalism and the Rewriting of History in Ngũgĩ and Mũgo's 'The Trial of Dedan Kimathi.'" *History in Africa* 28 (2001): 225–37.

Olick, Jeffrey K., Vered Vinitzky-Seroussi, and Daniel Levy. Introduction to *The Collective Memory Reader,* edited by Olick, Vinitzky-Seroussi, and Levy, 3–62. Oxford: Oxford University Press, 2011.

Osborne, Myles, ed. *The Life and Times of General China: Mau Mau and the End of Empire in Kenya.* Princeton: Markus Wiener, 2015.

———. "'The Rooting Out of Mau Mau from the Minds of the Kikuyu Is a Formidable Task': Propaganda and the Mau Mau War." *Journal of African History* 56, no. 1 (2015): 77–97.

O'Shea, Helen. *Ireland and the End of the British Empire: The Republic and Its Role in the Cyprus Emergency.* London: I. B. Tauris, 2014.

Otieno, Wambui Waiyaki. *Mau Mau's Daughter: A Life History.* London: Lynne Rienner, 1998.

Parker, Ian. *The Last Colonial Regiment: The History of the Kenya Regiment (T.F.).* Kinloss: Librario Publishing, 2009.

Peiris, G. L. "The Admissibility of Evidence Obtained Illegally: A Comparative Analysis." *Ottawa Law Review* 13, no. 2 (1981): 309–44.

Peterson, Derek R. *Creative Writing: Translation, Bookkeeping, and the Work of Imagination in Colonial Kenya.* Portsmouth, NH: Heinemann, 2004.

———. *Ethnic Patriotism and the East African Revival: A History of Dissent, c. 1935–1972.* Cambridge: Cambridge University Press, 2012.

———. "The Intellectual Lives of Mau Mau Detainees." *Journal of African History* 49, no. 1 (March 2008): 73–91.

———. "Writing in Revolution: Independent Schooling and Mau Mau in Nyeri." In Atieno Odhiambo and Lonsdale, *Mau Mau and Nationhood,* 76–96.

Presley, Cora Ann. *Kikuyu Women, the Mau Mau Rebellion, and Social Change in Kenya.* Boulder: Westview, 1992.

———. "The Mau Mau Rebellion, Kikuyu Women, and Social Change." *Canadian Journal of African History* 22, no. 3 (1988): 502–27.

Pugliese, Cristiana. *Author, Publisher and Gĩkũyũ Nationalist: The Life and Writings of Gakaara wa Wanjaũ.* Bayreuth: African Studies Centre, 1995.

———. "The Organic Vernacular Intellectual in Kenya: Gakaara wa Wanjaũ." *Research in African Literatures* 25, no. 4 (1994): 177–97.

Radstone, Susannah, and Katharine Hodgkin, eds. *Regimes of Memory.* London: Routledge, 2011.

Ranger, Terence. "Nationalist Historiography, Patriotic History and the History of the Nation: The Struggle over the Past in Zimbabwe." *Journal of Southern African Studies* 30, no. 2 (2004): 215–34.

Rasmussen, Jacob. "Mungiki as Youth Movement: Revolution, Gender and Generational Politics in Nairobi, Kenya." *Young: Nordic Journal of Youth Research* 18, no. 3 (2010): 301–19.

Rosberg, Carl G., Jr., and John Nottingham. *The Myth of "Mau Mau": Nationalism in Kenya.* New York: Praeger, 1966.

Roszak, Theodore. *Person/Planet: The Creative Disintegration of Industrial Society.* London: Gollancz, 1979.

Rutherford, Jock. *A History of the Kikuyu Guard.* Edited by John Pinney. 1957. Reprint, Herstmonceux: Mawenzi Books, 2003.

Sanders, Ethan R. "The African Association and the Growth and Movement of Political Thought in Mid-twentieth Century East Africa." PhD diss., University of Cambridge, 2012.

Santoru, Marina E. "The Colonial Idea of Women and Direct Intervention: The Mau Mau Case." *African Affairs* 95, no. 379 (1996): 253–67.

Schmidt, Peter R. "Postcolonial Silencing, Intellectuals, and the State: Views from Eritrea." *African Affairs* 109, no. 435 (April 2010): 293–313.

Scott, James C. *Domination and the Arts of Resistance: Hidden Transcripts.* New Haven: Yale University Press, 2008.

Siméant, Johanna. "Three Bodies of Moral Economy: The Diffusion of a Concept." *Journal of Global Ethics* 11, no. 2 (2015): 163–75.

Smith, Sir Sydney, and Frederick Smith Fiddles. *Forensic Medicine: A Textbook for Students and Practitioners.* London: J. and A. Churchill, 1949.

Sorrenson, M. P. K. *Land Reform in the Kikuyu Country: A Study in Government Policy.* Nairobi: Oxford University Press, 1967.

Spear, Thomas T. *The Kaya Complex: A History of the Mijikenda Peoples of the Kenya Coast to 1900.* Nairobi: Kenya Literature Bureau, 1978.

Spivak, Gayatri Chakravorty. Translator's preface to *Of Grammatology* by Jacques Derrida. Baltimore: Johns Hopkins University Press, 1977.

Spencer, John. *KAU: The Kenya African Union.* London: KPI, 1985.

Stewart, Laura. "Why Were There No Levellers in Scotland?" *History Today* 65, no. 9 (2015): 33–39.

Stone, I. F. *The Trial of Socrates.* New York: Anchor, 1989.

Sypnowich, Christine. "Law and Ideology." In *The Stanford Encyclopedia of Philosophy.* Edited by Edward N. Zalta. Winter 2014 ed., http://plato.stanford.edu/archives/win2014/entries/law-ideology.

Tamarkin, Mordecai. "The Loyalists in Nakuru during the Mau Mau Revolt and Its Aftermath, 1953–1963." *Asian and African Studies* 12, no. 2 (1978): 247–61.

Taxidou, Olga. *Tragedy, Modernity and Mourning.* Edinburgh: Edinburgh University Press, 2004.

Thiong'o, Ngũgĩ wa. "Born Again: Mau Mau Unchained." In *Writers in Politics: Essays.* London: Heinemann, 1981.

———. *Dreams in a Time of War: A Childhood Memoir*. London: Harvill Secker, 2010.
———. *Matigari*. Translated by Waugũi wa Goro. Nairobi: East African Educational Publishers, 1987.
———. *Petals of Blood*. London: Heinemann, 1977.
———. *Something Torn and New: An African Renaissance*. New York: BasicCivitas Books, 2009.
———. *Weep Not, Child*. London: Heinemann, 1964.
Thiong'o, Ngũgĩ wa, and Mĩcere Gĩthae Mũgo. *The Trial of Dedan Kimathi*. London: Heinemann Educational Books, 1976.
Throup, David. *Economic and Social Origins of Mau Mau, 1945—1953*. Athens: Ohio University Press, 1987.
Veilleux-Lepage, Yannick, and Jan Fedorowicz. "The Mau Mau Revolt in Kenya, 1952–1956." In *A History of Counterinsurgency: From South Africa to Algeria, 1900 to 1954*, edited by Gregory Fremont-Barnes, 177–204. Santa Barbara: Praeger, 2015.
Vernant, Jean-Pierre. "The Tragic Subject: Historicity and Transhistoricity." In *Myth and Tragedy in Ancient Greece*, edited by Vernant, and Pierre Vidal-Naquet, 237–48. Translated by Janet Lloyd. New York: Zone Books, 1988.
Wachanga, H. K. *The Swords of Kirinyaga: The Fight for Land and Freedom*. Edited by Robert Whittier. Nairobi: East African Literature Bureau, 1975.
Waciuma, Charity. *Daughter of Mumbi*. Nairobi: East African Publishing House, 1969.
Waller, Richard. "Ethnicity and Identity." In *The Oxford Handbook of Modern African History*, edited by John Parker and Richard Reid, 94–113. Oxford: Oxford University Press, 2013.
Wamue, Grace N. "The Politics of the Mungiki." *Wajibu: A Journal of Social and Religious Studies* 14 (1999): 15–16.
Wamweya, Joram. *Freedom Fighter*. Nairobi: East African Publishing House, 1971.
Wanjaũ, Gakaara wa. *Mau Mau Author in Detention*. Translated by Paul Ngigĩ Njoroge. Nairobi: Heinemann Kenya, 1988.
———. *Uhoro wa Ugurani*. Karatina: African Books Collective, 1946.
Watene, Kenneth. *Dedan Kimathi*. Nairobi: Transafrica, 1974.
Warren, Charles. *The Supreme Court in United States History*. 2 vols. Boston: Little, Brown, 1926.
Weber, Samuel. *Theatricality as Medium*. New York. Fordham University Press, 2004.
White, G. Edward. "The Evolution of Reasoned Elaboration: Jurisprudential Criticism and Social Change." *Virginia Law Review* 59, no. 2 (1973): 279–302.

White, Luise. "Separating the Men from the Boys: Constructions of Gender, Sexuality and Terrorism in Central Kenya, 1939–1959." *International Journal of African Historical Studies* 23, no. 1 (1990): 1–25.
Wickham, Chris. Conclusion to Coss, *Moral World,* 240–49.
Wiener, Martin J. *An Empire on Trial: Race, Murder, and Justice under British Rule, 1870–1935*. Cambridge: Cambridge University Press, 2009.
Willis, Justin. "Two Lives of Mpamizo: Understanding Dissonance in Oral History." *History in Africa* 23 (1996): 319–32.

Contributors

David M. Anderson is Professor of African History, in the Global History & Culture Centre at the University of Warwick, and Research Associate in History at Stellenbosch University. He has published widely on the history and politics of eastern Africa, including *Histories of the Hanged (2005).* His present research focuses on empire and violence, and on insurgency in Africa, and in 2018 he will publish a further volume on the history of the Mau Mau rebellion, based upon new documentary evidence.

Simon Gikandi is Robert Schirmer Professor of English at Princeton University and is affiliated with the Department of Comparative Literature, the Department of African American Studies, and the Program in African Studies. He was editor of *PMLA*, the official journal of the Modern Languages Association (MLA), for five years (2011–16). He is the author of many books, including *Slavery and the Culture of Taste*, the cowinner of the James Russell Lowell Award given to the best book by a member of the Modern Languages Association and of the Melville J. Herskovits Award for the most important scholarly work in African Studies. He has recently edited Volume 11 of *The Oxford History of the Novel in English: The Novel in Africa and the Caribbean since the 1950s* (2016).

Nicholas Kariuki Githuku holds a PhD from West Virginia University in African history with a focus on Eastern Africa in general, and contemporary political history of Kenya in particular. His research interests include the history of capitalism; British national and imperial history; the intricate, inescapable, and dialectical link between power or government legitimacy and resistance in the generic African state; and military, and (colonial and postcolonial) legal, history. Dr. Githuku is an assistant professor at York College, CUNY, Queens, New York.

Lotte Hughes is a historian of Africa and empire, specializing in Kenya. She is currently Senior Research Fellow at The Open University, UK. Her research interests include cultural rights and constitutional change in contemporary Kenya, memory studies, heritage, identity, and indigenous peoples' rights.

John Lonsdale is Emeritus Professor of Modern African History at the University of Cambridge. He is coauthor of *Unhappy Valley: Conflict in Kenya and Africa* (1992); coeditor, *Mau Mau and Nationhood* (2003); coeditor, *Writing for Kenya: The Life and Works of Henry Muoria* (2009); coeditor, *Ethnic Diversity and Economic Instability in Africa* (2012); editor, S. H. Fazan, *Colonial Kenya Observed* (2015).

Julie MacArthur is an assistant professor of African history at the University of Toronto. She is the author of *Cartography and the Political Imagination* as well as numerous articles. She has also worked extensively in African cinema, both as a curator and an academic.

Mĩcere Gĩthae Mũgo, poet, playwright, essayist, scholar, and community activist, retired from Syracuse University in 2015 as Meredith Professor for Teaching Excellence after forty-two years of university teaching in Africa and America. She has published widely and served on numerous international boards.

The Honorable **Willy Mutunga** was Kenya's Chief Justice and President of the Supreme Court from 2011 to 2016. Recently he has served as Secretary General of the Commonwealth special envoy to the Maldives, and a distinguished scholar-in-residence at Fordham Law's Leitner Center for international Law and Justice School.

Ngũgĩ wa Thiong'o, Distinguished Professor of English and Comparative Literature at the University of California, Irvine, is one of the leading writers at work in the world today. His books include the novels *Petals of Blood; A Grain of Wheat;* and *Wizard of the Crow;* the memoirs *Dreams in Time of War; In the House of the Interpreter;* and *Birth of Dreamweaver;* the essays *Decolonizing the Mind; Something Torn and New; Globalectics;* and *Secure the Base: Making Africa Visible in the Globe.* Ngũgĩ is a member of the American Academy of Arts and Letters and the American Academy of Arts and Sciences. He is the recipient of many honors, including the Nicolas Guillean award of Caribbean Philosophical Association; UCI Medal; and twelve honorary doctorates from universities in Africa, Europe, America, and New Zealand.

Index

Page references in italics denote illustrations on those pages.

CPSIA information can be obtained
at www.ICGtesting.com
Printed in the USA
BVHW081303220120
569805BV00001BA/2

9 780896 803176